Keynes on Monetary Policy, Finance and Uncertai͏̈

T0330679

This book provides a reassessment of Keynes' theory of liquidity preference. It argues that the failure of the Keynesian revolution to be made in either theory or practice owes importantly to the fact that the role of liquidity preference theory as a pivotal element in Keynes' *General Theory* has remained underexplored and indeed widely misunderstood even among Keynes' followers and until today. The book elaborates on and extends Keynes' conceptual framework, moving it from the closed economy to the global economy context, and applies liquidity preference theory to current events and prominent hypotheses in global finance.

Jörg Bibow presents Keynes' liquidity preference theory as a distinctive and highly relevant approach to monetary theory offering a conceptual framework of general applicability for explaining the role and functioning of the financial system. He argues that, in a dynamic context, liquidity preference theory may best be understood as a theory of financial intermediation. Through applications to current events and prominent hypotheses in global finance, this book underlines the richness, continued relevance and superiority of Keynes' theory of liquidity preference – with Hyman Minsky standing out for developing Keynes' vision of financial capitalism.

Researchers in monetary economics, macroeconomics, international finance, monetary policy, Keynesian and Post Keynesian economics, Keynes and Minsky will find this book of interest, as will financial market participants with an academic curiosity in economics, finance and philosophy.

Jörg Bibow is Associate Professor of Economics at Skidmore College, New York, USA and Research Associate at the Levy Economics Institute of Bard College, Annandale-on-Hudson, New York, USA.

Routledge Studies in the History of Economics

Keynes on Monetary Policy, Finance and Uncertainty

Liquidity preference theory and the global financial crisis

Jörg Bibow

Routledge
Taylor & Francis Group

LONDON AND NEW YORK

First published 2009
by Routledge
2 Park Square, Milton Park, Abingdon, Oxon, OX14 4RN

Simultaneously published in the USA and Canada
by Routledge
270 Madison Avenue, New York, NY 10016

Routledge is an imprint of the Taylor & Francis Group, an informa business

First issued in paperbackin 2011

Typeset in Times New Roman
by HWA Text and Data Management, London

British Library Cataloguing in Publication Data
A catalogue record for this book is available from the British Library

Library of Congress Cataloging in Publication Data
Bibow, Jörg.
  Keynes on monetary policy, finance and uncertainty: liquidity preference theory and the global financial crisis / Jörg Bibow.
      p. cm.
  Includes bibliographical references and index.
  1. Liquidity (Economics) 2. Keynesian economics. 3. Monetary policy.
  4. Financial crises. I. Title.
  HG178.B53 2009
  339.5–dc22   2008054275

ISBN13: 978-0-415-35262-8 (hbk)
ISBN13: 978-0-415-61647-8 (pbk)
ISBN13: 978-0-203-17053-3 (ebk)

Meinen Eltern

Contents

Figures

1 The triumph of Keynesianism?

The key role of liquidity preference theory in Keynes' heresy[1]

1.1 Why it should not take a global financial crisis to remind us of the continued relevance of Keynes

In the fall of 2008, the international financial system finds itself in severe crisis and the global economy appears to be on the brink of recession. The financial turmoil had its origin in the US subprime mortgage sector more than a year earlier. Following a lending boom and years of rapid property price increases, home prices stalled in 2006 and were falling nationwide by 2007, heralding serious troubles for borrowers and lenders alike. Equity markets reacted unfavorably with a sell-off in late February 2007 in response to a heightening of mortgage delinquencies. Calm quickly returned though and global equity markets reached new highs in the spring of that year. Many observers feared at the time that the US economy might be slowing, but hopes were high that the global economy might be able to "decouple" from its former growth engine.

Darker clouds emerged in the summer of 2007 with massive dislocations in global money markets and another sell-off in equity markets. Central banks around the world started pouring emergency liquidity into money markets and some also quickly eased policy interest rates. Remarkably, equity markets took off once again, despite the fact that money markets remained under strain and property prices continued to fall too. A decisive break in confidence came with the failure of Bear Stearns in March 2008, the first of a series of major Wall Street investment banks to go under in that year. In subsequent months more and more credit market segments experienced blockages while equity market prices continued to fall. Monetary and fiscal authorities initiated emergency efforts in response to these extraordinary events. The US Government was forced to put mortgage giants Freddie Mac and Fanny Mae under conservatorship as their securitized assets' prices plummeted and to bail out the insurance giant American International Group who had sold insurance on complex financial instruments now plunging in value through innovative financial derivatives known as credit default swaps.

September 2008 will be remembered for bringing fundamental change to Wall Street's landscape: major investment banks either defaulted (Lehman), or were absorbed by large commercial banks (Merrill Lynch by Bank of America), or turned themselves into bank-holding companies (Goldman Sachs, Morgan Stanley). Commercial banks, both small and large, felt increasing stress too, with Washington Mutual failing only days later. With hindsight, Lehman's default proved to be the really decisive systemic event: money and credit markets seized up completely in its aftermath. As even some large money market funds "broke the buck," i.e. their assets fell below the par value of their supposedly safe monetary liabilities, US authorities stepped up their efforts to contain the risk of a spreading banking crisis. Congress passed the "Troubled Asset Relief Program" (TARP) only after a very short and ambiguous bill was turned down on first try. The Federal Reserve began establishing a mechanism to buy investment grade commercial paper to prevent what could have been a financial strangulation of the corporate sector which relied on the sale of commercial paper to keep their daily operations afloat. As market confidence had taken a decisive hit following TARP's initial rejection, these measures came too late to prevent an equity market crash. In Europe and elsewhere governments were forced to come to the rescue of ailing banks as well. TED and Libor-OIS spreads reached historical highs as money and credit markets remained stymied in a crisis of confidence centered in global interbank lending.

Accordingly, their net worth being depleted by falling asset prices, households and corporations increasingly felt an unfolding "credit crunch" impacting their cash flows. With banks struggling under a worsening meltdown in their capital positions, talk of a systemic financial meltdown became louder. In the eyes of more and more observers the global "credit crisis" was approaching ever closer to a situation rivaling the Great Depression precipitated by the Wall Street crash of October 1929.

What diagnosis and policy advice does today's economics profession have to offer to prevent a repeat of the earlier disaster? In what way do today's policy responses differ from those pursued in the 1930s? According to the 94-year-old, but still active, long-time market participant Mr Seth Glickenhaus, there is indeed one "conspicuous difference" observable today: "In the '29 break you had [President] Hoover and [Treasury Secretary] Andrew Mellon contracting all the way. They believed that it wasn't the role of the government to get involved. This time, the government is moving heaven and earth to reverse the cycle." (*Wall Street Journal*, 6 Oct. 2008: "A Street Longtimer speaks").[2] Arguably, today's policy initiatives deliberately *counter* the forces that make for contraction of credit and private spending – rather than standing by or even reinforcing them – owing to the so-called Keynesian revolution in economics initiated by the publication of John Maynard Keynes' *General Theory* in 1936.[3]

Even if a lasting impact of what is perceived as the Keynesian revolution on today's policy response to a severe crisis is discernible, this book raises the issue that Keynes' supposed revolution in economic theory and policy, widely interpreted as having been inspired by, and offered as an explanation of, the Great Depression, was only very partially successful. As a related matter this book argues that it is wrong to consider Keynes' contribution as limited to offering helpful advice at times of severe crisis. Keynes titled his book *The General Theory* for good reason for, indeed, he identified a fundamental flaw in the mainstream "classical" theory which limited its scope to addressing economic questions where full-employment output existed at all times. As that condition was rarely met in practice Keynes was compelled to generalize the limited classical theory in order to provide the basis for theoretical coherence and valid policy prescription. In that regard, this book argues that Keynes did indeed provide us with a framework for understanding, among other things, the circumstances and developments that led up to today's crisis, one that is far superior to the "fair weather" mainstream model which guided policymakers around the world straight into that very crisis. It is remarkable that today's fair weather mainstream model is still essentially based on the same classical ideas that Keynes diagnosed as flawed in 1936.

In particular, this book argues that among the most important reasons for the failure of the Keynesian revolution to be made in either theory or practice is the fact that the role of liquidity preference theory as a pivotal element has remained underexplored and indeed widely misunderstood even among Keynes' followers and until today. The failure to appreciate the revolutionary character of Keynes' theory of liquidity preference is lamentable because with careful inspection it is clear that it provided the framework by which he conceptualized and analyzed the workings of the financial system with the banking system at its core – the very core that seems to be the culprit of today's crisis.

1.2 Banks and liquidity preference theory as a theory of financial intermediation

Keynes' *General Theory of Employment, Interest and Money* has been highly controversial ever since it was published in 1936. This should not be surprising, given the heretical nature of the book. For it denies the existence of an inherent tendency of "individualistic capitalism" towards some unique and optimal long-period equilibrium, the revered pinnacle of the economic discipline. Of the core constituents of Keynes' *General Theory*, launched by its author to revolutionize economic theory and policy, the theory of liquidity preference probably stands out as the most controversial element of all. Keynes presents liquidity preference theory in *The General Theory* as a "liquidity [preference] theory of interest," a theory that is supposed to fill the vacuum left by what he regarded as the flawed classical "savings theory of interest" (and its equally flawed "loanable funds" cousin).

This book offers a reassessment of liquidity preference theory. It argues that, in a dynamic context, liquidity preference theory is best understood as a theory of financial intermediation. Liquidity preference theory represents Keynes' attempt to rebuild monetary theory on the basis of a conception of banks as financial intermediaries, as institutions at the heart of capitalistic production and accumulation, a project prompted by institutional changes he observed and which he thought would necessitate an adaption of monetary theory. Already in his earlier *Treatise on Money*, Keynes (1930a, JMK 5: 27) observes that "current money is predominantly bank money" and then argues that "[i]t will, therefore, simplify the argument, without seriously detracting from its generality, if we assume not only that all the central bank money is held by the member banks, but also that *all the current money in the hands of the public is member bank money, i.e. bank deposits.*"[4]

Numerous confusions have emerged from the fact that liquidity preference theory appears in a rather static form in *The General Theory*. It is important to remember what *The General Theory* sets out to explain though, namely, the determinants of the level of employment for the economy as a whole at any moment in time. And when viewed from that particular perspective, liquidity preference theory, in a way, "collapses" into a theory of interest – as a portfolio equilibrium that balances the desire to hold liquid assets with the available pool of liquidity provided by the banking system. In this simplest, but also most essential form, the liquidity (preference) theory of interest is presented as "a purely logical step" that is needed to fill the important gap identified in the "classical" system with its flawed "savings theory of interest." The logical step pinpointed by Keynes is indeed a fundamental one. Alas, as presented in *The General Theory*, the critical role of the banking system's behavior remains somewhat hidden.

The critical role of banks takes place largely behind the scenes in Chapter 17 of *The General Theory* which he calls "The essential properties of interest and money." Exploring liquidity preference theory as a theory of asset price determination and how these impact on capital accumulation in a monetary production economy, Keynes identifies the "own rate of money interest" as "ruling the roost" of economic activity via its effects on the prices of riskless money debts of different maturities in particular (a sort of benchmark rate of interest) and on the structure of asset prices and, hence, interest rates in general. This illuminates the link between money and capital accumulation, and may in fact be seen as the culmination of Keynes' monetary thought (cf. Townshend 1937). This book argues that Keynes' (1936a, JMK 7: 293) dictum *"For the importance of money essentially flows from its being a link between the present and the future"* assigns a role of real and lasting influence to the behavior of financial intermediaries, at least in the kind of environment his analysis is referring to, namely growing and changing monetary production economies.

In a way, financial intermediaries provide the monetary complement to the key actors on the real-economy side in Keynes' vision, namely, entrepreneurs. According to his theory of effective demand, the level of employment is not determined in labor markets but is based on producers' assessments of expected sales proceeds relative to "known" supply conditions, i.e. profit maximization at a given level of effective demand. Demand in product markets includes new orders for investment goods by entrepreneurial investors facing "fundamental (or: Keynesian) uncertainty" – identified as the root cause behind the potential volatility of such commitments and their financing. In contrast with mainstream theory there is no presumption about expectations being held with certainty or certainty about probability distributions (certainty equivalence). Keynes emphasizes that the future of a changing economy is inherently unknowable. Entrepreneurs and their financiers are shaping what will unfold as the as yet unknown future, unknowable at the time their decisions are taken. In contrast to mainstream theory it is not households, functioning as consumers and providers of labor services, but rather entrepreneurs who are at the core of Keynes' microfoundations and the basis for his concept of equilibrium. Furthermore, it is financial intermediaries, rather than savers, who constitute the essential element in Keynes' vision of the process of capitalist production and capital accumulation. The point is that production in monetary production economies requires command over money – not saving! – to go ahead.[5]

The monetary theory of production features producers (and entrepreneurial investors) who need to secure finance, i.e. money required to pay the factors of production, to effectuate their production decisions. Because production requires command over money to go ahead effective demand in product markets and the level of employment are always and everywhere conditioned by the "terms of finance" as set by the financial system. The point is that in setting the terms of finance as currently prevailing in financial markets and conditioning production, those with control over finance are not in any way pinned down by those magical real forces which, according to the classics and today's mainstream alike, provide the underlying real anchors of the system; with money and finance as add-ons of convenience and mere surface phenomena. Instead, those in control of finance may follow whatever ideas or instincts they wish (or "animal spirits") when engaging in financial markets organized with a view of providing *liquidity* of investments (which "are fixed for the community as a whole"). In short, money and finance condition the real economy, not the other way round (as the "classics," old and new, would have it). Therefore, in Keynes' view, there is no dichotomy between monetary and real factors since "money plays a part of its own and affects motives and decisions and is, in short, one of the operative factors in the situation, so that the course of events cannot be predicted, either in the long period or the short, without knowledge of the behavior of money between the first state and the last" (Keynes 1933b, JMK 13: 408–9).

Within his "monetary theory of production" and broader vision of capitalism, liquidity preference theory captures Keynes' understanding of the working of the financial system encompassing financial markets and intermediaries as well as the monetary authorities, and featuring the separation between ownership and control of corporations. The rate of interest is set within the financial system in an ongoing, two-way interaction between financial market players (especially banks) and the monetary authorities (also in their role as financial regulators). Finance shapes the real economy landscape in lasting and sometimes disruptive fashions. As Minsky (1975) made clear in his critique of standard Keynesian interpretations, synthesizing Keynes' ideas as a special theory applicable to depressions only, *The General Theory* is not about some stable well-behaved system occasionally shocked by temporary disturbances, but about the inherent instability of finance and capitalism with its proneness to severe crises unless tamed by appropriate government policies.

Keynes' (and Minsky's) vision of money and banks as factors shaping the real economy is in stark contrast to modern monetary theory, which is dominated by the (neo-)Walrasian general equilibrium exchange paradigm with its highly acclaimed Arrow-Debreu icon. It is also well known that this "best developed model of the economy cannot find room for [money]" (Hahn 1982: 1).[6] And I may promptly add that the same holds for banks too. There is not even any real surprise here as the need to secure finance in order to obtain command over production is a nonissue within the Walrasian exchange paradigm. Thanks to some magical "auctioneer" intertemporal prices are such that markets clear through all time while compatibility of lifetime budget constraints is simultaneously assured. Within this peculiar exchange paradigm "saving" simply means ordering capital goods rather than consumption goods, with capital goods being "financed" out of planned future income; ruling out bankruptcies by assumption along the way too.[7] If macroeconomic models until the 1990s nevertheless usually included "money," they did so by some *ad hoc* assumption, and then typically referred to so-called "outside money" only (cf. Blanchard and Fischer 1989: 478; Hellwig 1993; Sargent 1987: 11, for instance).

More recent vintages of policy-oriented modeling exercises have mostly abandoned – redundant – money altogether, which seems only logical for a paradigm that cannot see any rationale for it anyway. Today's state-of-the-art modeling exercises typically use some monetary policy "reaction function" for the short-term rate of interest instead, which has the additional advantage of conforming with the actual practice of monetary policy. The policy prescription emerging from today's dynamic stochastic general equilibrium (DSGE) models is that a price-stability-focused central bank should use an appropriately tuned reaction function that has the interest rate instrument respond to (forecasted) deviations from policy goals owing to exogenous shocks. The point is, however, that while the short-term rate of interest is today acknowledged as being set by monetary policy, the "natural" or equilibrium rate of interest remains uniquely anchored by the underlying real forces of productivity and time preference – providing vivid testimony to the fact that Keynes' supposed revolution was aborted. Modern New Keynesian macroeconomics incorporates the loanable funds theory of interest, diagnosed as flawed by Keynes in the 1930s.

This book offers a reassessment of liquidity preference theory that highlights its validity and essential role in Keynes' heresy. To underline its continued relevance, we will also apply liquidity preference theory to recent developments in global finance, including the "saving glut hypothesis" and the ongoing global financial crisis. The remainder of this chapter is an attempt to compare Keynes' monetary theory in relation to both mainstream "New Keynesian" positions and some prominent Post Keynesian tenets.

1.3 "A managed currency is inevitable" – today's orthodox approach to monetary policy is Keynesian in nature

Already in his *Tract on Monetary Reform* in 1923 Keynes declared that attempts at restoring the supposedly automatic gold standard were misguided and that a "managed currency [was] inevitable" (Keynes [1923] 1971, JMK 4: 159).

Arguably, it is in this one respect, the inevitability of a managed currency, that Keynesianism has been triumphant as hardly anyone today seems to question the need for deliberate monetary policy management of fiat currencies. In fact, in both theory and practice, today's orthodox approach to monetary policy is basically Keynesian by nature.

Today's mainstream's monetary policy research agenda represents a quest for optimal stabilization policy through deliberate manipulation of the interest rate as policy instrument (see for instance Clarida *et al.* 1999; Romer 2000; Taylor 2000). Suitably dubbed the "reaction function approach" by Allsopp and Vines (2000), this approach to optimal stabilization policy aims at price stability as well as full employment. Undeniably, the reaction function approach is nothing else but a deliberate attempt at fine-tuning the economy. This is of utmost importance since the feasibility of fine-tuning has been at the heart of the "rules versus discretion" debate. The point is that once policymakers embark on manipulating the rate of interest as their policy instrument there is no sense in doing anything else but fine-tune the policy instrument in line with evolving economic conditions, a point expressed well by Alan Blinder:

> There is indeed a bright line between attempting to stabilize the economy and forsaking the whole messy business. But once you leave the realm of nonreactive rules and opt for some tuning, I fail to see any bright line – and maybe not even a dim one – between coarse-tuning, which is what central bankers are supposed to do, and fine-tuning, which is what they are supposed to avoid. Don't you always do the best you can, mindful of all the uncertainties and aware that perfection will not be achieved?
>
> (Blinder 1997: 12)

Note that Blinder refers to "nonreactive rules" and "forsaking the whole messy business" as the true alternative to fine-tuning. Proponents of this alternative worried that fine-tuning involves judgment and hence the risk of misjudgment and policy mistakes, let alone of deliberate misuse.

Of course the case for discretion has never been based on any idea of perfect success in fine-tuning policy goals. Perfect success at the goal level may be rare in practice. But proponents of discretion see worse policy performance arising under some automatic regime or, like Keynes, doubt that establishing an automatic regime is an option anyway – making a managed currency inevitable. The point is that aiming at minimizing a social loss function through interest rate policies inevitably requires fine-tuning the policy instrument. Failure to adjust the instrument as best as possible in the light of changing circumstances amounts to deliberately blocking market processes and de-stabilizing the economy. And this is exactly why conservative economists traditionally abhorred the "whole messy business" of interest rate policy in the first place.

Take Milton Friedman, for instance. The figurehead of monetarism proposed his famous "k-percent rule" not as some intermediate target strategy, but as an alternative to deliberate interest rate policies. Friedman strongly criticized any attempts to implement monetary "rules" indirectly through interest rate policies. His whole point was to make sure that central bankers abstain from that "whole messy business" but implement his favored rule directly as a strictly quantitative "base rule." The following quotation nicely captures this crucial point:

> the Fed currently attempts to control the money supply indirectly, by controlling a particular interest rate (the federal-funds rate). ... The alternative procedure is to let all interest rates be determined by the market – as they already mostly are – and instead control the money supply by controlling the amount of reserves available to the banking system.
>
> (Friedman 1975: 235–6)[8]

The situation is very similar for another very prominent conservative economist who proposed a conservative alternative to Keynes' "managed currency." In contrast to Friedman, who may be seen as standing in the line of thought of the historical currency school, F. A. von Hayek's alliance was with free banking. Hayek rejected monetary rules but favored reliance on the rule of the law and currency competition instead. The following quotation nicely captures Hayek's views on interest rate policies:

> With the central banks and the monopoly of the issue of money would, of course, disappear also the possibility of deliberately determining the rate of interest. The disappearance of what is called "interest rate policy" is wholly desirable. ... The whole idea that the rate of interest ought to be used as an instrument of policy is entirely mistaken.
>
> (Hayek 1976: 106–7)

We may also add the German economist Walter Eucken to this list of prominent conservative economists that represented the opposition to Keynes. Eucken may be less well known internationally, but his ideas have been very influential in shaping the German "Ordoliberalist" tradition, which in rather dubious ways influences monetary policymaking in continental Europe until this day. I say in dubious ways because his apparent disciples in Bundesbank and ECB circles have been rather disingenuous in calling on Eucken as their apparent inspiration for "stability-oriented" monetary policies. In practice, Eucken's principle of "primacy of currency policy" is seen as apparently justifying delays in interest rate easing when the economy slumps. By contrast, no such "caution" is ever applied when it comes to tightening policy (see below). However, and similar to Friedman and Hayek in spirit, Eucken's message was that central bankers should not be trusted with exercising any such discretion. While Eucken's views as to actual policymaking and implementation were less clearly expressed, including at times support for a commodity-reserve currency, his essential idea was one of implanting an "automatically working monetary stabilizer," as he called it, into the monetary system. Eucken did not want to rely on central bank's interest rate policy since "ignorance, weakness vis-à-vis interest groups and public opinion, flawed theories, all this influences the leaders [of the central bank] much to the damage of the task they are entrusted with" (Eucken 1952: 257; my translation).

Put in a nutshell, Keynes' conservative opponents argued for foregoing that "whole messy business" which mainstream theory today prescribes central bankers to engage in fully. In this one respect, then, it is undeniable that Keynes has proved triumphant over conservative ideas. There is little acknowledgement of the total defeat of conservative ideas of foregoing interest rate policies though. Instead, the "rules versus discretion" debate has taken a peculiar twist that presents discretion as the realm of lunatics.

And it is not clear to me whether this peculiar twist owing to "new classical" contributions is a deliberate attempt to cover up today's realities as just described, or whether it reflects a general state of ignorance prevailing among today's mainstream economists about some fundamental issues in monetary economics. The fact is that the mainstream completely misconstrues the quest for optimal stabilization policies through interest rate fine-tuning as something else than discretion, i.e. the Keynesian "managed currency" realm. I am referring here to the literature on the so-called time-inconsistency problem which alleges superiority of "rules" over "discretion."

I shall not elaborate on this point since I have critiqued this literature in detail elsewhere (Bibow 2004b; see also Forder 1998, Goodhart 1994a). According to what has proved to be highly influential new classical thinking on the matter, a time-inconsistency problem is said to give rise to an inflationary bias in monetary policy whenever central bankers have discretion at their disposal. This is because within the chosen model setup the general public has reason to rationally expect the policymaker, if equipped with discretion, to renege on the optimal zero-inflation policy and to spring deliberate "inflation surprises" upon them. Not only is "discretion" modeled (and mocked) as an utterly foolish attempt at chasing the moon, it must be sadly acknowledged that the time-inconsistency literature overlooks some rather fundamental issues and therefore ends up going seriously astray.

In the new classical world policymakers are envisioned to be equipped with an "inflation surprise" instrument. In other words, central banks do not set interest rates but simply flip their inflation surprise switch whenever they choose. Remarkably, this literature sets out to make the case for rules, but completely omits Friedman's long and variable lags. If this omission seems just a little outlandish, consider that the ultimate cause of all troubles in this imaginary world of inflation surprise policy switches is the postulate that policymakers aim at a more-than-full level of employment. Only inflation surprises can have real effects in this new classical world. But since the rationally expecting public understands what policymakers with "discretion" are after, the poor policymaking creatures are chasing the moon and only create an inflationary bias. What is needed to overcome the problem is a commitment to a rule, one that precludes the deleterious effects wrought by discretionary policy. And central bank independence (CBI) quickly emerges as the favored commitment device of many who allowed themselves to get fooled by this no-sense approach.

The irony is, of course, that CBI represents a policy of "discretion rather than rule," which is exactly why Friedman and other conservative economists generally rejected it (see Bibow 2002b, 2004b, 2008b, 2009b). Keynes, by contrast, as Chapter 6 below shows, supported the idea of CBI as a way of enhancing the efficiency of monetary policy. Exemplifying the remarkable confusions that afflict the debate on this issue, De Long (2000) suggested that today's dominant "New Keynesian" paradigm was really the "Triumph of Monetarism" under a different name (see Dalziel 2002). If we owe anything to those aforementioned prominent conservative economists, it is an unshakeable faith in the invisible hand's ability to equilibrate all markets, leading them to embrace a pertinacious urge to liberalize, deregulate, and privatize any market that prevents the invisible hand from working its magic. As far as monetary structure and policy approach are concerned, only Keynes' monetary thought can rationalize CBI and the quest for optimal stabilization policy through "feedback rules" for deliberate interest rate policies.

Furthermore, I must add here that there is no disagreement with today's mainstream whatsoever as to the ultimate policy goals of full employment and price stability. The true differences between "Keynes and the classics," then and now, concern the role that money plays in their respective conception of economies, or the functioning of monetary economies. The imaginary world of inflation surprise policy switches and policymakers keen to chase the moon is not Keynes' world; instead it is a new classical fiction. Importantly, however, the vision underlying these new classical ideas and today's mainstream thought resemble old classical ideas in important ways, those very classical ideas about the functioning of the economy that Keynes was attacking. And this is where the Keynesian triumph therefore ends: Keynes' attack failed to properly revolutionize our ways of thinking about the functioning of monetary economies. The reaction function approach may be Keynesian in nature, but orthodoxy remained stuck with the classical money neutrality postulate.

1.4   Stuck with the "money neutrality postulate"

In fact, in the end, it all boils down to the mainstream's steadfast adherence to the money neutrality postulate. The idea that money is neutral in "the long run" is the cornerstone of modeling exercises and policy advice alike. Vertical supply curves and Phillips curves as prominent representations of uniquely determined real underlying attractors of long-run equilibrium reflect the neutrality postulate. In the long run, money only determines the price level and monetary policy can only act as nominal anchor. A related prominent belief is that inflation has to be near zero to avoid detrimental effects on economic performance, as money may *not* be *super-neutral*.

While analytical convenience may explain in part the postulate's popularity in modeling exercises, it is even more difficult to see how one might honestly attribute any practical relevance to it. Here it is of great interest that we may actually consult the authority of Milton Friedman on this matter, the very economist who may have done more than anyone else in resurrecting the neutrality postulate in monetary economics. While Friedman was keen to resurrect the quantity theory of money and the neutrality postulate in theory, when it came to policy he merely suggested that his proposed k-percent rule would avoid *systematic* policy errors. It was precisely because of his concerns about a strong real effect of monetary policy in "the short run" (which he defined as a period of up to ten years) that he wanted to prevent central bankers from conducting interest rate policies, which, in his view, were prone to produce systematic policy errors (and cumulative effects). So when a prominent modern central bank politician, Otmar Issing, suggested to him that the neutrality postulate might provide guidance as well as comfort to the practical central banker, Friedman corrected him in the following highly illuminating way:

> Taken seriously, monetary neutrality means that central bankers are irrelevant: real magnitudes – which are what ultimately matter to people – go their own way, independently of what the central banker does. Central bankers are important in so far as money is not neutral and does have real effects. Neutrality propositions give little if any guide to effective central bank behavior under such circumstances. Perhaps they offer comfort to central bankers by implying that all *mistakes will average out in that mythical long run* in which Keynes assured us "we are all dead." Keynes went on, "Economists [central bankers] set themselves too easy, too useless a task if in tempestuous seasons they can only tell us that when the storm is long past the ocean is flat again."
>
> (Friedman 2002; emphasis added)

It is one thing for someone with a firm belief in or a strong mission to propagate, for political reasons, the neutrality postulate to be corrected on this point by Milton Friedman, and even with a reference to Keynes' famous remark on the long run. What a punishment for politically motivated wishful thinking! Another, however, is to take seriously the definition of neutrality as applicable for practical purposes that Friedman provided in this context, referring to a state in which "all mistakes will average out." While one might perhaps suppose that *random* mistakes will average or cancel out, in some sense, the same could hardly be expected for *systematic* mistakes stemming from a *policy bias*. Friedman's neutrality definition, which includes the need to avoid systematic mistakes, clearly allows for the possibility of a policy bias having real effects in the long run.

The conventional wisdom on money neutrality and shocks as embedded in mainstream New Keynesian models does not take this possibility seriously. Demand shocks are said to pose no conflict or trade-off between output and inflation stabilization anyway since monetary policy, working through aggregate demand only, acts like a demand shock itself. The optimal policy reaction is thus to offset fully any shocks to aggregate demand. By contrast, the response to supply shocks is more complex, reflecting an output–inflation variability trade-off. For instance, as an extreme form of inflation targeting, the policymaker would focus on stabilizing inflation only and ignore any concomitant degree of output instability caused by supply shocks.

There is an obvious problem with this view: if monetary policy is supposed to work through aggregate demand, which includes investment spending, supply-side effects cannot be denied. Any impact on the capital stock and productivity growth will not simply disappear after a couple of quarters. Kahn ([1958] 1972: 139) aptly warned against fighting inflation by causing unemployment:

> The economic waste involved in such a policy is particularly great if demand is regulated by restricting productive investment, as will be the main result of relying on monetary policy. Not only is there the loss of potential investment. But the growth of productivity is thereby curtailed, thus narrowing the limit on the permissible rate of rise in wages and increasing the amount of unemployment required to secure observance of the limit.

From a Post Keynesian view both actual and potential output is dependent on effective demand and the natural rate of growth of output is endogenously responsive to macroeconomic policies (Setterfield 2002, 2006; Lavoie 2006a). Monetary economies are inevitably characterized by path dependency and hysteresis, implying that monetary policy can lastingly depress employment and growth *unless policy errors cancel out over time*. It is remarkable how mainstream research practices deal with the conspicuous logical inconsistency in their theoretical framework: standard trend filtering techniques (à la Hodrick-Prescott, for instance) impose the "averaging out of mistakes" condition; which amounts to proving money neutrality by assuming it to be true.

The vital point at issue here also pertains to debates on the optimally low target rate of inflation. While mainstream thought offers inconclusive advice on this point, empirical evidence on the growth–inflation trade-off suggests that the target rate can actually be too low (Ahearne *et al.* 2002; Ball 1997; Ghosh and Phillips 1998; Pollin and Zhu 2006). For practical policy purposes the issue is not just about the optimal equilibrium rate of inflation but also about the best strategy to re-attain the target rate if inflation is above it, or how aggressively to respond to the perceived risk that this might occur. It is thus of great interest that the two most important central banks in the world, the US Federal Reserve and the European Central Bank (ECB), despite by all appearances being equally attuned to mainstream money neutrality beliefs when judged by standards of official rhetoric, follow starkly opposing approaches when it comes to practical policy.

For instance, when the Federal Reserve in the 1990s was facing a situation of economic growth at slightly above "comfort zone" inflation, ideas emerged from inside the Fed about the possibility of an "opportunistic approach to disinflation" (see Orphanides and Wilcox 2002). By contrast, when the ECB's chief economist at the time, Otmar Issing, addressed the suggestion that in the presence of hysteresis or persistence monetary policy should practice caution in tightening policy, his advice was that aggression rather than caution was required when dealing with perceived upward risks to inflation:

The existence of persistence in unemployment makes it even more important to ensure that the central bank avoids a situation in which disinflation becomes necessary. Given the favorable starting position of the ECB, this militates towards a forward-looking and pre-emptive approach which prevents inflation from emerging in the first place and in particular avoids inflation becoming ingrained into people's expectations.

(Issing 2001: 196)

Note the contrast: opportunism at the Federal Reserve was about not risking a recession despite the fact that actual inflation was higher than desired, while aggression at the ECB was about willingly risking recession as a pre-emptive measure to counter the possibility that inflation might rise from its current low level above some tolerable ceiling rate. A related issue concerns the respective inflation measures that provide the policy focus of the two central banks: The Federal Reserve focuses on core inflation and practices more tolerance towards "supply shocks" that push up headline inflation (such as the energy price boom in recent years). With the ECB's focus on headline inflation such leniency is more difficult, explaining why the bank still hiked its policy rate in July 2008 despite the fact that the Euroland economy was already in recession. This once again underlined that the opposing kinds of mindsets of American and continental European central bankers show up clearly in their actions as well. More generally, the Federal Reserve is known for its aggressive reactions to financial instability and economic weakness – dubbed the "Greenspan put" by outsiders, and explained as a "risk management approach" to monetary policy by Fed insiders. The ECB, on the other hand, is known for its urge for aggressive, "pre-emptive" tightening, paired with a pronounced tendency to "fall behind the curve" when it comes to monetary easing. ECB officials claim that they strictly follow their mandate, which in contrast to the Federal Reserve's is not a "dual mandate" featuring both price stability and maximum employment, but instead, in the words of the ECB's president Jean-Claude Trichet: "there is one needle in our compass and it is price stability" (*Reuters*, 24 Jan. 2008). And they notoriously assert that their "stability-oriented" (price-stability-only) approach is the best available anyway for maintaining price stability *as well as growth*.

It should be observed that business cycles on either side of the Atlantic are conspicuously different. While the US cycle is typically characterized by long upswings and brief downturns, Euroland's business cycle (following Germany's example) is characterized by protracted periods of domestic demand stagnation and belated and brief – export-driven – upswings. Are these transatlantic stylized facts of business cycles unrelated to monetary policy, as the money neutrality postulate would seem to suggest? Or is it not justified to suspect that the ECB's asymmetrical approach of aggressive tightening and "cautious" easing is bound to produce an "anti-growth bias" (Bibow 2002b, 2004b, 2006a), representing a case of *systematic* policy mistakes that do not cancel out over time but instead cause permanent real damage?

Addressing this question has gained a new urgency with the ongoing global financial crisis. I argued elsewhere (Bibow 2007, 2008a) that the above transatlantic clash of policy traditions has been one key contributing factor in the emergence of "global imbalances." Continental Europe's protracted domestic demand stagnation (under Germany's leadership) for much of the 1990s and again from 2001 until 2005 meant freeloading on external growth. As will be analyzed in detail in Chapter 8, since the 1990s and for differing reasons, other countries or regions of the world as well became overly reliant on external growth. The result was that the US for long came to act as sole global growth engine, running up an enormous external deficit along the way. Since their peak in 2006, global imbalances have finally started to reverse course – together with the implosion of the global credit structures underlying them. And since the fall of 2008 policymakers around the world are desperately trying to come to grips with the causes of and adequate policy responses to the ongoing crisis.

In this context, another aspect of the above transatlantic clash in policy traditions has come to the forefront of debates: is it wiser to pre-emptively prick asset market bubbles by tighter monetary policy as soon as they arise (the Bundesbank or ECB position), or is it better to let them pop on their own and concentrate on mopping up the mess afterwards (the Fed's position or Greenspan doctrine). The case for the latter approach was prominently reconfirmed in 2002 by no other than today's Federal Reserve Chairman Bernanke, arguing against the idea of pre-emptive tightening in 1997, as this "would have throttled a great deal of technological progress and sustainable growth in productivity and output" (Bernanke 2002). It is one thing that today the pendulum may be swinging away from the Greenspan doctrine, an issue to which we will return in the concluding chapter following an analysis of the global monetary and financial order (cf. Kohn 2008). It is quite another that Bernanke's above quotation also throws some interesting light on the money neutrality position. For in there Bernanke explicitly states that finance and monetary policy have a lasting impact on the supply side of the economy too. And this is the point I am driving at: the money neutrality postulate is at the heart of the matter. Modern mainstream modeling exercises steadfastly adhere to the classical principle Keynes attacked in his *General Theory*, backed up by dubious analytical constructs and empirical proofs which *assume* the postulate's validity (and hence prove nothing whatsoever). Practical central bankers around the world publically proclaim their (convenient) belief in the neutrality of their actions. But at times at least some of them seem to doubt whether finance and monetary policy really are of no real consequence beyond "the short run" which they reduce, conveniently, to just a couple of quarters.

In the light of the ongoing global financial crisis, then, does it not seem quite heroic to assume that the real economy disruptions witnessed around the world may be unrelated to finance and money (broadly defined to include monetary policy as well as national and international financial regulation), and that any real consequences might quickly evaporate as if nothing has ever happened? The real trouble is that modern mainstream theories of finance and the macroeconomy are of little if any use in understanding the functioning of monetary economies.

This book argues that Keynes has provided an alternative and much superior framework for monetary theory, which, among other things, rejects the money neutrality postulate. The next section illustrates some key analytical dividing lines between mainstream New Keynesians (or orthodoxy) on the one hand, and Keynes and Post Keynesians on the other.

1.5 Money neutrality versus Keynesian uncertainty and liquidity preference

If money neutrality is the cornerstone of monetary orthodoxy, do not miss that belief in the postulate is intimately related to the denial that situations of Keynesian uncertainty are fundamentally different from risk. In mainstream theory situations that are not certain are nonetheless generally reducible to probabilistic risk. By contrast, Keynes emphasized that in monetary economies the future is intrinsically unknowable: "defeat[ing] the forces of time and our ignorance of the future" (Keynes 1936a, JMK 7: 157) poses a serious challenge to economic decisions that involve commitment on the part of the decision maker and the possibility of bankruptcy.

> By "uncertain" knowledge, let me explain, I do not mean merely to distinguish what is known for certain from what is only probable. The game of roulette is not subject, in this sense, to uncertainty; nor is the prospect of a Victory bond being drawn. Or, again, the expectation of life is only slightly uncertain. Even the weather is only moderately uncertain. The sense in which I am using the term is that in which the prospect of a European war is uncertain, or the price of copper and the rate of interest twenty years hence, or the obsolescence of a new invention, or the position of private wealth owners in the social system in 1970. About these matters there is no scientific basis on which to form any calculable probability whatever. We simply do not know.
>
> (Keynes 1937c, JMK 14: 113–4)

It is in this kind of environment that liquidity attains value from the perspective of the holder. And it is in this kind of environment that the providers of liquidity, banks, attain real significance. Accordingly, Keynes pointedly observed that "the rate of interest is, on my theory, essentially an uncertainty phenomenon" (Keynes 1936e, JMK 29: 221).

By contrast, the mainstream's preoccupation with probabilistic risk *only* explains why the "best developed model of the economy cannot find room" (Hahn 1982: 1) for money or banks. Money seems largely superfluous and economic performance seemingly dependent on those legendary real forces only. Chapter 4 clarifies the important distinction between risk and uncertainty and its relevance in different contexts that involve different kinds of economic decisions. The remainder of this section will highlight that the contrasting treatment of uncertainty is crucial to some key dividing lines between "Keynes and the classics."

Uncertainty and wage flexibility

The first such dividing line concerns wage flexibility. While New Keynesians have provided microeconomic explanations for wage rigidities, ultimately their position is not much different from either traditional or modern "classical" views of wage flexibility as key adjustment mechanism and wage rigidities as the ultimate root cause of all troubles. In the classical world perfect wage (and price) flexibility is supposed to assure full employment. Patinkin (1956) felt confident to proclaim that Keynes got it all wrong because the "real balance effect" would anchor long-run equilibrium under perfect price–wage flexibility. It was never any trouble for theorists like Patinkin that this line of reasoning supposed money exclusively in the form of "outside" (or better gold) money – when their model world cannot make sense of money other than by *ad hoc* assumption in the first place. Obviously, this was not the kind of world that Keynes was considering.

Keynes viewed stickiness of money wages first of all as a policy-relevant empirical fact. In "The economic consequences of Mr. Churchill" Keynes emphasized that money wages tend to adjust much more slowly than most other prices; a fact that inspired his later emphasis in *The General Theory* on the "wage unit" and on money wages as the anchor of the whole structure of prices. Keynes was also keenly aware that money wage trends were not only influenced by macroeconomic conditions, but also by institutional and conventional factors, as reflected in his distinction between "profit inflation" (deflation) and "income inflation" (deflation) in the *Treatise*. Accordingly, keeping income inflation in balance required instruments other than monetary policy: "The task of keeping efficiency wages reasonably stable (I am sure they will creep up steadily in spite of our best efforts) is a political rather than an economic problem" (Keynes 1943f, Letter to B. Graham of 31 Dec. 1943, JMK 26: 38).[9]

But in Chapter 19 of *The General Theory* Keynes also judges *aggregate* (macro) money wage flexibility as an unreliable and risky adjustment mechanism. His argument squarely focuses on the uncertainties this would create for entrepreneurs and households, as well as for financial institutions. In denial of any sense in the supposedly equilibrating real balance effect,[10] Keynes understood too well that aggregate price instability would create financial system problems owing to the existence of bank money and money debts. In particular, in 1931, in the midst of the Great Depression, Keynes (1931a, JMK 9: 157) observed that "there is a degree of deflation which no bank can stand … . If nothing is done, it will be amongst the world's banks that the really critical breakages will occur."

Related to his emphasis on the unit-of-account function of money, Keynes stressed the need for a "stable measuring rod" (or aggregate stability of prices) to avoid unnecessary uncertainties and random bankruptcies. Stickiness of aggregate (not relative!) money wages (adjusted for productivity) are in his view not an obstacle blocking efficient adjustments, but the basis for price stability and the effectiveness of monetary policy management of the economy – through avoidance of uncertainty.

Uncertainty, loanable funds and monetary policy communication

Uncertainty is also key to the second fundamental dividing line concerning interest rate determination, financial markets and monetary policy. I observed above that an important innovation in New Keynesian monetary policy modeling exercises is to be seen in the use of the interest rate as policy instrument (as this better accords with actual monetary policy practice than the prior use of some money stock; not to mention the new classical "inflation surprise" fantasy instrument). It may thus at first appear as if the rate of interest in these modern models were wholly policy determined rather than driven by some market mechanism. This interpretation would differ fundamentally from the older "savings theory of interest" that Keynes attacked in the *General Theory*, according to which some "loanable funds (market!) mechanism" provided an inherent tendency for the rate of interest to move in line with the real anchors of productivity and thrift. Yet, while the short-term rate of interest is acknowledged as being set by monetary policy, the underlying structure in New Keynesian models is essentially of a real business cycle (i.e. new classical) kind, featuring the "natural" or equilibrium rate of interest as anchored by real forces. In the end, then, monetary policy remains a (neutral) surface phenomenon. The fact that liquidity preference theory has not replaced the classical or loanable funds theory of interest is most vivid testimony to the failure of Keynes' supposed revolution.

While diagnosed as flawed by Keynes in the 1930s, the loanable funds theory of interest continues to dominate theory and policy debates today. For instance, the idea that the rate of interest is ultimately determined by productivity and thrift underlies (current Federal Reserve Governor) Bernanke's (2003) "saving glut hypothesis" and (former Federal Reserve Governor) Greenspan's (2004, 2007) observations on the related "bond market conundrum." In their view increased global savings, in East Asian countries in particular, flooded the global capital market and thereby depressed interest rates, even as the US Federal Reserve tightened its policy rate. Based on Keynes' insights the analysis offered in Chapter 8 of this book denies the validity of these prominent hypotheses, presenting alternative liquidity preference theoretical explanations instead. Our analysis will also highlight the connection between "global imbalances" and today's global financial crisis.

The continued liveliness of the loanable funds theory of interest is also clearly reflected in modern textbooks, with Gregory Mankiw's bestselling *Principles of Economics* taken here as representative. According to Mankiw (2009: 584)

> the supply of loanable funds comes from people who have some extra income they want to save and lend out. This lending can occur directly, such as when a household buys a bond from a firm, or it can occur indirectly, such as when a household makes a deposit in a bank, which in turn uses the funds to make loans. In both cases, saving is the source of the supply of loanable funds.

Note here immediately that behind this approach is a vision of saving as financing investment, of saving being there first, to be then passed on to investors or to banks which then lend out the deposits to prospective borrowers of those funds. Liquidity preference theory denies the validity of this vision when applied to monetary production economies.

True, liquidity preference theory, in some form at least, has found its way into modern textbooks, although the form that it takes in a New Keynesian–New Classical synthesis of kinds is rather odd, to say the least. Again citing Mankiw:

> the two different theories of the interest rate are useful for different purposes. When thinking about the long-run determinants of interest rates, it is best to keep in mind the loanable-funds theory, which highlights the importance of an economy's saving propensities and investment opportunities. By contrast, when thinking about the short-run determinants of interest rates, it is best to keep in mind the liquidity-preference theory, which highlights the importance of monetary policy.
>
> (Mankiw 2009: 782)

Note here the connection drawn by Mankiw between the interest rate question and the assumed neutrality of money in the long run, confirming what we said above about monetary policy as a mere surface phenomenon compared to those real underlying forces.

As another variation on this theme Stiglitz and Greenwald (2003: 151) even argue "for a return to the pre-Keynesian emphasis on 'loanable funds'." These prominent New Keynesian economists suggest that what they attack as the traditional monetary paradigm, featuring the Hicksian *IS/LM* model, followed Keynes' liquidity preference theoretical lines. Still, and whatever the merit of Stiglitz and Greenwald's research agenda on the role of credit and information problems in finance in general,[11] their example further underlines my fundamental contention that liquidity preference theory and its role in Keynes' heresy have been thoroughly misunderstood.

We therefore need to re-emphasize here that our above claim for a Keynesian triumph over competing classical, traditional conservative ideas only referred to the general nature of the "reaction function approach." By contrast, the underlying structure of New Keynesian modeling exercises is anything but Keynesian. Even the Wicksellian heritage, as implied in the title of Woodford's (2003) influential work *Interest and Prices,* is questionable given the dubious treatment of "investment" in these models (see Spahn 2007). Perhaps a Fisherian flavor may be seen in depicting monetary policy communication and credibility as referring to inflation expectations only. There certainly is no room for liquidity preference of nonbanks or banks, just as there are no banks present anyway, and therefore also no bank failures possible, in this peculiar non-Keynesian model world. I am reminded here of Keynes' observation on economics as "a science of thinking in terms of models joined to the art of choosing models which are relevant to the contemporary world" (Keynes 1938b, JMK 14: 296). Perhaps it is fair to say that the economics profession today shows excessive ambitions on the science part, which is almost exclusively understood in terms of mathematical-deductivist modeling exercises of apparent sophistry, joined by an almost complete lack of any artistry in choosing relevant models. No real-world central bank has any inflation surprise switch at its disposal. But as the ongoing crisis highlights, bankruptcies, including bank failures, are highly relevant in the contemporary world. Policymakers are well advised to practice care in choosing models that do take those nasty realities seriously.

Unfortunately the interest rate question is an area lacking consensus even among Post Keynesians. A long-standing dispute concerns the endogeneity of credit money and how that relates to Keynes' liquidity preference theory. To be sure, Post Keynesians follow Keynes in rejecting loanable funds theory, but at the same time support for liquidity preference theory is widely lacking. I shall hope to rectify this omission in this book.

The endogenous money approach rightly emphasizes that monetary policy sets the short-term rate of interest, thereby influencing effective demand and potential growth – the neutrality of money argument is never taken seriously in Post Keynesian models. But little is said about how setting the short-term rate relates to financial markets and interest rates in general (other than through "mark-ups"). Banks appear strangely passive in this approach and liquidity does not seem to play any significant role, while little is said about policy communication either.

Chapter 5 sets out to explore Keynes' supposed exogenous money approach and how it relates to active bank behavior. Keynes understood perfectly well that the short-term rate was easily under the authorities' control. His concern was that steering longer term interest rates and financial conditions in general represents a much more complex and difficult task. Keynes argued that guiding and anchoring financial market expectations required skilful policy communication and was dependent on the authorities' credibility. In this regard, Keynesian policymakers should understand that market players generally care about inflation as well as growth. Keynes suggested that the authorities may have to back up their words by deeds, i.e. apply open market operations in long-term securities, to control rates beyond short-term ones. And Keynes also advised that under exceptional conditions the authorities must stand ready to greatly expand the central bank's balance sheet if the banks' support for credit expansion cannot be secured – all measures that are highly relevant today in the aftermath of an asset price boom and bust that has left bank capital severely impaired.

Uncertainty, asset prices and financial regulation

What follows from the previous argument is the question as to how uncertainty relates to another key dividing line, namely asset price determination and financial regulation. Asset price boom-and-bust cycles sit awkwardly with orthodox "efficient market theory." According to efficient market theory market prices of assets are always uniquely correct in reflecting all available information, i.e. they correctly reflect the realities of the underlying real economy. Financial markets absolve their allocative function efficiently, on this view, but they do not seem to shape the economy in any meaningful sense; finance (or saving?) smoothly follows those real fundamentals which yield uniquely correct signals in complete detachment from anything monetary. It seems quite natural, then, to "deregulate, liberalize, and privatize," and trust market discipline at all times. With so much faith in free and efficient markets it would seem odd to suppose that there might nonetheless be any role for a lender of last resort or even scope for fiscal bailouts.

Before rejecting the soundness of efficient market theory as a reliable tool to understand finance and the working of financial markets let me add here that mainstream theory has seen valuable innovations, particularly in the form of the asymmetric information approach (for instance in the work of Greenwald and Stiglitz 2003) and the behavioral finance literature (see e.g. Shefrin 1999; Shiller 2000; Shleifer 2000). The former approach offers important insights into the role of credit and banks despite their continued adherence to a loanable funds theory of interest. The latter innovative approach brings the analysis of financial markets closer to Keynes' emphasis on ignorance, conventions and mass psychology. And yet, these approaches cannot let go completely of the vision that money and finance provide a mere surface layer covering, perhaps sometimes distorting, the underlying real fundamentals of the economy.

To repeat, Keynes' vision is the opposite one of money and finance shaping the real economy. Financial conditions are a key determinant of economic activity and employment, and by influencing capital formation they also shape our future production possibilities in lasting fashion. Acting under Keynesian uncertainty the key actors, entrepreneurial investors and their financiers, are shaping a future that is unknowable at the time their decisions are taken. Informed by Keynes' experience as a successful professional financial investor, Chapter 12 of *The General Theory* highlights the role of "beauty-contest-like" asset-market play and conventional – rather than uniquely correct – asset valuations in markets organized for their liquidity.

An inherent instability of credit and asset markets emerges from Keynes' insightful account of the working of the financial system. One must bear in mind that Keynes wanted to protect and nourish the "advantages of individualism" against the threat of the totalitarian state when he at the same time warned that "when the capital development of a country becomes the by-product of the activities of a casino, the job is likely to be ill-done" (Keynes 1936a, JMK 7: 159). Faith in the invisible hand is unfounded when, under a thick fog of uncertainty and ignorance, players engage in herd-like gambling. Asset prices are inherently restless and financial markets endogenously breed instability. Among Post Keynesians Hyman Minsky stands out for developing Keynes' vision of financial capitalism (see also Kregel 1998).

Keynes' vision of a monetary production economy where finance matters cries out for a careful market-stabilizing regulation of the financial system. A lack of pre-emptive regulatory interference is bound to end up in *ex post* repair work. It is ironic that all too blissful faith in unrestrained free markets should end up leading to more rather than less government involvement, through nationalization of previously deregulated, but failed, banks, for instance. Since the 1980s the zeal for financial liberalization has extended its global reach, laying the ground for numerous crises in emerging markets and also the linkages through which the current crisis that hit the center of global finance in 2007 has spread worldwide. Chapter 7 shows that Keynes also saw an important role in regulating international capital flows.

Uncertainty, monetary policy and macro policy mix

It is not surprising then that Post Keynesians take issue with the "new consensus" view on monetary policy and the macro policy mix (see Arestis and Sawyer 2005; Fontana and Palacio-Vera 2007; Lavoie 2004; Palley 2007). Underlying the new consensus view is the money neutrality postulate and complete neglect of Keynesian uncertainty, explaining its severe limitations as highlighted in the above. The new consensus view has monetary policy playing the lead role for price stabilization and consequent full-employment growth, leaving at best a supporting role for fiscal policy. In line with the liberalization zeal fiscal action is probably perceived as a threat to the "small government" ideal. The postulated long-run neutrality of monetary policy seems to make this kind of interventionism more palatable. Policy coordination is not needed, or may even be harmful. In strict New Keynesian fashion, the new consensus view on monetary policy blames the existence of sticky wages (and perhaps other institutional flaws) as hindering the effectiveness of monetary policy in creating price stability and full-employment economic growth.

Post Keynesians do not deny that monetary policy offers flexibility in adjusting policy stance, which may be an important advantage when quick action is required. In this regard, a "risk management approach" of taking out insurance against low-probability events that carry calamitous consequences, as developed by the Greenspan Fed, is principally welcome (even if "low probability" may not be numerically expressible). But it should then also be acknowledged that sticky money wages actually provide a safety net against the greatest calamity of all: deflation. More generally, stable money wages (adjusted for productivity) establish the basis for effective stabilization policies. I argued above that Keynes' concern was that aggregate wage flexibility creates uncertainty for entrepreneurs and households as well as financial institutions. The same holds for policymakers as well. By contrast, a money wage anchor to the price system simplifies the task of policymakers, by reducing uncertainty. Post Keynesians generally do not favor leaving the entire stabilization burden on the central bank's shoulders, but consider active fiscal policy to be essential. This includes taking more seriously Keynes' (1936a, JMK 7: 378) hunch of "a somewhat comprehensive socialization of investment" as a strategy to foster recovery and stabilize the economy at full employment.

Overall, Post Keynesians show a much greater concern for proper policy coordination, aiming at some sound mix of policies also including debt management policies and financial regulation.[12] While closer *pre-emptive* cooperation would be preferable, it has been of great interest to observe more of an alertness and openness to coordinate among policymakers as the current crisis struck. As regards policy measures, one is tempted to remark that it is sometimes hard to see how certain actions could possibly be justified on the basis of popular mainstream models that seemed to guide policymaking under pre-crisis conditions.[13] But as noted at the start of this chapter, comparing the policy reaction to the Great Depression and today's crisis, something of a Keynesian revolution does seem to have happened. The Keynesian triumph in theory and policy has proved a very limited one, though, as the remainder of this chapter illustrated.

In summary, today's New Keynesian mainstream appears to recognize that a "managed currency is inevitable." Despite the prevailing free market faith orthodoxy accepts that shocks need to be countered by deliberate policy. Yet, while the "reaction function approach" to policy is Keynesian in nature, the money neutrality postulate deflects the policy task from the real issue; the consequent collateral damage (as experienced in today's crisis, for instance) is very real. It is also through the money neutrality postulate that the mainstream gets rid of liquidity preference theory. And while at least some New Keynesians attach a heightened importance to credit, loanable funds theory continues to enjoy widespread popularity. By contrast, Post Keynesians reject both the money neutrality postulate and loanable funds theory, but then manage to throw out liquidity preference theory, too, namely by adhering to what may be called the "credit simplicity postulate," a simplistic endogenous money view that – as Chapter 5 below argues – in its extreme form amounts to "reverse monetarism" (without neutrality).

This book argues that ignoring the key role of liquidity preference theory in Keynes' heresy is dangerously bound up with the continued teaching of classical ideas that are "misleading and disastrous if we attempt to apply [them] to the facts of experience" (Keynes 1936a, JMK 7: 3). Liquidity preference theory captures Keynes' vision of money and finance as conditioning effective demand and shaping the real economy (rather than just being a reflection of it). In monetary production economies money itself *is* a real factor as money enters directly into the calculation of real economic decisions, while the determination of financial conditions takes place in a complex, ongoing, two-way interaction between the authorities and financial market players, and without any links to the real economy other than through the ideas and models that may guide (or misguide) those actors.

1.6 Overview of the book

In a variety of ways Chapter 2 sets the theme for this book, which is appropriate given that Keynes regarded what he called the finance motive for the demand of money as the "coping stone" of liquidity preference theory. The finance motive highlights the lead role of money and banks – rather than savers – in enabling growth in a monetary production economy. The aim of Chapter 2 is to illustrate how the finance motive fits into the conceptual framework of Keynes' monetary analysis. The great beauty of the finance motive is to be seen in the fact that it breathes some life into the *seemingly* static framework of analysis of *The General*

Theory, thereby illustrating how the various motives for the demand for money *and* the behavior of financial intermediaries are related in liquidity preference theory (though we do not explicitly deal with uncertainty and the speculative motive here).

In the context of the finance motive debate Keynes made it clear that saving can never be a source of finance for investment. By implication, having more of "it" (of what really?), i.e. a "rise in thrift," cannot be expected to – *directly and immediately* – make the financing of investment any easier. Keynes' following remark beautifully pinpoints the "loanable funds fallacy":

> Increased investment will always be accompanied by increased saving, but it can never be preceded by it. Dishoarding and credit expansion provides not an *alternative* to increased saving, but a necessary preparation for it. It is the parent, not the twin, of increased saving.
>
> (Keynes 1939b, JMK 14: 281)

It may almost seem unwarranted that we move on to push loanable funds theory to *reductio ad absurdum* in Chapter 3, which concentrates on the central proposition of loanable funds theory that a "saving decision" is sufficient to affect interest rates. Yet Keynes' fierce stance on the "savings theory of interest" ("definite error," "nonsense theory," "formal error;" Keynes 1936a, JMK 7: 178–9) has not found many followers, not even among economists who are generally sympathetic to his work – to some extent, perhaps, because the finance motive, which represents Keynes' *coup de grâce* against orthodox error, was not properly understood. The distinguishing feature of our approach is that we apply *disequilibrium analysis* to the "rise in thrift," to highlight what loanable funds theorists ever since Dennis Robertson stubbornly refused to see, namely that there is always a counterpart to the "saving decision" (*ex ante* and *ex post*) as there are always two sides to any economic transaction.[14]

Chapter 4 concentrates on the uncertainty aspects central to liquidity preference theory but which are largely neglected in Chapters 2 and 3. For Keynes the notion of uncertainty means that the expectations and beliefs about the future which influence agents' assessments of their present situation will be partial and vague and that there will typically be a variety of opinion about the outcome of the events about which they are uncertain. A lot has been said about the fact that by "very uncertain" Keynes does not mean the same thing as "very improbable" (cf. Keynes 1936a, JMK 7: 148n), but it is usually not made clear what the economic implications really are in light of the term.

On our reading, uncertainty may give rise to certain motives that would *not* exist without it and changes in uncertainty, as perceived by economic agents, may affect the strength of these motives, while certain institutional arrangements provide the route or, perhaps, the "valve," through which agents' motives and decisions affect the economic situation. Foremost among these motives are the incentives to liquidity, i.e. the attractions which liquidity affords in such an environment, which provide the basis for Keynes' "liquidity theory of interest."

Whereas Chapter 3 is concerned with the question of interest rate *adjustments*, Chapter 4 concerns the phenomenon of interest itself. I first approach the issue via the liquidity preference schedule and then via Keynes' "own-rates analysis" featuring the concept of the "liquidity premium."

I argue that it is important to distinguish clearly between different types of decisions, in particular between portfolio decisions on the one hand, and spending and production decisions on the other. This distinction is important, first, because the macroeconomic implications of the different types of decisions are very different and, second, because, owing to the institutional arrangements of modern monetary economies, they are typically taken by different types of "players." The difference mainly consists in the "default option" available to the respective decision maker, where the "default option" is that position which involves the lowest level of commitment on the decision maker's part.

For consumers, producers, and entrepreneurial investors the default option is "not spending/producing," when exercising this option has direct income effects. For portfolio investors and banks the default option is "liquidity," which means holding bank deposits or central bank deposits, respectively (ignoring Treasury bills for simplicity's sake). Exercising this option does not have direct income effects. Instead, a general attempt to become more liquid affects interest rates (or spreads) and asset prices in the first instance, with the possibility of markets freezing up under extreme conditions. Banks are seen to be in a pivotal position. On the asset side of their balance sheet a refusal to roll-over or extend new loans can cut off other units from finance, with either direct income effects or repercussions within the financial system. On the liability side, their willingness to take assets in general off the market determines the quantity of liquidity available to soothe nonbanks' anxieties. At one remove this point also applies at the bank–central bank relationship and banks' own liquidity preference. In a systemic banking crisis it may be vital that the central bank substitutes in for banks in providing finance to nonbanks while supplying emergency liquidity to banks.

The "crisis in confidence" analysis in Chapter 4 is not only relevant and applicable to the current financial crisis. The crucial point brought out by our analysis is of more general validity and importance: the pace of capital accumulation is dependent upon *two* sets of factors while coordination between them may not be easily, certainly not automatically, attainable. Entrepreneurial investors' willingness to initiate capital projects despite the precariousness of their knowledge concerning the projects' prospective yields represents one factor, their financiers' willingness to part with liquidity the other. Furthermore, if the rate of interest is a *free parameter*, then the resulting level of economic activity is *indeterminate*, and the orthodox remedies, or rather avowed panaceas, of being "more thrifty" and/or of "cutting wages" are derived from faithful beliefs rather than anything else. "I should, I think, be prepared to argue that, in a world ruled by uncertainty with an uncertain future linked to an actual present, a final position of equilibrium, such as one deals with in static economics, does not properly exist" (Keynes 1936e, JMK 29: 222). Chapter 4 illuminates the role of uncertainty and highlights that money *is* the link between the present and the future.

Chapter 5 sets out to explore head on the role of banks in liquidity preference theory. There is the widespread view that *The General Theory* features money exogeneity and passive banks, a view that became established through the Hicksian IS/LM model. The examination of Keynes' view on banking behavior and the central bank–bank relationship as they evolved from his *Tract* to *The General Theory* sheds some interesting light on this issue. The main result is that Keynes' exogenous money view of *The General Theory* features exogeneity due to bank behavior, a distinct position that runs counter to both the old neoclassical synthesis picture of monetary policy as controlling the money stock (or verticalism) as well as to the Post Keynesian endogenous money approach (or horizontalism).

In particular, active bank behavior is identified as the driving force behind the "Keynes effect," which, I argue, should better be called the "Keynes mechanism." The Keynes effect arises when the "pool of liquidity" as provided by the banking system changes relative to the level of economic activity. For this to occur in a slowing economy, for instance, banks need to expand their business by buying other assets, thereby offsetting declines in the demand for loans that arise (although perhaps not immediately) as the economy slows. In any case, this vision of banks stands in sharp contrast to the endogenous money view of banks as *passive* conduits of loan demand.

The analysis in Chapter 5 also reveals how bank behavior matters in the central bank–bank relationship, the core channel in the transmission of monetary policy to the economy through the financial system. My analysis highlights that a "liquidity trap" can arise at any level of policy interest rate whenever the banks refuse to support the central bank's efforts, which may show up most prominently in surging deposits held by banks at the central bank. Banks are most likely to refuse to "follow their leader" either for fear of prospective losses in doing so or because past losses have left their capital impaired. It may then be left to the central bank to step into the banks' shoes and expand its balance sheet instead. Keynes considered policies to control interest rates beyond short-term rates through policy communication and open market operations. That these issues are highly relevant to the global financial crisis that started in 2007 needs no stressing.

Chapter 6 investigates an aspect of Keynes' monetary thought that has received conspicuously little attention: the structure, as opposed to the conduct, of monetary policy. The structure of monetary policy concerns the regulation of central banks and their relation to the state in matters of monetary policy. The popular concept of central bank independence belongs to the realm of monetary policy structure, and my analysis reveals that, perhaps to the surprise of today's mainstream proponents of the CBI idea, Keynes actually saw some positive scope for CBI. The chapter reviews Keynes' evolving views on the matter starting with his *Indian Currency and Finance* of 1913. But his perhaps most instructive contribution in this area is unearthed from a response to a policy pamphlet by the Labour Party of 1932. In his response Keynes provides an outline of what he considered a sound structure of monetary policy that would both enhance the efficiency of monetary policy while being in line with the general democratic traditions in his country as well.

I mentioned above the somewhat paradoxical 180 degree turnaround from traditionally conservative opposition to CBI towards uncritically embracing CBI as a "commitment device" or "rule." The problem is that the time-inconsistency case for CBI is derived within new classical modeling routines that have no relation to the real world. By contrast, it is actually less of a surprise than may seem at first that the liberal economist who believed that "a managed currency was inevitable" should also think carefully about how best to regulate the authority in charge of that management and its relation to the state.

The analysis through Chapter 6 pays little explicit attention to international considerations. Chapter 7 extends the analysis to the global context, focusing on Keynes' ideas and global vision as laid down in his plan of the early 1940s for an "International Clearing Union." This extension illustrates the application of liquidity preference theory when international interdependencies are taken into account and the ways in which Keynes thought his ideas could be best mastered for policy purposes through the design of adequate international institutions. Keynes proposed the establishment of an international monetary order based on "supranational" bank money. One concern of his was to implant a chiefly rule-based adjustment mechanism towards balance of payments equilibrium into the new global order featuring *symmetric* pressures for adjustment on both current account surplus and deficit countries. Another concern was to create sufficient national policy space that would enable countries to achieve domestic stability whilst abiding by the new international rules of the game and abstain from beggar-thy-neighbor strategies. Capital controls featured prominently in Keynes' proposal.

Following up on the previous chapter, Chapter 8 discusses the evolution of the international monetary order as actually set up at Bretton Woods in the light of Keynes' monetary thought and Clearing Union proposal. The analysis then addresses some prominent themes in policy debates of recent years. These include the emergence of global imbalances and seemingly paradoxical capital flows, the "Bretton Woods II" hypothesis and eruption of the ongoing global financial crisis, and the "saving glut hypothesis" as well as Greenspan's "bond market conundrum." It is argued that continued adherence to the loanable funds theory of interest has led to flawed diagnoses and policy prescriptions. An alternative liquidity preference theoretical reading of developments and events emphasizes the nth country role of the reserve currency issuer and the resulting "global dollar glut." Chapter 8 also outlines an appropriate policy response to counter the financial crisis based on our reading of Keynes' monetary thought. Chapter 9 concludes the book.

2 Some reflections on Keynes' "finance motive" for the demand for money[1]

2.1 Introduction

The introduction of the "finance motive," shortly after the publication of *The General Theory of Employment, Interest and Money*, arose in connection with the debate on interest rate determination between Keynes, D.H. Robertson (1936, 1937, 1940) and Bertil Ohlin (1937a, b). This debate soon developed into the infamous "liquidity preference versus loanable funds" controversy (LP–LF). While Robertson thought that the two theories amounted to virtually the same thing, Keynes repeatedly insisted on the differences between them, thereby highlighting liquidity preference theory as a fundamental component of his *General Theory*.[2]

In fact, the LP–LF controversy is still essentially unresolved and remains a source of much confusion in modern macroeconomics.[3] Keynes regarded the finance motive as the "coping stone" of liquidity preference theory. The purpose of this chapter is to show that a proper understanding of this coping stone helps to dissipate some of the confusion that afflicts modern macroeconomics.

I shall argue that Keynes' discussion of the finance motive is essentially an *addendum* to the transactions motive, albeit an important one, which he extended later on. The argument proceeds in three steps. First, in Sections 2.2 and 2.3, I shall review Keynes' presentation of the transactions motive in *A Treatise on Money* and *The General Theory*, and the explicit introduction of the finance motive in his post-*General Theory* writings. My aim is to illustrate the close link between the transactions motive and the finance motive. The second step, in Section 2.4, consists of a critical evaluation of Davidson's (1965) interpretation of the finance motive. Davidson's approach is to encapsulate the finance motive within the framework of the static Hicksian IS/LM equilibrium model. I shall argue that Davidson's analysis is flawed because the finance motive is clearly a *disequilibrium concept,* which makes for serious problems when attempts are made to squeeze it into an equilibrium framework such as the IS/LM model. The third step, in Sections 2.5 and 2.6, consists of analyzing the finance motive in a dynamic context. In particular, I shall consider its implications in relation to changes in income and wealth and the (dual) function of financial intermediaries in the process of economic growth. Asimakopulos's (1983) discussion of the finance motive in relation to the unfolding of the multiplier process is taken as a point of departure. I shall attempt to disentangle the confusions that his discussion, and the controversy it sparked off, involves. I suggest that the same confusions can be traced right back to D.H. Robertson's criticisms of Keynes. Section 2.7 concludes that, although Keynes' analysis of the motives to liquidity preference in *The General Theory* is, in some sense, incomplete, the finance motive, once included in the theoretical apparatus of *The General Theory*, does *not* invalidate this apparatus. Rather, it highlights the important role of financial intermediaries in a changing and growing economy.

I should warn the reader that the chapter abstracts from the uncertainty aspects central to liquidity preference theory, and that I shall not directly address the related "endogenous money" debate. As the title suggests, what follow are first of all reflections on a motive for the demand for money.[4]

2.2   The transactions motive for the demand for money

Keynes distinguishes between three different motives for holding money in *The General Theory*: the transactions motive, the precautionary motive and the speculative motive. I shall here concentrate on the transactions motive, which Keynes further divides into the "income-motive" and the "business-motive," relating to income-recipients in general and to businesspeople and dealers respectively. Both sub-categories of the transactions motive arise out of the imperfect synchronization of receipts and payments. Money, i.e. bank deposits, held (primarily) to satisfy the transactions motive serves to bridge the intervals between incoming and outgoing payments. The strength of this motive, Keynes argues, depends on various mainly institutional factors such as, for example, the length of the period between income payments, the structure and organization of industry, the value of current output, the cheapness and reliability of methods of obtaining cash when it is required and, to some extent, on the relative cost of holding cash (cf. Keynes 1936a, JMK 7: 195–6).

It is partly due to Keynes' (static) short-period equilibrium method in *The General Theory*, tailored to "discover what determines at any time the national income of a given economic system and ... the amount of its employment" (Keynes 1936a, JMK 7: 247), that sight is sometimes lost of the fact that these transactions deposits are held and reconstituted to *finance* expenditures (or rather transactions in general). Another reason is that the discussion of the transactions motive in *The General Theory* is clearly only a sketch of the elaborate analysis of the "cash deposits" Keynes presents in his earlier *Treatise on Money*, and which he thought unnecessary to repeat in much detail.[5]

What is important here is that, as far as the role of money as a transactions medium is concerned, Keynes' line of reasoning clearly follows the Cambridge tradition, as expressed in the Marshallian k.[6] However, Keynes applies this method to cash deposits only and not to the total of bank deposits which include "savings deposits" as well. Furthermore, in the *Treatise on Money* he concentrates on the fact that cash deposits are held to facilitate various different kinds of transactions, which is then reflected in his various sub-divisions of the broad category of cash deposits.[7] In this context he develops his notion of "true velocities" (i.e. disaggregated transactions velocities of circulation) as an expression for the velocity of cash deposits *held for a particular purpose* (he uses the concept of the transactions velocity of cash deposits and the Marshallian k interchangeably). He conjectures that observed fluctuations in the velocity of (total) cash deposits may be explained by fluctuations in the proportions of deposits employed in different uses while the *true* velocities of the deposits held for any particular purpose remain relatively stable (Keynes 1930b, JMK 6: 30, 38). Correspondingly, fluctuations in the (overall) Marshallian k of cash deposits may be due to changes in the relative weights of the different kinds of transactions to be facilitated while the respective Marshallian ks of the various sub-categories of cash deposits as such remain rather stable.[8] Keynes stresses that, given the imperfect synchronization of economic transactions and the corresponding money flows they give rise to, a particular level of economic activity requires *ceteris paribus* a certain amount of cash deposits to finance this volume of transactions.

Now apart from the change to the (static) short-period equilibrium method of *The General Theory*, the same views on money as a transactions medium specified with such care in the *Treatise on Money* underlie Keynes' analysis in the later book. In *The General Theory* Keynes re-emphasizes his view that the notion of the income-velocity of money is only applicable to this part of the total stock of money (Keynes 1936a, JMK 7: 194, 201). The change in method, however, leads to the transactions motive being defined as a (static) *equilibrium concept*. In any given short-period equilibrium a part of the total stock of money is accountable for the role of money as a transactions medium. Yet, there is no longer any explicit consideration of the use of transactions deposits to "finance" transactions and of banks as providers of credit. Nevertheless, the reader is asked to visualize the banking system's business of providing credit and the use of transactions deposits to "finance" what is under certain conditions a *continuous* circular flow of economic transactions at a given level of (actual) economic activity.

Robertson's (1936: 181, n. 7; 1937: 432; 1940: 12 ff.) critique concentrates on Keynes' assertion that the transactions demand for money depends on *current* output (income) only. The question of how to provide finance for *ex ante* investment, which may differ from *current* investment, is for him the hub of the whole debate about liquidity preference. And, indeed, in *The General Theory* we find that:

> In normal circumstances the amount of money required to satisfy the transactions-motive and the precautionary-motive is mainly a resultant of the general activity of the economic system and of the level of money-income.
>
> (Keynes 1936a, JMK 7: 196)

Keynes (1936a, JMK 7: 197) explicitly says there that it is "the actual occurrence of a change in the general economic activity and the level of incomes" which gives rise to a change in the transactions and precautionary demand for money. Ohlin and Robertson's critique forced Keynes to clarify his position and led to the introduction of the finance motive.

2.3   The finance motive for the demand for money

In replying to Ohlin (1937a) in his 1937 "Alternative theories of the rate of interest," Keynes (1937e) acknowledges that in *The General Theory* he had not considered that "an accumulation of unexecuted or incompletely executed investment decisions may occasion for the time being an extra special demand for cash" (Keynes 1937e, JMK 14: 208). It is important to bear in mind that the finance motive is a motive for the demand for money. As a solution to the problem of providing the *extra finance*, therefore, what is needed, according to Keynes, is a "technique to bridge this gap between the time when the *decision* to invest is taken and the time when the correlative investment and saving actually occur" (Keynes 1937e, JMK 14: 208). But he stresses that, if investment is proceeding at a steady rate, the finance needed is itself a "revolving fund."[9]

We see here the connection between the finance motive and the *equilibrium view* of the transactions motive as stated above. For a given level of economic activity, each expenditure (or transaction in general) has to be planned and before it can be executed finance has to be secured. Seen from this perspective, the recurring need to finance a particular volume of planned investment at a particular level of general economic activity is part of the continuous circular flow of transactions and, hence, is one of the factors that is covered by the transactions motive and the Marshallian *k* analysis, *no matter what kind of planned expenditure actually has to be financed*. Keynes later expresses this in a somewhat different way when he divides this circular flow – to be facilitated by "active balances" (i.e. cash deposits) – into *two time lags*:

> The active demand … falls into two parts: the demand due to the time lag between the inception and the execution of the entrepreneurs' decisions, and the part due to the time lags between the receipt and the disposal of income by the public and also between the receipt by entrepreneurs of their sale proceeds and the payment by them of wages, etc.
>
> (Keynes 1938a, JMK 14: 230)

In equilibrium, that is, when planned activity is equal to actual activity, "finance" is not a problem at all, as there is indeed no *extra* finance demand in this situation. The finance motive only comes into the picture once there is a *change in planned activity*:

> An increase in activity raises the demand for cash, first of all to provide for the first of these time lags in circulation, and then to provide for the second of them. Thereafter the demand for cash falls away unless the completed activity is being succeeded by a new one. A given stock of cash provides a revolving

fund for a steady flow of activity; but an increased rate of flow needs an increased stock to keep the channels filled.

(Keynes 1938a, JMK 14: 230)

The last sentence of this quotation makes it clear that, *ceteris paribus*, a greater volume of transactions requires in equilibrium a greater amount of active balances to accommodate it. The point which is brought out by the finance motive is that this additional need for money arises *even at the stage of planning*, when the relevant decision has been made and finance has to be secured before the planned activity can become actual, that is, when the level of actual activity has not yet been affected. *Finance balances represent the prior provision made to finance the planned addition to actual activity.* The volume of active balances, which support the original – still unchanged – level of (actual) activity, can hardly be drawn upon (though Keynes did not assume *k*, or rather the *true* velocities, to be constant). Therefore, "inactive balances" have to be attracted, at the cost of an increase in the rate of interest. This increase in the rate of interest reflects the fact that the satisfaction of the additional demand for as yet inactive finance money balances requires *ceteris paribus* (in particular a constant money supply) some other agent, for the time being, to become less liquid. Once expended, however, the finance balances become part of the active circulation, or revolving fund, and can be used for any purpose over and over again.

The fact that the *additional* finance motive is a transitory, disequilibrium phenomenon, important during the interregnum period of transition, is clearly brought out by the following statement:

It follows that, if the liquidity preferences of the public (as distinct from the entrepreneurial investors) and of the banks are unchanged, an excess in the finance required by current *ex ante* output (it is not necessary to write "investment", since the same is true of *any* output which has to be planned ahead) over the finance released by current *ex post* output will lead to a rise in the rate of interest; and a decrease will lead to a fall. I should not have previously overlooked this point, since it is the coping-stone of the liquidity theory of the rate of interest. I allowed, it is true, for the effect of an increase in *actual* activity on the demand for money. But I did not allow for the effect of an increase in *planned* activity, which is superimposed on the former, and may sometimes be the more important of the two, because the cash which it requires may be turned over so much more slowly.

(Keynes 1937f, JMK 14: 220)[10]

D.H. Robertson viewed Keynes' elaboration on the need to finance planned (investment) expenditure as contradicting Keynes' former position that the rate of interest is not determined by productivity and thrift but by monetary factors instead. According to Robertson, the finance motive proved that these "real" factors have a *direct and immediate* influence.[11]

So far I have tried to illustrate that the finance motive is closely linked conceptually to the transactions motive. It merely emphasizes that *even only planned* changes in the level of economic activity will be accompanied by corresponding changes in the volume of transactions deposits needed to facilitate them. Moreover, as far as the demand for money as a transactions medium is concerned, Keynes' analysis bears a close resemblance to the traditional Marshallian *k* analysis.

2.4   The finance motive within the Hicksian IS/LM model: Paul Davidson's interpretation

Davidson (1965) complains that Keynes' finance motive is unduly neglected in the Keynesian literature and that this neglect has led to an unwarranted dichotomization into independent monetary and real subsets in "Keynesian models." Davidson's own conclusions on this issue, if correct, would be of far-reaching importance for macroeconomics, for he suggests that *the finance motive provides a possible reconciliation of the LP–LF controversy*, which, he says, is "mainly a semantic confusion between movements along the demand schedule for money and shifts in the schedule" (Davidson 1965: 60). Davidson provides an interpretation of the finance motive which yields the astonishing conclusion that:

> when there is an increase in planned investment, for example, the equilibrium quantity of money demanded will *ultimately* increase for two reasons: (1) a shift in the L_t^* function (i.e.) finance motive, and (2) a movement along the new L_t^* function as output increases and induces further spending via the multiplier. It is the shift in the L_t^* function which puts *additional* pressure on the rate of interest.
>
> (Davidson 1965: 52–3; my italics)[12]

In terms of the Hicksian IS/LM model, according to Davidson, and except in very special conditions, consideration of the finance motive would imply that the IS and LM curves are not independent of one another but would generally shift simultaneously.

Since the IS/LM model is a tool for comparative-static equilibrium analysis this would imply that according to Davidson's interpretation the finance motive causes a *lasting additional* demand for money. Reflection on this result in the light of the analysis in the previous section, which emphasized the transient nature of the finance motive, raises questions about the logical consistency of Davidson's interpretation. Indeed, in what follows I shall argue that this interpretation of the finance motive is logically inconsistent or, alternatively, that it has nothing to do with Keynes' finance motive. But how does Davidson get his results?[13]

In order to introduce the finance motive into the IS/LM model[14] Davidson defines the demand for money as a function of (planned) expenditure and not, as according to him is usually the case, as a function of income (output). Furthermore, he distinguishes between investment and consumption expenditure, defining a *constant* Marshallian *k* for each of the respective components of expenditure (his parameters α and β). *This, it turns out, is the only true modification of the IS/LM model Davidson actually makes.*

Davidson analyzes the case of an increase in investment expenditure. In terms of the traditional IS/LM model and assuming a constant money supply, this would be represented as an outward shift of the IS curve along a given upward sloping LM curve. The observed increase in the rate of interest arises due to the need to facilitate a higher level of income with a given money stock, that is, it depicts the working of the transactions motive. In Davidson's modified IS/LM model, however, *additional* pressure on the rate of interest arises due to an upward shift in the LM curve itself. Davidson's argument is based on the fact that solving the two simultaneous equations of his modified IS/LM model yields the comparative-static result that the two curves shift *simultaneously* except in the special case where his parameters α and β (the respective Marshallian sub-*k*s) are equal. Davidson interprets this result to mean that *owing to the finance motive* the demand for money – except in this special case – *increases at each level of output*. In his graphical presentation *this* is what leads to the *upward* shift in the LM curve.

However, a logical slip has crept into Davidson's reasoning here. When Davidson interprets the comparative-static solution of his simultaneous equations model he looks at the two equations separately. First, as far as the IS curve is concerned, he agrees with the usual result that an increase in autonomous investment *ceteris paribus* leads to an outward shift of this curve. But second, when he concentrates on the LM curve, to analyze what happens *at each level of output* in the case of an increase in autonomous investment expenditure, Davidson seems to overlook in his verbal reasoning that this necessarily implies a corresponding decrease in another component of aggregate expenditure. But then, by implication, we are plainly looking at a change in the composition of total expenditure and as he rightly says the requirement for the LM curve to remain unchanged in this case is that α is equal to β.[15] This only proves that the aggregate Marshallian *k* would change together with a change in the composition of total expenditure if the respective Marshallian *k*s of the components involved are not equal, an interesting but not surprising result. A *change-in-composition-effect* of this kind may appropriately be dealt with in terms of Keynes' concept of *true velocities* as presented in Section 2.2 above. Notwithstanding its possible practical relevance, this case clearly comes under the transactions motive and has nothing to do with Keynes' finance motive.

Nevertheless, Davidson's analysis brings out an important point very clearly – it highlights the limitations of the IS/LM model and the method it employs as a tool to represent Keynes' monetary thought. There is nothing wrong with Davidson's account regarding the demand for money as a function of (planned) expenditure.[16] In equilibrium, however, when planned and actual expenditure and output are equal, as they necessarily are in the context of comparative-static equilibrium analysis of the IS/LM model, it does not make any difference.

Correctly understood, Keynes' finance motive cannot produce a *lasting* additional demand for money apart from the transactions demand for money. At the new (higher) equilibrium – where planned expenditure again equals current output or, put differently, planned activity equals actual activity – all that is involved is a need for a greater amount of transactions balances as indicated by the Marshallian k. For the rate of interest to remain constant the money stock has to be increased by an appropriate amount, that is, the LM function in this case shifts to the right (monetary accommodation). Given a constant money supply, by contrast, the additional requirements for transactions purposes are squeezed out of inactive balances through an increase in the rate of interest, the degree of which is indicated by the slope of the LM curve. In this latter case there is a shift in the IS curve along a *ceteris paribus* unchanged upward sloping LM curve. To this limited extent the interdependency of the monetary and real sectors of the economy *is* captured by the orthodox comparative-static equilibrium analysis (financial crowding-out effect). How we get from one equilibrium to another cannot be brought out by a set of (static) simultaneous equations. Hence, the finance motive does not enter the scene at all, and does not provide an *extra* demand for money.

So the problem really stems from trying to force Keynes' *disequilibrium conception* of the finance motive into the equilibrium IS/LM model for the purpose of doing comparative-static analysis. The finance motive is a *transient phenomenon*. If we squeeze it into the graphical exposition of the IS/LM model, which may be helpful to illustrate the contrast to Davidson's interpretation, we have to visualize the *sequence* of events demonstrated by Figure 2.1.[17]

We start from the equilibrium *point A*. Consider Davidson's case: entrepreneurs decide to increase investment expenditure while the money supply remains unchanged. In order to actualize this increase in planned activity the entrepreneurs have to secure (the additional) finance beforehand. This means that there is a

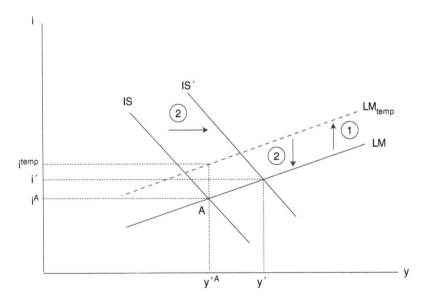

Figure 2.1 Sequence of events

temporary upward shift in the LM curve *prior* to the shift of the IS curve. The level of actual activity is still unchanged at its former equilibrium but, even at this stage, someone has to become less liquid than before, for the time being, in order to provide the finance. The upward shift in the LM curve indicates that this will generally require an increase in the rate of interest even *at an unchanged level of output*, and hence the *disequilibrium character* of the whole situation now becomes quite apparent. Once the *extra finance* is expended and the shift in the IS curve actually occurs, however, the LM curve shifts *ceteris paribus* back to its previous position since there is no longer any *additional* finance motive at work and the pressure arising due to the transactions motive when *actual* activity increases has been captured by the upward slope of the LM curve all along.

Among those factors that would lead to a more enduring change in the position of the LM curve is a change in the composition of total expenditure (output) if the respective Marshallian ks are unequal, which is, as we saw, just the case Davidson actually discusses. To conclude, Davidson's results do not depend on defining the demand for money as a function of *planned* expenditure. In comparative-static equilibrium analysis his definition does not make any difference and there is, strictly speaking, no finance motive.

Davidson was criticized immediately in 1966 by Horwich who argued that the dislocation of the LM curve would be temporary only. Davidson (1967, 1978, 1994) remained unconvinced by this attack, and indeed his modified IS/LM model generally produces simultaneous and lasting shifts in both curves.[18] This result, however, does not involve the finance motive at all but directly follows from his disaggregated demand for money function and, hence, his interpretation of Keynes' finance motive does *not* provide a reconciliation of liquidity preference theory and loanable funds theory.

2.5 The finance motive in a dynamic context – Asimakopulos on finance and the multiplier

In the previous section we dealt with the difficulties in integrating Keynes' disequilibrium concept of the finance motive into comparative-static equilibrium analysis. In this section and the next we shall enter a more dynamic setting and follow up on the adjustment processes involved. Furthermore, it should be remembered that the above analysis in terms of the IS/LM model makes the usual assumption that liquidity preference remains unchanged and abstracts from the implied changes in stocks and, correspondingly, in wealth. In what follows I shall concentrate on the latter aspect which will, even when considered alone, turn out to be critical to understanding the full breadth of Keynes' finance motive and its bearing on the LP–LF controversy. Shifts in liquidity preference due to uncertainty, in addition, may either (over- or partly) compensate or, as the situation may be, aggravate possible tensions arising during the process of economic change between the financial system, on the one hand, and spending units deciding upon repeated or newly contemplated expenditure plans, on the other.

Asimakopulos' (1983) discussion of Keynes' finance motive directs attention to the dynamics of adjustment and for this reason provides a useful starting point. Asimakopulos' overall approach is to analyze the finance motive in relation to the gradual unfolding of the multiplier process. Indeed, his main point is that Keynes' "revolving fund of finance" is based on very special assumptions which do not allow for the fact that the multiplier requires time to work itself out in full or, put differently, to establish its relation to our discussion in the previous section; as he sees it the whole problem hinges on the implicit assumption of an "instantaneous multiplier" in comparative-static equilibrium analysis. This line of reasoning leads Asimakopulos to the conclusion (and he is roughly in agreement with Robertson on this point) that there is a crucial error in Keynes' analysis as far as his notion of the revolving fund of finance is concerned. On his reading, the revolving fund notion refers to the liquidity of the bank, the initial liquidity position of which can only be restored once the multiplier has run its full course. Only then is saving at a level which is exactly equal to the amount of bank loans which have to be repaid. In his discussion Asimakopulos raises a number of issues related to the finance motive, in particular that Keynes described the practice of finance as a "twofold process" and that he implicitly assumes an unchanged term-structure of interest rates. The final upshot of Asimakopulos' analysis is that the introduction of the finance motive contradicts Keynes' stance on the complete independence of investment from saving. In short, Asimakopulos questions the general validity of this central insight of Keynes' monetary thought. The overall drift in Asimakopulos' argument is clearly reflected in his following statement:

> Keynes is assuming implicitly that the full multiplier operates instantaneously, with a new situation of short-period equilibrium being attained as soon as the investment expenditure is made. Such a situation is a necessary, even though not a sufficient, condition for the initial liquidity position to be restored. It is not enough to have *ex post* saving equal to *ex post* investment (this result holds, of course, at all times as a result of the national accounts identities) in order for saving to be potentially available to repay the bank loans which made possible the increase in investment.[19]

Asimakopulos' discussion of the finance motive sparked off a huge controversy. However, no agreement was reached and a lot of confusion remains.[20] In my view the confusion stems, on the one hand, from the disputants being distracted by Keynes' reference to a particular institutional arrangement and practice of finance, thereby diverting attention from the essence of the finance motive as a theoretical conception, while, on the other hand, ignoring some important logical implications of this conception and thereby leaving its full dimension completely in the dark. Let me substantiate the second part of this statement, to which I shall return in more detail in the next section, before I address the first part.

First of all, the deeper reason for the confusion appears to arise from the disputants' shared tendency to abstract from changes in the transactions demand for money when *actual* activity changes, and thereby to scorn the intimate affinity between the finance motive and the transactions motive as outlined above.[21] Furthermore, I should like to re-emphasize that Keynes' conception of the finance motive belongs to the sphere of *changes* in the level of economic activity, that is, changes in the level of income – and wealth, as we shall see. Hence, to abstract from the implications of such changes leaves the whole point of this theoretical conception meaningless from the start.

Addressing the first part of the above statement will serve as a kind of ground clearing to disentangle a few aspects related to the finance motive which are enmeshed in Asimakopulos' discussion. The argument in this section evolves in a number of stages and various aspects of the conceptual framework of Keynes' monetary analysis discussed in previous sections will slot into place in due course. Then, on the basis of this kind of ground clearing I shall in the next section reflect upon the implications of the finance motive in their full dimension. The important role of financial intermediation in a changing and growing economy is unearthed as the crux of the whole issue.

i. First, there is Keynes' description of investment finance as a "twofold process." For Keynes it was simply "convenient to regard the twofold process as the characteristic one" (Keynes 1937f, JMK 14: 217), which represents, we may conjecture, what was usual practice in the City at that time. The twofold process involves first obtaining short-term finance (from banks) and the subsequent long-term issue of securities in order to fund the short-term obligations. But as Keynes says, "this makes no difference to the amount of 'finance' which has to be found by the market as a whole, but only to the channel through which it reaches the entrepreneur" (Keynes 1937f, JMK 14: 217). Asimakopulos' allegation that Keynes implicitly assumes an unchanged term-structure of interest rates is far off the mark (cf. Asimakopulos 1983: 226). Keynes clearly says that – *under this particular institutional arrangement* – the entrepreneur who contemplates investing has to be satisfied on the two points involved in the twofold process. Therefore, by implication, an expected unfavorable change in the term-structure is just the case which may provide the investor with the motive to depart from this twofold process. However, it is no surprise that Keynes thereafter concentrates on the first stage of this process, i.e. on short-term finance, since the prior provision of money to finance the planned addition to the expenditure flow is the crucial point sought to be brought out by the finance motive. Although expectations about the stage two funding enter into the decision, whether or not any change in the term-structure actually occurs prior to the eventual long-term funding of an already undertaken investment project can obviously no longer affect this project, apart from the windfall profit or loss due to an unexpected change in the cost of its finance.[22]

ii. Unfortunately the twofold process leads Asimakopulos to a second misunderstanding, namely to regard "finance" as a synonym for bank credit, which contains an obvious confusion between the two sides of a bank's balance sheet. When Keynes discusses finance he means the investor's command over money, i.e. bank deposits. *The finance motive is a motive for the demand for money*. Finance is *not* a synonym for bank credit.[23] Rather, the whole point is that finance may become a problem just in case no *additional* bank credit is provided. Keynes makes an interesting "*obiter dictum* ... which may help illustrate the nature of the argument" (Keynes 1937f, JMK 14: 222), as he puts it, to the influence of "unused overdraft facilities." He regards this as the usual practice in business finance in Great Britain and appraises this practice as mitigating the effects arising from pressures to secure *ex ante* finance. Keynes (1937e, JMK 14: 223) concludes that this is an "ideal system" since "there is no superimposed pressure resulting from planned activity over and above the pressure resulting from actual activity." Thus, in an overdraft system the theoretical concept of the finance motive lacks any *practical* importance. The required additional finance-money is provided by additional bank credit just when it is expended. In an overdraft system no extra demand due to the finance motive exists, not even temporarily, since we have a simultaneous change in *actual* activity and money demand right from the beginning, a case satisfactorily captured by the transactions motive.[24] Let us instead consider the case where no additional bank loan is provided which requires the investor to procure the finance through the new issue market.

If the finance reaches the investor through this alternative channel it means that he has to attract money from inactive balances, which are thereby set aside to be "transformed" into active balances. They are, however, at this stage still inactive in the sense that they are not used to facilitate the current level of actual activity. Their "transformation" into active balances is only complete once they are expended.[25] Once they are expended, Keynes says, *liquidity is automatically restored*.

iii. This is where the third and crucial confusion arises. Asimakopulos' (1983: 228; 1985: 406–7) whole argument hinges on the idea that the restoration of liquidity requires the repayment of the (short-term) bank loans. Yet, for Keynes the notion of the restoration of liquidity refers to the liquidity of the economy as a whole. He coins the appropriate term "pool of liquidity," which is provided by the banking system, and the restoration of which means that it is becoming available again in its full initial volume to be drawn upon for whatever purpose. The additional pressure *due to the finance motive* existed only temporarily. But since "the same money" may be used again straight away for the same purpose – in this sense – *finance is a revolving fund*. Of course, additional pressure now arises *owing to the transactions motive*. But this is an accompaniment of the change in *actual* activity and was considered in Keynes' analysis all along. The transactions motive takes over as the planned expenditure is realized and the multiplier process has set in, and the finance motive in this way "merges" with the transactions motive.

2.6 The finance motive and the dynamics of financial intermediation

So much for ground clearing. Obviously it is rather unfortunate that the close link between the two motives was generally suppressed in this controversy, supposedly in order to highlight the role of the finance motive, while, I think, it can only be properly understood in the context of its relation to the transactions motive which captures the same aspect of the importance of money as far as changes in *actual* activity goes. *For the crux of the matter is that the finance motive is a concept of change and we end up in utter confusion when we do not fully embrace the implications of the changes involved.* The changes involved are first of all in the level of income and secondly, though not necessarily, in wealth.[26] This change in wealth and the related portfolio aspects are abstracted from in the usual IS/LM analysis and their inclusion makes things far more complicated.[27] However, the "wealth effect" has to be taken into account when positive net investment occurs, since this implies an increase in the physical capital stock and hence in wealth. By wealth effect, let me explain, I mean that at any time the net investment, or rather its financial counterpart, has to be held *in some form* by someone.

It is due to this additional complication that Keynes regarded the case of an increase in the production of consumption goods (i.e. the case of an increase in the level of income due to a rise in the propensity to consume at an unchanged level of investment) as an easier example. Furthermore, the increase-in-consumption case was meant to underscore that it is really an increase in any kind of planned (and actual) expenditure which gives rise to an increased demand for money, and, hence, leads *indirectly* to pressure on the rate of interest (cf. Keynes 1939b, JMK 14: 283–4). Clearly, in this case too there is *ceteris paribus* a lasting increase in the need for transactions deposits to facilitate the higher level of income which, in order to be met without disturbing financial markets in a given state of liquidity preference, requires the banking system to acquire some kind of asset (presumably additional working capital loans to consumption goods industries).

It is however the case of the prior provision of additional investment finance for a planned increase in investment expenditure which features in the controversy over the finance motive.[28] In order to understand this case, which involves a change in wealth and, hence, the precautionary motive which is partly a function of wealth,[29] it is important not to conflate what Keynes in his *Treatise on Money* called "the dual functions of bankers."[30]

The first function of the banking system is to provide *payment transmission facilities* which typically consist of chequeable deposit liabilities ("transactions money"), thereby acting as a clearing house in transferring current payments by means of book entries. Their second function is *intermediation*, thereby providing "asset money" (or rather indirect monetary and non-monetary liabilities in general). Though bank liabilities, no matter of what kind and for what particular purpose they are predominantly held, are in any case part of the holder's wealth portfolio, it is useful to keep these two functions of the banking system conceptually distinct.

An increase in the level of income affects the first function of banks – to provide more transactions money and its approximate counterpart of working capital loans (as we previously saw, even in the increase-in-consumption case). Changes in wealth, however, have a bearing on the second function as well. A consideration of these factors will shed some light on the "error" that Asimakopulos, and before him Robertson, believed to have spotted in Keynes' analysis.

In a modern economy, part of the capital stock is held indirectly through intermediaries, that is, in the form of liabilities issued by financial intermediaries.[31] This is the second function of banks Keynes was referring to. In a growing economy we would *a priori* expect to see such holdings increase together with the aggregate wealth of the economy. This implies that, structural changes in the various forms of finance of industry apart, the outstanding volume of bank credit will grow over time owing to both of the dual functions of bankers. Asimakopulos, and before him Robertson, although both concentrating on the case where the additional "investment finance" is provided by additional bank loans, interpret Keynes' revolving fund of finance, i.e. the claim that liquidity would be automatically restored and could be used over again once the finance is expended, to apply to the bank (or the banking system as a whole we may presume) which provides the additional loans and the "liquidity" of which is on their account only restored once the additional loans were "paid back."[32]

Obviously, this (bank's assets-) revolving fund interpretation requires that the ratios of indirect and direct finance change in a growing economy in a very peculiar way. Structural changes in these ratios will indeed occur over time but for manifold reasons which, however, do *not* prove Keynes' notion of the (bank's liabilities-) revolving fund of finance to be wrong.[33] To see this remember that Keynes' point is that: "A *given stock* of cash provides a revolving fund for a *steady flow* of activity; but an increased rate of flow needs an increased stock to keep the channels filled" (Keynes 1938a, JMK 14: 230; my emphasis). Clearly the revolving fund notion is a general notion which not only applies to the revolving fund of investment finance. It applies to the whole "pool of liquidity," and it underlies the equilibrium conception of the transactions motive as outlined in Sections 2.2 and 2.3 above.[34]

I have stressed the transient, disequilibrium nature of the finance motive and its close relation to the more general transactions motive in Keynes' scheme. Finance is a revolving fund for a steady flow of investment while a greater flow of investment *ceteris paribus* requires a greater revolving fund of finance. Asimakopulos', and Robertson's, position on the revolving fund of finance, which presupposes the repayment of the (additional) bank loans, is untenable since it requires either structural changes in the financial system of a very peculiar sort,[35] or an unchanged level of income (and wealth). But then, by definition, there is no point in discussing the finance motive in the first place since there is no extra finance motive apart from the transactions motive. The finance motive only matters when changes in the level of income (and/or wealth) occur and, we must add, when we are interested in the period of transition, i.e. in disequilibrium states.

However, as I mentioned above, according to Keynes the demand for monetary assets due to the *precautionary motive* would generally increase together with increases in wealth, and this is the counterpart of the second function of bankers.

It is in his "The Process of Capital Formation," a comment on the Committee of Statistical Experts' report published in 1939, that Keynes goes into more detail about the role of financial intermediaries in the growth context, and thereby somewhat enlarges on his conception of the finance motive. At the beginning the finance motive is restricted to the provision of *money* for changes in activity at the stage of planning and is hence related to the first function of bankers only. In this last article on the finance motive Keynes describes it as being one aspect of the second function of banks, i.e. intermediation, that the financial system must be flexible enough to provide the form in which wealth holders currently wish to hold their savings. Decisions how to employ *additional* savings may take some time and this lag can only be bridged by financial intermediaries.[36] The finance motive is now meant to include this bridging function and is therefore understood as being related to the second function of bankers and the precautionary motive as well.

At some points it appears as if Asimakopulos had something of this sort in mind. But reflection on the second function of banks in an environment of a growing economy reveals a confusion in his position. His misapprehension of the twofold process is related to the idea of some kind of "saving constraint" which is relaxed only when the multiplier has run its course and, for this reason, the stage two funding may represent a practical problem for the investor and, more important, a theoretical problem for Keynes' stance on the independence between investment and saving. Asimakopulos seems to hold the view that there is a difference in kind between the (equilibrium) saving used to take up the securities issue and the short-period or disequilibrium saving represented by bank deposits. The point is, however, that once the investment expenditure has been made and "the investment," in a physical sense, is realized, "the saving" has been done *pari passu* with it.[37] In what form "the saving" will be temporarily or permanently held pertains to the eminent *second decision* of an act of saving, the portfolio decision, which forms the center of the liquidity preference domain. Nevertheless at any moment and, if we want, at any stage of the multiplier process, the additional saving will in some form be part of somebody's wealth portfolio. Given the twofold-process practice investors have to contemplate beforehand on what terms the conversion of their additional indebtedness may be achieved when the time comes and they have to bear the risk of being mistaken on this. But still, once the expenditure has been made, the saving has been done too.[38]

A central proposition of liquidity preference theory is that the decision about the form in which wealth is currently held refers to the portfolio of wealth as a whole, i.e. to the whole of past savings plus current saving which is usually only a small addition to the total. This enlargement of the theoretical conception of the finance motive, first introduced as merely an *addendum* to the transactions motive, then also as an associate of the precautionary motive, makes it clearer how *all* the motives for the demand for money *and* the behavior of financial intermediaries are related in liquidity preference theory. Indeed, consideration of the implied changes in stocks and of possible shifts in liquidity preference owing to uncertainty yields us the clue for an understanding of the critical impact of the behavior of financial intermediaries on economic activity.[39]

Ultimately Asimakopulos' (and unfortunately not only his) confusion stems from both an attachment to a conception of saving which is inappropriate for a growing monetary economy and from a misapprehension of the role played by financial intermediaries in such an environment. A "saving constraint" is only meaningful in the sense of a physical constraint, i.e. full capacity utilization. When Asimakopulos discusses the funding of investment expenditure by a long-term issue it is not a "saving constraint" which may cause the problem but the possibility of a financial constraint. But this is what the finance motive is all about. If the financial provision for a planned increase in expenditure has to be secured beforehand without a corresponding increase in the pool of liquidity, this may lead to a disruption in the market. In this situation somebody else has to become less liquid and the terms on which that investor is willing to do so may cause the contemplated increase in expenditure not to occur in the first place – the lack of finance may act as a restraint on expansion. But is this not the essence of liquidity preference theory? The terms on which finance for any expenditure is available are determined by liquidity preference which thereby affects, most importantly, the volume of the flow of current investment expenditure and saving, the latter being usually obscured by such non-explanatory conceptions as *ex ante* or *ex post* saving or "loanable funds." Asimakopulos draws the wrong conclusion when he asserts that the finance motive shows that investment is not independent from saving. It merely highlights that the Keynesian investment dog does not bite its own tail but instead requires liquidity in order to wag it or, put differently, that monetary factors – as expressed by liquidity preference theory – have effects which are very real indeed. So truly, the finance motive *is* the coping stone of liquidity preference theory.[40]

2.7 Concluding remarks

The essence of the "finance problem" as brought out by the finance motive is that for finance not to interrupt the growth in *actual* activity, an amount of money has to be set aside which is neither used to facilitate the current level of actual activity nor necessary to calm the disquietude of wealth holders. If this requires *additional* finance it can *ceteris paribus* only be provided by banks *prior to the actual emergence of the additional investment and saving*. That this issue was of pivotal importance for Keynes is clear: "The investment market can become congested through shortage of cash. It can never become congested through shortage of saving. This is the most fundamental of my conclusions within this field" (Keynes 1937f, JMK 14: 222).

I have presented an analysis of Keynes' monetary conceptual framework which was shown to be both consistent and to reflect a high degree of continuity in its development from the *Treatise on Money* to the post-*General Theory* writings. I have argued that Davidson's attempt to squeeze the finance motive into the IS/LM model for the purpose of comparative-static equilibrium analysis is unsuccessful, and hence that there is no reconciliation of the LP–LF controversy (which will be further discussed in Chapter 3 below) along the lines he suggests. His approach nevertheless highlights, once again, the limitations of the IS/LM model, and of comparative-static equilibrium analysis in general, in illuminating Keynes' insights. In particular, the neglect of the role of financial intermediation in current macroeconomic analysis with its characteristic preoccupation with equilibrium states restricts the explanatory power of macroeconomic theory immensely. In equilibrium, and this to an extent includes the short-period equilibrium analysis in *The General Theory*, liquidity preference theory in its static version "collapses" into a theory of the rate of interest while, indeed, liquidity preference theory is a theory of financial intermediation as well. Hence, the analysis shows not only that D.H. Robertson's criticism of Keynes' theory of the rate of interest, to the extent that it focuses on the finance motive, is besides the point, but that liquidity preference theory actually has a much wider scope than that. The failure to see this is reflected in Asimakopulos' conflation of liquidity and saving. Contrary to his conclusion the finance motive does not show that investment is dependent on saving. Instead it highlights that investment depends on liquidity – and this is what liquidity preference theory is all about. Money really matters.[41]

3 The loanable funds fallacy

Exercises in the analysis of disequilibrium[1]

3.1 Introduction

The predominant view on the issue of interest rate determination – widely inspiring economic policies of the past and the present – is that a rise in (private or public) investment raises interest rates, whereas an act of (private or public) thrift lowers them. And since virtually all modern macroeconomic models feature "the" rate of interest as being determined – *in equilibrium* – by technology on the one hand and agents' time preferences on the other, this view would seem to be well-founded in economic theory.

Yet modern theory remains conspicuously silent about the mechanism(s) by means of which intertemporal prices are believed to attain their equilibrium values. Getting interest rates right, for the most part, appears to be left to the Walrasian auctioneer, the famous guarantor of the perfect working of the price mechanism. Interestingly, and in stark contrast to the modern preoccupation with equilibrium analysis, proponents of loanable funds theory were never quite satisfied with tacitly assuming that some such mechanism exists, without ever actually investigating the issue. Instead, they concentrated on the disequilibrium processes during which interest rates are supposed to move towards their equilibrium values. And according to loanable funds theory, the market mechanism does generally function properly and, hence, intertemporal prices tend to reflect fundamentals. If correct, loanable funds theory would thus appear to justify the faith that so many modern theorists have in the elegant Walrasian fiction.

That said, the orthodox view on the rate of interest as an essentially real phenomenon, apparently affirmed by loanable funds theory, stands in stark contrast to Keynes "liquidity [preference] theory of interest" of *The General Theory*. According to liquidity preference theory, the rate of interest is a purely monetary and conventional phenomenon (Keynes 1936a, JMK 7: 203). And liquidity preference theory strictly denies that *changes* in the "real forces of productivity and thrift" *directly and immediately* affect interest rates. Amazingly, after being hotly debated for many years, and spawning a vast literature ever since the 1930s, the profession finally seems to have lost sight of this crucial interest rate issue altogether. This is all the more remarkable as the infamous "liquidity preference versus loanable funds" (LP–LF) controversy was apparently abandoned while still unresolved (Leijonhufvud 1981; Maclachlan, 1993).

Given that abandonment without resolution hardly represents a tolerable state of affairs, this chapter freshly investigates the issue of interest rate determination, approaching it from an angle we believe to be suitable to pinpoint an important analytical flaw in loanable funds theory. We focus on the question whether a "rise in thrift" *directly and immediately* lowers the rate of interest, as loanable funds theory predicts (and as, for instance, the "global saving glut hypothesis" critiqued in Chapter 8 suggests). Our aim is to illustrate that loanable funds theory is *logically inconsistent* and should thus be abandoned.[2]

I must stress here that this critique is not aimed at any particular model of loanable funds theory, but at the logical consistency of loanable funds theory in general, the essence of which will be outlined in simple terms in Section 3.2. This is not to deny that a remarkable variety of loanable funds models has been constructed to "prove the case" mathematically. The point is that the LP–LF debate gives ample testimony to the fact that model-building is often a pretty vain exercise. For, notwithstanding its apparent methodological sophistication and technical elegance, any model is bound to be much beside the point when the model builder fails to make sure beforehand that s/he properly understands the problem the model is supposed to represent. Saying this, and in the context of the LP–LF debate, of course, it is Hicks' (1936, 1939) famous "drop-one-equation" type of "equivalence proof" which immediately comes to mind. And yet, Hicks' "proof" dominated the (ever more dominant) neo-Walrasian position on the LP–LF issue for the subsequent forty years!

While this particular example hardly reflects well on the neo-Walrasian model-building tradition in monetary theory, this is not to say that all model building is necessarily barren. In fact, I shall argue below that the modern "financial buffers approach" throws some light on particular aspects of liquidity preference theory which are relevant to the LP–LF issue. Yet, as there are severe limitations afflicting this approach too, we shall indicate some appropriate generalizations. Furthermore, our analysis shows that sound *ex ante* thinking is a necessary but not sufficient precondition for illuminating model building. For care must also be taken with vigorous *ex post* interpretation of what a model actually proves, and what it does not.

These issues will be illustrated step by step in our analysis of the logical and methodological considerations involved, beginning, in Section 3.3, with the within-the-period (disequilibrium) sequence of events that are generated by a rise in thrift that is not anticipated by producers. Focusing on manufacturing industries, the interplay between real and financial buffer adjustments are analyzed for various forms of finance of production. Section 3.4 then goes beyond the single period in which the disequilibrium first occurs, and follows up on the likely cumulative adjustments in production and spending. Having thus identified and clarified the types of market signals and adjustment mechanisms involved, an analytical short-cut to solving these complexities will be proposed in Section 3.5. This short-cut is based on the assumption of correct anticipations on the part of producers, thereby allowing them to move directly to the final equilibrium position. Clearly, the *General Theory* case of (generally) fulfilled "short-term expectations" of Section

3.5 describes, in some sense, an "equilibrium" (adjustment). But it remains to be seen how all this relates to the neo-Walrasian general equilibrium paradigm, an issue addressed in Section 3.6, where we introduce service industries and discuss flexibility of prices and wages. The absence of *real time* in the neo-Walrasian approach underlying modern macroeconomics turns out to be a crucial shortcoming, given that the question at issue concerns intertemporal rather than atemporal coordination. Section 3.7 summarizes the positive implications of our analysis by briefly outlining the alternative liquidity preference theory of interest, taking the post-*General Theory* "finance motive" into account as well.

3.2   Loanable funds and the interest rate mechanism: a framework for disequilibrium analysis

According to loanable funds theory, a rise in thrift *directly and immediately* lowers the rate of interest unless obstructed by either one of two specific interfering factors, namely, a simultaneous rise in hoarding or credit contraction. Different versions of loanable funds theory were proposed, and a considerable variety of specific models put forward, but the essence of loanable funds theory may be suitably expressed in terms of the following simple loanable funds market equation:

(1) $S + \Delta M - H = I;$

with S and I standing for net national saving and net national investment over some period of time, and ΔM and H for changes in the stock of money and net hoarding respectively and over the same period of time.[3]

Note immediately that loanable funds theory portrays a peculiar vision of capital accumulation. This vision features a "genuine" saving fund, the classical (or "real") fund of investment finance, as being either augmented or diminished by either one of two "monetary" funds. On the one hand, saving may be "abortive" in a monetary economy if the savings were hoarded, i.e. withheld from the loanable funds market by the general public, or if they "disappeared in the banking system," i.e. fell prey to a contraction of credit by the banks. On the other hand, the banks may deliberately expand credit, thereby artificially augmenting genuine saving by what was once widely discussed under the heading of "forced saving." Seen in this way, a rise in thrift, by adding genuine saving to the supply of loanable funds, directly and immediately lowers the rate of interest unless monetary factors artificially obstruct the "loanable funds mechanism" (Leijonhufvud's 1981 term). The key issue here does not turn on a comparison of equilibrium solutions for the *level* of interest, for instance at varying rates of time preference. Rather, the key issue concerns the actual *disequilibrium processes* during which the rate of interest is believed to *change* in the right direction and towards its (natural) equilibrium level. If the proper working of the loanable funds mechanism could be established, this would seem to lend some support to the belief that the price system automatically grinds out *the* equilibrium rate of interest.

In this section we present a framework for disequilibrium analysis. We take a simple economy consisting of a household sector and a business sector. For our purposes, it is not necessary to consider labor markets in any detail, except for the fact that labor services are contracted in terms of *money* wages; i.e. the firms enter into unconditional commitments to pay money wages over a period of time, which is assumed to correspond to the length of their production (and distribution) process. Households make *spending decisions* regarding their expenditures on consumption goods and services. The management of firms make spending decisions too, deciding on expenditures on newly produced capital goods. In view of the proposition investigated here, entrepreneurial investors may be seen as awaiting the appropriate market signal, namely, a fall in the rate of interest, which would encourage them to increase investment spending. It will not affect the argument, but simplify the analysis, if we assume that the ordering of the production of a new capital asset and the actual production thereof is undertaken by one and the same business unit. These expenditures occur within the business sector, and capital goods are largely produced to order.

By contrast, in the consumption goods sectors goods and services are, in general, not produced to order. At least, this is the case when we ignore the part played by the trade and distribution industries, and assume that the producers do the selling and storage business themselves. (This simplification does not affect the essence of the argument.) *Production decisions* are thus based on the management's *expectations* about the price at which finished goods (or services) can be sold. These "short-term expectations" are formed at the time when the management commits itself to starting the process of production. Once the rate of production (and employment) has been decided, the firm's money outlays over that period are largely determined as well. Ignoring intra-business-sector sales and purchases, a firm's outlays consist of money wages payable to hired labor and money payments to the creditors and owners of the firm from whom money was raised through the sale of financial instruments of various forms. Naturally the firms' outlays are the incomes earned by households for labor services sold to firms and money lent or sold to them through the purchase of various forms of financial instruments.

Finally, we need to consider the *portfolio decisions* of both households and firms regarding the portfolio composition of assets and liabilities. We focus on financial assets, since we are particularly interested in the issue of interest rate determination, i.e. the prices of securities. While securities are traded in organized markets and thus have uncertain prices, there is one particular type of financial instrument which, in a sense, has a certain money value: money itself. A specific service industry thereby enters into play, namely financial intermediaries.

Financial intermediaries issue their liabilities by buying assets. For instance, financial intermediaries buy loans from firms and households which they finance by selling their own liabilities. These liabilities include money, i.e. bank deposits, the value of which, as we have already noted, is fixed in money terms and which are conventionally accepted as the final settlement of any money contract. Securities may be of fixed-coupon or dividend-paying types. Since the discussion of the interest rate issue usually concentrates on the former type, we shall follow that tradition. We define "the" rate of interest, i.e. the whole complex of rates of interest, in terms of a security's coupon over its price (i.e. running yield). Interest rates must be such that all (liquid) financial instruments, securities and money, are willingly held – a *portfolio equilibrium*. All money in this economy is of the "inside" type, and all markets are competitive.[4]

The basic framework for our disequilibrium analysis is now in place, and it may be helpful to begin by applying it to a simpler case where there is *no* actual rise in thrift, i.e. no net reduction in consumer spending, but merely a redirection of aggregate consumption expenditure. To start with, we concentrate on manufacturing industries only. Let us say, then, that there is a shift in consumption expenditure away from producer A towards producer B. If consumption goods producers A and B do not foresee this change in composition of aggregate consumption expenditure, and thus fail to adjust the structure of production in time, the following signals, most likely in the form of inventory changes, will arise: an unplanned rise in A's inventories and a fall in B's.

Yet, importantly, this is not all there is. For these changes in *real buffers* have their financial counterparts. Disequilibria between spending and production decisions imply changes in *financial buffers* as well, i.e. precautionary holdings of liquid financial instruments. In particular, while A suffers a cash-flow shortfall that needs to be covered somehow, B enjoys a cash-flow surplus, which has to be held in some form too. Our framework for disequilibrium analysis stresses the two-sidedness of economic transactions, and features the role of financial buffers in accomplishing the matching of stocks and flows, in particular when planned flows do *not* match.

Notice that this shift-in-consumption example features an *atemporal* coordination failure: a lack of correspondence between the goods produced for *present* consumption on the one hand and the composition of *present* consumption expenditure on the other. And the market mechanism appears to work properly as far as the goods markets' signals are concerned: changes in real buffers (inventories) signal to producers that consumers' preferences concerning the direction of present consumption have shifted. Producers' incentives to respond to such changes in preferences are of an immediate monetary kind too, as unplanned changes in financial buffers mirror unplanned changes in real buffers. And, interestingly, even in the case of atemporal coordination failures, additional signals may arise in financial markets, namely, owing to changes in financial buffers, reflecting cash-flow shortfalls or surpluses, respectively.

This second type of signal, the interest rate signal, is at the heart of the loanable funds issue. But the focus now turns to the intertemporal plane of analysis, asking: Does the market mechanism provide the right *intertemporal* signal when a shift in preferences in favor of *postponing* consumption occurs, inducing entrepreneurial investors to change their activities accordingly? We are now ready to take a closer look at the loanable funds mechanism, which we may approach in two different ways. One route may be described as an *equilibrium case*, the other route as a *disequilibrium case*, depending on whether or not producers' (short-term) expectations about the price at which finished goods and services can be sold at are fulfilled. We begin with the latter case, where producers "get it wrong." The type of disequilibrium thus again features a mismatch between production and spending decisions. These types of decisions are carried out by different players, and there is no *a priori* reason why they should always and automatically match. We continue to concentrate on manufacturing industries for the time being, but the argument put forward will be extended without difficulty to include service industries more generally, apart from financial intermediaries, in Section 3.6 below. Importantly, in the next section we look at the sequence of events within one single production period only.

3.3 A rise in thrift and the loanable funds fallacy

Suppose that we start out from an equilibrium in period 1 in which the expectations of firms (sales proceeds) as well as households (incomes) were fulfilled and now enter period 2 in which a disequilibrium first arises (see Figure 3.1). Corresponding to the increase in households' "planned saving" is a drop in consumption spending over the current period 2 we are looking at. A disequilibrium arises if the consumption goods industries do not anticipate the incipient drop in sales revenues but continue to produce the same amount of consumption goods. The key question is how the increase in inventories, which arises over this period, will be financed "eventually" or, put differently, how firms close the unexpected gap that arises between their sales revenues and their production outlays over period 2, *if they can close this gap at all.*

Notice that when I stated the key question about the financing of the increase in inventories, I put the word "eventually" in inverted commas to avoid misleading the reader. For it would be wrong to suggest that unplanned inventories have to be financed only once they arise. The inventories, as is the case for production in general, had to be financed when their production was ordered. What I meant, then, is that the unplanned nature of this increase in inventories implies that some unplanned financial adjustments must be undertaken as well: whatever mode of finance for (this part of) production was chosen, the output was expected to yield sales revenues which, in the event, did not materialize. Let us specify the mode of finance of our firms' production outlays.

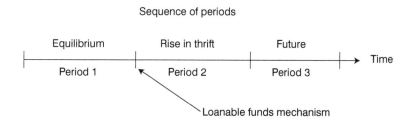

Sequence of periods

Figure 3.1 Time and the loanable funds mechanism

For instance, if the consumption goods industries held no "liquid reserves" and were to finance the whole of their current production with bank loans to be repaid by the end of the current period, the following situation will then arise. The difficulty is that at the end of period 2 firms will be unable to repay their loans. In other words, they will go bankrupt, *unless* they have access to additional (emergency) borrowing, an example of which would be the situation in which the banking system extended new loans to them. Note, however, that this is not a normal roll-over of loans, since the roll-over to continue production in the subsequent period has not been taken into account. Firms, in the present case, in fact become more indebted to banks over the current period 2. In fact, nothing in the argument depends on how the various actors may adjust their behavior beyond period 2 (which will be discussed in Section 3.4 below).

The managements of firms typically do not relish the prospect of illiquidity and bankruptcy, and they know that mistakes in sales forecasts may quite easily occur. They will therefore want to make sure of having access to some form of *liquidity*. So far I have considered only one way of preventing bankruptcy: firms having access to emergency borrowing from banks. Except for unused overdraft facilities, this would, however, leave firms at the mercy of their banker, given that it is the latter who has to *decide* whether to extend additional loans (and under what conditions) in the event of a firm getting into difficulties of the kind described above. Even in the case of overdraft facilities, the borrower, once again, becomes dependent upon the banker as soon as the limit of the pre-arranged credit line is reached. (Furthermore, a sudden rise in overdraft indebtedness signals information to the overdraft provider which the user may not be too keen to disclose under all circumstances. Lenders are on the watch for conspicuous behavior, which borrowers thus try to avoid.) Hence, the management may well prefer to (partly) hold some form of liquidity which it can be sure of being able to resort to when needed.

We may therefore allow our firms both to *hold* securities as liquid reserves and to acquire finance by *issuing* securities rather than taking out bank loans. Such behavior does not necessarily involve corporate saving. Rather, firms (partly) abstain from buying liquidity services from specialists and (to that extent) operate like financial intermediaries themselves (although this is an option typically unavailable to small firms). From the perspective of the firm this implies that it would actually be able to avoid bankruptcy at the end of the period without having to appeal to its banker.[5]

The crucial point is that over the period (the current period 2) in which the unforeseen "rise in thrift" occurs, firms must increase their net indebtedness in order to close the unexpected shortfall in sales revenues, either by selling some (liquid) assets or by increasing their gross indebtedness, i.e. issuing more liabilities.

How then does this unanticipated rise in thrift affect interest rates? According to loanable funds theory, it all depends on whether the savers buy securities or bank deposits. In the former case, savers supply their loanable funds, and interest rates are predicted to fall. In the latter case, savers are said to "hoard," and interest rates are meant to remain unchanged since the additional loanable funds are kept away from the loanable funds market. In addition, banks may interfere by contracting credit. In short, interest rates move in the right direction, unless either hoarding or credit contraction stall the loanable funds mechanism.

If the reader accepts the consistency of the disequilibrium analysis presented here – and who would want to deny the economic *logic* that there are always two sides to any economic transaction? – then the falsity of the core prediction of loanable funds theory just described cannot be denied either. The loanable funds fallacy consists of the following fatal oversight: loanable funds theory completely overlooks the fact that – in one way or another – the firms facing the unexpected rise in thrift will be "in the loanable funds market" to cover their unexpected cash-flow shortfalls. Indeed, what loanable funds theorists see as an additional supply of loanable funds is *exactly* matched in *size*, but possibly not in *composition*, by the additional demand for loanable funds due to distress borrowing – of one form or another – on the part of those having to cope with the unexpected rise in thrift.

Beware here not to confuse the issue: loanable funds theory predicts that a rise in thrift *directly and immediately* lowers interest rates, except for two specific interfering factors. In the light of our own disequilibrium analysis, there clearly is the possibility that interest rate adjustments may occur in an *indirect* way, depending on the portfolio preferences of the households and firms, and possibly financial intermediaries, involved in this redistribution in wealth. We said above that a portfolio equilibrium requires interest rates to be such that all (liquid) financial instruments are willingly held. And a redistribution in wealth may well disturb any given portfolio equilibrium. For there is no *a priori* reason why the composition of assets and/or liabilities sold by firms in order to finance the unexpected shortfall in sales proceeds should exactly meet wealth holders' preferences at current rates of interest. Hence, the rate of interest may actually change to match *portfolio decisions* of households and firms. Yet no *a priori* case can be made for interest rate changes, in so far as there are any, in any particular direction.

In order to settle the LP–LF issue we therefore need to clarify the role of hoarding and bank behavior. In this section we concentrate on the former, and simply assume that a contraction of credit does not occur. In other words, we assume, for the time being, that the size of the banking system's balance sheet remains constant. Nevertheless, we should note here that the portfolio reshuffles involved in this unexpected rise in thrift on the part of households and firms may, in principle, be partly or wholly facilitated through financial intermediaries, possibly, though not necessarily, in ways which affect some conventionally defined measure of bank deposits (i.e. the credit counterpart). Specifically, if the closing of the cash-flow shortfall is accomplished through the banking system, the size of the banking system's balance sheet rises relative to the rate of production, unless households reduce their overdrafts with banks correspondingly, or banks simultaneously sell other assets. The possible involvement of financial intermediaries in disequilibria of the kind discussed here thus also has important implications for the behavior of monetary aggregates which have played such a prominent role in the theoretical and applied work in monetary economics since the 1970s.

It is therefore of particular interest that the "buffer-stock" variety of monetarism was considered to have some bearing on the LP–LF issue.[6] For instance, Laidler (1984: 24–5) maintains that "the theory of the interest rate which underlies the [money] buffer stock approach is a loanable funds theory and not a liquidity preference theory." Among other things, our disequilibrium analysis shows that this claim is incorrect. If money acts as the sole financial buffer, producers – in the event of a disequilibrium between production and spending decisions as discussed above – by assumption run down their money balances only. If the savers decide to hoard their planned savings, i.e. accumulate bank deposits, a case of passionate concern to loanable funds theorists, interest rates would remain unchanged – exactly as loanable funds theory would seem to predict.

The crucial point is, however, that while the money buffer-stock approach features both sides of the disequilibrium situation in which (only) money balances are supposed to act as a buffer, loanable funds theory focuses on one side only – the saver – but ignores the counterpart, i.e. the producer. Consider thus the following case. If the producers were to cover their cash-flow shortfalls through selling securities, while savers, as before, prefer to hoard their planned savings, interest rates would actually tend to *rise*. Notice that this result is in blatant contradiction of loanable funds theory, which predicts that interest rates would remain unchanged if a rise in thrift occurs while hoarding rises simultaneously. Loanable funds theory is therefore flawed: it simply overlooks that the books must somehow be balanced over the current period and microeconomic decisions reconciled in the aggregate. This is what I call the loanable funds fallacy.

While this example proves that loanable funds theory is flawed (while buffer-stock monetarism is at least *logically* consistent), it also illustrates an important shortcoming of buffer-stock monetarism à la Laidler: is there really any reason to believe that money acts as the sole financial buffer?

Interestingly, a widening of the type of (financial) assets acting as buffers was proposed by Bain and McGregor (1985). They interpret the results of their so-called "financial buffers approach" as follows: "long-term interest rates on non-buffer assets are indeed likely to be determined in accordance with loanable funds theory ... [while] short-term interest rates on buffer assets are likely to be determined in accordance with liquidity preference theory" (Bain and McGregor 1985: 386). In our view, this interpretation is erroneous. Two related criticisms should be distinguished here.

First, Bain and McGregor confuse the *logical* issue in the loanable funds debate with particular *empirical* assumptions. In contrast to loanable funds theory, which simply overlooks that *something* must act as a buffer by *logical necessity*, their results are based on particular *empirical assumptions* concerning the types of assets functioning as buffers on the one hand, and the types of assets acquired for purposes of portfolio investment on the other. They apparently confirm the predictions of loanable funds theory by simply *assuming* that savers acquire certain non-buffer assets, which Bain and McGregor (1985: 391, n. 15) call "bonds," while their counterparts are *assumed* to run down bills, which "stand for all interest-bearing financial buffers" (rather than non-interest-bearing money only). Whatever the *empirical* relevance of the specific empirical assumptions underlying either of the buffer-stock approaches may be, importantly, they do *not* rescue loanable funds theory from being *logically* inconsistent.

Secondly, Bain and McGregor (1985: 393) justify their particular empirical assumptions concerning financial buffers and non-buffer assets as stemming from *differences* in transactions costs. For one thing, portfolio considerations, such as differences in transactions costs, never explicitly featured in loanable funds theory as affecting the savers' decision to either hoard or buy securities. It is thus somewhat peculiar to offer this case as a rationale behind the portfolio choices of the savers' counterparts, which were altogether ignored by loanable funds theory in the first place. More importantly, from a liquidity preference perspective, which explicitly treats portfolio decisions as being based on a balancing of relative attractions, differences in transactions costs are certainly important, but other portfolio considerations such as market conditions, relative yields, expectations, etc. must be taken into account as well. There can be neither any presumption that firms necessarily always *hold* financial instruments as buffers of a shorter maturity than savers may wish to acquire, nor that firms necessarily only *use* short-term financial instruments when trouble actually arises. Depending on market conditions, expectations, etc., the ranking of assets in their capacity as buffers may change. Indeed, firms may just as well *not* use up their most liquid (i.e. price certain) buffers, if alternatives still exist, but keep them as their ultimate buffers.

Correctly interpreted, then, the financial buffers approach, generalized to the extent that no specific empirical assumptions about buffers and non-buffers are made, confirms the liquidity preference view that a rise in thrift may affect interest rates *indirectly*. At least such an *indirect* effect may arise if portfolio preferences between the parties concerned in such a redistribution of wealth do not match at current rates of interest. The point is that we are only allowed to conclude that "change-in-composition-effects" may change interest rates *in either direction*. This result in itself is in stark contradiction of loanable funds theory. At a logical level, it is enough to point out that the core predictions of loanable funds theory regarding a rise in thrift do not feature the possibility that interest rates may actually *rise* under any circumstances. One counterexample should be sufficient to falsify a theory. At an empirical level, one certainly cannot exclude the possibility that the savers' counterparts sell securities rather than running down bank deposits.[7]

3.4 A cumulative deflationary process and where it ends

Apart from proving that loanable funds theory is fatally flawed, the previous section served to clarify that a disequilibrium between production and spending decisions, due to an unanticipated rise in thrift for instance, may *immediately* produce market signals in the sphere of *two* types of markets, namely goods markets and financial markets. The nature of these market signals is very different, though. On the one hand, interest rates may be affected *indirectly*, depending on the liquidity preference of the parties involved in the resulting redistribution of wealth. Interest rates may change *in either direction* though, and the sought-after interest rate signal – the central issue in the LP–LF debate – is therefore ambiguous. On the other hand, a rise in thrift *directly* leads to downward pressure on consumption goods prices, a clear-cut market signal to producers.

The most likely repercussion of this second market signal is that the firms which were hit by an unforeseen drop in sales proceeds attempt to cut back on their production outlays, either through cost savings and/or scaling down of their output *in periods subsequent* to the one disequilibrium period we have been looking at so far. If, as is not unlikely, the rise in thrift thereby initiates a cumulative downward adjustment in production, complex processes of simultaneously falling levels in production and spending result. Whether this cumulative deflationary process comes to an end before a complete collapse of consumption goods production depends on the relative rates of decline in production and spending respectively. If, at some point at least, spending falls off by less than production, a new stable position may be attained at which producers' production outlays once again match their expected sales proceeds at that level of output. At this point the hitherto clear-cut market signal would vanish, and producers' incentive to reduce output further due to *this* signal would vanish with it.

What happens to the interest rate signal during a cumulative deflationary process? What we may say is the following. As long as the savers stay ahead of the producers in the downward cumulative race, with the latter attempting to bring their production outlays back into line with their falling sales proceeds, the former will, no doubt, increase their savings and acquire assets of one type or another (the savers will be increasingly less successful at adding to their savings though, as incomes fall *exactly* in line with production outlays). In short, all along, following a rise in thrift, the savers will acquire additional assets of one type or another, and producers will sell and/or issue financial instruments of one type or another in order to cover their cash-flow shortfalls.

A point of particular interest which we mentioned before, and which we elaborate upon in this and the subsequent section, is that the two parties may not interact directly: financial intermediaries may come into play. For instance, if savers add (primarily) to their securities holdings, these securities may be bought either directly from the troubled firms, or via intermediaries reducing their portfolios of securities. Notice here that not only the size, but also the composition of the banking system's balance sheet may change. For instance, the banking system could keep the size of its balance sheet constant if the banks simultaneously reduced their portfolio of securities in line with *additional* loans purchased from the troubled firms. In this case, savers "supply their loanable funds" by buying securities from the banks (i.e. not-hoarding). Bank credit to firms would expand (as one component of overall credit), and even yet interest rates would – as a first approximation – remain unchanged. Alternatively, if the savers prefer to stay in bank deposits (i.e. hoarding) while firms cover their cash-flow shortfalls via securities sales/issues, the resulting tendency for securities prices to fall may prompt banks to take additional securities off the market, thereby expanding overall credit and, hence, hoards available to the savers. Such *credit expansion* – at the discretion of banks! – may (partly) offset the tendency of rising interest rates which itself, as noted above, falsifies loanable funds theory.

Of course, any mixture of these alternative routes of adjustment is a possibility. Savers may prefer a particular type of financial instrument at one time and another type at some other time. In practice, these choices are never restricted to the new savings made during any particular period but typically refer to the whole portfolio of wealth. Similarly, firms, i.e. the distress borrowers in our rise in thrift example, may at one time prefer to cover their cash-flow shortfalls (primarily) through one particular channel, and take recourse to another source on other occasions. Much depends on institutional arrangements, market conditions, on balance sheet positions and the flexibility options these still contain.

In summary, during the cumulative deflationary process precipitated by the rise in thrift, the firms' net indebtedness tends to rise relative to their business activities, thus leading to a deterioration of their balance sheet position compared to the initial one, whatever it was. Yet, *at no point during this process* does a rise in thrift *directly and immediately* depress interest rates. All along, financial market signals remain ambiguous as far as the change-in-composition effects featuring here are concerned, while the goods market signals are as clear-cut as before: pointing towards business contraction.[8] One may therefore envisage a cumulative process of numerous disequilibrium periods until at some point production outlays catch up with falling expenditures, *and activity thus once again stabilizes at that level*. The next section follows an analytical short-cut strategy and focuses on the final equilibrium only.[9]

3.5 Correct anticipations and bank behavior

Assume now that entrepreneurs correctly anticipate the incipient drop in consumption spending – and hence sales revenues – which a rise in thrift bestows upon them. In other words, we altogether abstract from the above (type of) disequilibrium processes and move straight away from the initial to the final position at which entrepreneurs, once again, get their sales forecasts right. We may call this short-cut strategy the "equilibrium case," describing the case where entrepreneurs' short-term expectations are always fulfilled. (As before, we assume that expectations of both firms and households were fulfilled in the initial period 1.) The equilibrium case is not meant to suggest that entrepreneurs always "get it right." The disequilibria of Section 3.3 occur all the time in practice, and may easily evolve into the Section 3.4 type of cumulative processes. Nevertheless, the analytical short-cut seems appropriate and fruitful for a number of reasons.

First, the likely direction of change in economic activity due to disequilibria between spending and production decisions would appear to be indisputable anyway: a clear-cut market signal. Yet, if there are reasons to believe that cumulative deflationary processes do not necessarily lead to a complete collapse in output, but may stabilize at *some* level, a new chapter of economic analysis would seem to have opened up before us: if activity may stabilize at *any* level, it makes sense then to concentrate on the question of what determines the level of economic activity in the first place. As a side-effect, the interest rate issue appears in a different light too. It does not primarily concern the *signaling* question anymore, an issue already settled, but the question "what determines the rate of interest at any time."[10]

Secondly, from the point of view of producers, the analytical short-cut strategy offers an interesting variation on the theme of the previous two sections. For in the case of a correctly anticipated rise in thrift, what we have just referred to as a rather clear-cut market signal does not actually arise either, since the signal, so to speak, had been correctly anticipated. The equilibrium case thereby illustrates that actual surprises may not represent the only motivation for changing output plans – plans which turn out to be optimal plans given some particular level of effective demand.[11]

Finally, the short-cut strategy also helps to clarify the notion of "credit contraction" as an interfering factor in the loanable funds mechanism in particular, and the role of bank behavior more generally. In this regard, our analysis points towards *two* alternative channels through which interest rates may be affected *indirectly*. We have already referred to the change-in-composition channel above. Another channel is financial intermediaries, which may step in and (partly) facilitate redistributions in wealth. And if they do, any corresponding changes in the pool of liquidity and overall credit made available thereby, available to satisfy the general public's liquidity preferences and financing needs, will generally overlap with the first, the change-in-composition effects. The point is that the analytical short-cut allows us to separate the two channels. As redistributions in wealth due to mistaken expectations are precluded in the equilibrium case, change-in-composition type of indirect effects on interest rates due to differences in liquidity preference *within* the general public are ruled out as well. The investigation may thus focus on the effects on interest rates due to changes in the size and composition of the banking system's balance sheet alone. And these may well arise at any time and quite independently of change-in-composition effects anyway.

In the equilibrium case, expectations of producers are fulfilled and sales revenues of, and incomes earned in, the consumption goods industries in the current period fall by the same amount. As *ex ante* and *ex post* sales revenues match, this time round it is not the firms which are presented with an unpleasant surprise, but households' income expectations which are disappointed instead. Moreover, saving plans would appear to be disappointed by the same amount as income expectations. It therefore becomes important at this point to unravel what loanable funds proponents actually mean by "planned savings" and how a rise in planned saving is supposed to *directly and immediately* lower interest rates, thereby providing the market signal for increased investment. It turns out that loanable funds proponents simply confuse *money* and *saving*. There are two versions of loanable funds theory we need to distinguish here.

One version, due to the Swedish economist Bertil Ohlin, defines "planned saving" with reference to expected future incomes. At first one might think that this version may be safely neglected today. For it appears that even loanable funds proponents took Keynes' (1937f) criticism of Ohlin's concept of "*ex ante* saving" as conclusive. Ohlin's version thus died quietly, at least for a while.[12] Curiously, however, Ohlin's version rose from the grave again in the 1970s when a new generation of neo-Walrasians challenged the earlier neo-Walrasian "drop-one-equation" type of equivalence proof à la Hicks (1936, 1939; cf. also Patinkin 1958, 1965) – which had reigned for some forty years or so. Foley (1975) and Buiter (1980) prove that the two theories employ rather different equilibrium notions and that they are only equivalent under very specific conditions, in particular perfect foresight. Remarkably, however, these later neo-Walrasian contributors do not appear to be troubled in the least by the question how *planned saving* out of expected future incomes may possibly provide the *money* which the investor needs *today*.[13] Although certainly of value in clarifying the usefulness of general equilibrium-only analysis, these attempts at resuscitation of a loanable funds corps can thus hardly be seen as successful.

Another version of loanable funds theory, due to Keynes' former pupil and long-time friend Dennis Robertson, was blessed with a longer life among loanable funds followers. Robertson (1940: 6), although in agreement with Ohlin that "in the analysis of the market for loanable funds it is some kind of intentional or 'ex-ante' concept of saving that is required," defines "planned saving" as referring not to future but to current income. More precisely, due to the "Robertsonian consumption lag," it is the income earned in the previous period. In other words, the saving plan for the current period takes its cue from last period's income. The point is, however, that the savers' wishful thinking does not predetermine incomes in the current period. Current income is determined by effective demand, that is, production *decisions* rather than saving *plans*. If entrepreneurs correctly anticipate the rise in thrift, the savers' saving plans remain forever nothing but wishful thinking. Robertson too confuses *saving* and *money*.[14]

The essential difference between the two loanable funds versions is the following. While Ohlin (and his belated neo-Walrasian followers) portray some visionary world in which *saving plans* may – by some miraculous device – channel *money* to entrepreneurial investors for the financing of today's production, Robertson's savers transfer "something," also called "planned saving," to investors which they do seem to actually have at hand already. But what is it that they transfer? Clearly, just as savers cannot possibly supply their envisioned future savings on some Ohlinian loanable funds market, they can hardly supply past savings on some Robertsonian loanable funds market either. What "savers" may supply, of course, is *money*. That is, they may wish to part with liquidity in exchange for some other claim or asset at current rates of interest, the amount of their savings being wholly unaffected by such a portfolio swap.

In other words, one may envision "savers" who at the beginning of the period wish to add bonds to their portfolio of wealth. And they may even arrive at this wish on the basis of their incomes earned in the previous period, not knowing, at this point, how much income they are going to earn over the current period and, hence, what planned saving is going to be *ex post*. It will not be denied that such a *change in liquidity preference* may affect interest rates, with various further repercussions being possible. Alas, it would seem to be particularly hard to predict the savers' reaction when the basis for their changed liquidity preferences turns out as having been wishful thinking. At least, this time round, producers will not be seen as distress borrowers in the loanable funds market.

Accordingly, we altogether deny the idea that planned saving may somehow disappear in the banking system, or that the loanable funds mechanism may get stalled because the banks contract credit. For the rise in thrift, if accurately anticipated by the consumption goods industries, will never be more than wishful thinking. The *planned* saving simply does not materialize. Thus the rise in thrift is not being "aborted" by credit contraction, but planned saving is being aborted by being anticipated.

Nevertheless, bank behavior can surely make a real difference, and quite independently of whether or not a rise in thrift occurs. Consider the following two cases, which feature changes in the size and/or composition of the banking system's balance sheet. One example may be seen as representing endogenous money, the other exogenous money. Beginning with the former, suppose that firms adjust their borrowing from banks exactly in line with their business activities, which, incidentally, may be a reasonable assumption, at least as a first approximation. As, this time round, there arises no need to take recourse to emergency borrowing, the size of the banking system's balance sheet would change *pari passu* with the level of economic activity. At least such an outcome would appear to arise if banks restricted their activities to *passively* responding – perhaps via overdrafts – to their borrowers' needs only. Money would be *endogenous*, driven by credit demand only.

Alternatively, assume that the quantity of money remains constant, rather than shrinking exactly in line with economic activity as in the previous case. *Assuming* a constant and given stock of money may seem arbitrary at first sight, but it illustrates the following point. By implication, if loan demand falls off in line with economic activity, banks must expand their activities in other directions – otherwise the size of their balance sheets could not remain unchanged. In particular, banks may decide to take additional securities off the market, thereby driving up securities prices (i.e. lowering their running yields). In short, the *exogenous* money case highlights that banks always have the choice of managing their balance sheets *actively* and adjusting them in whatever way pleases them.

Let me pinpoint the crucial differences at issue here. Endogenous money proponents like Moore (1988), for instance, are certainly right to reject the prehistorical "deposits-make-loans" view of banking (cf. Chick 1993), along with the related loanable funds fallacy that savings deposited with banks may somehow disappear in the banking system. Banks issue their liabilities by buying assets, including (overdraft) loans. So far so good. Yet, it hardly seems any more fruitful to caricature banks as "doing" nothing else but passively taking on whatever volume of loans their borrowers may wish to take out at the current short-term rate of interest (while depositors conveniently lend to banks however much is being borrowed from the banks). Replacing monetarism by what is effectively "reverse monetarism" is not a particularly illuminating way of thinking about monetary control and the role of bank behavior in a world which values liquidity. Endogenous money proponents, while avoiding one,[15] thereby commit another interest rate fallacy. Central banks do *not* set those interest rates which liquidity preference theory is concerned with. Typically, they set the overnight rate (cf. Borio 1997; Bindseil 2004), which still leaves "the" rate of interest "in the air."[16]

Unfortunately, it has been widely misunderstood that money exogeneity plays a peculiar role in the "liquidity [preference] theory of interest" of *The General Theory*. Essentially, assuming a constant and given stock of money allows Keynes (1936a) to concentrate on the simpler partner in the liquidity preference pair of scissors, the liquidity preferences of the general public, leaving the far more difficult and complex part to take place behind the scenes, bank behavior and banks' interaction with the monetary authorities.[17]

Obviously, this is not to suggest that banks, in the occasion of a rise in thrift for instance, must always follow the particular banking policy of keeping the size of their balance sheet exactly constant while the level of economic activity is changing. The point is to illustrate the following: interest rates may be affected *indirectly* and even in the desired direction, if, to put the point in the most general terms, banks expand their balance sheets *relative* to the level of economic activity, and if the general public's propensity to hold deposits does not simultaneously rise sufficiently to offset this *liquidizing effect*. Clearly such a liquidizing effect, a change in the amount of liquidity available *relative* to the level of economic activity (and wealth), is independent of any rise in thrift as such and, moreover, not easily interpreted as an *automatic* market mechanism of the sought-after type. Rather, it *may* simply represent the optimal response on the part of the banks in respect of the size and composition of their balance sheets (which is not to suggest that banks must always and necessarily be responding to changes elsewhere in the economy rather than initiating changes).

This liquidizing effect is generally referred to in the (Keynesian) literature as the "Keynes effect" (Cottrell 1994). Yet the focus in the literature is usually on the part played by the general public's demand for liquidity alone, and sometimes the Keynes effect is interpreted unnecessarily narrowly (cf. Leijonhufvud 1968: 325). In contrast with the non-existent loanable funds "mechanism," it may actually be more appropriate to call this liquidizing effect on interest rates the "Keynes mechanism." For the Keynes mechanism describes an indirect interest rate channel *caused by a tendency on the part of banks* to try to prevent a falling-off in profits due to slack business in any one particular direction by expanding their activities in alternative ones instead, and *vice versa*. Notice that this alternative interest-rate mechanism along liquidity preference lines presupposes both agile behavior on the part of banks as well as a roughly unchanged state of the general public's liquidity preferences, in particular.[18]

3.6 Price flexibility and real time

The disequilibrium analyses of Sections 3.3 and 3.4 concentrated on manufacturing industries and treated inventories as bearing the initial brunt of mismatches between spending and production decisions. Market signals in the form of unplanned changes in these real buffers were treated there as prompting producers to respond in ways which lead to cumulative processes of simultaneously falling production, spending, and inventory investment. In fact, as Blinder and Maccini (1991: 73) report, empirically: "inventory movements are dominant features of business cycles." It is thus of some interest that the New Keynesian "credit view" has motivated research which links these empirical findings on the cyclical behavior of inventories to the issue of business finance.

According to the credit view (cf. e.g. Bernanke and Blinder, 1988, 1992; Bernanke and Gertler, 1995), bank loans are "special" from the point of view of at least some borrowers, so that credit too, and not just money, may represent an additional (lending) channel in the monetary transmission mechanism. Kashyap *et al.* (1994) and Gertler and Gilchrist (1994), for instance, investigate firms' inventory demand behavior in recessions by size of firms. Their work is based on the presumption that small firms may be bank-dependent and thus more likely to be liquidity constrained than larger firms. Indeed, their findings seem to indicate that small firms' inventory investment responds at a faster pace in recessionary periods as compared with larger firms. More generally, Gertler and Gilchrist (1994: 327) find that "[s]hort-term debt mirrors the response of inventories." In other words, this line of research focuses on a particular case of disequilibria between spending and production decisions, with inventories acting as real buffers, and bank loans as financial buffers. On the one hand, there is a clear relationship between the credit view and our above financial buffers approach. On the other hand, the specific empirical question at issue in this credit view research on inventory responses is whether at least some firms face restrictions with regard to the sources available to cover the corresponding cash-flow shortfalls.

Until now we concentrated on these cash-flow shortfalls as the *logical* counterpart of disequilibria between spending and production decisions. We may now further generalize our disequilibrium analysis with regard to the *original* goods market disequilibrium. For inventory changes represent only one of two possible immediate adjustment strategies of producers who "get it wrong," the other being changing *current* prices. In effect, allowing for flexible goods prices amounts to extending the analysis to include service industries, where, naturally, inventories and inventory changes cannot occur in the first place and the actual rate of production is not predetermined. Nevertheless, at least as long as the (potential) production of services is organized along capitalistic lines, cash-flow shortfalls may arise just as easily. For the outlays of service industries over the period will be largely predetermined by the contracts/commitments entered into in order to set up the organization which is capable of accomplishing the production of services, no matter how much production/consumption actually takes place over the same period.

From an empirical point of view, it is thus immediately clear that while microeconomic decisions must always be reconciled in the aggregate *in some way*, there is no one-to-one correspondence to be expected between changes in real buffers on the one hand, and changes in financial buffers on the other. Firms' adjustment strategies may differ not only by size of firm (the credit view criterion), but across manufacturing and service sectors, and their strategies may also vary over time. Furthermore, there is little reason to expect the structure of the economy to be homogeneous through time, particularly the structure of the financial system. Finally, firms' degree of foresight with regard to incipient changes in demand will vary too, with our "equilibrium case" of Section 3.4 as a limiting case. And the analysis has shown that balance sheets of both financial intermediaries and the general public may well adjust in this case too – with some interesting implications concerning the interest rate issue. We can only indicate here the complexity of implications of our disequilibrium analysis for financial data analysis.

From a purely theoretical point of view, however, nothing in our argument concerning the determination of interest rates hinges upon whether or not service industries are included, or to what extent goods prices rather than inventories adjust. This merely amounts to allowing for (perfectly) flexible goods prices in addition to financial assets prices. Neither adjustment strategy offers a real solution to the underlying problem of the cash-flow shortfall.[19] We may thus pinpoint what exactly distinguishes our exercises in the analysis of disequilibrium from the standard neo-Walrasian approach to monetary theory.

The point is that even if *current* factor prices were perfectly flexible – no doubt, a blatantly counterfactual assumption – we should still not get rid of the cash-flow shortfall featuring in our disequilibrium analysis in this way. Flexibility of today's factor prices simply won't do, we need to go further (backwards in time) than that. One way of avoiding this problem altogether is to assume that *past* factor prices are perfectly flexible as well. I mean those prices which were "relevant," or so it would seem, at the time when "commitments" to starting the production process were made. Clearly, if we make this tricky *assumption*, we are safely in the realm of the neo-Walrasian "recontracting" world – a world of "pre-reconciled choices" (Shackle 1972) from which *historical* (or, real) time is absent (Robinson 1970).

Effectively, the recontracting device collapses the future into the present. If the possibility of *ex post* disappointment, which is inherent in the vagaries of organizing the process of production along capitalist lines in the face of an uncertain future, is ruled out *ex ante by assumption*, then production effectively becomes a timeless "process." Unfortunately, we thereby abstract from the crucial empirical fact and core institutional feature which characterizes the type of economies monetary theory is presumably referring to. The potentiality of cash-flow shortfalls arises due to the fact that capitalistic production involves fixed commitments to pay out sums of money. By the very nature of the organization of production in market economies, entrepreneurs enter into all sorts of contractual commitments in order to gain control over the process of production, money-wage contracts in particular. These contracts are typically non-recontractable.

These *contractual* linkages through time characteristic of the real world are entered into by entrepreneurs in the face of uncertainty about future demand. But they do not seem to pose any serious coordination problem when we write down an equation which links agents' time preferences to some imagined intertemporal price mechanism. This *imaginary* linkage is most easily established by simply including expected future incomes into the budget constraint upon which Walras' law is set to work. A decision not to consume today then appears to involve the placement of a substitute order for future consumption, while the production of capital goods may even be "financed" out of saving *plans*. Unfortunately such imaginary transactions through time appear to be not from this planet, and *historical time* thereby silently slips through our analytical hands together with the intertemporal coordination problem *by assumption*. Perhaps it is no surprise that neo-Walrasian general equilibrium theorists have never been able to settle the LP–LF issue, an issue which concerns *disequilibrium* adjustments in *intertemporal* prices. At any rate, the loanable funds fallacy poses a formidable challenge to neo-Walrasians: to justify the idea that – by *some* mechanism other than the elegant Walrasian fiction – intertemporal prices correctly reflect technology and time preferences.

3.7   Filling the gap – the liquidity preference theory of interest

The main message of this chapter is a negative one: the loanable funds mechanism which loanable funds theorists believe to *directly and immediately* lower interest rates when a rise in thrift occurs was shown to be a mere *mirage*. Keynes' analysis in the *Treatise* already establishes the logical inconsistency of what went on to become loanable funds theory, a result which we corroborated in Section 3.3 by means of a generalized financial buffers approach. However, it was not until a few years later that Keynes himself completed his alternative vision of the process of capital accumulation in monetary production economies. In *The General Theory*, the principle of effective demand is shown to be the key to the level of economic activity at any time, while the rate of interest – one determinant of effective demand – is "determined *exogenously* with respect to the income generation process" (Pasinetti 1974: 47). In particular, interest rates are determined independently of the real forces of productivity and thrift believed to be the anchor and steering forces behind the loanable funds market.

No doubt, Keynes' vision of capital accumulation is diametrically opposed to the loanable funds one. Starting from an older vision of capital accumulation in corn economies, with a *real* saving fund as the classical source of investment "finance," loanable funds theorists merely annex hoarding and banks, i.e. *monetary* factors, to the usual corn economy picture. From the loanable funds vision the "genuine" saving fund of investment finance may be either augmented or diminished by either one of two "monetary" funds, namely hoarding/dishoarding and credit expansion/ contraction. Keynes was at pains to point out that the augmented corn economy vision had outlived its time, beautifully depicting the loanable funds fallacy:

Increased investment will always be accompanied by increased saving, but it can never be preceded by it. Dishoarding and credit expansion provides not an *alternative* to increased saving, but a necessary preparation for it. It is the parent, not the twin, of increased saving.

(Keynes 1939b, JMK 14: 281)

In short, in monetary production economies the classical saving fund is to be written out of the play. At any time, the investor's need for cash can only be satisfied out of two alternative sources, either by attracting already existing deposits, or by the banks' new creation of them. (Over time both credit and hoards will have to grow.) By contrast, additional saving, i.e. a rise in thrift, cannot possibly alleviate the investor's need for *money* (not saving!). On the one hand, an unanticipated rise in thrift (Section 3.3) merely redistributes existing wealth without adding anything to it. On the other hand, a correctly anticipated rise in thrift (Section 3.5) does not add any net saving to the loanable funds market either, as the planned saving is simply "frustrated" by being anticipated.[20] Clearly, Keynes was getting a bit bored with the loanable funds corn economists who, then and now, stubbornly refuse to understand their corn-economy illusion:

If there is no change in the liquidity position, the public can save *ex ante* and *ex post* and *ex* anything else until they are blue in the face, without alleviating the problem [i.e. the demand for *money*, not *saving*] in the least – unless, indeed, the result of their efforts is to lower the scale of activity to what it was before.

(Keynes 1937f, JMK 14: 222)

The second part of this devastating verdict spotlights the "Keynes mechanism," leading us to the positive implications of our exercises in the analysis of disequilibrium.

The Keynes mechanism describes an interest rate channel featuring a liquidizing effect caused by a tendency on the part of banks to try to prevent a falling-off in profits due to slack business in any one particular direction by expanding their activities in alternative ones instead, and *vice versa*. Interest rates may thus tend to change in the desired direction after all. Yet, if they do, this would not be the *direct and immediate* effect of any rise in thrift itself, but a possible accompaniment of the fall in incomes induced by such a drop in spending. The Keynes mechanism can thus hardly be interpreted as an *automatic* market mechanism which assures appropriate intertemporal prices and equilibrium between saving and investment. But it will at least tend to lessen the deflationary effects of increased thriftiness. By contrast, the other channel of *indirect* interest rate effects, change-in-composition-effects, may in principle move interest rates in either direction.

Our disequilibrium analysis thus clarifies the forces which definitely do not, and *some* of the forces which may indeed, move interest rates away from what they were before.[21] But the analysis does not explain why the level of interest rates was what it was in the first place. The rate of interest is simply left "in the air." This is a rather serious matter. On the one hand, the Wicksellian notion of *the* "natural rate of interest," as determined by the real forces of productivity and thrift, is irreparably undermined as the anchor of the system. On the other hand, the principle of effective demand implies that the system may be in a state of rest at any level of activity. The market rate of interest, determined by whatever forces (but exogenously to the income-generating flows of the system), then appears to hold a prominent role. Indeed, when the classical (LF-augmented) corn economy play is being recast in the context of a monetary production economy, money, which was all along used to playing only a junior (and mainly nominal) part, is suddenly seen as "ruling the roost" of real activity and accumulation.

However, it is not a very big step – but is it not a straightforward logical step? – to require that at any time interest rates must be such that the general public's desire to hold money rather than other financial instruments ceases at the margin, given the amount of liquidity the banking system decides to provide. And this is just the way Keynes states the issue in *The General Theory*:

> [T]he rate of interest at any time, being the reward for parting with liquidity, is a measure of the unwillingness of those who possess money to part with their liquid control over it. ... It is the 'price' which equilibrates the desire to hold wealth in the form of cash with the available quantity of cash.
>
> (Keynes 1936a, JMK 7: 167)[22]

Hicks' (1939) and Robertson's (1940) critique that Keynes leaves the rate of interest "hanging by its own bootstraps" misses the point. With the "real" bootstraps of orthodoxy shown to be imaginary rather than real, Keynes is simply stating the monetary principle from which to start in order to fill the gap left thereby. In his view, the liquidity preference theory of interest is plainly a piece of pure logic, filling the gap, but in itself leaving some important questions unanswered.[23] In particular, the liquidity preference theory of interest neither explains why the general public's *propensity* to hoard is what it is at any time, nor why the banking system provides a certain amount of liquidity at any time, and neither more nor less.

But Keynes also added some flesh to his logical starting point. In particular, he has some very illuminating things to say in *The General Theory* about the various motives of liquidity preference (or, the incentives to liquidity) and on market psychology (e.g. the role of expectations, confidence, animal spirits and conventions as the driving forces behind the behavior of financial market participants). He is less explicit on the possibilities and limitations faced by the monetary authorities in molding these factors and deliberately steering longer term interest rates towards some desired level, apart from setting short-term ones. Indeed, most of the time, as in the quotation from *The General Theory* just referred to, he simply takes the pool of liquidity provided by the banking system (or, the stock of money) as a given constant in that book. In this regard, the "finance motive debate" (cf. Chapter 2) offered him an important opportunity to clarify the role of the banking system, leading up to the following – more symmetric – statement:

> one could regard the rate of interest as being determined by the interplay of the terms on which the public desires to become more or less liquid and those on which the banking system is ready to become more or less unliquid. This is, I think, an illuminating way of expressing the liquidity preference theory of the rate of interest; but particularly so within the field of "finance".
>
> (Keynes 1937f, JMK 14: 219)

Just as in the rise in thrift case we concentrated on above, where interest rates would tend to fall if thriftiness results in a lower scale of activity, Keynes argues there that a rise in productivity tends – *indirectly* – to lead to higher interest rates, namely through putting additional pressure on a given pool of liquidity. In principle, the working of the Keynes mechanism is symmetric. Keynes emphasizes, however, that such an outcome is neither natural nor inevitable, as the classical savings fund vision would seem to suggest. For, in principle, the banking system is in the position to offset the additional pressure on the pool of liquidity by simply expanding the provision of liquidity accordingly.

A point of particular interest emerging from the finance motive debate is the fact that a rise in economic activity may give rise to additional pressure on the pool of liquidity even at the stage of planning, i.e. even before "anything real" has happened at all. Keynes referred to this point as the "coping stone of the liquidity theory of the rate of interest" and thought it would "buttress the liquidity theory of interest against the savings theory of interest" (Keynes 1937f, JMK 14: 220–1). And rightly so. For it highlights that an increase in planned investment spending (or rather, spending and activity in general) does not affect interest rates *directly* through drawing on some given pool of saving, but only *indirectly* and in so far as it adds to the pressure on the pool of liquidity. A plan to invest may thus be defeated by giving rise to financial market congestion, reflecting a shortage not of saving, but of liquidity. In fact, increased saving – *ex ante* and *ex post* and *ex* anything else – would do nothing to alleviate this shortage – unless it somehow affects the liquidity position, perhaps by crowding out activity. Instead, the provider of the pool of liquidity is found in a key position, potentially posing a *liquidity* constraint on *real* activity. Note that the classical fund of saving proper is not merely annexed by supplementary monetary funds; the saving fund is out.

Seen in the light of the LP–LF debate, Meade's (1975) metaphor of the Keynesian investment dog wagging its savings tail, which he contrasts to an older vision where the reverse order was held to be the true model of reality, is both right and wrong. Meade is right in pinpointing the key message of Keynes' "revolution:" the strict denial of the orthodox saving–finances–investment vision of capital accumulation, whether LF-augmented or not. This outdated vision Keynes replaced by the diametrically opposed vision of a monetary production economy, where capital is produced and production is dependent not on prior saving, but on liquidity. Meade is wrong, however, to believe that Keynes succeeded in shifting economists' view of the world to fully embrace the world in which we actually live. Countless "proofs" of the equivalence of the two theories, barren attempts at reconciling the unreconcilable, give ample evidence of the aborted revolution.[24]

Clearly, Leijonhufvud (1994: 155) gets things the wrong way round in his suggestive and derogatory remark about the "strong conviction" of Richard Kahn and Joan Robinson on the interest rate mechanism as "a central tenet of Cambridge faith (among the faithful)." Indeed, his remark is both regrettable and could not be further off the mark. For the LP–LF debate concerns a *logical* rather than an *ideological* point. Pretending to live in an (LF-augmented) corn economy though, is purely a matter of faith.[25]

Appendix

Pre-*General Theory* roots of the liquidity preference versus loanable funds controversy, and the loanable funds fallacy

In tracing Keynes' identification of the loanable funds fallacy, it is in fact useful to go back to the 1920s, a period of close cooperation between Keynes and Dennis Robertson, his student and friend (cf. Presley 1979, 1992; Bridel 1987). Robertson's (1926) *Banking Policy and the Price Level*, featuring the notion of "abortive saving" (or, lacking), may be considered the background to the first round of liquidity preference versus loanable funds (LP–LF) controversies that followed upon the publication of *A Treatise on Money*. In that book, Robertson developed a rather complex scheme of thought and terminology for analyzing the saving–investment nexus and the role of the banking system in the trade cycle. His scheme features both the possibility of saving somehow "getting lost" for investment, i.e. the old hoarding idea (or "abortive lacking" in Robertson's colorful terminology), as well as the possibility that the saving fund may somehow be augmented by the banking system. The latter idea was much discussed at the time, broadly under the heading of "forced saving." In essence, the idea was that genuine saving as the "classical" source of investment funds may be either augmented or diminished by supplementary sources.

Clearly, the Robertsonian picture of saving being either diminished or augmented as a fund for investment was just one step away from the later loanable funds perspective where a change in saving would cause a change in interest rates unless there was a simultaneous and offsetting change in either hoarding or bank credit. It was Keynes in the *Treatise* who shifted the focus to the role of the rate of interest that was going to be at the heart of the LP–LF debate. The point is that the *Treatise* analysis already denied the existence of what Axel Leijonhufvud (1981) fifty years later dubbed the "loanable funds mechanism" and illuminated the loanable funds fallacy. Robertson's first published response to the *Treatise* and Keynes' rejoinder, the opening shots in the "buckets in the well" fallacy, highlight the crucial point at issue.

Robertson's (1931) "Mr. Keynes' theory of money" turns on the notion of hoarding, and since he states that he has "no doubt that Mr. Keynes is right in laying stress on 'hoarding' as a dominant feature of trade depression" (409), it might at first appear as if the whole issue is a matter of terminology only: "What I am urging is that one thing, and one thing only, can make it occur, namely, an increased desire on the part of somebody to 'hoard,' that is, to keep resources idle in the form of bank deposits" (401; notice here that Robertson refers to hoarding "in the form of bank deposits"). Robertson also explicitly refers to Keynes' argument about the need to finance "losses" and states "but the fact which this argument suppresses is that such a state of affairs cannot come about except as the result of an act of 'hoarding,' i.e., of holding back unspent part of a stream of money which is normally spent, on the part of some one" (400).

Robertson's assessment of the behavior of producers – facing the losses – and their "alleged sale of assets" is of interest here. According to his "highly simplified numerical illustration," these producers sell assets "in order to maintain the scale of their operations unchanged" (Robertson 1931: 402). Robertson even states that he thinks "Mr. Keynes has done a real service in calling attention to their [i.e. loss-makers' asset sales] existence" (402, n. 1), but believes the financing of losses to be quantitatively unimportant compared with alternatives open to entrepreneurs, such as cutting down personal expenditures or the scale of their operations. The crucial question is, however, *when* are those changes in the scale of operations, as one alternative open to entrepreneurs, supposed to happen?

In the ensuing debate, Robertson went on to become the great champion of period analysis (or the "step-by-step" method as he called it). Do his above statements imply that the entrepreneur cuts down his personal expenditure or the scale of operations *in the same period* in which the losses would otherwise occur? And is it only because the entrepreneur refuses to follow these other alternatives that he then has to sell assets in order to maintain the scale of his operations *in the subsequent period(s)*? Before we move on to Keynes' (1931) rejoinder, it is worth looking at a later statement by Robertson in which he proposes essentially the same argument as in 1931 and which brings, in my view at least, the whole problem to a head. Robertson's following remark was made in the context of his discussion of liquidity preference theory as presented in *The General Theory* and then even after Keynes' introduction of the finance motive. Interestingly, in this remark Robertson himself refers back to the earlier buckets-in-the-well debate (the "old ghost"). Robertson (1940: 19, n. 1) remarks that

> debate on this matter has sometimes been hampered by the ghost of an old argument, dating from the days of the *Treatise on Money*. According to this argument the loss-making tailor, in order to avoid restricting either his personal consumption or the scale of his business, will sell securities to the same amount as I buy them. Obviously, so long as such a situation continues, the rate of interest will not fall nor the formation of capital equipment be stimulated; but neither, so far as the mere maintenance of total income (other than the tailor's) and employment goes, is it necessary that they should. Evidently, however, this can only be a transitional situation and it is not instructive to stop short at it.

Keynes' rejoinder concentrates on Robertson's crucial mistake, reflected in "Mr Robertson's view that the price levels of consumption goods and investment goods will move in *opposite* directions – like buckets in a well" (Keynes 1931d, JMK 13: 223). The following statement illuminates Keynes' essential point: all transactions within any one period and their corresponding money flows must always match. This must be the case in equilibrium and in disequilibrium. In the latter case, situations of disappointed sales expectations on the part of producers, the financial counterparts of such disequilibria may well have an impact on interest rates. However, depending on the liquidity preferences (portfolio decisions) of the parties involved (including the banking system, the role of which is made explicit), the direction of change is ambiguous. Nothing can be said *a priori*; interest rates may even rise. According to Keynes (1931d, JMK 13: 224–5),

> An increase in saving relatively to investment during any period means that the savers find themselves at the end of the period with an increase of wealth, which they can embark at their choice either in liquid or in non-liquid assets, whilst the producers of consumption goods find themselves with an equal decrease of wealth, which must cause them to part at their choice either with liquid or with non-liquid assets which they previously possessed. Unless the propensity to hoard of the savers is different from the propensity to hoard of the entrepreneurs – and if it is different, it will mean that there is a change of hoarding propensity for the community as a whole, which change is as likely *a priori* to be in one direction as in the other – it follows that the excess of saving has *in itself*, and apart from its repercussions on the aggregate propensity to hoard, no tendency to cause any change at all in the price of non-liquid assets. Nor, of course, has it any tendency to cause a change in the volume of inactive deposits, except in so far as the banking system may be influenced by changes in the business deposits to fix the total deposits in such a way as to change the amount of the inactive deposits.

We can thus see what the problem is. Robertson (1931, 1940), although clearly admitting that Keynes has a point, albeit only a minor one in his view, appears to think that Keynes' argument refers to a situation in which a "loss-making tailor" sells securities in order to finance his excessive personal consumption and/ or continue his loss-making business on the same scale in subsequent periods. The point, however, is that Keynes is concerned with the question of how the cash-flow shortfall incurred in the current period is met, and it has to be met somehow, failing which the tailor will default on his commitments. Keynes' argument is based on the simple economic truth that there are always two sides to any economic transaction. People cannot save, that is, realize an excess of current income over current expenditure, and acquire securities, for instance, out of thin air. Savers must have a counterpart; there must be a "deficit unit" whose expenditure (outlays) exceeds income (revenue). In a disequilibrium case such as the present example, it is the loss-making tailor who needs somehow to balance the books. And the loss-making tailor needs to balance the books in the same period, the current period, in which the savers are supposed to save more than thin air, at least insofar as the savers are actually going to be successful in doing so.

Robertson, by contrast, ignores the redistributional effect between producers and consumers that Keynes had drawn attention to. His notion of hoarding not only confuses saving (rather, non-spending) and portfolio decisions; his whole argument overlooks the necessary counterpart to these decisions. It overlooks that over any period of time the books must always be balanced. It is not that the loss-making tailor only enters the "loanable funds market," if he enters it at all, to finance his, perhaps, unchanged scale of activities planned to be carried out in subsequent periods. He is in the market at any rate, namely to cover the cash-flow shortfalls inflicted upon him by the savers in the current period. These flows, saving and losses, exactly match and cancel out. There is thus no addition to saving that could depress interest rates.

Clearly, Keynes' (1931) argument does not depend at all on how agents may adjust their behavior in periods subsequent to the one disequilibrium period he is looking at. As Figure 3.1 highlights, Keynes restricts his argument to the one, current period in which the disequilibrium (first) occurs. Indeed, he explicitly explains in a footnote that

> I did not deal in my book, and I am not dealing here, with the train of events which ensues when, as a consequence of making losses, entrepreneurs reduce their output. This is a long story, though not, I think, fundamentally different, which I intend to treat in detail in due course. Its only bearing on the present argument is that a change in output affects the demand for active deposits, and may therefore (according to how the banking system behaves) affect the supply of hoards.
>
> (Keynes 1931d, JMK 13: 229, n. 7)

In summary, then, the early debate between Robertson and Keynes probably contains everything that needs to be said about the loanable funds fallacy and, for that matter, the LP–LF debate. But note also Keynes' above observation on the role of the banking system's behavior featuring the possibility that the supply of hoards (inactive deposits) may be affected if the demand for active deposits, but not the supply of total deposits, moves in line with output. The envisioned bank behavior would seem to open up the possibility of another interest rate channel, an *indirect* interest rate channel that was going to become an integral part of *The General Theory* with its assumption of an exogenous stock of total deposits (the subject of Chapter 5 below). Keynes' observation therefore gives a good indication of the direction he was subsequently going to take with regard to liquidity preference theory and the behavior of the banking system. It is essential that any impact on interest rates potentially arising through this channel has got nothing to do with any rise in thrift as such, but *may* arise if loss-making entrepreneurs adjust their scale of activities in response to the losses inflicted upon them by such a rise in thrift, for instance, while banks expand their business in other directions instead.

While the Keynes effect (Cottrell 1994) was already present in the *Treatise*, the key shortcomings of that book concerned output adjustments. Key inspirations in Keynes' move toward *The General Theory* came from the Cambridge Circus and Richard Kahn in particular as well as Ralph Hawtrey (see Harcourt 1994; and Kahn 1984, 1985, 1989 on the former; and Davis 1980 and Deutscher 1990 on the latter). With the discovery of the principle of effective demand the role of liquidity preference theory was going to change fundamentally, although the substance of liquidity preference theory remained essentially unchanged and was already fully developed in the *Treatise*. Bibow (2000) discusses these issues in more detail (see also Bibow 2006b).

4   On Keynesian theories of liquidity preference[1]

It might be more accurate, perhaps, to say that the rate of interest is a highly conventional, rather than a highly psychological, phenomenon. For its actual value is largely governed by the prevailing view as to what its value is expected to be. *Any* level of interest which is accepted with sufficient conviction as *likely* to be durable *will* be durable; subject, of course, in a changing society to fluctuations for all kinds of reasons round the expected normal. In particular, when M_1 is increasing faster than M, the rate of interest will rise, and *vice versa*.

(Keynes 1936a, JMK 7: 203–4)[2]

4.1 Introduction

This chapter sets out to offer a macroeconomic perspective on the interaction between the financial system and the level of economic activity, focusing on the relationship between liquidity preference, investment and the role of confidence.

We shall proceed as follows. Section 4.2 discusses the role of uncertainty and interest rate determination in relation to the "liquidity preference schedule." The analysis of interest rate determination is then extended in Section 4.3 in terms of Keynes' "own-rates analysis," which provides a general equilibrium framework to study the interaction between interest rates and the level of economic activity. In Section 4.4 we apply this framework to analyze a "crisis in confidence" and illustrate that the likely impact of uncertainty on the level of economic activity works through two channels. Two key points emerge here. The first, on a theoretical level, is the importance of distinguishing clearly between portfolio decisions on the one hand and production and spending decisions on the other. The second, on a practical level, is that in modern monetary production economies the financial system represents an important factor in determining the level of economic activity. Sections 4.5 and 4.6 critically assess two prominent Keynesian theories of liquidity preference, those of Tobin (1958) and Hicks (1974), in the light of this framework. While I shall argue that both of these theories need to be qualified in important ways, there nevertheless appears to be scope for an interesting "synthesis." The distinction between risk and uncertainty looms large throughout the analysis, which is concluded in Section 4.7.

4.2 The liquidity preference schedule[3]

In this section we study the determination of securities prices at any one point in time, in terms of the aggregate "liquidity preference schedule," that is, the *potentiality* in the minds of the public towards retaining certain amounts of their total resources in the form of "money" in different sets of circumstances. Although any individual is only required to take a single decision with regard to his *actual* money holdings, the aggregate amount of which, importantly, is not determined by the public, we may usefully consider the individual's decision to be the composite result of the following three incentives to liquidity: the transactions, the precautionary and the speculative motives for the demand for money.[4] Taking the level of economic activity as given allows us to abstract from the first, the transactions motive for the demand for money. The transactions motive takes account of the fact that an economy of the kind we are interested in requires an "accounting network," given that payments and receipts are typically imperfectly synchronized and that agents therefore hold and reconstitute part of their wealth in a form that can facilitate their transactions. When changes in the level of economic activity occur the corresponding adjustments needed to satisfy the transactions motive or, otherwise, the repercussions on securities prices caused by such changes would also have to be considered. The transactions motive thereby provides the link between the money wage – "the fulcrum which supports the price-structure" (Kahn 1984: 126) – and the rate of interest, i.e. the whole complex of the various rates of interest (current yields) on securities in general and on debts of different maturities in particular.

   The precautionary motive is partly related to the transactions motive and, hence, to the level of economic activity, but refers more intimately to wealth and the portfolio (investment) decision by expressing "the desire for security as to the future cash equivalent of a certain proportion of total resources" (Keynes 1936a, JMK 7: 170). We may distinguish a number of sub-motives which affect the strength of the precautionary motive. To begin with, there is the objective of being prepared to make unforeseen expenditures arising either in the form of contingencies or opportunities. Then there is the desire to preserve one's wealth at a predictable value in order to meet (perhaps to some extent anticipated) subsequent liabilities. Put differently, portfolio investors, aware that alternative positions differ in terms of risk, prefer both to avoid putting the whole of their wealth at risk and to keep their options open to some extent. "Cash," i.e. bank deposits and their equivalents, play an important role as a means towards these ends. Yet much depends on institutional arrangements. The existence of organized securities markets and easy access to some temporary borrowing facility, for instance, will tend to diminish liquidity preference due to the precautionary motive. Whilst we may presume that the strength of both the transactions and the precautionary motives depends – *to some degree* – on the opportunity costs of holding cash, we propose that, given these institutional arrangements, the interest elasticity of the demand for money does not primarily arise from these liquidity motives.

This leads us, finally, to the speculative motive for the demand for money. There are two necessary conditions for the speculative motive to be of any practical relevance. The first concerns uncertainty about the future rate of interest, and also applies to the precautionary motive. The second condition refers to the existence of organized securities markets. Uncertainty about the future rate of interest naturally exists in a "changing society" and the uncertainties besetting a changing society will generally give rise to a variety of opinion about what is uncertain; different investors will hold different expectations as to the future rate of interest, for instance. Organized securities markets provide the playing field that allows portfolio investors to bet on their views. In particular, investors may try to anticipate changes in the "market views" as expressed in current market quotations. It is here that the speculative motive emerges. If the portfolio investor is confident enough to bet on his "knowing better than the market what the future will bring forth" (Keynes 1936a, JMK 7: 170), and if his view is that securities prices will fall as soon as the market finds out about it, he may rationally (desire to) hold money speculatively. Depending on the investor's degree of conviction and market organization, a "bear" may even take short positions while "bullishness" may give rise to leveraged long positions. We take open-market operations as an example to illustrate the existence of the speculative motive and the possibility of deriving a downward-sloping aggregate liquidity preference schedule from it.

Consider the following proposition. In our view the monetary authority may affect "the rate of interest," i.e. the whole complex of rates of interest, through two channels. The first channel is changes in the supply of money available to satisfy the speculative motive in a *given state of expectations*. By "state of expectations" we mean here the amalgam of beliefs held by the participants in financial markets with respect to those factors they consider relevant in affecting the future course of prices of existing financial instruments. In particular, the state of expectations includes beliefs about the future policy of the monetary authority and views on how this relates to the future course of interest rates. Correspondingly, market participants will have views as to what they consider a "fairly safe level" of the rate of interest in the light of these expectations.

The second channel is the possibility of the monetary authorities precipitating a *change* in the state of expectations itself, thereby giving rise to discontinuous changes in the rate of interest with an unchanged stock of money and, possibly, without any transactions taking place. Such discontinuities occur in this (pure) form when wealth holders come to a general reassessment of the situation when their expectations are generally changing in the same direction. A *general* strengthening of the speculative motive for the demand for money at the current rate of interest would change that rate forthwith. This could be envisaged as a shift in the liquidity preference schedule. Clearly, this second channel does not yield a smooth liquidity preference schedule.

The first channel, by contrast, does yield such a schedule. We may take open-market operations as an illustration of the speculative motive in a given state of expectations. Most commonly the monetary authority, a dealer in money and debts, does not stand ready to buy and sell at stated prices along the whole complex of interest rates. Rather, it concentrates its monetary management at the very short end of the money market.[5] Given what we may call the "stance of monetary policy," it is then left for financial markets to grind out the whole complex of interest rates. Any influence of the monetary authority at the long end of the market is of an indirect form only, working mainly via expectational factors and the behavior of financial institutions. In principle, however, the monetary authority may also attempt to influence the whole complex of interest rates more directly by conducting open-market operations at the long end of the market too.[6] For instance, if the monetary authority were to bid up bond prices by taking additional securities off the (open) market without giving rise to a change in the state of expectations, i.e. without disturbing the general view as to what is a safe level of the rate of interest, this would generate a smooth liquidity preference schedule. At rising bond prices certain portfolio investors may wish to increase the amount of cash in their portfolio due to two factors working in the same direction. First, any rise in the degree of divergence of the rate of interest from what the investor considers a fairly safe rate raises the risk of illiquidity. Second, less earnings are available to compensate for this increased risk, since the yield on bonds falls relative to cash. The induced adjustment in exposure may be gradual or swift depending, as noted above, on the individual investor's views on future rates and the degree of conviction with which they are held. At the margin certain "bulls" join the "bear" brigade in the face of rising bond prices.

While we may envision this liquidity preference schedule as a continuous curve over a certain range, there are a number of pitfalls to be avoided. To begin with, and to repeat, the present thought experiment refers to a given state of expectations, i.e. that there is no change in the general view as to what is a fairly safe level of the rate of interest (which is more likely to be the case if there exists a variety of opinion about what is uncertain). However, the scope for "deliberate action" on the part of the monetary authority to move along a given liquidity preference schedule may be very limited. A point may quickly be reached at which portfolio investors agree, for instance, that it is preferable at the current rate of interest to increase without limit the amounts of cash at the expense of securities in their portfolios. In such a situation the monetary authority has lost effective control over the rate of interest. In other words, the system is then in a "liquidity trap" and the speculative motive becomes absolute for a given stance of monetary policy and *in a given state of expectations*. Furthermore, shifts in the schedule itself, perhaps when such attempts are overdone, may be counterproductive if they lead to an adverse change in the state of expectations concerning the future monetary policy, in particular. Worse still, deliberate action may induce increased uncertainty about the future more generally, thereby strengthening the precautionary motive (which, being interest inelastic, takes a discontinuous jump in yields to be satisfied).[7] The important point which emerges from this is that there may be a multiplicity of liquidity traps. (Milton Friedman (1970) correctly stresses the importance of liquidity trap(s) in Keynes' theory, but he should have insisted on the plural.) Indeed, financial markets may produce a liquidity trap at *any* level of interest rates. More generally, it is possible to argue that there is no stable and well-defined liquidity preference schedule at all, since in a changing society it is not only monetary policy but all sorts of events which may prompt a general reassessment of the situation and revisions in expectations. Yet, whatever market "consensus," in the sense of a state of expectations embodying a variety of opinion, emerges, given that there is some variety of opinion, there will also be *some* scope for open-market operations to play on this delicate balance between the "two views" ("bull–bear" position; cf. Keynes 1930a, b). It is the speculative motive which is responsible for the interest responsiveness of the demand for money and which thereby provides the basis for determinacy in the sense of some degree of stability in the rate of interest.

The practical limitations of this thought experiment may be severe, but the theoretical implications are far-reaching nevertheless: the speculative motive highlights that the rate of interest is a purely monetary phenomenon. The rate of interest is the market's expression for the terms on which "the public" is at the margin willing to become more or less liquid when either the banking system with the monetary authority at its core takes corresponding actions and/or the real economy draws on the given (pool of) liquidity to finance an *increase* in the level of economic activity. We shall now extend these results in terms of a general portfolio allocation approach, thereby attaining a proper macroeconomic perspective of the interaction between the rate of interest and the level of economic activity.

4.3   The structure of asset prices and the concept of the "liquidity premium"

A general portfolio equilibrium is a state in which no wealth holder has an incentive to reshuffle his portfolio at the current structure of asset prices. We propose that different types of assets possess the following attributes in different degrees: (default-risk-adjusted) yield q, carrying cost c, and what we shall call a "liquidity premium" l. To determine the expected returns on different types of assets over a period of time, in addition, the expected percentage appreciation or depreciation a relative to some standard of value, which we may take to be money, is required. Hence, the total expected return on an asset, or its "own rate of (money) interest," is the sum of these four elements: $R_i = q_i - c_i + l_i + a_i$.[8] It then appears that an equilibrium requires the demand prices of all different types of assets to be such that their total expected returns ("own-rates") are all equal.

In the previous section, we discussed the various motives which, with varying strength, affect the desire to hold "money." Money also holds a pivotal position from the perspective of the general portfolio allocation approach developed here. To begin with, the yield on money, the short-term rate of interest, is set by the monetary authorities – a datum for the economy. Apart from any net yield $q - c$, and there does not seem to be any disagreement in the literature about this point, money is *par excellence* "liquid." And this is what we mean by money bearing a substantial "liquidity premium," the yield foregone "for the potential convenience or security given by this power of disposal," as Keynes (1936a, JMK 7: 226) puts it.[9]

It is clear then that the liquidity premium is not an actual yield but a notional reward, an amount of actual yield the wealth holder is willing to forego for having cash at his disposal instead of other less liquid assets. This does not mean that other assets may not have liquidity premiums, merely that money, being *par excellence* liquid, bears the highest liquidity premium. Next in line in respect of liquidity premiums are probably marketable securities which have to be further distinguished, first, according to their own characteristics such as maturity and default risk, etc., and, secondly, by how well the market in which they are traded is organized.[10] By contrast, most capital goods, property and other physical assets (except for a few commodities and gold, in particular) will have a low or zero liquidity premium under normal circumstances. Customized capital equipment, in particular, is typically not resaleable at all. Notice that the generalized portfolio allocation approach pursued here includes all kinds of assets and durable commodities, not just financial assets, and all assets are so far on the same footing. In equilibrium asset prices must be such that *all existing* assets are willingly held. This brings us to the crucial institutional aspect we mentioned in the previous section, which reflects the separation between the management and ownership of the means of production: organized securities markets.

The management of a firm is concerned with managing the means of production under its control (although typically owned by others) in a way which allows it to retain control over the process of production. To achieve this objective the management must keep the level of the firm's financial commitments in line with the firm's overall balance sheet position. Its decisions concern, first, at what rate to use the existing capital equipment, since this *production decision* largely determines the firm's level of financial commitments, i.e. contracted and/ or conventionally agreed pay-outs to the factors of production, and, second, the size (and composition) of the stock of capital equipment, i.e. investment *spending decisions. Financial decisions*, i.e. the management of the firm's balance sheet in support of its production and spending decisions, include, first, decisions about what type of financial instrument to issue before either type of the above "real" decisions can be carried out and, second, what margin (and form) of liquidity to hold relative to the magnitude of commitments entered on the basis of these "real" decisions.

In forming estimates of the expected rates of return on potential projects the management is constrained by the fact that the investment horizon of any given project is typically shorter than the (principally) *infinite* horizon of the firm as an institution, the continued decision-making of which the incumbent management wants to stay in control of. In short, the management's estimates of the terms it can afford to pay on finance raised in order to continue and/or expand the firm's activities will be made with a view to the continuance of the firm as an ongoing concern.[11] From the viewpoint of the management, the expected rates of return on projects (marginal efficiencies of capital) and the terms of finance acceptable to go ahead with them are closely related. The valuation of capital assets (demand price), in conjunction with the costs of newly producing them (supply price), determine the extent to which additions are made to the existing capital stock, i.e. the management's investment spending (and production) decision.[12]

Yet, except for whatever influence on the firm's credit rating the management may have, the "terms of finance," i.e. the terms on which business in general may raise finance at any one time, are beyond the control of management. The terms of finance are determined on financial markets. Forming views on the expected returns on projects is difficult, even more difficult for outsiders not in control of managing them. The point is that due to the prevailing separation between ownership and management of the means of production, a rather delicate situation arises. The owners of wealth, being granted the opportunity of holding their wealth in the form of financial assets traded on organized securities markets, no longer have to face the definite commitment which the production of physical capital (and the organization set up around it in order to use it) necessarily involves. The dangers associated with the illiquidity of physical capital disappear from their minds since they are able to dissolve their commitment and "get out" at any time. As a result, participants on financial markets may be less concerned with the expected rates of return on projects than with the "own rates of (money) interest" on marketable financial instruments. As we have noted before, investors may try to anticipate changes in the "market view" as expressed in current market quotations. "Liquid" markets invite speculation. If investors primarily concern themselves with anticipating what the likely market views are going to be, securities prices will be based on "conventional valuation." *Any* convention may hold firm at times, but may also suddenly break down, perhaps without immediately precipitating a new one. It is not surprising, then, not only that the general level of interest rates in the economy, being the outcome of a process of conventional valuation, may be "wrong," in the sense that the general level of interest rates so determined may be incompatible with the, supposedly, unique long-period full employment equilibrium of the economy, but that securities prices may be subject to sudden swings in market sentiment as well.

The point is that the option of staying *par excellence* liquid is always open to the portfolio investor. As we saw in the previous section, the terms on which the portfolio investor is willing to *part with liquidity* forms the margin of substitution affecting the prices of securities while the aggregate amount of liquidity is not determined by the public. These prices are important because management must sell financial claims on the expected cash flows *before* they can continue and/ or expand their business. While we may interpret the outcome as the markets' expression of what, on the markets' view, "business can bear," the views of both parties involved clearly do not have to coincide. Yet, the markets set the pace, whatever it may be, to which business must adapt or perish.[13]

It is a key proposition of liquidity preference theory that there is no automatic market mechanism which adjusts the general level of interest rates so as to stabilize economic activity when changes in the "real sphere" occur, thereby providing the system with a tendency towards some unique and optimal level (as classical and loanable funds theories of interest would suggest; see Bibow 2000 and Chapter

3). However, we shall here concentrate on a more specific case in which interest rates may actually move in the wrong direction in response to a rise in general *uncertainty*.

Risk and uncertainty

Subjective expected utility (SEU) theory (cf. Ramsey 1926; Savage 1954) is widely accepted as the cornerstone of the economics of uncertainty. In terms of this approach, "probability" is understood as "degree of *subjective* belief," and it is assumed that a decision maker can assign exact numerical probabilities representing his degree of belief as to the likelihood of each possible "state of the world" upon which the consequences of his choices are contingent. Any attempt to distinguish between "risky" situations in which probabilities are available to guide choice, on the one hand, and "uncertain" situations in which information is in some sense too imprecise to be summarized by probabilities, on the other, is thus ruled out right from the start. Rational choice is always "as if" informed by numerically definite subjective probabilities. Risk and uncertainty become synonymous.

However, there exists a general agreement that "uncertainty" (as distinct from risk) plays an important part in Keynes' monetary thought, in particular in *The General Theory*. A significant literature has appeared which argues not only that Keynes' approach to probability differs distinctly from the subjectivist interpretation of probability associated with the orthodox SEU model, but also that this difference is crucial for a proper understanding of his economic writings (cf. Carabelli 1988; O'Donnell 1991; Lawson 1985; Runde 1990, 1994, 1996). It is therefore useful to consider briefly the significance of Keynes' theory of uncertainty, particularly as it relates to his liquidity preference theory.

In *A Treatise on Probability* Keynes analyzes probability as a *logical* relation between two sets of propositions, the conclusion of an argument h on the one hand, and a specific body of evidence e on the other. The rational degree of belief warranted – *objectively*, in Keynes' view – by a knowledge of such relations ranges between the extreme of certainty at one end (where h is a logical consequence of e) and impossibility at the other end (where h stands in a contradictory relation with e). Typically, however, the relation between h/e is only one of *partial* implication warranting some degree of belief between these two extremes. According to Keynes these degrees of belief are generally not numerically definite. Indeed, his theory concentrates on binary comparisons between relations of partial implication, where new probability comparisons may sometimes be derived from others already given.

An important feature of Keynes' theory is that probability is always relative to a specific body of evidence e, where the magnitude of the probability depends, so to speak, on the balance between the favorable and unfavorable evidence relevant to the conclusion of an argument. But in Chapter 6 of the *Treatise* Keynes suggests that we might also want to compare probability relations in terms of the extent, in some sense, of the evidence on which they are based. To this end, he introduces his concept of evidential "weight," metaphorically, the balance between the "*absolute* amounts of relevant knowledge and of relevant ignorance respectively" (Keynes 1921, JMK 8: 77), which he variously defines as a measure of the amount or degree of completeness of the specific body of evidence which forms the basis of the judgment of probability. He suggests that, other things being equal, when using probabilities as a guide to conduct, we should prefer the probability relation with greater evidential weight.

Clearly, these elements combine to make a complex picture of choice under uncertainty (particularly when, as Keynes does, *risk* is taken into account too). For instance, additional relevant evidence may either increase or decrease the magnitude of the probability of an argument, depending on whether the new knowledge strengthens the unfavorable or the favorable evidence, but it will typically increase the weight of the argument, since the conclusion now rests on a more substantial basis of evidence. Yet, given Keynes' definition of weight, the revised assessment of the completeness of the evidence underlying some belief may go either way. There also exists the possibility where additional relevant evidence leaves the magnitude of the probability of an argument unchanged (or affects it in either direction), while the weight of an argument actually *decreases*. New evidence may convince the decision maker that he is more ignorant than previously believed (cf. Runde 1990).

How does all this relate to Keynes' economics and rational conduct under uncertainty? A lot has been said about the fact that by "very uncertain" Keynes does not mean the same thing as "very improbable" (cf. Keynes 1936a, JMK 7: 148n.), but it is usually not made clear what the economic implications really are.

In Section 4.2 above, we saw that Keynes' speculative motive, the core element in his "liquidity [preference] theory of interest," depends both on the institutional setting of organized securities markets and on heterogeneous beliefs among investors. Furthermore, in this case, uncertainty does not prevent but, rather, provokes the portfolio investor into taking a "speculative" position, to bet on her views, so to speak. By contrast, the precautionary motive for the demand for liquidity is more closely related to the idea that uncertainty may lead agents to (desire to) "abstain from commitments" and to refuse to bet, an idea which is central to the argument developed further below. This element of liquidity preference theory is, perhaps, most beautifully expressed in Keynes' following remark:

> our desire to hold money as a store of wealth is a barometer of the degree of our distrust of our calculations and conventions concerning the future ... The possession of actual money lulls our disquietude; and the premium which we require to make us part with money is the measure of the degree of our disquietude.
>
> (Keynes 1937c, JMK 14: 115–16)

The "crisis in confidence" of Section 4.4 below illustrates how Keynes' "own-rates analysis," the general portfolio equilibrium approach yielding a structure of asset demand prices discussed in this section, relates to actual economic decisions. I would like to introduce here the concept of the "default option" available in any particular decision-making context.

The concept of the default option

By default option we mean that position or action which involves the lowest level of commitment on the part of the decision maker. By "commitment" we mean the decision maker's risk of being constrained in some way in the future (so that the magnitude of the loss in flexibility involved must be weighted against the prospective benefits). Yet, *the default options available in different decision-making contexts differ in terms of their effect on the level of economic activity.* It is mainly for this reason that it is important to distinguish clearly between portfolio decisions on the one hand, and production and spending decisions on the other. We added some organizational and institutional structure to Keynes' "own-rates analysis" here in order to highlight this point. Participants in financial markets make portfolio decisions, and thus do not have to concern themselves with making production and spending decisions. These types of ("real") decisions are made by the management of firms, the financial decisions of whom are, however, dependent upon the terms of finance as determined on financial markets at any one time. Moreover, the financial decisions of firms necessarily *precede* the implementation of their "real" decisions, which is what makes the portfolio decisions of financial institutions so important. Our aim is to show that there are effectively two different channels through which an increased desire to *abstain from commitments* may affect economic activity, channels which are different in kind, but which nevertheless work in the same direction – they reinforce each other and are therefore twice de-stabilizing (Trevithick 1992: 58n.). One represents a direct interruption of the circular flow of production and spending based on a view that does not even have to take any possible adverse change in the terms of finance into account – "opt-out effects," as we would like to call them. The second channel makes the continuation and expansion of the circular flow of production and spending seem even less attractive in terms of the costs of financing it.

A word of warning may be in order here concerning the increasing financial activities of firms, a widely observed fact which may seem to contradict the proposed distinction between different types of decisions. In fact, large firms typically enjoy considerable leeway in adjusting their finances and to an extent behave like financial intermediaries themselves. In particular, some large firms (or groups of firms) have what may be seen as their own "in-house bank" or include financial divisions the activities of which (i.e. portfolio decisions) may go far beyond the financial management of the core ("real") business of the firm (i.e. financial decisions). Such (non-core) financial activities may have significant effects on the overall profitability of the firm, in either direction. Furthermore, firms' investment plans will typically include estimates of the terms of finance expected to prevail over their planning horizon.

It follows that the grouping of decisions and institutions proposed in this section must not be interpreted too literally. Firms may well be among the players who make portfolio decisions in a wider sense too. Yet, whatever the effect of such activities on the firm's overall profitability may be, and whatever influence the management may have on the firm's credit rating, the general level of interest rates in the economy (or "terms of finance") is beyond the control of management. Let us now examine the likely events in a "crisis in confidence."

4.4 A "crisis in confidence"

We interpret uncertainty here as affecting the "state of confidence," where confidence refers to the decision maker's trust in the reliability of his calculations and anticipations about what the future will bring forth. This form of uncertainty is most usefully conceived in terms of low weight, i.e. at the second level of Keynes' two-tier theory of rational belief. A decline in confidence tends to make the available default option appear relatively more attractive in the mind of the decision maker. In terms of the general portfolio allocation approach of the previous section, a general rise in uncertainty would tend to increase the liquidity premium on money relative to all other assets (and money debts). This is how confidence is related to the concept of the liquidity premium.

Consider the management of some firm currently reviewing the production capacity of the firm under its control. Suppose that the firm is in the business of producing consumption goods. Two aspects are best distinguished: first, replacing worn-out equipment and machinery in order to maintain a given capacity; and second, expanding capacities by making positive net investments. Consider the former case, and assume that the investment project whose replacement and continuation is currently under review has thus far fulfilled the profit expectations which gave rise to it in the first place. Assume that financial provisions (typically in the form of liquid financial assets) were made over the years for the amortization of principal in accordance with the depreciation plan of the worn-out machinery, which is, however, not yet completely worn out.

In this case the entrepreneur may nevertheless decide that it would still be best to "wait" and postpone renewing commitments, perhaps even though the continued use of the nearly worn-out machine involves extra costs/risks as compared with a new replacement for it. The accumulated financial provisions are available, as the case may be, to retire securities, repay bank loans or remain invested in financial assets. As long as the production of the replacement equipment has not been ordered, the firm would not have to roll-over its bank loans, issue new securities (liabilities) or sell liquid securities (assets). This situation may occur even in the absence of disappointed sales expectations or any profound new information leading to a revision of the estimated profitability of the replacement. Rather, the idea is simply that due to a lack of confidence the entrepreneur postpones renewing his "commitments." He might not, or no longer, want to act on the basis of his possibly unchanged best guess about what the future may hold.

When we apply our generalized portfolio equilibrium approach to this case of physical assets which are not traded on organized markets, the initial effect of a crisis in confidence would not be directly observable. Rather, it would be "reflected" in the minds of those who run these (productive) assets as a diminished feeling of comfort with their given level of commitments to pay-outs relative to their existing balance sheet position. When the "demand prices" for existing physical assets then fall below their supply price our generalized portfolio perspective indicates a disequilibrium. The new production of those assets falters while those in control of the existing stock of such assets are simply "stuck in disequilibrium."[14] Yet, given that there will be some correspondence between the structure of the economy and the length of the depreciation period of productive capital, the postponement of the replacement order represents an immediate loss in revenue and income to the industry producing the equipment. The default option of not-spending/not-producing directly affects the level of aggregate incomes. The probable repercussions in the form of further reductions in spending by those affected by these opt-out effects would then tend to vindicate the lack of confidence which started the trouble in the first place. The process becomes cumulative; once started it feeds on itself.

Since our main concern is to analyze the impact of an increase in general uncertainty at the onset of a crisis in confidence, imagine now that wealth holders are hit by a deterioration in the state of confidence at the same time. A "refusal to act," or a desire to "stay liquid," in the context of the portfolio decision cannot give way to a more drastic default than holding money (*par excellence* liquid) – the available bottom-line default option. In the case of an individual portfolio investor a change in liquidity preference may be satisfied by a portfolio reshuffling at unchanged market prices if someone else takes the opposite view. However, a more widespread rise in liquidity preference must affect market prices unless, and only to the extent that, the banking system takes the opposite view and meets a widespread rise in liquidity preference by taking more securities off the market and thereby enlarging *at its discretion* the (otherwise "given") amount of liquidity available.[15] In short, a change in the relative l_i must translate into a change in securities prices until, at some new structure of asset prices, the desire to stay liquid vanishes at the margin. This will occur, of course, when portfolio investors are once again content in the aggregate with the composition of their portfolios at changed net yield $(q_i - c_i)$ differentials relative to money and possibly changed a_i terms as well – when the own rates of (money) interest are in a new equilibrium.[16]

The hesitating entrepreneur will find little encouragement to go ahead and order the replacement equipment in the face of falling securities prices, i.e. deteriorating terms of finance. For in this case it has become more expensive to roll-over the bank loan or (re)issue new securities as the case may be, but more lucrative to stay invested in liquid securities. It is quite clear, then, that at the onset of the disequilibrium, precipitated by a "crisis in confidence" which causes an increased desire to postpone investment spending, changes in the general level of interest rates would at the same time, if anything, prove de-stabilizing. As the direct opt-out effects start feeding through the economy, such asset price movements would tend to exacerbate the developing disequilibrium. The expectations which originally precipitated the production and installation of the current capital stock may be disappointed on a massive scale, and firms' attempt to bring their level of financial commitments into line with their deteriorating balance sheets may go a long way before the level of economic activity stabilizes *at some level*. (Keynes' "fundamental psychological law" that spending does not immediately adjust in full when income changes prevents the system from being highly unstable.) All along, while the principle of effective demand is "taking its toll" on incomes, there is no reason why wealth holders should *automatically* become more confident in holding their wealth in a form other than perfect liquidity. Furthermore, their appetite for holding assets which involve a greater default risk, as well as their assessment of the default risks involved in holding different forms of wealth, may change as well.

Portfolio decisions and the banking system

Our "crisis" story has concentrated on the entrepreneurial decision of whether or not to replace a worn-out piece of capital equipment. The argument can easily be generalized to include capacity expansion. In particular, in a growing environment the business sector's requirement for *additional* external finance must be taken into account. This factor adds complexity. In particular, the crucial role of the banking system as the source of liquidity comes to the forefront. A growing capital stock requires *ceteris paribus* a growing amount of liquidity, unless wealth holders become continuously more willing to hold their wealth in ever more illiquid form. Yet, the role of the banking system is no less important in the simpler case discussed above, though it might be less apparent. We assumed above that a roll-over of bank loans (as one possible form of finance considered there) would depend only on the decision of the entrepreneur. However, the bank may equally deny the roll-over. And again this may be the case not because the loan failure statistics which form the basis of the bank's profit expectations indicate any deterioration in prospective loan performance, but because the banker feels "less confident" about the reliability of these statistics as a guide to the future. In other words, the "confidence factor" may be relevant in the banker's decision-making process as well, and we may extend our "crisis" to include bankers' behavior. So, when we said above that the default option of the portfolio decision is to hold money, we must take into account that the amount of that particular medium which allows wealth holders to choose this default option depends on what the banking system is doing. In our example, the bank's default option, i.e. a refusal to roll-over the loan, *ceteris paribus* diminishes the amount of liquidity available to the same extent. Of course, this does not have to be the case, if the bank expands its business in other directions instead. Furthermore, the loan refusal would not seem to matter if the firm affected can easily resort to alternative sources of finance. In short, banks are doubly important, first, as providers of liquidity to the economy and, second, in so far as their denial of credit (roll-over and/or expansion), for whatever reason, may directly cause a disruption of the circular flow of production and spending. It is therefore not only the size of the liabilities side of the banks' balance sheet that seems to matter, but also the composition of the assets side. Both may be (partly) a reflection of bank, rather than non-bank, behavior. From the perspective of bank borrowers, changing degrees of rationing may be felt, both within a particular class of borrowers and among different classes.[17]

To conclude, uncertainty affects economic activity through two channels. In the case of a crisis in confidence, liquidity preference theory shows that, if anything, the "financial channel" would reinforce the economic implications of the opt-out effects due to not-spending/not-producing, in the form both of falling securities prices and stiffer credit rationing. The banking system holds a pivotal position. This completes our analysis of the relationship between liquidity preference, investment and the role of confidence or, put differently, between the rate of interest and the marginal efficiency of capital in affecting the level of economic activity. The following two sections discuss the most prominent Keynesian theories of liquidity preference, those of Tobin (1958) and Hicks (1974), in the light of our reading of Keynes.

4.5   Liquidity preference as aversion to risk

Tobin's (1958) main concern is to provide microfoundations for the downward-sloping *aggregate* liquidity preference schedule. He discusses two different sets of assumptions regarding the behavior of individual decision makers which, in his view, may generate this schedule from Keynes' "speculative motive" for the demand for money. Let us start with his representation of the "original Keynesian explanation."

On Tobin's reading, Keynes' theory of liquidity preference builds on the two crucial propositions that interest rate expectations are assumed to be inelastic and held with certainty, and that expectations about future interest rates (nevertheless) differ among investors. Tobin's analysis takes place in a two-asset context of "cash" and "consols," where consols are assumed to dominate cash in terms of "yield" (current interest rate).[18] Yet, the portfolio decision depends on the "expected holding period returns" on both assets, which includes expected capital gains or losses on consols. In particular, the investor calculates the "critical level of the current rate" which is that rate of interest at which the expected capital losses are equal to the excess yield on consols over cash. Investors make a simple all-or-nothing choice on the basis of their critical yields. Whereas each individual investor holds an undiversified portfolio, aggregating over a large number of investors – who differ in their opinions about the future interest rate and, hence, in their critical yields – produces (at least approximately) a smooth downward sloping aggregate liquidity preference schedule. It is quite clear then that Tobin's representation of the original Keynesian explanation refers to a given state of expectations.

Tobin's theory of risk-averse behavior departs from the original Keynesian explanation, first of all, by assuming that interest rate expectations are independent of the current rate of interest. What I shall call Tobin's "standard model" assumes that the mean value of the expected capital gain on consols is zero. (Hence interest rate expectations are implicitly assumed to immediately adjust in a way which leaves the expected capital gain on consols equal to zero and risk constant, unless stated otherwise, at all times.) As a result, *heterogeneous beliefs* about the future interest rate play no part in the standard model, or rather there are no heterogeneous beliefs about the expected value of the future interest rate, since Tobin assumes, second, that expectations are generally not point-valued. Uncertainty is understood as the dispersion of possible returns around the mean value and is measured by the standard deviation of some (symmetrical) probability distribution.

How does risk aversion affect the portfolio decision? First, and to repeat, cash is the only "riskless" asset available in the model and is *by assumption* dominated by consols in terms of yield. When it is further assumed that the expected value of the capital gain on consols is zero, then their expected holding period return always exceeds the return on cash. Hence, maximizing the expected return on the portfolio would imply investment in consols only. Yet, given that investors do not hold point expectations about the future rate of interest, the all-consols position also involves maximum *risk*. It is here that the investor's attitude towards risk comes in. While investing in cash instead of consols reduces the expected portfolio return, it also reduces the risk of potential capital losses (and actuarily equal gains). Investors, well aware of this risk–return trade-off, are assumed to maximize expected utility instead of simply maximizing expected monetary returns. The portfolio decision depends on, first, the shape of the investor's utility function, reflecting his degree of risk aversion, and, second, his perception of the price of this trade-off currently prevailing in the market. The typical risk-averse investor is a "diversifier," i.e. someone who holds some combination of cash and consols, rather than one to the exclusion of the other.

As a change in the yield on consols involves both a substitution effect and an income effect, the investor's reaction is generally ambiguous. Yet, in the case of the typical risk-averse diversifier, the substitution effect will be stronger than the income effect. With rising opportunity costs of holding cash the (typical) risk-averse investor will (by definition) be willing to hold more consols relative to cash for a given amount of wealth. An inverse relationship between the demand for cash and the rate of interest thereby emerges. In this way risk-averse behavior is applied as the rationale for deriving the downward-sloping microeconomic liquidity preference schedule. If it is accepted that portfolio investors are predominantly risk averse, then, it seems, the *aggregate* liquidity preference schedule would be downward sloping as well. Notice that the risk aversion theory explains the downward slope in the liquidity preference schedule without having recourse to heterogeneous beliefs and inelastic interest rate expectations.

A rather serious shortcoming of Tobin's standard model is that it cannot explain an inverse "term-structure of interest rates," since the long rate exceeds the short rate *by assumption*. (More precisely, in this two-asset context, time deposits cannot offer a higher yield than consols.) When the yield on consols falls short of the yield on cash a risk-averse investor would have no rationale for holding consols, so long as she holds the expectation of a zero capital gain. The investor would tend to hold an all-cash portfolio and his undiversified portfolio choice, moreover, would not be due to the speculative motive either. Under these circumstances cash dominates consols both in terms of risk and expected mean holding period return. Yet, as all outstanding consols are always held by someone, this raises the question of who would hold them. The downward slope of the liquidity preference schedule, then, is derived within a model that excludes the possibility of a descending yield curve, a phenomenon which does occur from time to time.

However, Tobin mentions that his approach would work just as well with a non-zero expected value of capital gains. If we relax the assumption of zero expected capital gains (essentially a means of excluding heterogeneous beliefs) to get a "generalized model" of Tobin's theory of risk aversion, the supposed complementarity to the "original Keynesian explanation" emerges. Tobin's "original Keynesian explanation" shows that an investor who is sufficiently "bearish" about consols on the basis of his "critical yield" holds money *speculatively*. Yet, his risk aversion theory shows that, even with a zero mean expectation of capital gains, i.e. without some more or less confidently held belief that securities prices are about to fall, uncertain beliefs as such will induce the typical risk-averse diversifier to hold money. So what exactly is the role of risk aversion? Interestingly, our solution to the "inverse-yield-curve puzzle" may shed some light on this question.

In the event of an inverse yield curve an incentive for holding consols arises as soon as the expected mean capital gain is sufficient to compensate for the lower yield on consols relative to cash. A risk-neutral investor would be indifferent when these two measures coincide. With a group of investors sufficiently "bullish" about the prospects of consols, consols will still be held even when the term structure *is* inverse.[19] Hence, *if* heterogeneous beliefs are allowed for, the generalized model allows for the possibility of an inverse yield curve. Notice however that a risk-averse investor would require an expected mean capital gain on consols which *exceeds* the differential in yields by some "premium" he attaches to holding cash.

Risk versus uncertainty again

Let us then consider the question about the role of risk aversion somewhat further by (re)turning to a particular criticism that has often been leveled against Tobin's risk aversion theory of liquidity preference, namely that it fails to come to grips with *uncertainty*, but deals with *risk* only. There are different layers to this argument, one of which concerns the question whether situations of uncertainty and uncertain beliefs can be appropriately captured by means of probability distributions (cf. e.g. Chick 1983; Carabelli 1988; Davidson 1988, 1991; Weisman 1984). Clearly, Tobin's analysis refers to risky/uncertain situations in which all possible outcomes are (believed to be) known and can be described by some probability distribution. The concept of the default option may help us to see what is at issue here.

We have already discussed Tobin's derivation of a downward-sloping microeconomic liquidity preference schedule. Tobin undertakes a similar exercise to analyze the consequences of an increase in the perceived risk of consols. In this case the results are unambiguous: an increase in perceived risk induces a fall in consol prices. The yield differential between consols and cash widens or, put differently, the "premium" on cash rises, thereby reflecting the increased perceived riskiness of consols. A similar outcome, it seems, would result from an increase in the degree of risk aversion. Presumably the direction of change in securities prices would be exactly the same in the case of an increase in *uncertainty* (crisis in confidence), even if we allow for the possibility that uncertainty about the expected volatility of consol prices may not be expressible in terms of probability distributions.

Hence, whether we ascribe the situation at issue as being due to an increase in uncertainty, perceived risk, or the degree of risk aversion respectively may not matter *in terms of their economic effects*. They all seem to entail an increased desire to move towards the default option and to abstain from less liquid positions. The resulting behavior is essentially the same, namely, an attempt to shift out of "more risky" instruments into "less risky" ones. In other words, all of these factors seem to precipitate a rise in the "liquidity premium" on cash, the default option available in the context of the portfolio decision concerning a given amount of wealth, as in Tobin's model. At least in a modeling sense, then, Tobin captures correctly an essential element of the theory of liquidity preference (cf. Cottrell 1993, for a similar view).

To conclude, we must qualify Tobin's (1958) theory of risk aversion as an explanation of "the" downward-sloping aggregate liquidity preference schedule. The risk aversion theory, i.e. the standard model which highlights risk-averse behavior to the exclusion of heterogeneous beliefs, derives the downward slope of the liquidity preference schedule in a way that precludes the possibility of an inverse term structure. It follows that risk aversion alone cannot be the whole story. Indeed, in the light of our reading in Section 4.2 above, inelastic interest rate expectations in conjunction with diverse participants in organized investment markets are preconditions for Keynes' speculative motive and responsible for his downward-sloping aggregate liquidity preference schedule. However, a schedule so derived, and similar to Tobin's "original Keynesian explanation," refers to a given state of expectations. Given that the state of expectations may easily shift itself, taking uncertainty seriously thwarts the possibility of a stable and well-defined liquidity preference schedule in the first place.[20]

Yet Tobin's proposal of considering his risk aversion theory as a complement rather than a substitute for the "original Keynesian explanation" may nevertheless be justified in the following sense: his theory may be seen as contributing towards explaining the "liquidity premium" on money, namely in terms of risk aversion. In other words, risk aversion appears to concern the pricing of "risky" instruments relative to less risky ones. It may however not itself give rise to *actual* money holdings, in particular when relative asset prices are believed to be in equilibrium, unless the desired risk–return mix cannot be achieved otherwise. By implication, if we interpret Tobin's comparative-static results to refer to the performance of the economy *over time*, the degree of financial intermediation may matter if capital markets are imperfect.[21] By contrast, *at any moment in time* changes in the liquidity premium (reflecting changes in the state of expectations or, perhaps, the degree of risk aversion) do *not* yield a downward-sloping *aggregate* relationship between the amount of cash and the opportunity costs of holding cash in the first place.

In addition, I would like to extend the defense of Tobin's analysis in respect of another layer in the risk versus uncertainty argument, which will then lead us on to Hicks' (1974) (re)interpretation of liquidity preference. The point at issue refers to the relevant *investment horizon*, or whether Tobin's treatment of *time* captures uncertainty in a satisfactory way. Hicks (1974: 38, 41) argues that by concentrating on single-choice situations "liquidity slips through," that "there is an element in risk-bearing *over time* which escapes from the conventional presentation" (such as Tobin's). Hicks argues that the investor's awareness of the *time after* the single finite investment period will affect the choice in the first period by giving rise to liquidity considerations of another type. However, Tobin (1958: 67, n. 2) too remarks that his fixed investment period is only a "fiction." He refers to the possibility of reshuffling one's portfolio *before* the end of the planned investment horizon and argues that "the fact that this possibility is always open must influence the investor's decision." Both Hicks and Tobin are then effectively concerned with the same issue, namely that the investor *may* learn something new over the (planned) investment period which might prompt him to reassess the attractiveness of the initial portfolio composition chosen. Both of them argue that liquidity considerations of this type will matter *ex ante*. In Tobin's modeling procedure, since the portfolio *is* fixed over the investment period, these *ex ante* liquidity considerations must affect the composition actually chosen (rather, prices) either via the investor's attitude towards risk or the perceived riskiness (expressed by probability distributions) of the instruments available.

The important point to notice is that, according to Tobin's (1958: 66) interpretation, liquidity preference theory concerns itself with the investor's choice of allocating a given amount of wealth among cash and alternative financial assets. In other words, Tobin strictly concentrates on *portfolio decisions* alone. Hicks' (1974) "waiting theory" of liquidity preference, to which we now turn, goes beyond the realm of the portfolio decision – with rather serious consequences for the theory of liquidity preference.

4.6 Hicks' "waiting theory" of liquidity preference

Hicks (1974) starts from Keynes' (1930a) notion of liquidity which refers to, and compares, the degrees of liquidity of different assets according to the criterion of being "more certainly realizable at short notice without loss." On the basis of this ranking, Hicks argues that investment in physical equipment amounts to taking a non-marketable and hence highly illiquid position. Investment in financial assets, by contrast, involves taking a marketable position which, in principle, can be easily dissolved. But not all marketable positions are equally liquid. Some financial assets, e.g. bonds, are price unstable, while other assets such as short-dated securities (bills) exhibit more stable prices and are therefore very liquid. So far so good. Then, however, Hicks (1974: 38–9) considers time in this context: "For liquidity is not a property of a single choice; it is a matter of a sequence of choices, a related sequence. It is concerned with the passage from the known to the unknown – with the knowledge that if we wait we can have more knowledge." Taking an imperfectly liquid position, Hicks argues, narrows the band of opportunities available to the holder, whilst "staying liquid" leaves all options open to benefiting from information becoming available later on.

On the basis of this time-related concept of a liquid position Hicks interprets liquidity (preference) as a choice for *flexibility*, or as a choice of postponing commitments which cannot easily be dissolved as more is learned in the mean time. In the same way Hicks (1974: 57) concludes that the "social function of liquidity is that it gives time to think." I call this Hicks' "waiting theory" of liquidity preference. But there is a serious problem with this theory since the economic implications of "waiting," or rather the strength of the "desire to wait," depend crucially on what type of decision and hence which default option one is referring to. In other words, the question is whether these *ex ante* liquidity considerations concern the potential revision of a position initially taken or whether they include the possibility of deferring taking any position altogether. These default options are very different in nature.

Consider Hicks' (1974: 52) following microeconomic statement: "When a firm undertakes real investment, it acquires a non-liquid asset; but it loses a liquid asset (or incurs a corresponding liability) on the other side. In either case, its liquidity is diminished." Yet, this does *not* follow at all. Presumably Hicks is looking at some, let us say, manufacturing firm, an entity which will typically employ physical equipment in its production process which forms its "running assets" (Hicks' term). But at the same time, Hicks argues, such a firm will also hold some "reserve assets" – *liquidity*. At some starting point the firm's balance sheet may show a certain desired ratio between running and reserve assets, and as their counterpart it will also show liabilities of some form (including equity stakes). Now imagine the management of the firm decides to purchase additional running assets, i.e. to order the production of capital. The point is that, contrary to Hicks' above statement, there is no *a priori* reason why this firm's balance sheet should then necessarily end up showing financial ratios, in particular its running assets/reserve assets ratio, different from what they were initially. The firm's business and its balance sheet, theoretically speaking, could expand while all financial ratios remain unchanged. The reason this is the case is that there are specialist firms which "produce" reserve assets – banks. *Banks are in the business of providing liquidity.* The point is *not* that firms must necessarily accept a deterioration in their liquidity position when undertaking real investment, but that firms must acquire finance *before* they can spend on new investment – *this is the link between investment and finance*; the link which is not brought out by Hicks' analysis. Interestingly, the above observation about the effects of investment on the liquidity position of an individual firm is equally true for the economy as a whole, though the outcome clearly depends on the *behavior* of the banking system.[22]

To conclude, "staying liquid," in the sense used by Hicks, i.e. taking a liquid position in money or bills instead of investing in physical equipment, involves more than a decision in what form to hold existing (titles to) wealth: it also extends to the choice of whether or not to make additions to the existing stock of wealth. "Staying liquid" as used by Hicks then has direct "opt-out effects" on the level of economic activity and incomes. In short, Hicks' waiting theory of liquidity preference involves a fudging of portfolio decisions and spending (and production) decisions, since the bottom-line default option available in his waiting theory is "not spending"/"not producing."

Jones and Ostroy's (1984) attempt to apply Hicks' waiting theory of liquidity preference in a macroeconomic context by formalizing the notion of flexibility encounters the same difficulties. They model a three-period two-choice sequential decision problem in order to derive the relation between the "variability of beliefs" and "flexibility." Their analysis of the optimal investment strategy yields the following "behavioral principle:" "The more variable are a decision-maker's beliefs, the more flexible is the position he will choose" (1984: 13). Importantly, switching out of a non-monetary position, which may become opportune because of revised second-period yield expectations, incurs a liquidation cost. They find that holding money can be *rational*. In particular, they find that reductions in the expected yield on alternative assets, and similarly increases in the liquidation cost of these assets, enlarge "the set of beliefs for which money is the optimal first period asset" (1984: 23).[23] In their view, these results show that "liquidity has value because it permits profitable exploitation of information not yet received" (1984: 24). They conclude that:

> From a macroeconomic perspective ... the tantalizing prospect of portraying the connection between business cycles and public confidence as a relation between flexibility induced shifts in asset demands (away from capital investment and towards more liquid assets, especially money) and uncertainty is too compelling to be ignored.
>
> (Jones and Ostroy 1984: 26–7)

In short, they too view the portfolio allocation problem as a choice between liquidity and *new* physical assets which misrepresents the portfolio decision as a choice between spending/producing and not-spending/not-producing.

Risk versus uncertainty once more

I questioned above the relevance of a particular criticism widely leveled against Tobin, that his theory of risk aversion, by using probability distributions and comparative-statics, both conflates risk and uncertainty and, moreover, fails to capture the *time* element appropriately. In the context of the portfolio decision (concerning financial instruments), this criticism appears to miss the point.

The fact that all existing assets must always be held – *at some price* – poses an important constraint on the sought-after meaningful distinction between risk and uncertainty, the corollary of which is that in the context of the portfolio decision a "refusal to act" cannot give way to a more drastic default than holding money (if it is accepted – *conventionally* – that money is the available default option, a convention which may break down, however).

Jones and Ostroy's formalization of Hicks' new interpretation of uncertainty as a *sequential* decision problem, in which liquidity preference features as a choice for flexibility, broadens the scope of the analysis in various ways. First, notice that, like Tobin, Jones and Ostroy use probability distributions as a measure of uncertainty. More precisely, however, Jones and Ostroy attempt to *explicitly* model the possibility of learning after the initial choice (an *ex ante* consideration Tobin mentions too) in terms of their concept of "variability of beliefs." They define that the more the decision-maker *expects* to learn at an intermediate stage, and the more final risk is resolved thereby, the greater the variability of his beliefs. Interestingly, they even relate their concept of variability of beliefs to Keynes' (1921, 1936a) notions of "degrees-of-belief" and "confidence of beliefs," and argue that "the degree-of-belief in a prior distribution over states increases as the variability of [an information structure] decreases" (Jones and Ostroy 1984: 24).

Second, Jones and Ostroy widen the range of assets to include not only financial instruments, but physical assets as well. Clearly, this does *not* present any problem. Indeed, our own-rates analysis extends the portfolio decision both by widening the spectrum of *existing* assets to include physical assets, thereby opening up the possibility of severe portfolio disequilibria for those in charge of these assets, and by explicitly including the balance sheets of banks too, thereby embracing bank behavior as a distinct force.

Finally, however, when Jones and Ostroy establish connections between the variability of beliefs regarding the riskiness of payoffs *over time* on the one hand, and a wider spectrum of assets ordered in terms of their flexibility, on the other, their spectrum of assets ranges from money as a *store of value* to *new* capital goods. In terms of the (orthodox) economics of uncertainty and information, which Jones and Ostroy's modeling procedure represents an example of, placing a capital goods order stands for making the terminal move while *holding* money, "the most liquid asset," which stands for the "perfectly flexible position," means taking informational actions (rather, waiting for new evidence).[24] An error has crept in here.

The point is that holding money or other alternative *existing* assets versus spending on (i.e. ordering the production of) *new* as yet *non-existing* capital goods represent altogether different economic categories. The time element is indeed important – different types of decisions are involved. The decision not to order the production of new capital goods (i.e. a *not*-spending/production decision) does *not* require a decision to *hold* money (or any other financial instrument) *instead*. The potential entrepreneurial investor either does or does not already hold these financial instruments anyway. In the former case, switching between alternative forms of existing instruments would still be a possibility, a portfolio decision. In the latter case, a decision not to spend/produce may well involve a corresponding decision not to borrow money either. This would be felt, primarily, by the banking system, the provider of (credit) money. And, again, this concerns portfolio decisions, for both parties concerned. At any rate, by constructing a "pseudo-choice" between something already existing and something as yet non-existent, "liquidity slips through," to recall Hicks' initial motivation.[25] Put differently, in deciding about ordering the production of new capital goods money is involved, not as an alternative *store of value*, as both Hicks and Jones and Ostroy seem to suggest, but as a *standard of value*. And a decision *not* to order the production of *new* capital goods amounts to not taking any position whatsoever.

Yet, while the above pseudo-choice does not actually exist, a need to secure finance *before* ordering the production does so. This will involve a comparison of yields, not an absolute choice, but a balancing of relative attractions. In this way, the yields on financial instruments, i.e. the rate of interest, provide a floor to the expected rate of return on potential capital projects awaiting to be produced, or not.[26] Note that this leads us back to the question discussed in Section 4.2 above. An important question which the "real options approach to investment," to which we now turn, also fails to address: what determines interest rates?

The real options approach to investment

The basic argument of this "new view," an application of option pricing theory to investment spending, is that if investment is irreversible but can be delayed in order to gain additional information, the value of this "flexibility option" as calculated in the mind of the investor affects the optimal investment strategy (cf. e.g. Pindyck 1991; Dixit and Pindyck 1992; Hubbard 1994). Clearly the underlying idea is similar to Hicks' (1974) "waiting theory," while these authors make it clear that the issue concerns a spending rather than a portfolio decision. Perhaps the most interesting implication of this *partial* equilibrium approach is that the value of the "flexibility/waiting option" is not affected if there exist opportunities for "hedging" in futures markets. The point, however, is that one will always tend to know more about any particular investment project "later" and best *ex post*, so that "waiting" in this sense, if possible, is *always* valuable. Hence, it is only *changes* in the value of such "flexibility options" that may contribute towards explaining *fluctuations* in (aggregate) investment spending, for instance. But who is short in these "real options"? Clearly the issue needs to be studied from a general equilibrium perspective, and the issue of interest rate determination needs to be brought in as well.

A synthesis – risk premiums and "animal spirits"

It is quite clear, then, that "liquidity preference theory" in the Hicksian form has ceased to be concerned with the question about the form in which to hold existing wealth but, instead, has become a theory of investment spending under uncertainty, where uncertainty is understood to give rise to the desire to wait and postpone the *spending/production* decision. While the possible fruitfulness of such an approach to the theory of investment spending cannot be denied, it is also quite clear that it loses sight of the question that liquidity preference theory proper was supposed to answer in the first place: how are interest rates determined? In Hicks' waiting theory any discussion of this question is subverted because finance and investment are not properly distinguished to begin with.[27]

Indeed, the primary role of Keynes' (1936a) liquidity preference theory is to fill the gap left by the flawed classical theory of interest. In his view, the instability of investment spending in monetary production economies is largely due to fluctuations in the marginal efficiency of capital. Interest rates present a problem, in a sense, because they are (relatively) stable.[28] An interesting synthesis emerges here. In our view, Tobin's theory of risk aversion concerns the relative pricing of risky financial instruments traded in organized securities markets. Hicks' waiting theory, by contrast, concerns the pricing of those "real options" featuring in the "new view" on investment spending. This synthesis includes the possibility that the entrepreneurial investors' spontaneous urge to action rather than inaction (waiting) may be dimmed just when portfolio investors' lack of confidence leads to rising risk (aversion) premiums and interest rates.

Keynes does not suggest, however, that entrepreneurial investors always lack the confidence to play their part. Far from it. As in the context of the portfolio decision, the strength of the desire to wait and postpone a spending/ production decision is the outcome of a balancing of relative attractions. There are counterbalancing propensities at work, what Keynes called "animal spirits." These may be easily disturbed, however, since the basis of our knowledge about the future is so flimsy.

In short, Keynes does not assume agents are ignorant about their own ignorance, although their degree of awareness and concern about this fact varies considerably over time, being under the continuous influence of multifarious factors including institutional and (mass) psychological ones. Indeed, Keynes' agents are "too rational" to simply believe in averages, calculated on the basis of knowledge however vague and scanty, sharing the faith that some auctioneer works out *ex ante* that particular vector of prices which makes their most probable forecasts turn out right, at least on average *ex post*. Averages may not matter so much if bankruptcy is a real possibility. Disequilibria and the option to "stay liquid" are too important facts to assume away, at least for serious agents, including serious economists such as Maynard Keynes.

4.7 Conclusion

Tobin's (1958) risk aversion theory offers neither a rationale for Keynes' speculative motive nor for "the" sought-after downward-sloping *aggregate* liquidity preference schedule, although it may be seen as contributing towards explaining the "liquidity premium" on money, namely in terms of risk aversion. Strictly speaking, Hicks' (1974) waiting theory has nothing to say about liquidity preference theory proper and conceals rather than reveals the relationship between liquidity preference and investment spending. Nevertheless, it may yet offer a potentially fruitful approach to a theory of investment spending, much along the lines of Keynes' "marginal efficiency of capital." While both partial equilibrium theories of liquidity preference thus offer illuminating insights into particular aspects of Keynes' monetary thought, in our view, they both effectively refer to elements different from their respective author's intention. Furthermore, only parts of the overall picture are illuminated. Keynes' own-rates analysis encapsulates the whole picture and offers a general equilibrium perspective of the role of uncertainty and confidence in financial markets and investment spending.

In general, a lack of confidence tends to make the available "default option" appear increasingly attractive. We concentrated here on the question of how, in the event of an increase in general uncertainty, the increased desire to "stay liquid" is resolved in the aggregate. In the context of portfolio decisions and securities markets non-action is not possible in the aggregate, as prices adjust instantaneously until all existing claims are willingly held. The desire to abstain from commitment then takes on an altogether different meaning in the context of spending and production decisions. Here the available default option allows non-action. It is important to keep the portfolio decisions separate, conceptually, from spending and production decisions. In fact, destabilizing interest rate movements due to the desire to stay liquid in the former sphere may be superimposed on the macroeconomic effects due to non-action in the latter.

The assumption that *all* prices adjust instantaneously appears to offer a neat way out of such complexities. Following a change in perceptions of *risk*, for instance, the new market clearing price vector is found instantaneously at which agents' *decisions of all types and through all times* are once again made consistent with one another. Yet there is a problem here if the notion of *uncertainty* includes the possibility that "waiting" might be optimal at least for some actors, i.e. if these "actors" attach a value to the "waiting option" which it may not be possible to compensate by adjustments in the vector of equilibrium prices. (Notice that I do not suggest that prices may not adjust anyway, and that this stickiness may actually be optimal.)

Liquidity preference theory argues that the prices of money debts move in rather limited bands. While the general level of interest rates may be *anything* within these bands and while, furthermore, interest rate adjustments may actually be destabilizing, the speculative motive and conventional influences will at least keep interest rates bounded within these bands. By contrast, there may be no speculative motive at work to keep the expected profitability of potential investment projects within the limited band of interest rate fluctuations as determined on financial markets. The system may get stuck at some suboptimal level of economic activity at which agents either lack the incentive to deviate from their plan of actions in the light of current prices or lack the power to bring about change.

5 On exogenous money and bank behavior

The Pandora's box kept shut in Keynes' theory of liquidity preference?[1]

5.1 Introduction

Debates on endogenous versus exogenous money are a recurrent theme in monetary theory. Given that Maynard Keynes and Milton Friedman are probably the two most influential monetary thinkers of the twentieth century, it is of some interest that Desai identifies an apparent similarity of exogenous money views underlying both Keynes' *General Theory* as well as the monetarist theory of Friedman: "The banking system is a passive agent in this view and given the cash base is always fully loaned up" (Desai 1989: 149).

Perhaps this also explains why many monetarists and Keynesians happily discussed money matters in terms of IS/LM (Hicks 1937). Indeed, according to this *exogenous* money interpretation of *The General Theory*, monetarists and Keynesians part company only when it comes to the velocity of circulation, with the latter attributing crucial importance to the interest elasticity of *demand* for money. Expressed in Hicksian terms, the interest elasticity of money demand is however all a matter of degree concerning the steepness of the slope of *LM*, an empirical question of whether it was vertical or near-vertical, but generally taken to be upward-sloping at any rate. On the one hand, except for some floor to the rate of interest at which *LM* becomes horizontal, due to money demand becoming infinitely interest-elastic, the central bank could thus always control "the" rate of interest by simply changing the quantity of money. On the other hand, a rise in investment would seem to put upward pressure on interest rates just as in the world of the "classics."

The exogenous money position underlying the synthesis, and apparently shared by Keynes and Friedman, was challenged by Kaldor (1970, 1982, 1983) and Moore (1988); the former merely arguing (as part of his attack on monetarism) that Keynes should have embraced endogenous money, the latter going so far as to claim that Keynes had actually come close to doing so in his earlier monetary writings. Following their lead, endogeneity of money has become a central theme of post-Keynesianism, widely identified today with a horizontal *LM* at any level of interest the central bank chooses to peg (Cottrell 1994). For one thing, "horizontalists" tend to discard entirely Keynes' "liquidity theory of interest." For another, the supply of money is seen as purely credit *demand*-driven; with banks featuring, once again, as passive agents.

This chapter attempts to provide a fresh examination of Keynes' views on banking behavior and the central bank–bank relationship as they evolved from his *Tract on Monetary Reform* to *The General Theory*. Our objective is to clarify in what sense money may be "exogenous" in *The General Theory*. We shall employ the following working definitions. Money supply exogeneity means that changes in the supply of money can occur or do normally occur, presumably at the discretion of the monetary authorities or the banks, independently of changes in the variables affecting the demand for money. Money becomes endogenous, by contrast, to the extent that changes in the supply of money are caused by changes in the demand for money, i.e. are dependent upon variables affecting the demand for money. Such endogeneity may be a matter of degree, as in practice both ways in which the supply of money may change are relevant. But it is also a question of principle when we need to decide upon the role of monetary policy and the part played by banks in the money-supply process. For, as Desai (1989) observes, the exogeneity of a variable is often conflated with the extent to which it can be controlled by policy. In fact, there can be little doubt that the money stock is treated as "given" in *The General Theory* most of the time. The crucial question concerns the authorities' degree of control over bank behavior and thus the determination of this exogenous variable.

Our main result is that Keynes' exogenous money view of *The General Theory* features exogeneity due to bank behavior. We identify a distinctly Keynesian position on the money-supply process and show that the exogeneity position presented in *The General Theory* runs counter to both verticalism and horizontalism.

The chapter is organized as follows. Section 5.2 reviews the *Tract*, beginning with a discussion of the conceptual apparatus and monetary theory underlying that work, before turning to the more technical control aspects of banking policy – our central concern here. We follow the same approach when we move on to the *Treatise* in Sections 5.3 to 5.5 and to *The General Theory* in Sections 5.6 and 5.7, respectively. In each case fundamental changes in Keynes' monetary thought are shown to have occurred at the theoretical and conceptual level of analysis, whereas his discussions of technical control aspects take the form of refinement in the light of these new theoretical breakthroughs. In fact, with regard to banking policy, we find a high degree of continuity in the evolution of Keynes' monetary thought. Section 5.8 concludes.

5.2 *A Tract on Monetary Reform* – currency management aimed at stable internal prices

The drastic fluctuations in the value of money between 1914 and the early 1920s, and the detrimental effects on economic performance these were having in Britain and elsewhere, provide the background to *A Tract on Monetary Reform*. The key question Keynes investigates here is whether Britain (and other countries) should return to a gold standard, or what "alternative aim(s)" should be pursued instead. And, at a time when the profession and public opinion seemed to have had no more urgent aim than the restoration of gold, Keynes is ready to proclaim: "In truth, the gold standard is already a barbarous relic" (Keynes 1923, JMK 4: 138). For, in his view, events since 1914 had brought about changes which could not easily be, and should not be, reversed:

> A regulated non-metallic standard has slipped in unnoticed. *It exists.* Whilst the economists dozed, the academic dream of a hundred years, doffing its cap and gown, clad in paper rags, has crept into the real world by means of the bad fairies – always so much more potent than the good – the wicked ministers of finance.
>
> (Keynes 1923, JMK 4: 138)

There was thus no escape from addressing a new *management problem*: "We have reached a stage in the evolution of money when a 'managed' currency is inevitable" (Keynes 1923, JMK 4: 159).[2] But there was a need to adapt monetary theory and practice to the changed circumstances.

As regards theory, the quantity theory of money – as he had inherited from Marshall and Pigou and himself taught to undergraduates at Cambridge – still had a firm grip on Keynes when he wrote the *Tract*: "This theory is fundamental. Its correspondence with fact is not open to question" (Keynes 1923, JMK 4: 61). Keynes presents his arguments in terms of a "real balance" (or, Cambridge) version of the quantity theory of money: $n = p(k + rk')$; where n stands for currency notes or other forms of cash in circulation with the public; p for the index number of the cost of living (called "consumption unit"); k for the amounts of consumption units the public requires having a purchasing power over in the shape of cash and k' held at their banks against cheques; and r for the "proportion" of their potential liabilities (k') to the public the banks keep in cash.

Although Keynes regards his real balance equation as an appropriate tool to analyze the "few, definite, analyzable influences" (Keynes 1923, JMK 4: 68) that govern the general price level, he also warns of an "error often made by careless adherents of the quantity theory" (Keynes 1923, JMK 4: 64). The error is to assume that the public's habits in the use of currency notes and banking facilities as well as the banks' reserves practices are independent of changes in the quantity of currency, an assumption which, he argues, is contradicted by the facts. The reactions on the other variables r, k, and k' to changes in n may be either stabilizing or de-stabilizing, and Keynes (1923, JMK 4: 66–7) ventures that these effects may perhaps even last permanently.

But the affairs of the dead – the so-called "long run" – were never his métier. He is far more interested in the short-run phenomenon of the credit cycle, which he analyzes via his real balance equation, advancing the following diagnosis. Credit cycles, he argues, are characterized – and caused, it seems – by systematic changes in the demand for real balances, namely:

> a tendency of k and k' to diminish during the boom and increase during the depression, irrespective of changes in n and r, these movements representing

respectively a diminution and an increase of 'real' balances (i.e. balances, in hand or at the bank, measured in terms of purchasing power).

(Keynes 1923, JMK 4: 67)

Given that credit cycles are accompanied by cumulative price level changes, inflations and deflations, both having vastly detrimental effects on the working of a system of capitalistic individualism based on money contracts, the monetary authorities should aim at taking compensatory measures in order to avoid cyclical fluctuations and stabilize the price level. His outline of the broad principles of currency management too is, at this stage of the argument, expressed in terms of the variables of his real balance equation:

> Two of these, n and r, are under the direct control (or ought to be) of the central banking authorities. The third, namely k and k', is not directly controllable, and depends on the mood of the public and the business world. The business of stabilizing the price level, not merely over long periods but so as also to avoid cyclical fluctuations, consists partly in exercising a stabilizing influence over k and k', and, in so far as this fails or is impractical, in deliberately varying n and r so as to *counterbalance* the movements of k and k'.
>
> (Keynes 1923, JMK 4: 68)

His own diagnosis of the credit cycle, and the policy advice derived from it, Keynes contrasts to the position of the "[o]ld-fashioned advocates of sound money" who:

> have laid too much emphasis on the need of keeping n and r steady, and have argued as if this policy by itself would produce the right results. So far from this being so, steadiness of n and r, when k and k' are not steady, is bound to lead to unsteadiness of the price level. Cyclical fluctuations are characterized, not primarily by changes in n or r, but by changes in k and k'. It follows that they can only be cured if we are ready deliberately to increase and decrease n and r, when symptoms of movement are showing in the values of k and k'.
>
> (Keynes 1923, JMK 4: 69)

A more detailed discussion of monetary control follows in Chapter 5: "Positive suggestions for the future regulation of money." To begin with, the control of the creation of currency, Keynes argues, should *not* be of any direct concern to the authorities, as used to be the advice in former (Currency School and Cunliffe Committee) times: "Cash, in the form of bank or currency notes, is supplied *ad libitum*" (Keynes 1923, JMK 4: 145) by the monetary authorities, simply providing however much cash the public demands at the prevailing internal price level.[3] Instead, Keynes advises that the authorities should watch and control the volume of (internal) credit, that is, the *creation of credit by banks* and the corresponding volume of *bank deposits*, as the main determinant of the internal price level. A point of utmost importance to us here is that Keynes employs a broad definition of credit, including not only bank loans in a narrower sense (advances), but also such items as banks' holdings of bills and longer term securities (investments). According to Keynes:

> The internal price level is mainly determined by the amount of credit created by the banks, chiefly the Big Five; though in a depression, when the public are increasing their real balances, a greater amount of credit has to be created to support a given price level … than is required in a boom, when real balances are being diminished. The amount of credit, so created, is in its turn roughly measured by the volume of the banks' deposits – since variations in this total must correspond to variations in the total of the investments, bill-holdings, and advances.
>
> (Keynes 1923, JMK 4: 142)

The banks' aggregate monthly returns provide the empirical basis for Keynes' investigations into the banks' demand for "cash," the first step in his analysis of how the authorities may establish their *indirect* control over the creation of credit. Although there were no legal reserve regulations in place at the time, Keynes finds that the banks' (aggregate) cash-to-deposits "proportion" (or, "reserve ratio" in *Treatise* terms), apart from some window dressing in their half-yearly statements, and despite widely varying conditions, fluctuated only little over the preceding two and a half years. His explanation for this finding features conventional behavior as well as a trade-off between considerations of safety and profitability. On the one hand, a bank would risk its reputation if its actual proportions fell below the current *convention* about what is a "safe" proportion; on the other hand, a bank's earning power is unnecessarily impaired if it rises above it. Although Keynes is fully aware that banks have discretion with regard to the form of their credit creation, and despite his empirical finding of ample variations in advances-to-deposits ratios, i.e. variations in the composition of banks' asset portfolios, his attention focuses on cash-to-deposits proportions. The stability of this ratio would seem to provide the focal point of control over the banks' (overall) credit creation:

> In recent times their aggregate deposits have always been about nine times their 'cash.' Since this is what is generally considered a 'safe' proportion, it is bad for a bank's reputation to fall below it, whilst on the other hand it is bad for its earning power to rise above it. Thus in one way or another the banks generally adjust their total creation of credit in one form or another (investments, bills, and advances) up to their capacity as measured by the above criterion; from which it follows that the volume of their 'cash' in the shape of bank and currency notes and deposits at the Bank of England closely determines the volume of credit which they create.
>
> (Keynes 1923, JMK 4: 142)

The second step in Keynes' analysis concerns the management problem of establishing control over the quantity of banks' cash reserves. Keynes stresses that the respective policies pursued by the Treasury and the Bank of England are interdependent and hence need to be coordinated. He presents an elegant description of the interrelatedness of their balance sheets. The Treasury's overall funding policies, including borrowing from the Currency Note Account, Ways and Means advances, Treasury bill issues, and longer dated loans, may affect the banks' cash positions in complex ways; directly by affecting the Bank of England's assets, and indirectly through changing the amount of the banks' holdings of T-bills (seen as their "second-line reserves" or "cash at one remove"). He affirms that "the capacity of the joint stock banks to create credit is mainly governed by the policies and actions of the Bank of England and of the Treasury," and his overall view is that "the control, if they choose to exercise it, is mainly in their own hands" (Keynes 1923, JMK 4: 144).

Keynes' discussion of the Bank of England's alternative options of control over the volume of its own assets, and hence liabilities, emphasizes what we now call "open-market operations" as a particularly effective instrument. Apart from Ways and Means advances to the Treasury and her gold holdings (immobilized under the post-1914 arrangements until the return to gold in 1925), he divides the Bank of England's assets into two categories: advances to its own customers and bills of exchange on the one hand, and her gilt-edged and other investments on the other. The volume of advances and bills, he argues, is only indirectly, but still "adequately," controllable by varying the price charged, i.e. bank rate. The other category (including gold holdings) is immediately and directly controllable. For the bank "can increase or decrease at will her investments and her gold by buying or selling the one or the other" (Keynes 1923, JMK 4: 144–5). Keynes regards open-market operations as being both more direct in its effect on banks' reserves and more open to deliberate and unconstrained variation, where this *additional* instrument may either neutralize or strengthen bank rate policy:

> It is often assumed that the bank rate is the *sole* governing factor. But the bank rate can only operate by its reaction on … the Bank of England's assets … . Thus a low bank rate can be largely neutralized by a simultaneous reduction of [Ways and Means advances] or [the Bank's investments] and a high bank rate by an increase of these. Indeed the Bank of England can probably bring the money market to heel more decisively by buying or selling securities than in any other way; and the utility of bank rate, operated by itself and without assistance from deliberate variations in the volume of [the Bank's investments], is lessened by the various limitations which exist in practice to its freedom of movement, and to the limits within which it can move, upwards and downwards.
>
> (Keynes 1923, JMK 4: 145, n. 1)

All in all, Keynes appears to be satisfied with the possibility of controlling the banks' credit creation. In view of his outline of the principles of currency management expressed in terms of his real balance equation, his more detailed analysis of the existing facts, and comments on them, are nevertheless somewhat surprising – particularly with respect to the variable r, i.e. the banks' proportion. For, obviously, *conventional* reserve ratios are not under the authorities' direct control – as they "ought to be." Yet, he neither proposes to establish legal reserve requirements, nor does he return to the issue of using variations in reserve ratios as a policy tool, a possibility, it would seem, implicit reference was repeatedly made to in terms of his real balance equation. His advice of adding to the Bank of England's "usual method," consisting of deliberate variations in bank rate with a view of exercising a stabilizing influence over k and k' (apart from whatever influence the authorities may have over "the mood of the public and the business world more generally"), other more direct means of control over n and r reduces – in effect – to one variable only: the quantity of banks' cash. Keynes is aware, however, that the possibility of the banks' departure from conventional behavior leaves a residual, or more than residual, unpredictability. His summary of a policy of controlling the banks' credit creation mentions the possibility of opposing bank behavior:

> Therefore it is broadly true to say that the level of prices ... depends in the last resort on the policy of the Bank of England and of the Treasury ...; though the other banks, if they strongly opposed the official policy, could thwart, or at least delay it to a certain extent – provided they were prepared to depart from their usual proportions.
>
> (Keynes 1923, JMK 4: 145)

The authorities' job to counterbalance instabilities in the public's demand for real balances which would otherwise lead to credit cycles and fluctuations in the price level seems to be complicated by the fact that they need to convince the banks *not* to oppose them, but to follow suit. Clearly, even bank regulation in the form of *minimum* reserve requirements would, at best, reduce the banks' discretion in one direction only.

5.3 *A Treatise on Money* – the "excess-bearish-factor" version of liquidity preference theory

The *Tract* is mainly concerned with the *consequences* of fluctuations in prices and the *policy objective* of *internal* price stability. It does not provide a thorough investigation into the *causes* of the credit cycle and the *practice* of monetary control over price stability. The *Treatise* is aimed at filling this gap. Again, Keynes attempts to encapsulate the phenomenon of the credit cycle, and to give a *causal explanation* of it, within the realm of monetary theory. But no longer does he regard the monetary theory of the day as fit for that purpose: the quantity theory in its usual forms, he argues, is useless for anything but describing equilibrium positions. Credit cycles represent disequilibria though, and policy decisions must be based on a causal theoretical analysis of what happens out of "long-run equilibrium." Nevertheless, the idea of some *unique* long-run equilibrium towards which the economy is tending remains one of the building blocks of the *Treatise*.

We may take Keynes' critique of his own real balance equation of the *Tract*, which he formerly regarded as an appropriate analytical tool to tackle those "few, definite, analyzable influences" that govern the price level, as our starting point. Keynes detects two faults in his earlier treatment. Notwithstanding the possible appropriateness of the "consumption unit" as a measure of the purchasing power of money, he sees the "great fault" in relating this particular price index to a monetary aggregate which is used for much else than expenditures on this particular index. Its "second fault" lies in limiting the possible causes of variations in the deposits-to-currency proportion to changes of habits on the part of the public, a factor which is only relevant for those bank deposits serving the public's income purposes ("income deposits"), but not for bank deposits broadly defined. Yet, even after restating his argument in a "form which is formally free from these objections," Keynes dismisses the revised version of his real balance equation too:

> Formerly I was attracted by this [quantity-theoretic] line of approach. But it now seems to me that the merging together of all the different sorts of transactions – income, business and financial – which may be taking place only causes confusion, and that we cannot get any real insight into the price-making process without bringing in the rate of interest and the distinctions between incomes and profits and between savings and investment.
>
> (Keynes 1930a, JMK 5: 205)

This critique captures the character of the *Treatise* innovations with respect to the motives for holding bank deposits as well as to the hub of his new conceptual apparatus, designed for *causal* analysis of disequilibria.

Essentially, Keynes' new analysis of money demand is undertaken in terms of disaggregation by type of transaction and actor. Underlying his disaggregated analysis in the *Treatise* is a clear, albeit indirect, distinction between various motives for the demand for money, in the sense that these motives are identified by type of deposits used and type of transactions executed by various actors. This approach contrasts with his later *General Theory* where the "incentives to liquidity" are analyzed directly and without any such explicit classification of types of deposits.[4] Yet, the contrast with the analysis of the *Tract* is even greater. In the *Tract* too, the "demand for real balances" appears to be a function of various determinants, including the levels of activity and prices, wealth, confidence, etc. But the causes and effects of changes in the demand for real balances, playing such a central part in that book, are treated in a completely undifferentiated way – a crucial source for Keynes' later dissatisfaction with it.

Instead, he proposes a classification scheme for decomposing the broad money holdings of the general public. The total volume of deposits created by the banking system falls into the requirements of the *industrial circulation* with the remainder forming the *financial circulation*. The former covers the provision of finance, and the facilitation of payments, which relate to "real" economic activity, including households' "income deposits" and "business deposits A" (or, "industrial deposits") of firms. The financial circulation covers the facilitation of purely financial transactions through "business deposits B" (or, "financial deposits") and the provision of "saving deposits A and B" which, roughly, stand for the precautionary and speculative motives of *The General Theory* respectively. Interestingly, the public's demand for "cash" is seen as being of no essential relevance to the analysis. For simplicity, he says, and since "current money is predominantly bank money," Keynes generally assumes "not only that all the central bank money is held by the member banks, but also that *all the current money in the hands of the public is member bank money, i.e. bank deposits*" (Keynes 1930a, JMK 5: 27).

The point is that the composition of a given broad monetary aggregate may change both systematically, due to fluctuations in the requirements of the industrial circulation over the cycle, in particular, as well as unsystematically, owing, for instance to sudden changes in the "state of bearishness" of the general public and to the extent that these are met by the banking system. In addition, the corresponding disaggregated velocities may differ both in magnitude and degree of stability. By "covering up" these matters through aggregation and by neglecting the role of the rate of interest and of profits, the traditional quantity theory fails to shed any light on the price-making process and the causal factors at work during cycles. Velocity used in this way, Keynes says, is an "omnibus conception" (Keynes 1930b, JMK 6: 5).

The "excess-saving factor" and the "excess-bearish factor" summarize the relevant causal factors which Keynes believes to be at work in such *disequilibrium* situations. The former explains the determination of the consumption goods price level, the latter that of capital goods. We must restrict ourselves here to a brief discussion of the excess-bearish factor which in many ways encapsulates, or represents an early version of, the liquidity preference theory of *The General Theory*. The point we wish to stress here is that this early version is both more complex and more general than its (reduced-form) successor version. The excess-bearish factor concerns the interaction between the demand for, and the supply of, money.

As in *The General Theory*, in the *Treatise* this interaction is seen as determining the "market rate of interest." Yet, in the *Treatise* the portfolio decisions not only of the general public, but also of the banks enter explicitly into the play; where both parties' portfolio decisions are seen as being based upon a balancing of "relative attractions" of the various forms in which wealth may be held (including expectations about future securities prices, which may be "bullish" or "bearish" in nature and of varying degrees). It is made explicit here that the banks may *decide* to adjust their portfolios, either in size and/or composition, both over the cycle as well as in the event of sudden changes in the "state of bearishness" of the general public, for instance. The outcome, i.e. the stock of money in existence at any time, always depends on the banks' portfolio decisions.

For instance, the banking system of the *Treatise* may facilitate a changing degree of diversity of opinion within the general public ("two views") by providing advances ("financial loans") to the "bulls" who therewith buy out the "bears," the latter being content, for the time being, with holding more savings deposits at rising securities prices. Furthermore, the banks themselves may, perhaps, disagree with the public and take a varying amount of securities off the market (at some price). In particular, only to the extent that the banking system does *not* meet the changing requirements on the part of the public will such changes affect securities prices, the "*excess*-bearish factor," which includes the possibility that the banking system not only fails to compensate for, but might even aggravate, such changes. The excess-bearish factor represents a theory of the "market rate of interest" in terms closely similar to the liquidity preference schedule of *The General Theory*, albeit featuring the general public *and* the banking system the role of which is not hidden behind the assumption of an "exogenous" quantity of money:

> It follows that the actual price level of investments is the resultant of the sentiment of the public and the behavior of the banking system. This does not mean that there is any definite numerical relationship between the price level of investments and the additional quantity of savings deposits created. The amount by which the creation of a given quantity of deposits will raise the price of other securities above what their price would otherwise have been depends on the shape of the public's demand curve for savings deposits at different price levels of other securities. [*Footnote*: The rate of interest offered by the banking system on savings deposits also comes in, of course, as a factor influencing their relative attractiveness.]
>
> (Keynes 1930a, JMK 5: 128)

Notice that the conception of the excess-bearish factor carries over the message from the *Tract* that the banking system's job was to accommodate fluctuations in the public's demand for real balances. But this time round, the argument is expressed and analyzed in terms of the equilibrium rate of interest rather than the equilibrium volume of real balances. In the *Treatise* long-run equilibrium entrepreneurs earn "normal profits" and are thus under no motive to either increase or decrease their levels of activity; while the system is in its *unique* saving-equals-investment equilibrium. Essentially, when expressed in Wicksellian terms, monetary factors work through their impact on the "market rate of interest," a departure from the "natural rate" of which sets off saving–investment *disequilibria* and, hence, profit inflations/deflations. The authorities should thus aim at making the market rate of interest match the natural rate (Keynes 1930a, JMK 5: 139).[5]

As we saw above, the authorities' control over the banks' creation of credit (and the corresponding volume of deposits) was not simply taken for granted in the *Tract*, but seen as being dependent upon institutional arrangements and practices. Similarly, the monetary authorities' control over the market rate of interest is not taken for granted in the *Treatise* either. In particular, the *Treatise* not only identifies the various motives for the public's demand for money by distinguishing various types of deposits provided by banks to meet these motives, but also offers an analysis of the process of supply of these deposits along liquidity preference lines: the *Treatise* features a liquidity preference theory of bank behavior. In fact, the supply side of liquidity preference theory is dealt with in great detail in that work, both analytically and institutionally.

The next section resumes the discussion of the banks' demand for reserves, analyzed, in the *Treatise*, in terms of a liquidity preference theory of bank behavior and as one aspect of the banks' overall portfolio choices. The provision of the quantity of reserves available to the system is the subject of Section 5.5. The rich treasure of institutional detail of the *Treatise* offers some interesting refinements with regard to technical monetary control aspects and the determination of the market rate of interest.

5.4 A liquidity preference theory of bank behavior

A preliminary analysis of the behavior of banks of the "fully developed modern type" (Keynes 1930a, JMK 5: 20), operating within a system equipped with a clearing house dealing with inter-bank claims, is provided in Chapter 2: "Bank money." Keynes rejects there the idea – held by "practical bankers" – that the whole initiative in banking business lies with the depositors, and he stresses the banks' interdependency instead. This interdependency arises due to the fact that the expansion of business on the part of any one particular bank, i.e. the creation of deposits by making loans or purchasing assets, will involve payments to depositor-customers of other banks. As a result, the individual bank faces an effective limitation. For, in Keynes' view, it "cannot raise its own deposits relatively to the total deposits out of proportion to its quota of the banking business of the country" (Keynes 1930a, JMK 5: 26–7). For the system as a whole, however, there is no such limitation, at least as long as the banks move forward in step. Rather, the very interdependency of banks leads to a "tendency towards sympathetic movement on the part of the individual elements within a banking system" (Keynes 1930a, JMK 5: 23).

Keynes illustrates his case by discussing the banking arrangements in a hypothetical closed and cashless society in which, moreover, "banks do not find it necessary in such circumstances to hold cash reserves but settle inter-bank indebtedness by the transfer of other assets" (Keynes 1930a, JMK 5: 23). He argues that such a system would be capable of "violent movement," as there was no check on banks as a whole. The system's overall stance would just be whatever "average behavior" of banks (not depositors!) happens to be:

> the behavior of each bank, though it cannot afford to move more than a step in advance of the others, will be governed by the average behavior of the banks as a whole – to which average, however, it is able to contribute its quota small or large. Each bank chairman sitting in his parlour may regard himself as the passive instrument of outside forces over which he has no control; yet the "outside forces" may be nothing but himself and his fellow-chairmen, and certainly not his depositors.
>
> (Keynes 1930a, JMK 5: 23)

Actual monetary systems differ from this hypothetical case mainly in the following way: a central bank takes on the roles of clearing house and bankers' bank. It issues deposits that (member) banks use to settle clearing house differences, and which can also be encashed to accommodate changes in the public's demand for "cash."[6] In short, the (member) banks regard their deposits at the central bank (and vault cash) as their "reserves."[7] Much in line with his earlier *Tract* position Keynes argues that any individual bank first of all decides on some prudent "cash proportion" to aim for. If the central bank is in control of the volume of reserves, it may take on the role of "conductor of the orchestra." For "it is the aggregate of the reserve resources which determines the 'pace' which is common to the banking system as a whole" (Keynes 1930a, JMK 5: 26).

Yet, Keynes does not assume this to be the case. Rather, he investigates *how* this state of affairs may best be achieved. Although he confirms his *Tract* finding about the stability of banks' reserve ratios for the whole period from 1921 until 1929, he now proposes to have the banks' reserve ratio fixed by law rather than by custom and convention. In fact, he even recommends that: "the central bank should have the power to vary within limits the reserve requirements of its member banks" (Keynes 1930b, JMK 6: 334). These recommendations are closely related to another proposal though, namely, that the volume of reserves be controlled via open market operations. Legal reserve requirements are seen as auxiliary means to ensure the effectiveness of open-market operations under exceptional circumstances. For, as Keynes sees it, the central bank's strength and ability to enforce its will on the market largely depends on its earning capacity and market share.[8] The *Treatise* offers some interesting extensions and clarifications concerning the role of open-market operations in controlling bank behavior, to which we return in a moment. Even more interesting, perhaps, is the analysis of bank behavior itself: Keynes no longer just concentrates on the banks' reserve policies.

The empirical fact of *stable* reserve ratios at *some* conventional level which is not correlated with either the state of trade or with bank rate is important to falsify the competing view (attributed to Pigou's *Industrial Fluctuations*) that the banks vary their reserve ratios in accordance with the state of trade. But another finding, observed but otherwise ignored in the *Tract*, now receives his attention too: the variability of the composition of banks' assets. In a way, Keynes' analysis of the banks' overall portfolio choices is an extension of his analysis of their reserve policies, concentrating on institutional and conventional factors as well as a trade-off between prospective profitability and "liquidity" of alternative forms of lending. Put the other way round, banks' reserve policies are now seen as one aspect of their overall banking policies, and the availability of highly liquid interest-yielding assets (Treasury bills, in particular) is explicitly identified as a necessary condition for the stability of banks' reserve ratio at some conventional or legal level.

The core of Keynes' liquidity preference theory of bank behavior is worked out in a most remarkable section on "The interchangeability of non-reserve bank assets," from which we need to quote here at some length.[9] Clearly, banks are pictured there as *actively* managing their balance sheets. In deciding about the form of their lending, or the division of their resources in different forms of investment available to them, they balance profitability considerations as against liquidity (i.e. market risk) considerations. In an uncertain world, moreover, this balancing job represents a "never-ceasing problem," since the strength of various considerations is continuously varying over time with changing circumstances:

> Apart from the rare occasions of a deliberate change in the conventional [reserve] ratio, ... and from the possibility of the member banks being in a position to influence the amount of their own reserves ... what bankers are ordinarily deciding is, not *how much* they will lend in the aggregate – this is mainly settled for them by the state of their reserves – but in *what forms* they will lend – in what proportions they will divide their resources between the different kinds of investment which are open to them. Broadly there are three categories to choose from – (i) bills of exchange and call loans to the money market, (ii) investments, (iii) advances to customers. As a rule, advances to customers are more profitable than investments, and investments are more profitable than bills and call loans; but this order is not invariable. On the other hand, bills and call loans are more "liquid," than investments, i.e. more certainly realizable at short notice without loss, and investments are more "liquid" than advances. Accordingly bankers are faced with a never-ceasing problem of weighing one thing against another; the proportions in which their resources are divided between these three categories suffer wide fluctuations; and in deciding upon their course they are influenced by the various considerations mentioned above.
>
> (Keynes 1930b, JMK 6: 59)

Keynes offers some explanations for these fluctuations in banks' portfolio proportions. In particular, these fluctuations may be due to variations in the banks' customers' *demand for advances*. But notice that he views banks as applying judgment to the issue of whether or not to accommodate their customers' changing requirements. He distinguishes between trade customers and "speculative movement[s]," and points out that banks' judgment appears to concern both microeconomic and macroeconomic issues, and that banks' own liquidity preference may change. Most importantly, notice that even to the extent that banks accommodate the variations in their customers' demand for advances, this would at best make one component of their overall balance sheet *endogenous*. For in Keynes' view banks would try to compensate such endogenous variations in their loan business by employing their resources in alternative directions. Keynes continues:

> When, for example, they feel that a speculative movement or a trade boom may be reaching a dangerous phase, they scrutinize more critically the security behind their less liquid assets and try to move, so far as they can, into a more liquid position. When, on the other hand, demands increase for

advances from their trade customers of a kind which the banks deem to be legitimate and desirable, they do their best to meet these demands by reducing their investments and, perhaps, their bills; whilst, if the demand for advances is falling off, they employ the resources thus released by again increasing their investments.

(Keynes 1930b, JMK 6: 59–60)

Finally, notice that Keynes' analysis of bank behavior takes the aggregate amount of reserves, or, the stance of monetary policy, as given; while the possibility of banks' access to reserves and their discretion to deliberately vary their conventional reserve ratio appear as provisos in the above. We have thus reached the issue of the authorities' control over bank behavior.

5.5   Controlling bank behavior and the market rate of interest

In many ways Keynes' analysis of the monetary authority's influence over the market rate of interest in the *Treatise* represents a more detailed and refined analysis of its control over credit creation in the *Tract*. Again, his analysis refers partly to particular institutional arrangements existing at that time, mainly in Britain and the US, but also pertains to institutional arrangements and practices of an "ideal central bank of the future" (Keynes 1930b, JMK 6: 233). In fact, Keynes' key question is how a central bank can best frame and use "means of establishing an unchallengeable centralized control over [the banks'] aggregate behavior" (Keynes 1930b, JMK 6: 190).

As in the *Tract*, Chapter 32 of the *Treatise* starts from the idea that controlling bank money (or, credit creation) presupposes the central bank's control over its own balance sheet. Yet, this time round it is not just the total volume of reserves which matters to him, but also the channels through which these reserves are made available to the banks. Keynes is particularly interested in the possibilities of providing reserves in a way that *directly* influences *longer term* rates of interest. He divides the central bank's assets into categories which broadly correspond to the policies he investigates, namely, "investments" which the central bank purchases on its own initiative on the one hand, and "advances" which the central bank has purchased "in virtue of an obligation, of law or custom, to purchase such an asset if it is tendered or specified conditions" (Keynes 1930b, JMK 6: 202) on the other.[10] The latter concern bank rate policy directed at the short-term rate of interest, the issue here is how bank rate can be made "effective." The former concern open-market policies, and their use as an *additional* policy instrument which may be directed at shorter *and* longer term rates.

As regards bank rate policies, Keynes praises the virtues of what he calls the "London technique." Given that the tendering of eligible assets for which the central bank is willing to make advances occurs at the banks' discretion, it would at first appear as if the central bank has no control over the *volume* of its advances at all. However, for Keynes, making bank rate "effective" means directing short-term market rates for lending and borrowing of money in a way which leads to the desired volume of banks' reserves, namely, by making it *unprofitable* for banks to sell more eligible assets to the central bank than the latter intends to buy. The "London technique" describes the limiting case where bank rate is such that the Bank of England's advances to the member banks are normally nil and come into existence only temporarily. Obviously, in a changing society, policy carried out along these lines can only be effective as long as the central bank continuously "maintains touch with market conditions" (Keynes 1930b, JMK 6: 204).[11] A complex two-way interaction between the central bank and the banks thus results, and Keynes refers to the situation "when an increase of bank rate is anticipated in the near future" (Keynes 1930b, JMK 6: 203) as an occasion when advances may *temporarily* be positive. Nevertheless, if successful, making bank rate effective thus implies that the provision of the banks' reserves is made through the central bank's investment category only, i.e. business carried out at the latter's initiative.

This leads us to the central bank's policies regarding its "investments" and the question of open-market operations as an *additional* policy instrument in guiding the system in some desired direction. To begin with, Keynes does not deny the limits of carrying out bank rate policy and open-market policy along different lines. He argues though that "the *kinds* of effect produced by [them] are materially different" (Keynes 1930b, JMK 6: 225). One immediate limitation arises if the money market is indebted to the central bank, as, he observes, was normally the case in the US, but would not be if the London technique were applied. Another possible limitation arises, most likely in the case of restrictive open-market operations, if these measures evoke "the resistance of the banks both in their own interest and to avoid upsetting their customers" (Keynes 1930b, JMK 6: 226). Bank rate would then have to be raised in line with market rates in order to keep it effective. This is less likely to happen in the case of expansionary open-market operations. For Keynes ventures that the banks may often be able to "increase their loans and advances without a material weakening in the rates of interest charged" (Keynes 1930b, JMK 6: 226), an argument which appears to involve what he elsewhere calls the "unsatisfied fringe of borrowers" (cf. Keynes 1930a, JMK 5: 190; 1930b, JMK 6: 326–7).

Two factors underscore the special attraction of open-market policies: first, their *direct* effects on banks' reserves which, he ventures, would tacitly influence banks to move in step in the desired direction and, hence, "give the central bank a means of using the inherent instability of the system for its own purposes" (Keynes 1930b, JMK 6: 228), second, their potential to influence long-term rates of interest *directly*. Direct control over long-term rates is especially important when the preservation of international equilibrium constrains bank rate policies. And domestic equilibrium may be more dependent on long-term rates anyway.

Indeed, the emphasis on the role of longer term rates of interest in preserving (or, re-attaining) domestic equilibrium is one of the foremost innovations of the *Treatise*.[12] The "crux of the whole matter" is brought to its head in Chapter 37, which offers crucial insights into both the role of bank behavior itself and the effectiveness of open-market operations in influencing bank behavior. The influence of short-term rates on economic activity is presented here as being *indirect* in nature, working mainly through their influence on longer term rates. The influence of short-term rates on longer term ones, moreover, is seen as being driven largely by bank behavior.

In effect, Keynes applies here his liquidity preference theory of bank behavior to the varying proportions of short-term and long-term securities in banks' portfolios and the related issue of the yield curve. We saw above that banks' *active* management of their asset portfolios involves both a certain responsiveness to their customers' varying requirements as well as considerations of profitability and banks' own liquidity preferences. In the context of his remarkable discussion of the term structure of interest rates we find what is probably Keynes' clearest reference to the driving motive behind bank behavior:

> There are a number of financial institutions – amongst which the banks themselves are the most important … – which vary from time to time the proportionate division of their assets between long-term and short-term securities respectively. Where short-term yields are high, the safety and liquidity of short-term securities appear extremely attractive. But when short-term yields are very low, not only does this attraction disappear, but another motive enters in, namely, a fear lest the institution may be unable to maintain its established level of income, any serious falling off in which would be injurious to its reputation. A point comes, therefore, when they hasten to move into long-dated securities; the movement itself sends up the price of the latter; and this movement seems to confirm the wisdom of those who were recommending the policy of changeover.
>
> (Keynes 1930b, JMK 6: 320)

It is clear from this observation that Keynes views banks as being attentive to their own shareholders. Their reputation is linked to their established level of income. It is due to the banks' concern about their own profitability – and hence their capital base – that they respond to a falling-off in profitability in any particular form of lending, either due to slack demand (business cycle) and/or market yields obtainable (term structure), by looking for alternative kinds of investment. (Notice also the element of self-fulfilling prophecy in banks' credit creation.) This "motive," importantly, would appear to be at work no matter how the monetary authorities may decide to provide the reserves of the system.

All of this is also much in line with Keynes' view of banking business as extending well beyond the provision of working capital finance, itself being procyclical. In Keynes' view, the banking system has a "dual function," including a role in the financing of "fixed investment." The following observation links up nicely with what we said in Section 5.4 about the banking system's part in the excess-bearish factor:

> In actual fact the banking system has a dual function – the direction of the supply of resources for working capital through the loans which it makes to

producers to cover their outgoings during the period of production (and no longer), and of the supply *pari passu* of the current cash required for use in the industrial circulation; and, on the other hand, the direction of the supply of resources which determines the value of securities through the investments which it purchases directly and the loans which it makes to the stock exchange and to other persons who are prepared to carry securities with borrowed money, and of the supply *pari passu* of the savings deposits required for use in the financial circulation to satisfy the bullishness or bearishness of financial sentiment, so as to prevent its reacting on the value and the volume of new investment.

(Keynes 1930b, JMK 6: 310–11)

This observation is also noteworthy for Keynes' reference to "the banking system," without distinguishing between the roles played by the monetary authorities and the banks respectively. This distinction appears, however, in section (d) of Chapter 37 on "Open-market operations to the point of saturation." Keynes explains that up to that point he was dealing with "the normal and orthodox methods by which a central bank can use its powers for easing (or stiffening) the credit situation to stimulate (or retard) the rate of new investment" (Keynes 1930b, JMK 6: 331). He now turns to "extraordinary methods" which may have to be applied in "acute circumstances." Keynes proposes a "remedy in the event of the obstinate persistence of a slump" which consists of carrying out open-market operations in long-term securities "*à outrance.*" He believes that the central bank will normally be able to draw the banking system in the desired direction:

If the central bank supplies the member banks with more funds than they can lend at short term, in the first place the short-term rate of interest will decline towards zero, and in the second place the member banks will soon begin, if only to maintain their profits, to second the efforts of the central bank by themselves buying securities. This means that the price of bonds will rise unless there are many persons to be found who, as they see the prices of long-term bonds rising, prefer to sell them and hold the proceeds liquid at a very low rate of interest.

(Keynes 1930b, JMK 6: 333)

Notice here that this remark features the liquidity preference of the general public ("many persons"). For Keynes also refers to the development of "extreme situations," characterized by increased uncertainty and depressed financial sentiment and the emergence of a "very wide and quite unusual gap between the ideas of borrowers and of lenders in the market for long-term" (Keynes 1930b, JMK 6: 334); the latter seem to feature the banks' liquidity preference. The advice he gives only alludes to imposing a duty on the central bank:

How is it possible in such circumstances ... to keep the market rate and the natural rate of long-term interest at an equality with one another, *unless we*

> impose on the central bank the duty of purchasing bonds up to a price far
> beyond what it considers to be the long-period norm.
>
> (Keynes 1930b, JMK 6: 334)

Unfortunately, Keynes does not elaborate on what the central bank "considers to be the long-period norm," how it comes about, and whether it is some sort of *unique* norm. But it seems clear enough that Keynes is here referring to a situation in which the banks refuse to "second the efforts of the central bank" so that the latter is left quite on its own. It seems also clear that banks refuse to engage themselves beyond what *they* consider the long-period norm for fear that a future reversal of positions may involve a "serious financial loss." In other words, the expectation of a renewed future rise in interest rates prevents them from expanding their holdings of long-term securities. What is important in the *Treatise* in "extreme circumstances" only was going to receive a far more general importance in *The General Theory*, to which we now turn.

5.6   Bank behavior and the "Keynes mechanism" of *The General Theory*

Keynes of the *Treatise* believed that monetary management could guide the system towards its *unique* long-period full employment equilibrium by making the market rate of interest correspond to the natural rate. At the level of monetary theory, the fundamental break between *The General Theory* and the *Treatise on Money* is therefore well illustrated by his repudiation of the Wicksellian natural rate concept: "I am now no longer of the opinion that the concept of a 'natural' rate of interest, which previously seemed to me a most promising idea, has anything very useful or significant to contribute to our analysis" (Keynes 1936a, JMK 7: 243).

Owing to the discovery of the "principle of effective demand," Keynes reaches the conclusion that neoclassical theory is only valid and applicable under conditions of full employment, conditions which represent merely a special case that is *not* automatically attained through the working of market forces. There is thus no *unique* long-period position, but a multiplicity of natural rates. Each natural rate, if the market rate accords to it, would keep the level of activity – under given conditions – at some prevailing rate, whatever it may be: "merely the rate of interest which will preserve the *status quo*" (Keynes 1936a, JMK 7: 243). The system cannot be in equilibrium with the market rate being below that natural rate which corresponds to full employment (i.e. the "neutral rate"). For a state of "true inflation" would then develop. But the market rate can well be in equilibrium above the neutral rate, and the system would then be stuck in an "unemployment equilibrium."[13]

The natural rate having thus lost its analytical significance together with its uniqueness, the market rate of interest itself moves to the centre-stage position. As regards the *substance* of liquidity preference theory, there is no actual change involved. For already the excess-bearish factor of the *Treatise* encompasses a liquidity theory of the market rate of interest. Nevertheless, liquidity preference theory now takes on another *role*, namely primarily as a "liquidity theory of interest," replacing the classical "savings theory of interest" diagnosed to be flawed. Key changes occur at the level of *exposition* however. In particular, in *The General Theory* the analysis of the motives for liquidity *apparently* refers to the general public only. The behavior of banks, by contrast, is hidden behind some given quantity of money generally assumed to be constant in that book. The rest of this section examines the analytical role of this "constant-money-stock-assumption" (CMSA) and what it implies about the behavior of banks.

To begin with, and probably most importantly, the CMSA serves as an analytical device in Keynes' attack on the quantity theory. If a fall in effective demand depresses activity and leads to falling wages and prices, the classical economists Keynes is rebelling against would simply attribute falling prices to a declining money stock – *if* there were a decline. *By (CMS) assumption*, this traditional monetary channel is ruled out, highlighting instead the role of *real* demand and money wages in determining the levels of activity and prices, respectively. At the same time, as pointed out in Chapter 19, the CMSA allows for the possibility of an alternative channel through which falling money wages may at least *indirectly* tend to raise activity:

> The reduction in the wages-bill, accompanied by some reduction in prices and in money-incomes generally, will diminish the need for cash for income and business purposes; and it will therefore reduce *pro tanto* the schedule of liquidity-preference for the community as a whole. *Cet. par.* this will reduce the rate of interest and thus prove favorable to investment. … It is, therefore, on the effect of a falling wage- and price-level on the demand for money that those who believe in the self-adjusting quality of the economic system must rest the weight of their argument; … If the quantity of money is itself a function of the wage- and price-level, there is indeed, nothing to hope in this direction. But if the quantity of money is virtually fixed, it is evident that its quantity in terms of wage-units can be indefinitely increased by a sufficient reduction in money-wages.
>
> (Keynes 1936a, JMK 7: 263–6)

Let us then attempt to elaborate on the analytical role of the CMSA in the light of Keynes' earlier writings. On our reading, the CMSA has at least six more arguments to speak in its favor, given Keynes' *quaesitum* in *The General Theory*: to analyze the factors which determine the level of activity at any time.

First, as Joan Robinson (1970: 82) argues, there may have been some tactical considerations involved. Indeed, some critics of the *Treatise*, foremost amongst them Hayek (1931; cf. Keynes 1931b, JMK 13: 249–51), claimed that the disequilibria Keynes analyzes in the *Treatise* must necessarily be the result of the banking system's departure from neutrality. Clearly, this claim is diametrically opposed to Keynes' objective of showing that disequilibria may just as well originate outside the banking system, whereas the latter may, at least potentially, take on the role of a "balancing factor" (as already in the *Tract*). Perhaps, then, critics would accept the CMSA as representing "neutral money," whatever that may be (Keynes 1936a, JMK 7: 183).[14]

It is also clear, second, that the CMSA simplifies his analysis in a number of ways. Compared to the rather more complex analysis in the *Treatise*, the CMSA allows Keynes to concentrate on the income–expenditure part (excess-saving factor) while the excess-bearish factor, the element his critics had most difficulties with, is "set on neutral." The part played by liquidity preference is at the same time made even clearer. The rate of interest is established at any time at that level at which the desire for extra liquidity vanishes at the margin; an *attempt* to become more liquid changes the rate of interest forthwith. Why complicate matters by making allowance for banks' discretion to respond to the public's changed liquidity preferences, for instance, which the banks may or may not use? The new truncated excess-bearish version simplifies his analysis without distracting from the essence of his theory of effective demand, namely, that it is spending, and investment spending in particular, which is driving the system.

While the aim to simplify may have been a goal in itself, the CMSA, third, also helps to bring out another crucial analytical point: it makes clear that, for instance, an increase in the level of economic activity may affect interest rates *indirectly* simply due to the changing requirements of the industrial circulation (the transactions motive), *if* the banking system does not duly enlarge the pool of liquidity. Clearly this outcome would have nothing to do with a shortage of saving (Keynes 1938a, JMK 14: 231). Rather, it shows that purely *monetary* factors condition the equilibrium level of *real* activity. They do so not only at the new higher level of activity (perhaps prompted by a rise in the marginal efficiency of capital) which is sustainable even at higher interest rates, but also at the initial level of economic activity. By implication, there is no unique long-period equilibrium, independent of the "banking policy."[15] In short, the CMSA stands for a *particular* banking policy, which could be different, and in which case the long-period equilibrium would then likely be different too.

"Banking policy," crucially, includes both the policies of the authorities and the banks. And, fourth, the CMSA has pivotal implications for the behavior of banks. If, in a recession, firms manage to adjust their indebtedness to banks roughly in line with their shrinking business, the size of the banks' balance sheets would tend to shrink *pari passu*. At least, this would occur if banks did nothing else but *passively* accommodated firms' varying working capital requirements. Money would then be *endogenous*, purely credit demand-driven. And this would rule out the *indirect* effect on interest rates featuring in his own analysis and referred to in the literature as the "Keynes effect" (Cottrell 1994).

In the light of our reading we may try to clarify here the analytical content of this Keynes effect. First of all, there is no need to restrict its potential role to the case of changing money wages only. The point is far more general, referring to changes in the size of the pool of liquidity *relative* to the level of activity and prices, for whatever reason. The *Treatise* features procyclical variations in the requirements of the industrial circulation, the liabilities part of which (i.e. income and business deposits A) reappears in *The General Theory* under the heading of the transactions motive for money demand. The corresponding changes on the asset side of the banks' balance sheets are analyzed in detail in the *Treatise*, but left implicit in *The General Theory*.

Clearly, for the stock of money to remain constant when the demand for working capital is falling off, for instance, banks must expand their business activities in other directions. In particular, they may *decide* to buy more investments, thereby driving down the *long-term* rate. The CMSA presupposes bank behavior of this sort, *whether policy-controlled interest rates are adjusted or not* (see below). Perhaps we should better call this purely bank-driven interest rate channel the "Keynes mechanism."[16] Analytically speaking, the Keynes mechanism is driven by the banks' profit motive; it presupposes both agile behavior on the part of banks and unchanged liquidity preferences of the general public.

Yet, fifth, the CMSA and, hence, the Keynes mechanism, has some empirical content as well. It is not an arbitrary assumption simply made for analytical convenience. The liquidity preference theory of bank behavior of the *Treatise* was clearly related to Keynes' own empirical investigations in that book and his earlier *Tract*. And, indeed, so long as banks do not get into trouble themselves, what should stop them from investing in alternative directions when their normal clients are getting cold feet (see Table 5.1)?[17]

Last, but not least, the CMSA thereby also exemplifies the *generality* of *The General Theory*. Clearly a particular banking policy which keeps the money stock constant while the economy hits a recession is not a worst case scenario. Leijonhufvud's (1981: 166–7, n. 50) claim about widespread bankruptcies among banks is far off the mark. *The General Theory* is neither a depression theory, as Hicks (1937) convinced many, nor is it a disaster theory. The CMSA implies that the banking system is probably not, at least not yet, in major trouble itself. For, otherwise, the banks' resources may not be employable in alternative directions. This is not to suggest that Keynes was unaware of such calamitous possibilities (cf. Keynes 1931a, JMK 9).[18] Rather, he refers to what I would like to call "the most favorable case" of a more or less neutral banking policy in terms of which he analyzes the potential sources of "automatic relief," and against which the possibility of more aggressive "deliberate action" on the part of the monetary authorities is then compared. Importantly, while policy-controlled interest rates are likely to be reduced in practice, the Keynes mechanism may work at any given stance of monetary policy, that is, feature *money exogeneity due to bank behavior alone*.

5.7 On liquidity traps – a special type of coordination problems

In *The General Theory*, open-market operations are used mainly to illustrate Keynes' "new" liquidity preference theory of interest. Yet, Keynes' thought experiments also partly pertain to our main concern here: the central bank–banks relationship. In a way, Keynes continues his *Treatise* analysis of the question whether open-market policies provide an *additional* tool to influence longer term rates more directly. Bank rate policy is of no concern to him anymore, since the "short-term rate of interest is easily controlled by the monetary authority" (Keynes 1936a, JMK 7: 203), both in theory and common practice. Moreover, at the time, short-term rates were next to nothing anyway. The real problem was one of getting down the long rate too.[19]

Again, Keynes also contemplates some ideal or reformed state of affairs with an enlarged field of deliberate control, in which, he ventures, the monetary authority could establish a *direct* relationship between the complex of rates of interest and the quantity of money by being "prepared to deal both ways on specified terms in debts of all maturities" (Keynes 1936a, JMK 7: 205); but his discussion more generally refers to institutions and practices where this relationship is less direct. And he warns the reader that "in applying this theory in any particular case allowance must be made for the special characteristics of the method actually employed by the monetary authority" (Keynes 1936a, JMK 7: 206).

Central to his theory of the determination of interest rates is the speculative motive for the demand for money, defined as: "the object of securing profit from knowing better than the market what the future will bring forth" (Keynes 1936a, JMK 7: 170). The speculative motive is also seen as central to the working of open-market operations: "it is by playing on the speculative-motive that monetary management ... is brought to bear on the economic system" (Keynes 1936a, JMK 7: 196). For the interest-elasticity of "the" liquidity preference schedule is largely due to the speculative motive. However, analytically speaking, "the" liquidity preference schedule is based on some given state of expectations, and expectations are seen as an integral part of monetary management. In particular, expectations about the future policies of the central bank feature as a chief factor in molding "the" state of expectations. Open-market operations work through two channels:

> In dealing with the speculative-motive it is, however, important to distinguish between the changes in the rate of interest which are due to changes in the supply of money available to satisfy the speculative-motive, without there having been any change in the liquidity function, and those which are primarily due to changes in expectation affecting the liquidity function itself. Open-market operations may, indeed, influence the rate of interest through both channels; since they may not only change the volume of money, but may also give rise to changed expectations concerning the future policy of the central bank or of the government.
>
> (Keynes 1936a, JMK 7: 197; cf. also Chick 1983)

Clearly, Keynes does not believe in some *stable* and *unique* liquidity preference schedule being out there. Quite the opposite: "Certainly the liquidity preference curve is on the wobble," as he puts it in a letter of 13 December 1936 to Dennis Robertson (Keynes 1936c, JMK 14: 93). Indeed, the whole point about open-market policies directed at longer term securities appears to be that they must lead to a change in the state of expectations in the desired direction in order to be fully effective. Of course, open-market operations can hardly fail immediately to affect the prices of securities dealt in to some degree. For: "in normal circumstances the banking system is in fact always able to purchase (or sell) bonds in exchange for cash by bidding the price of bonds up (or down) in the market by a modest amount" (Keynes 1936a, JMK 7: 197). But he thought that there were rather narrow limits to playing on the speculative motive by moving interest rates away from what is considered a "fairly safe rate" – *in some given state of expectations.* Full effectiveness largely depends on the *credibility* of the actions undertaken, and the institution undertaking them; in particular, whether monetary policy "strikes public opinion as being experimental in character or easily liable to change," or whether it "appeals to public opinion as being reasonable and practicable and in the public interest, rooted in strong conviction, and promoted by an authority unlikely to be superseded" (Keynes 1936a, JMK 7: 203).

All his reasoning about actual and hypothetical practices of monetary control is, of course, based on his view of the rate of interest as a *conventional phenomenon* (Keynes 1936a, JMK 7: 203; Carabelli 1988; Ciocca and Nardozzi 1996; Vicarelli 1984); a conventional phenomenon, moreover, which has real effects *in the long run.* In the *Treatise,* he was merely concerned about the possibility of a *temporary* gap between the beliefs of borrowers and lenders. In *The General Theory,* the financial system could come up with too high a *convention* and get the general structure of interest rates wrong in the long run. The rate of interest could be "in equilibrium" at *some* natural rate level which keeps economic activity stable at a level which involves persistent unemployment and slack capital formation.

Keynes thought that such was the case in the 1930s. Thus, the task of the day was to steer the conventional view downwards. And, by and large, he ventures the view that "precisely because the convention is not rooted in secure knowledge, it will not always be unduly resistant to a modest measure of persistence and consistency of purpose by the monetary authority" (Keynes 1936a, JMK 7: 204). The British experience after the departure from the gold standard in September 1931, i.e. the relaxation of the external constraint which featured in the *Treatise,* followed by the successful War Loan conversion in 1932 seem to have encouraged this judgment. For Keynes uses this example to illustrate his case in *The General Theory.*[20]

"[M]odest falls" to which public opinion can be "fairly rapidly accustomed" are distinguished there from "major movements … effected by a series of discontinuous jumps." The former would appear to be the direct result of open-market purchases, playing – within limits – on the speculative motive in a given state of expectations. The minor movements so achieved successfully prepared the ground for the major ones, the "series of discontinuous jumps," corresponding to *shifts* in the liquidity function of the public (Keynes 1936a, JMK 7: 204).

Is there a limit to such policies? Well, Keynes repeatedly refers to what may be seen as some *absolute floor* below which interest rates, seemingly, could never fall. But he believes that: "whilst this limiting case might become practically important in future, I know of no example of it hitherto" (Keynes 1936a, JMK 7: 207). In fact, the point he is making about the limitations of monetary management is not at all restricted to this hypothetical absolute floor (whatever the practical or theoretical relevance of this limiting case itself may be; cf. Black 1987, 1995; Greenspan 1998). For the problem Keynes describes exists at *any* level of interest: if open-market purchases drive up securities prices, their running yields so reduced will compensate for *less* perceived risk of a renewed future rise in interest. Yet, in a given state of expectations, this risk *rises* the further the rate of interest deviates from what is considered a "fairly safe level" in that state of expectations. *Ceteris paribus* investors prefer to move into a more liquid position – the trade-off which provides the basis for the authority's playing on the speculative motive. *A* limit is reached when selling pressure due to securities holders' move into cash fully offsets the upward price pressure due to open-market trades. At that point the central bank has lost effective control: the system is in *a* liquidity trap. This condition may arise at *any* level of interest. There is correspondingly a *multiplicity* of liquidity traps (Leijonhufvud 1968; Chapter 4).

This problem would not arise, however, if the authorities managed to shift the state of expectations in the desired direction. The market participants' assessments of risk of capital losses largely depend on their expectations of future rates of interest. This risk would not rise with falling yields if participants trust that lower yields will stay low for some time. Best of all, views about the fairly safe level of interest fall together in line with market yields and a new convention as to the appropriate rate of interest gets established. Securities would then willingly be held at higher prices even without any increase in cash. In practice, open-market purchases of securities may, almost at the same time, move market yields directly, thereby *ceteris paribus* enlarging the liquidity of the system correspondingly (liquidity channel), and successfully steer the convention itself downwards too (expectational channel). In this case, the increased liquidity so-provided would not actually be required to make good for any rise in perceived market risk, i.e. to particularly satisfy the speculative motive, but to balance the reduced spread (opportunity cost of holding cash) instead, i.e. to satisfy the demand for liquidity more generally. But Keynes' theoretical observations also include the possibility that the state of expectations may move in the wrong way. In that case the expectational channel may *counteract*, and more than fully so, any effect on interest rates coming through the liquidity channel.

What happens, then, when the policy fails and the system is "trapped" by a general movement into cash of holders of securities? As in his *Treatise*, Keynes only speaks of "the banking system" when investigating open-market operations. Clearly, as far as the general public is concerned, moving into cash means moving into *bank deposits*. Keynes does not describe open-market purchases as leading to a banking panic: piling up currency notes underneath mattresses plays no part in his monetary thought whatever. Rather, he refers to a situation in which the central bank provides abundant "cash," while wealthy individuals, producers, institutional investors and other non-bank financial intermediaries wish to increase their holdings of *deposits*. By implication, if cash injections via open-market purchases *fail* to raise securities prices, while the general public increases their holdings of deposits, there must be a *tendency for banks' "cash" (i.e. their reserves in the form of central bank deposits) to be piling up correspondingly.* In other words, a liquidity trap describes a situation where the banks *refuse to* "second the efforts of the central bank by themselves buying securities."

Already in his *Tract*, Keynes had mentioned the possibility of such "opposing" behavior – "provided [the banks] were prepared to depart from their usual proportions" (Keynes 1923, JMK 4: 145). In the *Treatise*, he refers to a case in which the public's increased desire to move into liquid assets would tend to offset upward pressure on prices due to securities being taken off the market by the banking system; but this is not seen as an effective barrier. Rather, matters get serious only when the measures rest on the authorities' book alone: *the* liquidity trap as a special case where the expected rebound to *the* "long-period norm" of interest, and the corresponding prospect of financial losses, leads everyone else but the central bank to prefer to stay liquid.

Interestingly, a technical generalization of this special case is provided in the book in which, in general, "technical monetary detail falls into the background" (Keynes 1936a, JMK 7: xii); as a corollary of the generalization which occurred at the level of theory. Owing to the insight that "the" long-period norm is established by *some* convention, Keynes of *The General Theory* becomes far more alert to the complexity of influence of monetary policies on interest rates. In theory, the problem is that the convention the financial system comes up with may be wrong and the economy gets stuck in an unemployment equilibrium. In practice, "the" convention is molded largely by monetary policy itself, but the authority may fail to change it when needed – for failure to convince the banks to follow suit. *A* liquidity trap arises when the monetary authority – for lack of power and/or credibility – fails to communicate convincingly with the markets. For, if the central bank wants to guide the markets, it must successfully sell its policy and convince the markets. Actually, this may sound more difficult than it is, since normally the markets may want to be convinced by some *credible* leader. Essentially, liquidity traps represent *communication failures* between the central bank and her clients: the banks.[21]

5.8 Conclusion

In the light of our reading of Keynes' monetary thought as it evolved from the *Tract* to *The General Theory*, we conclude that neither the old exogenous money consensus of the neoclassical synthesis nor the more recent endogenous money challenge of Post Keynesianism pay due attention to a peculiar factor which, over time, seems to have attracted ever more of Keynes' own heed and concern: bank *behavior*.

The former view invokes a peculiar vision of central banking as deliberately operating through a "veil of banks" and along some given and stable liquidity preference schedule, easily controlling "the" rate of interest along these lines; except, of course, for *the* liquidity trap. Accordingly, that infamous special case, then, seems to provide the proper realm of Keynes' *Special (General) Theory* of "Slump Economics" (Hicks 1937), representing Keynes' core contribution to monetary theory (Friedman 1968, 1971).

Whilst starting from the correct observation that real world central banking has preciously little in common with the IS/LM fiction (cf. Borio 1997; Bindseil 2004), the latter view too disregards the fundamental importance of the theory of liquidity preference as pinpointing the source of long-run non-neutrality. Also, the endogeneity position incorrectly infers from the fact that banks issue their liabilities by buying assets that the quantity of money is endogenously determined by the general public, having no existence independent of demand (cf. Moore 1988, 1991).

By contrast, the vision of a liquidity preference theory of banking emerging from Keynes' monetary writings depicts banks as actively managing both sides of their balance sheets simultaneously. Working in a competitive environment, banks are driven by their profit motive and need to secure some conventional return on their capital base just like any other enterprise; and perhaps more so, given that banks are highly leveraged. At any rate, banks have ample discretion both over the size and composition of their balance sheet. Not even with regard to the industrial circulation did Keynes view banks as passive along horizontalist lines; but as applying judgment to the loan business they undertake. With regard to the financial circulation, Keynes saw banks as active players in organized securities markets. It thus seems reasonable to presume that at any time banks are satisfied overall with the size and composition of their balance sheets in the light of the current structure of rates of interest.[22]

That part of their liabilities conventionally called "money" may then be taken as a *given* in an analysis of the determination of the rate of interest which explicitly concentrates on the liquidity preferences of the general public only: "[The rate of interest] is the 'price' which equilibrates the desire to hold wealth in the form of cash with the available quantity of cash. ... This is where, and how, the quantity of money enters into the economic scheme" (Keynes 1936a, JMK 7: 167–8). (One must not forget here the *quaesitum* of *The General Theory*, i.e. the level of activity at any time with the rate of interest as one of the main determinants.)

If circumstances change, say, for instance, a rise in the marginal efficiency of capital points towards a rise in activity which involves *ceteris paribus* increased pressure on the given pool of liquidity provided by the banking system, interest rates would tend to rise – unless the pool of liquidity is enlarged accordingly. Lavoie (1996) correctly draws our attention to Keynes' objection to Hicks' suggested IS/LM interpretation that: "An increase in the inducement to invest *need* not raise the rate of interest."[23] But Lavoie is wrong to suggest that Keynes' objection lends support to horizontalism. Rather, it exemplifies the crucial point which was at the heart of the "finance motive" debate: in a monetary production economy capital accumulation *cannot* be constrained by the "supply of savings," as the "classics" and their loanable funds cousins would have it, but it *may* be constrained by *liquidity*: "in general, the banking system holds the key position in the transition from a lower to a higher scale of activity" (Keynes 1937f, JMK 14: 222).

In short, in *The General Theory* the quantity of money is *exogenous* in the sense that it is *not* necessarily under the control of the monetary authority (and, obviously, not under the general public's either[24]), but largely dependent upon *bank behavior*. Keynes was very much concerned about the institutional requirements and appropriate techniques to achieve sufficient control over banks, but he did not propose a theory based on the heroic and counterfactual assumption that such control as actually existed was sufficient to easily control the banks and, hence, "the" rate of interest.

Yet, while the complexity of interaction between the central bank and the banks and the role of bank behavior was carefully dealt with in his earlier monetary works, Keynes only fully grasped the far-reaching theoretical implications of the authority's lack of control over banks in his final work. The Keynes mechanism features truly *active* bank behavior, active behavior of a kind which may occur at any given stance of monetary policy (i.e. *short-term* rate of interest pegged at some level). And the concept of the liquidity trap illustrates the importance of communication in monetary policy, including the possibility of a *time-inconsistency* problem in financial markets which may disrupt the money-supply process. For the authorities may fail to direct (e.g.) longer term rates of interest in some desired way for failure of credibly communicating their future intentions to financial market participants, banks' perceptions in particular.

Nevertheless it remains true that in *The General Theory* the complex interaction between the authorities and the banks takes place largely behind the scenes, while the reader is only presented the outcome of their interaction, i.e. some *given* quantity of money – the Pandora's box kept shut.

Postscript

An abundant diversity of views continues to characterize "the" endogenous money view. In the above comparison with Keynes' exogenous money views featuring active bank behavior I singled out Moore's (1988, 1991) horizontalism, which probably represents one extreme of the spectrum of views. Extreme horizontalists like Moore follow Keynes in rejecting loanable funds theory as flawed, but at the same time reject liquidity preference theory as irrelevant; offering what is, in effect, a central bank theory of interest instead. Kaldor's endogenous money views are often seen as a key inspiration behind extreme horizontalism. And the fact that his endogeneity position was as much an attack on Friedman's "new monetarism" as it was on Keynes' *General Theory* would even seem to corroborate the conventional wisdom that Keynes and Friedman held similar views on money exogeneity cum "passive" banks (Desai 1989).[25] It is however noteworthy that *lack of control over banks* features prominently in Kaldor's (1970, 1982, 1983) critique of money exogeneity along monetarist lines. In any case, our reading of Keynes' monetary thought strongly rejects any idea of passiveness on the part of banks, whether as submissive reserve multipliers of Friedmanite helicopter drops or reactive conduits of credit-money drawings to finance working capital through pre-arranged credit lines by corporate borrowers.

Moore was directly challenged on particular aspects of his extreme horizontalism by Dymski (1988), Goodhart (1989), and Arestis and Howells

(1996), for instance. His loyal supporters include in particular Lavoie (1992, 1996) and Rochon (1999), who have also stressed important similarities or linkages with money circuit approaches (cf. Rochon and Rossi 2003, and earlier Deleplace and Nell 1996). Among Post Keynesian scholars who have contributed to this debate, including Arestis (1988), Hewitson (1995), Howells (1995), Kregel (1984–5), Graziani (1989), Messori (1991, 1995), Palley (1991), Rogers (1989), Smithin (1994), and Wray (1990, 1992), for instance, Chick (1983, 1992) and Dow (1996, 1997) may perhaps be singled out as representing the other end of the spectrum of views, arguing that banks too have liquidity preference and are dependent upon financial markets. Surveying the Post Keynesian literature on endogenous money, Fontana (2003) contrasts "accommodationist" and "structuralist" approaches (see also Dow 2006; Lavoie 2006b), but gives the impression that a lot of common ground may exist today in granting practical relevance to both money endogeneity as well as liquidity preference.

In fact, Chick and Dow propose a "nondualistic treatment" intended to demonstrate the "compatibility between the central tenet of the endogenous money story and liquidity preference" (Chick and Dow 2002: 594). They aim to overcome the usual textbook dualism between the interest rate and the money supply. And Lavoie (2008) proposes a novel Post Keynesian amendment to the "new [mainstream] consensus" titled "taking liquidity preference into account," with the amendment consisting of supplementing the usual monetary policy reaction function (featuring the short-term rate of interest only) by a "transmission mechanism equation" that shows the market rate of interest as a function of not just the policy rate, but also term and risk spreads. A "Minsky moment" (or "rush towards liquidity and riskless assets") is modeled as a rise in the risk premium. Lavoie concludes that monetary policy may have to react to turmoil in the financial system by easing monetary policy in order to shield the real economy.

I welcome these proposals. Bank behavior affects "the" rate of interest and liquidity simultaneously. The excess-bearish factor of the *Treatise* shows changes in the general public's liquidity preference as impacting on the rate of interest only to the extent that the banks do *not* offset such a move by enlarging the pool of liquidity. Nothing is automatic in all this though, but depends on the banks' own liquidity preference as well as profit (bank capital) considerations. Lavoie's novel amendment acknowledges that setting the overnight (policy) rate of interest is *not* equivalent to setting "financial conditions" (or "the" rate of interest Keynes was referring to in his analysis of price determination of debt securities and assets in general).[26] The next step would be to acknowledge that the banking system plays a key part in determining financial conditions, including bank credit and the stock of money[27] – or the "pool of liquidity" that is available at any time (and in that sense "given" and "exogenous") to satisfy the liquidity preference of the general public (including non-bank financial institutions), or to be drawn upon to finance any planned additions to current levels of economic activities. And the final step in meeting Keynes' vision would then be to realize that banks play an *active* part in setting financial conditions that is independent of the authorities' policy stance – posing a formidable challenge to the authorities to either marshal the banks' support, or offset their lack of such, in stabilizing the economy; a monetary production economy that is growing and evolving under conditions of true Keynesian uncertainty rather than probabilistic risk about known possible outcomes (somehow predetermined by the real forces of thrift and productivity through continuously clearing markets).

Apart from Keynes' pupils Joan Robinson and Richard Kahn as adherents to liquidity preference theory, Hyman Minsky can be singled out for adding illuminating insights to the vision of banks and finance as real forces in shaping economic growth and development in monetary production economies. In fact, Minsky's whole point is that forces inherent to the financial system, though in interaction with the real economy (namely, through interdependent cash flows and balances sheets), lead to *endogenous* financial instability – a disposition to be countered by appropriate policy actions. In returning to this issue in the concluding chapter I am going to emphasize that policy actions include macroeconomic policies as well as financial regulation.

Appendix

Table 5.1 Assets of London Clearing Banks, 1921–1936

Year	Absolute amounts (Annual averages, £million)				Shares of gross deposits (%)		
	Cash inc. balances at BoE	Total liquid assets	Invest-ments	Advances	Total liquid assets	Invest-ments	Advances
1921	211	679	331	833	37.5	18.3	46.0
1922	206	659	391	750	37.1	22.0	42.3
1923	197	582	356	761	34.8	21.6	46.3
1924	195	544	341	808	32.6	20.4	48.4
1925	196	539	286	856	32.4	17.2	51.5
1926	195	532	265	892	32.0	15.9	53.6
1927	198	553	254	928	32.3	14.8	54.2
1928	196	584	254	948	33.1	14.4	53.7
1929	194	568	257	991	31.6	14.3	55.1
1930	192	596	258	963	33.1	14.3	53.5
1931	182	560	301	919	31.8	17.1	52.2
1932	187	611	348	844	34.1	19.4	47.1
1933	212	668	537	758	34.2	27.5	38.8
1934	212	576	560	753	30.6	89.8	40.1
1935	215	623	615	769	31.2	30.8	38.5
1936	221	692	614	839	32.3	28.7	39.2

Source: Nevin and Davis 1970 (based on Bank of England Statistical Summary)

6 Keynes on central banking and the structure of monetary policy[1]

John Maynard Keynes' monetary works, from *A Tract on Monetary Reform* to *A Treatise on Money* and *The General Theory*, are well known for their insights into the functioning of monetary economies and the *conduct* of monetary policy in such a world, i.e. the appropriate goals of, and ways to implement, monetary policy. Less well known is that Keynes also thought carefully about the appropriate *structure* of monetary policy: the regulation of central banks in general and their relation to the state in matters of monetary policy.

In fact, in recent years discussions in monetary economics have often concentrated on the structure rather than the conduct of monetary policy. The notion of "central bank independence" in particular has received enormous popular attention as well as scientific support from a literature dealing with the so-called time-inconsistency problem allegedly afflicting "discretionary" arrangements in monetary policy.[2] While the notion of central bank independence is clearly meant to capture *some* elements of the relation between the central bank and the state implicitly held to be essential in solving the alleged time-inconsistency problem, it is often not made clear what the crucial responsibilities of an independent central bank exactly should be, and how and to whom it should be held to account on its performance. Yet it would seem to be of little use to claim anything for "independence" as such, and it may even be positively misleading to sell independence as a free lunch, when what really matters is the precise *form and degree* of independence.

It is thus of some interest that Keynes in 1932 provided an outline of a particular form and degree of independence that he thought would promote efficiency in the conduct of monetary policy and allow ultimate democratic control over policy to be retained at the same time. The analysis of Keynes' proposal of 1932 for a sound structure of monetary policy will be our main objective here.

However, as Keynes' proposal of 1932 itself is little more than a sketch of certain essential aspects, some of which may even sound ambiguous to the modern reader, I felt that some background might be helpful. We could then judge the proposal within the wider context of his monetary thought, particularly his evolving views on central banking and the structure of monetary policy. Section 6.1 therefore begins with a plan that Keynes had devised in 1913 for a central bank in India. Here the issue was whether a central bank should be established in the first place and, if so, what its functions and its relation to the state should be. Keynes' plan strictly refers to the classical gold-standard era and the Indian rupee's gold-exchange standard, conditions soon to be swept away.

Section 6.2 covers the monetary upheavals of World War I and its aftermath, leading first to Britain's return to gold in April 1925 and then to sterling's subsequent and final departure from gold in September 1931. While Keynes' views on the proper conduct of monetary policy were by then already strongly opposed to the nostalgic drive at monetary reconstruction that characterized the 1920s, we discuss further evidence on his views as to a sound structure of policy from this interim period, ending with the September 1931 sterling crisis. After discussing his proposal of 1932 in Section 6.3, the discussion in Section 6.4 briefly follows up on the early post-*General Theory* era, which saw Keynes as a director of the Bank of England between 1941 and 1946, and the bank's nationalization on 1 March 1946. Section 6.5 concludes.

Overall, the analysis shows that Keynes' 1932 proposal is an original contribution to the issue of central bank independence that is relevant to modern discussions. Not least, his proposal is of interest for its resemblance to the United Kingdom's new monetary arrangements introduced in May 1997 and enacted in the Bank of England Act 1998.

6.1 Keynes' plan for a central bank in India

Between 1906 and 1908, Keynes worked at the India Office in London. His appointment as a civil servant charged with Indian affairs led to *Indian Currency and Finance*, his first book, which was published in 1913, as well as his appointment to the Royal Commission on Indian Finance and Currency in the same year.

In *Indian Currency and Finance*, Keynes investigated the gold-exchange standard of the Indian rupee and its relation to sterling and the City of London, India's domestic banking system and money markets, and the organization of various central banking functions within India's existing multiple-reserve system. As regards currency arrangements, Keynes believed that "in her gold-exchange standard, and in the mechanism by which this is supported, India ... is in the forefront of monetary progress" (Keynes 1913a, JMK 1: 182). Any aspiration to establish a gold currency, in his view, would have been wholly unsuitable for India.

Keynes was less enthusiastic about banking arrangements in India. On the one hand, particular restrictions that had contributed to the banks' stability in the past came to present inefficiencies once stable currency arrangements became established. On the other hand, the spell of prosperity of the more recent past had been accompanied by strong deposit growth at declining cash reserve and at declining (paid-up) bank capital ratios, developments he considered dangerous in a country with a tradition of hoarding and bank runs.

Keynes' anxiety about the stability of the Indian banking system was closely related to his concern about the divorce between currency and banking authorities and the general lack of a central banking authority. Paying particular attention to the issue of crisis management, Keynes argued that in the absence of a central bank the government itself would have to act as lender of last resort by making its reserves directly available to the money markets in a crisis.[3] But in his view the issue of establishing a central bank went beyond the advantages of having a centralized pool of the government's reserves and the bankers' reserves when a crisis hits. A central banking authority would also provide a general direction for national banking policy and enforce prudence when it was needed. Moreover, the cooperation between banking and note issue would add elasticity to the system, thereby reducing interest rate volatility. Proposing that the issue of establishing a central bank would be a proper subject for inquiry by a Royal Commission, Keynes (1913b, JMK 15: 166) did not fail to convey his own preferences:

> At the present time the arguments in favor of a state bank for India are very strong ... The government have taken over so many of the functions of a central bank that they cannot wisely neglect the rest. A note issue of growing importance, the management of the government's cash balances, the regulation of the foreign exchanges – all these are controlled together and treated as a whole in a compact and admirably conceived scheme. But other benefits cannot be obtained easily, so long as these functions are utterly divorced from those of banking proper.

When *Indian Currency and Finance* was already in proof, Keynes was approached to serve on the Royal Commission on Indian Finance and Currency set up in May 1913. Keynes – aged 30 – came to play a conspicuous role on that commission, both in taking evidence from witnesses and in the drafting of the commission's report.[4] Yet, being highly controversial, the issue of establishing a central bank in India was not intended to be made a central subject of the commission's inquiry. The subject did not feature at all among the issues the commission had been appointed to study. Nevertheless, in their investigations the commissioners soon came to realize that the issue could hardly be ignored, although the Indian exchange banks, in particular, fearing competition from a new institution endowed with privileges, were strongly opposed to that idea. As a compromise the issue was excluded altogether from the main report but was dealt with in an annex, a "Memorandum on Proposals for the Establishment of a State [i.e. central] Bank in India." This memorandum was largely due to Keynes.[5]

Not surprisingly, then, the memorandum came down in favor of establishing an Indian central bank rather than continuing with the existing state of affairs with some central banking functions being performed by the "Independent Treasury System." For, Keynes argued, the state was already – in effect – bearing most central banking responsibilities, but it lacked a "suitable machinery" to meet them. Apart from its having direct advantages for the commercial world through, for example, reducing the range of fluctuation of the bank rate and its volatility, increasing bank branches and bringing sound banking facilities to remoter parts of India, Keynes (1913b, JMK 15: 197) stressed that he:

attach[es] great importance to the increased stability which a State Bank would introduce into the Indian banking system. India is not well placed at present to meet a banking crisis. The Presidency Banks are already banker's banks to an important extent, but they are not strong enough to support the whole burden. In effect the Government keeps a part of the banking reserves, but there is no machinery for bringing its reserves into normal connection with banking. With no central reserve, no elasticity of credit currency, hardly a rediscount market, and hardly a bank rate policy, with the growth of small and daring banks, great increase of deposits and a community unhabituated to banking and ready at the least alarm to revert to hoarding, even where it had been seemingly abandoned, there are to be found most elements of weakness and few elements of strength.

It is worth considering some details of the memorandum, the introduction to which begins with:

> A central bank must necessarily stand in a somewhat close relationship to Government. If the bank is to be useful, it must have the management of the Government balances and of the note issue. It would be contrary to experience elsewhere and to what seems reasonable for India to hand over these functions to a purely private institution. If Government is to interfere at all, it cannot help involving itself in ultimate responsibility for the bank, and if it is thus to involve itself, its powers must be sufficient to permit an effective supervision. From a Government with feeble powers and placed in the position of interested but irresponsible critics, there would be a greater likelihood of vexatious interference; while too great a dependence on the terms of the bank's charter must tend to make these too rigid and narrow for practice.
>
> (Keynes 1913b, JMK 15: 151)

Keynes' memorandum offers an "outline constitution" of the envisaged relations between the government, the central bank's decision-making bodies, and the shareholders. As regards shareholders, Keynes foresees a compromise role. On the one hand, he clearly regards as essential that the executive officials responsible for the policy and administration of the bank (the "central board") be appointed by government and rest under its ultimate responsibility. On the other hand, Keynes wishes to retain, and make use of, the commercial instincts and commercial knowledge of representatives of the shareholders – even if the banking business of the central bank may not be carried out with a purely commercial interest in view. Ownership of the central bank is thus to remain private, while the influence of shareholders would be chiefly consultative and advisory, and profits be partly due to the state. Keynes provides a detailed proposal on the capitalization of the central bank and the division of its profits, together with appendices on state banks and private capital and the division of the profits of the German Reichsbank. In his view, "Continental experience suggests ... that it is probably inadvisable for the Government to subscribe any part of the capital of the Bank itself" (Keynes 1913b, JMK 15: 165–6) – the rationale underlying this particular proposal being of some interest, not least since he changed his mind on this point later on. But in 1913, Keynes wrote:

> The presence of private capital is probably a considerable bulwark against some kinds of political pressure. Continental experience shows that private ownership of the Bank's capital, even although the shareholders have no more than advisory powers, is an important safeguard of the Bank's independence; and continental writers have laid great stress on this.
>
> (Keynes 1913b, JMK 15: 160)

As regards the central bank's decision-making bodies, one issue concerned the relation between the central board and the central bank's regional head offices. For Keynes saw it as a matter of great importance that in a large country like India a high degree of decentralization should be maintained in the day-to-day management of the bank. As a practical matter, Keynes proposed that the central bank should be erected upon the three existing "presidency banks"[6] that, as presidency head offices, then would become part of a decentralized central bank system. The "managers" of the presidency head offices would have much regional autonomy in conducting their local business, but along the guidelines set for them at the centre by the central board. The managers (or their deputies) would also serve as "assessors" on the central board, mainly for keeping the board in touch with local business conditions.

We thus turn to the core issue: the role of the central board and its relation to the government. As is apparent from his views on private ownership, Keynes was concerned about the central bank's "independence." He also states that "combin[ing] ultimate Government responsibility with a high degree of day-to-day independence for the authorities of the [central] Bank" (Keynes 1913b, JMK 15: 152) was one of the main difficulties he faced in devising a working constitution for that institution. But what form and degree of independence did he actually have in mind? What powers and duties, and what relationship *vis-à-vis* the government, did he foresee in practice? Fortunately, his outline is quite specific on these crucial questions, and his discussion of the "relation of the Bank to the Government" sheds some important light on its underlying rationale. In addition, annexed to the memorandum is another appendix titled "The Relation of State Banks to their Governments" (Keynes 1913b, JMK 15: 202–8), reviewing the situation in various countries.

The central board's projected duties "would be chiefly concerned with bank rate, with the remittance of funds from one Presidency to another, and between India and London, and with questions of general policy" (163). Of its three members the governor of the bank would act as chairman of the board, appointed for periods of five years (subject to an age limit but eligible for reappointment) by the king on the recommendation of the secretary of state, and removable in like manner. The other two members are one representative of government and a deputy governor, the former being an expert appointed by the viceroy, the latter being nominated by the other two court members.[7] In addition, there would be the assessors, namely three or more of the managers of the presidency banks, but who would have no voting rights. The central board's powers are wide but feature an escape clause:

Within the limits of the Bank Act, the Central Board shall have absolute authority, and the signature of the Governor supported by a majority vote of the Board shall be legally binding upon the Bank; save that the representative of the Government shall have discretionary power (for use in emergencies only) to suspend the carrying into effect of any decision until it has been reported to the Viceroy, with whom shall lie an ultimate right of veto.

(Keynes 1913b, JMK 15: 153–4)

Keynes explains in his discussion that the proposed method of appointment of the governor and deputy governor was "intended not to make them Government officials, but to place them in a position of considerable independence" (Keynes 1913b, JMK 15: 159). And he emphasizes that the two "should invariably be persons of commercial or banking, not of administrative or official, experience" (Keynes 1913b, JMK 15: 161). Furthermore, as regards the location of the central board, he mentions as an objection to Delhi that this would "place the Bank too much under the direct influence of Government" (Keynes 1913b, JMK 15: 163), although he does not appear to consider this as a decisive objection himself.

The core issue in securing the central bank's independence thus appears to be that of making sure that the execution of (central) banking business be under expert control. This was important, in Keynes' view, both to make the proposal acceptable to the commercial world and on efficiency grounds per se, as: "Banking business must be outside the regular Government machine, ignorant of 'proper channels,' and free of the official hierarchy where action cannot be taken until reference has been made to a higher authority" (Keynes 1913b, JMK 15: 160). At the same time, however, as Keynes emphasizes, the proposed arrangements would relieve the government of undue responsibilities, particularly:

As regards the Secretary of State's exposure to pressure or parliamentary criticism of an undesirable kind, the creation of a State Bank would, without question, improve and strengthen his position. Recent experience shows that he cannot, under the present system, resist cross-examination on minute details of financial management. ... The State Bank, on the other hand, would have a high degree of independence; and there would be numerous questions to which the Secretary of State's proper answer would be that it was entirely a matter for the Bank. He would never admit, for example, the faintest degree of responsibility for the precise level of the bank rate at a particular moment. The Secretary of State would be behind the Bank, but his authority would only come into play on rare and important occasions. On important changes of policy and on alterations of clauses in the Bank Act, the Secretary of State would have the last word and with it the responsibility.[8]

(Keynes 1913b, JMK 15: 158–9)

While bank rate policy would thus principally be part of the central bank's independence, i.e. discretion, it must be borne in mind here that Keynes' proposal refers to the peculiar situation of India at the time, with the Indian rupee being on a legal gold-exchange-standard link to sterling. Hence the Indian central bank that Keynes had in mind would not just have had to act in accordance with what was laid down for it in the Bank Act, but also within a fixed-exchange-rate constraint. Apart from the viceroy's veto right, ultimate responsibility over the currency would thus be vested with the state. In Keynes' view, the custody of the gold standard reserve should not be entrusted to the state bank either:

> Although the custody of the gold standard reserve and the ultimate responsibility for the maintenance of exchange must remain, in the most direct manner, with the Secretary of State, he should use the Bank as his agent in the actual sale in India of sterling drafts on London on the occasions in which the gold standard reserve is brought into play for the purpose for which it exists. The moment at which this reserve is brought into play ought not to depend, I think, upon anyone's discretion, but should be governed by rule. There should be a notification, that is to say, that the Government will at all times sell, through the Bank as its agent, sterling bills on London at [a certain price].
>
> (Keynes 1913b, JMK 15: 191–2).

6.2   The bumpy road from that "barbarous relic" to a "managed currency"

In *Indian Currency and Finance*, Keynes (1913a, JMK 1: 71) expressed the hope that the time may not be too far off when Europe "will find it possible to regulate her standard of value on a more rational and stable basis." In the event, martial circumstances abruptly ended the ancien régime (De Cecco 1974; Sayers 1976). Under such unfavorable conditions, though, the establishment of a more rational and stable basis for regulating the standard of value was bound to be intricate. Nevertheless, in late 1914, in a commentary on wartime financial events, Keynes (1914, JMK 11: 320) speculated optimistically about "the prospects of money:"

> If it proves one of the after effects of the present struggle, that gold is at last deposed from its despotic control over us and reduced to the position of a constitutional monarch, a new chapter of history will be opened. Man will have made another step forward in the attainment of self-government, in the power to control his fortunes according to his own wishes. We shall then record the subtle, profound, unintended, and often unnoticed influences of the precious metals on past historical events as characteristic of an earlier period. A new dragon will have been set up at a new Colchis to guard the Golden Fleece from adventures.

It took some 30 years and another world war before stability of currencies, internally and externally, was eventually regained. Under the Bretton Woods regime, gold was at last deposed from its despotic ruling over the world and reduced to the position of a constitutional monarch (with Keynes as one of the regime's chief architects; see Chapter 7). In Britain's case, however, the year 1931 marked another important watershed, as sterling finally went off gold and from then on became a genuinely "managed" currency. The purpose of this section is to survey his views on currency affairs in the years before the Keynesian revolution, ending almost concurrently with sterling's golden link, and at just the time when Keynes provided an outline of a sound structure of monetary policy for Britain. That outline will then be discussed in the next section.

At the beginning of the 1920s, Keynes the "dear money man" agitated against the inflationary boom of 1919–20 following World War I, favoring bank rate hikes sufficient to break inflation. As circumstances changed with the slump of 1921–2, Keynes strongly agitated against the opposite vice, deflation. There were ample opportunities for him to fight on the latter front until the onset of World War II (whereupon Keynes (1939a, JMK 9) favored preventing another wartime inflation by fiscal rather than monetary means).

What were at first the prospects, and then the actual protracted deflationary consequences, of sterling's return to gold at its pre-war parity, provided the background to both *A Treatise on Money* and *The General Theory*. But Keynes' position was already developed and most forcibly argued in *A Tract on Monetary Reform*: the proper aim of monetary policy should be to stabilize internal prices in general, rather than exchange rates in terms of gold in particular, both inflation and deflation must be avoided.

Unfortunately, the *Tract* remains altogether quiet on the issue of the structure of monetary policy, apart from Keynes' recommendation that the Bank of England and the Treasury should closely coordinate their monetary and debt management policies in order to secure proper control over banks' credit creation and the credit cycle. In fact, Keynes' dedication of the *Tract*, "humbly and without permission, to the Governors and Court of the Bank of England, who now and for the future have a much more difficult and anxious task entrusted to them than in former days" (Keynes 1923, JMK 4: xv), is almost conspicuous for avoiding the question of whether and what role government and Parliament should play in relation to the Bank of England, newly entrusted with that demanding task.

Nevertheless, it must be stressed that Keynes was swimming strongly against the current of the time in fully embracing the idea of a managed currency. For monetary orthodoxy was heading straight back to the gold standard. As one aspect of the general aspiration for a return to monetary stability, principally shared, of course, by Keynes (although not the suggested golden route), there were powerful calls for central bank independence in the 1920s.[9] The background to the popularity of that idea, however, was a budgetary rather than a purely monetary one, as some "wicked ministers of finance" had misused the printing press for "inflationary tax" purposes (analyzed with astute clarity in Chapter 2 of the *Tract*). Yet, returning to the *status quo ante*, restoring the old despot, that "barbarous relic," presented no choice of wisdom to Keynes. For, in his view, war events had brought about changes which could not easily be, and should not be, reversed:

> In truth, the gold standard is already a barbarous relic. All of us, from the Governor of the Bank of England downwards, are now primarily interested

in preserving the stability of business, prices, and employment, and are not likely, when the choice is forced on us, deliberately to sacrifice these to the outworn dogma, which had its value once, of £3. 17*s* 10.5*d.* Advocates of the ancient standard do not observe how remote it now is from the spirit and the requirements of the age. A regulated non-metallic standard has slipped in unnoticed. *It exists.* Whilst economists dozed, the academic dream of a hundred years, doffing its cap and gown, clad in paper rags, has crept into the real world by means of the bad fairies – always so much more potent than the good – the wicked ministers of finance.

(Keynes 1923, JMK 4: 138)

In short, there was in his view no escape from addressing a new management problem: "We have reached a stage in the evolution of money when a 'managed' currency is inevitable" (Keynes 1923, JMK 4: 159).

Interestingly, it was in the context of another Royal Commission on Indian Currency and Finance that Keynes, summoned to give evidence in late March 1926, provided some further insights into his views on the appropriate structure of monetary policy. After Britain's return to its pre-war gold parity on 28 April 1925, the Royal Commission was due to assess the wisdom of establishing a gold currency in India, replacing the existing system of practical stability of the rupee–sterling exchange without legal rate and with priority for preserving stability of internal prices when important external movements occurred. Not surprisingly, Keynes altogether rejected the wisdom of that proposal. Instead, his recommendation was to stick to the status quo and "do nothing whatever," commenting on the general state of currency affairs:

We are at the moment in a state of reaction on currency matters, not at all to be unexpected after the debauches of the War and post-war period. The world has seen the disadvantages and the abuses of unregulated currencies, and it is trying to seek salvation in conservatism, in going back, not in my opinion to the reality, but to the appearance of what existed in pre-war days. It is not impossible that out of this something wise may be evolved, but it is going to be very difficult. We are not at the end of currency discussions, but at the beginning of them. The future currency of the world is going to be determined not by what has happened in the last two or three years, but by what is going to happen in the next 10 years.

(Keynes 1926c, JMK 19: 491–2)

In the context of discussing the regulation of internal prices, Keynes was asked to whom the regulation of the currency should be entrusted. He replied that "the ideal arrangement is a central bank, which is in close touch with the Finance Department of the Government" (Keynes 1926c, JMK 19: 501). The discussion then turned to the relation of the bank to the government, and Keynes was asked whether he would be opposed to any suggestion that the central bank should work absolutely without any sort of direction from the Finance Department. Keynes answered, "I think it is very difficult. It is not desirable. The Indian finance Department is such a very big factor in the situation in their operations that it would be an inefficient way of conducting the bank not to be in very close touch with them, and if you are in very close touch with them it is impossible that they should not be taking a certain responsibility. That had better be faced at the outset" (Keynes 1926c, JMK 19: 504). His reply brought the commissioners on to an issue on which other witnesses seem to have laid much emphasis, namely, that in important European countries central banks were more or less independent of the government. Keynes (1926c, JMK 19: 504) suggested distinguishing between formal and informal arrangements, arguing that formally the Bank of England, being a private institution, was extremely independent, which, however, did "not in any way represent the facts." In practice, he argued, the government of the day would have the final word, even though the bank directors could make a great public scandal by resigning if they were strongly in opposition, summarizing the situation as

> a very transitional state in England in which the formal situation is more remote than it used to be from the actual situation. That is also the case in several other countries. There is a struggle going on as to where the equilibrium of power should lie. In the United States the precise relation of the Federal Reserve Board to the United States Treasury is in the process of evolution. It is impossible to make an up-to-date exact statement of what it is at any moment.
>
> (Keynes 1926c, JMK 19: 505)

The issue of the relation between the central bank and the government came up once more, with the commissioners questioning Keynes on whether responsibility for maintaining exchange should remain with the government, as Keynes had proposed in his memorandum of 1913, in which he had also recommended that the custody of the gold standard reserve should remain with the government. Keynes explained that his earlier proposal assumed a legal value of the rupee in terms of sterling, with the legal liability in relation to the currency remaining with the government. Furthermore, he also saw it as a compromise at the time as the central bank idea was not widely accepted. In 1926, by contrast, Keynes (1926c, JMK 19: 511) held that "if the central bank was, whilst administratively an independent entity, nevertheless in a sense a full organ of Government, then [he] should be inclined to centralize the whole thing and to put the whole matter in the hands of the bank." This reply led on to a most interesting exchange on the possibility of conflicts between the independent central bank charged with discount policy on the one hand, and another branch of government in charge of the exchange rate on the other. Clearly, this issue hinges on the kind of exchange-rate regime in place, and the norm under both the gold standard and the later Bretton Woods system of fixed (but adjustable) exchange rates, in Britain and most other countries, was that the central bank was neither in charge of legislating the price of gold nor of setting the exchange parity. Matters might be different though under flexible exchange rates, like in India in 1926 or Britain in 1932. Note, therefore, that although Keynes was interviewed on the particular case of India, his answers on the issue of conflict and coordination take a more general view, with Britain often serving as an illustrative example. Not so much the Britain of 1926 though, but how regulation might evolve there in the future. So when the commissioners wondered whether conflicts between the central bank and the Treasury might not arise if responsibilities were decentralized Keynes (1926c, JMK 19: 511) stressed: "I think it would be most important that they should be pursuing an agreed policy, wherever the final responsibility lay. It would be hopeless to have the bank responsible for the discount policy and pursuing a line which was not in accordance with the line of the Treasury in their responsibility for exchange." From this reply the commissioners inferred that in order to avoid possible conflicts both policies must be controlled by one body, "either the bank must take over both, or the Government must control the discount policy of the bank." Keynes' response to this suggestion is most revealing:

> I think in a sense that is true, but at any rate in English conditions, and I should have thought in Indian conditions, things are not quite so cut and dried in practice, and you can have two bodies which maintain their respective spheres of responsibility and of power and yet necessarily always work together. It is the fundamental question of the relation between any central bank and any Treasury. In a sense in any country it is quite unworkable that the two should be in antagonism. Therefore you might say, as a logical consequence of that, that one must be in subordination to the other, but I hope that is not true in practice, but that you can have two bodies neither of which is subordinate to the other but which must always act in co-operation with one another. It is a dilemma which you get in other spheres of government. My view in this country of the *future of regulation* would be that the Treasury and the Bank of England would be neither subordinate to the other but would always be pursuing the same policy. That may sound impossible, but I do not think it is.[10]
>
> (Keynes 1926c, JMK 19: 512; emphasis added)

And when the questioner tried to pin him down on whether or not the government would retain responsibility for varying the rate of exchange, Keynes affirmed and further elaborated:

> I conceive a central bank not as something which is independent of the Government in the sense in which a Bombay cotton mill is independent of the Government, but as an organ of the Government which has a certain independence of the executive; that is to say, that it is not a subordinate department of the Treasury, but is an organ of the Government on a level of authority with the Treasury. I think there is apt to be confusion between the Government as a sovereign body getting rid of responsibility, and some particular department of Government like the Finance Department, which at present has responsibility, having less responsibility. I think the change would mean that the Department of Finance would have less responsibility than it has now, but the Government of India, in a broad sense, would have just the same amount of responsibility as it has now. It is impossible to conceive a

sound system in which your central bank was really a private thing and was not subordinate to the sovereign instructions of the Government. ... I should not be able to conceive a situation in which the bank could fluctuate the exchange contrary to the wishes of the supreme authority of the Government.

(Keynes 1926c, JMK 19: 512–13)

In *The End of Laissez-Faire*, first published in July 1926, Keynes addressed the principal matter of state control in the economy head on. Among his most important *agendas* for state control, namely, "decisions which are made by *no one* if the state does not make them," the "deliberate control of the currency and of credit by a central institution" features prominently (Keynes 1926a, JMK 9: 291–2). Moreover, discussing the "ideal size for the unit of control and organization," Keynes singles out the Bank of England as an example of "semi-autonomous bodies within the State,"[11] the progress and recognition of which would, in his view, represent progress. Referring to a general tendency towards separation between ownership and control, the Bank of England is seen as an "extreme example," as it would be "almost true to say that there is no class of persons in the kingdom of whom the Governor of the Bank of England thinks less when he decides on his policy than of his shareholders" (Keynes 1926a, JMK 9: 290).[12]

The End of Laissez-Faire forms part of that episode in Keynes' life when he was involving himself not just in politics and economic policy matters generally, but also in the politics of the Liberal Party. In the summer of 1926, the Liberals charged a committee of experts to formulate a program of industrial policy the outcome of which appeared in January 1928, titled *Britain's Industrial Future*. According to Harrod (1951: 392), "Keynes' contributions were of central importance." Harrod particularly credits Keynes for drafting the chapter on currency and banking, Section 6.4 of which concerns the role of the Bank of England in the future of Britain as Keynes and the committee imagined it (cf. Moggridge 1992: 458).

On the issue of ownership, the Liberal Industrial Inquiry (1928: 414) clearly echoed Keynes' view of the Bank as "an admirable specimen of the 'semi-socialized' institutions which represent ... the true line of development," disagreeing with the idea of nationalizing the Bank of England. The key point is to make evident that the Bank is a national institution, acting in the national rather than in any special interests. In particular, shareholders' dividends should be permanently fixed at their present figure, and any surplus profits be either retained within the bank or be due to the Treasury.

On the issue of public control, the recommendation is that the Bank of England's control of the credit system "should be exercised more deliberately and systematically than hitherto" and that it "ought to become part of the recognized duties of the Bank of England to regulate the volume of credit, so far as possible [within its constraints *vis-à-vis* gold], with a view to the maintenance of steady trade conditions" (Liberal Industrial Inquiry 1928: 414). The overall drift of the argument, it seems, is one of clarifying the proper objectives and responsibilities of monetary policy, while changes in the formal constitution of the central bank, charged with bringing them into effect, are meant to strengthen rather than weaken the central bank's position, as "it is the aims and objects of the Bank rather than its position or its powers which need modification" (Liberal Industrial Inquiry 1928: 415). Finally, the program also suggests that the "co-operation between the Treasury and the Bank of England, which has inevitably become much closer than it was in pre-war years, should be expressly provided for in the inner Management of the Bank" (Liberal Industrial Inquiry 1928: 415).

Keynes' own relations with the Bank of England were often rather uncordial though. In May 1928, a Bill on the amalgamation of the wartime Treasury (Bradbury) currency note issue with that of the Bank of England appeared which attracted heavy criticism from Keynes, who argued that the Bill would inefficiently constrain the good judgment and discretion of the Bank of England's operation within the gold standard.[13] The Bank of England itself seems to have favored the Bill (Sayers 1976: ch. 12), for bad reasons, as Keynes' letter of 18 May 1928 to the editor of *The Times* suggests:

> The Bank of England thinks that it can burke discussion by not allowing the slightest change in outward forms, however obsolete and inconvenient. This is a great mistake. Besides, why should the Bank fear discussion? We do not want to be governed by masked men in false beards muttering "Mumbo Jumbo." But every wise reformer knows that the strength, prestige, and independence of the Bank of England are the corner-stones of a sound credit system in this country. Adequate profits, adequate reserves, adequate knowledge, and adequate freedom from interference by "interests," political and financial, are the necessary conditions for successful management. But the Bank will not, in the long run, increase its prestige or secure its future or avoid suspicion by putting forward a case which will not stand ten minutes' expert cross-examination, whilst its real reasons and motive, however praiseworthy, remain, like its profits and its statistics, secret and unavowed.
>
> (Keynes 1928a, JMK 19: 752)

Keynes' foremost academic preoccupation over the second half of the 1920s was his *Treatise on Money*, published in October 1930. The *Treatise* is a major work on monetary theory in general, and monetary control of the phenomenon of the credit cycle in particular. As regards the latter, Keynes' key concern is how the central bank, treated as an organ of national government, may best establish an unchallenged position of control over the banking system, which he regarded as crucial for the successful conduct of monetary policy. By contrast, Keynes makes hardly any specific proposals in the *Treatise* concerning the regulation of the central bank itself and its relation to the state, that is, the *structure* of monetary policy. In fact, the only discussion with a direct bearing on this issue is his critique of the existing regulation of the central reserves, particularly the note issue.

For one thing, Keynes (1930c, JMK 20: 235) argues that placing limits on the discretionary power of the central bank over the note issue, as an indirect means of avoiding its being subjected to imprudent financial demands of the government, was ill directed for that purpose, as "unfortunately an Act of Parliament is a very ineffective method of curtailing the powers of a government; and in almost every known case of stress and strain, in which the note regulations interfere with the wishes of the Government of the day, it is the former which have given way." But the existing note regulations were not merely useless in his view. Keynes thought them positively harmful. They represented an element of weakness rather than of strength in the central bank's position in relation to the banks by freezing the former's reserves from use; while, in Keynes' view, the idea that monetary management had to focus on controlling the note issue was obsolete anyhow. As to the "right principles of regulation," Keynes (1930c, JMK 20: 243) states:

> I believe that, in any civilized country today with a responsible government and a powerful central bank, it would be much better to leave the management of the reserves of the central bank to its own unfettered discretion than to attempt to lay down by law what it should do or within what limits it should act. What the law – or, failing the law, the force of a binding convention – should attend to is the regulation of the reserves of the member banks, so as to ensure that the decision as to the total volume of bank money outstanding shall be centralized in the hands of a body whose duty is to be guided by considerations of the general social and economic advantage and not of pecuniary profit.

The general drift of Keynes' argument here is clearly in favor of the central bank's discretion at the operational level. Particularly, he would not expect that "the rules of wise behavior by a central bank could be conveniently laid down – having regard to the immense complexity of its problems and their varying character in varying circumstances – by Act of Parliament" (Keynes 1930c, JMK 20: 234).[14] But Keynes did not want to leave it at the central bankers' discretion to decide what the "general social and economic advantage" would be. In light of his *Treatise* analysis, a policy directed at stable prices in general was the appropriate strategy to eliminate or dampen credit cycles and secure full employment of resources.[15] Accordingly, his final analysis of the possibilities of monetary control addressed the question: "Does it lie within the power of a central bank in actual practice to pursue a policy which will have the effect of fixing the value of money at any prescribed level? If, for example, the duty of preserving the stability of the purchasing power of money within narrow limits were to be laid upon a central bank by law, would it be possible for the central bank to fulfill this obligation in all circumstances?" (Keynes 1930c, JMK 20: 304). While Keynes did not specifically answer whether and how the central bank's objective(s) should be laid down *by law*, he clearly believed at the time that monetary policy would go a long way in controlling the rate of investment, which he saw as key to the overall stability of the system. And his following critique of the actual practice of monetary control at the time further corroborates how great an importance he attached to the need for transparency in the conduct of policy:

> The pre-war system did not do much to stabilize world prices or to ward off credit cycles – with such acts of God it did not consider itself in any way concerned. But it had one great advantage – everyone knew quite clearly what

principles would govern the Bank of England's actions and what they would have to expect in given circumstances. The post-war system has substituted a most efficacious "management" for the old "automatic" system which is all to the good; but, at present, no one knows exactly to what objects the "management" is directed or on what principles it proceeds. It can scarcely claim hitherto to have tried to apply scientific principles to the attainment of the economic optimum, in the light of day and with the assistance of expert discussion and criticism, but proceeds to unknown destinations by the methods described in the City as "the hidden hand."

(Keynes 1930c, JMK 20: 207)

During the final stages of his work on the *Treatise* Keynes became a member, and dominated the proceedings, of the Committee on Finance and Industry. Commonly known as the Macmillan Committee, it met from 1929 to 1931. In his own evidence to the committee Keynes made numerous proposals to strengthen the Bank of England's resources and its position in relation to the markets. For one thing, Keynes was concerned about the City's external short-term (net) indebtedness combined with a rather small amount of gold resources at the bank. As regards the bank's internal position, he thought that a larger mass of securities would better enable the bank "to force its will on the market." At the same time a larger portfolio of earning assets would raise earning power correspondingly, an insufficiency of which, Keynes feared, might otherwise embarrass the Bank of England in the pursuance of monetary policy, namely, in a long period of cheap money.

This particular point led on to some discussion – and guesses – about the bank's hidden (capital) reserves, and the role of private shareholders.[16] Keynes saw the following "dilemma." On the one hand, a private institution in a privileged position would be open to the charge of keeping excessive reserves if it disclosed its true resources. On the other hand, understatement of its true resources would risk the criticism that they were running on a low margin, a charge that would hardly help in fulfilling the bank's responsibilities. When the argument was then put forward that private shareholders would make it more difficult to apply pressure to the central bank than if it were a public institution, Keynes (1930c, JMK 20: 248) replied, "I think they are depending on a broken reed. The fact that there are certain shareholders in the background is worth nothing. It is one of those pretences that will never stand any strain." Cecil Lubbock, a Bank of England director (and deputy governor, 1923–5 and 1927–9), came back on this point and suggested that "the Bank does attach very great value to the fact that its position makes it independent and free from any political pressure – or as far as possible." And Keynes responded, "I think they do, but that does not depend on the fact that they have private shareholders" (Keynes1930c, JMK 20: 248).

But Keynes (1930c, JMK 20: 262) also held that public ownership and the bank's profits should not interfere with the pursuance of monetary policy, arguing that he "should be opposed to interesting the Treasury in any way in the profits of the Bank of England." Accordingly, he suggested that the payments of the bank to the Treasury should be fixed, the two departments be amalgamated, and the

Bank of England be given "absolute discretion over the form of the assets," rather than merely acting as trustee in the management of the securities of the Issue Department. Because the Chancellor of the Exchequer is interested in his revenue, the Bank of England "ought to have the whole of its assets at its disposal, at its unfettered discretion, for the sole objective of the safest and best management of the monetary system, not having to earn a revenue for interests that are committed to its charge" (Keynes 1930c, JMK 20: 241). In summing up his position, he said that he "should like to see [the Macmillan] Report centre round the magnification and evolutionary enlargements of the functions of the Bank of England" (Keynes 1930c, JMK 20: 241 265).[17] Finally, it is worth quoting at some length from that part of his evidence which deals with the role of transparency in central banking. For on this occasion Keynes elaborates on the underlying rationale of conducting monetary policy transparently:

> I attach enormous importance particularly in the long period to getting rid of unnecessary secrecy and mystery of all kinds. ... The more we get rid of unnecessary secrecy and mystery the more we can facilitate informed outside criticism. We increase the freedom with which the Bank officials can discuss the position and make use of collective wisdom. If everything is secret and everything has to be discussed in confidence the circle within which opinions can be freely exchanged is unduly narrowed. I think also that greater publicity of all kinds will lead to better understanding by the market of what the Bank's intentions are, and that will facilitate those intentions being carried into effect quicker and with more certainty. It nearly always pays the market to adapt itself to the real intentions of the Bank. So that the easier it is to interpret those, the quicker in effect will be the methods of control which the Bank uses. Publicity will also help to educate the public and the world and bring much nearer the day, which I am sure we should all welcome, when the principles of central banking will be utterly removed from popular controversy and will be regarded as a kind of beneficent technique of scientific control such as electricity or other branches of science are. ... It will, at any rate, be brought nearer by making possible a rational discussion of these subjects. The Bank of England by its mystery, I think not only retards scientific progress, but, instead of rendering itself less open to popular pressure and to dangerous charges, renders itself more open to these things.
>
> (Keynes 1930c, JMK 20: 241 262–3)

The Macmillan Report was published on 13 July 1931, the day of the Danat Bank's failure, with Germany having recourse to a two-day bank holiday. Severe and widespread banking crises were on the verge of developing, or already on the way, on the Continent and in the United States in particular, while sterling was also increasingly coming under pressure. Keynes was not far off the mark when on 13 August 1931 he wrote to Richard Kahn, "We should be off [gold], I should say, within a month unless heroic measures are taken" (Keynes 1931e, JMK 20: 594–5). On 21 September 1931 sterling went off gold. Economically, no doubt, sterling's early devaluation and fairly quick transition to a long run of easy money helped to save Britain from the worst calamities of the Great Depression as experienced elsewhere. Politically, sterling's final departure from gold was shortly preceded by the fall of the second Labour government for failure to cope with the soaring sterling crisis, followed by the first national government of August 1931, still with Philip Snowden as Chancellor of the Exchequer, then followed by the second national government of November 1931, again under Ramsay MacDonald but now with Neville Chamberlain as Chancellor. At any rate, sterling's de-linking from gold in September 1931 paved the way for a managed currency in Great Britain (see Moggridge 1972; Sayers 1976). And it provided the background to the Labour Party's policy pamphlet on *Currency, Banking and Finance* (1932), which provoked Keynes' critical review of Labour's ideas of bringing the Bank of England under public ownership and control.

6.3   Keynes' plan for a sound structure of monetary policy in a managed currency regime

Keynes seemed to be at pains to give the Labour Party's 1932 policy pamphlet on currency, banking and finance a favorable reception (see Moggridge 1992: 467–8). Although Keynes supported some Labour positions and therefore tried to make his criticisms sound gentle overall, he actually strongly opposed those particular proposals relating to the Bank of England's independence and structure of monetary policy. Contrary to the Chancellor of the second national government and the Bank of England's long-time Governor Montagu Norman, who both hung on to the idea of an ultimate return to gold, Labour favored a "managed sterling currency." Keynes (1932e, JMK 21: 129) considered it of "first-class importance that the progressive, experimental policy should be expressly endorsed by the second party in the state," namely that monetary policy should aim primarily at stability of value in terms of wholesale prices rather than in terms of an international standard such as gold. In fact, he argues, Labour's pamphlet sets "forth a moderate and quite practical monetary policy for adoption by the political party which represents the only organized body of opinion outside the National Government, and which will therefore be called on some day, presumably, to form an alternative government" (Keynes 1932e, JMK 21: 128).

Keynes' two-part critique appeared in the *New Statesman and Nation* on 17 and 24 September 1932, titled "The Monetary Policy of the Labour Party." While his positive response to Labour's first resolution on the managed sterling currency comes as no surprise, his reaction to Labour's second resolution relating to the nationalization of the Bank of England is of particular interest here. For it most directly concerns the *form and degree* of independence of the Bank of England that Keynes considers appropriate for managing the envisaged sterling standard. Again, Keynes starts on a positive note, judging it wise and prudent that Labour dropped their former proposal to nationalize not just the Bank of England but the joint stock banks (the "Big Five") as well, a measure that he thought was quite unnecessary for "the purpose of handling the vital controls." But he clearly does not approve of Labour's planned provisions for the Bank of England, although finding it "not unnatural, after what has occurred, that this resolution should have been so drafted," namely, "that the Bank of England should be brought under public ownership and control; and that the Governor of the Bank should be appointed by the Government and be subject to the general direction of a Minister of Cabinet rank, who should in turn be responsible to the House of Commons for banking policy; the day-to-day business of the Bank being carried on by the Governor and his subordinates" (Keynes 1932e, JMK 21: 130; here Keynes is quoting from what he refers to as a "penny pamphlet" by the Labour Party on currency, banking and finance).

Against this Labour proposal, Keynes then summarizes his own position in the form of "five propositions as embodying the essentials." The first proposition reads: "The interest of private shareholders in the profits of the Bank, nominal though it now is, should altogether cease" (Keynes 1932e, JMK 21: 131). Contrary to the orthodox view of 1932, public ownership was a clear-cut case to Keynes. His evidence to the Macmillan Committee makes it clear that he now considered private shareholders not only as playing no positive part in the management of the central bank at all (in contrast to his earlier views of 1913), but that the "pretence" actually weakened the bank. His second proposition underlines the first, stressing that the central bank be put on a secured track and that it be seen, as a disinterested public body, as pursuing nothing but the national interest: "The Bank should be expressly recognized as a national institution from which private profits and private interest are entirely excluded. The directorate should be selected on public grounds and should not stand for the interest of the City any more than for other national interests" (Keynes 1932e, JMK 21: 131).

Departing slightly from his ordering of propositions, in the light of the previous section it should come as no surprise, and require no further comment, that Keynes reserved one proposition especially for the issue of openness and transparency of conduct. Proposition 5 reads: "The day-to-day policy of the Bank, its statistics, its technique and its immediate aims and objects should be as public as possible, and should be deliberately exposed to outside criticism" (Keynes 1932e, JMK 21: 131).

The remaining propositions deal with the most delicate matter of all, the issue of public control of the central bank, describing the core principles of division of responsibilities. Clearly, Keynes disapproved of Labour's contemplated form of democratic control in which the governor of the central bank would be "subject to the general direction of a Minister of Cabinet rank, who should in turn be responsible to the House of Commons for banking policy." Already in his "Indian plan" of 1913 he disliked the idea that a minister should be in charge of, and have to answer to Parliament on, expert matters of (central) banking policy. The previous section provided more evidence from the 1920s for the interpretation that Keynes did not want the central bank to be directly subordinated to any minister, but to cooperate on an even level with the Treasury, both contributing in a coordinated way towards the government's general policy. His third proposition of 1932 reads: "The management of the Bank should be ultimately subject to the Government of the day and the higher appointments should require the approval of the Chancellor of the Exchequer" (Keynes 1932e, JMK 21: 131). In fact, Keynes' subsequent discussion shows that the crucial role of the government of the day was to lay down the "main lines of policy," which I presume in the light of the previous analysis to refer to the ultimate aims or goals of policy.

The government in turn would not be completely free in stipulating its main lines of policy though. The government of the day would need to consider the "norm" of the currency system, as Keynes' fourth proposition foresees that "the principles of the currency system, e.g., whether or not the standard should be gold, or whether stability of wholesale prices or of the cost of living or of some other index, is to be its norm, should be determined by Parliament" (Keynes 1932e, JMK 21: 131).

As if to balance these various checks on the central bank's scope for discretion, as imposed by Parliament's "norm," the "main lines of policy" of the government of the day, and informed outside expert criticism (if conduct is transparent), Keynes adds a sixth proposition, supposing the other five were accepted. The sixth proposition affirms his opposition to Labour's proposed form of democratic control, establishing a principle meant to guarantee that expert opinion dominate where it should. The principle reads: "The less direct the democratic control and the more remote the opportunities for parliamentary interference with banking policy the better it will be" (Keynes 1932e, JMK 21: 131).

The subsequent discussion sheds further light on Keynes' underlying rationale for his preferred structure of monetary policy, explaining (to the Labour Party, in particular) that the envisaged monetary policy would engage the Bank of England "in the practice of a very difficult technique, of which Parliament will understand less than nothing. A planned economy will be impracticable unless there is the utmost decentralization in the handling of expert controls" (Keynes 1932e, JMK 21: 131).

While central bank independence is thus seen as an appropriate means to an efficient conduct of monetary policy, namely, by protecting the monetary technicians in the handling of the expert controls, ultimate democratic control over monetary policy would nevertheless be retained. The monetary technicians will neither be directly accountable to Parliament nor to the public. Instead, they will be held to account by the government of the day, on the basis of the latter's prerogative to establish the main lines of policy (with exposure to outside criticism providing additional scrutiny). In turn, the government will be accountable on overall performance of economic policy to Parliament, and thereby also to the electorate. This, it would seem, is simply following the normal democratic principles, applied with a view to securing expertise in the conduct of a difficult technique. Keynes' following observation is noteworthy for its clear distinction between the "powers or structure" of the central bank on the one hand, and its actual conduct of monetary policy in recent years on the other. Interestingly, his verdict puts the ultimate blame for the poor conduct of policy not at the independent technicians' door, but at the door of the "higher authority" – for failing to prescribe clearly what the technicians' discretion should be aiming at:

> It has been the recent policy of the Bank of England, rather than its powers or structure, which has been at fault. Its independence and its prestige are assets. Nor, in spite of its origins and the opportunity for interested motives on the part

of the directorate, can its public spirit over the last decade be called in question. The demand for its subjection to the democracy largely arises, I think, out of peculiarities of recent years which will not characterize a normal regime. More often than not since the War the country has possessed no defined standard and not even a defined monetary policy laid down by Parliament; with the consequence that the Bank of England has been left free to exercise, though it has not been loath to exercise, a wider discretion than it ought to have or has had in the past or will have in the future, on matters which go far beyond the practice of a technique for the attainment of a purpose, the general character of which has been laid down by higher authority.

(Keynes 1932e, JMK 21: 132)

Keynes goes still further out of his way in defending the bank's Governor Montagu Norman, his expertise as a technician and disinterestedness as a public servant. Keynes had often severely criticized and strongly opposed Norman's advice as to the main lines of policy, "the choice of which, as distinct from the execution, was not properly [Norman's] affair at all but that of the Government of the day" (Keynes 1932e, JMK 21: 132; see Sayers 1957: 71). Keynes seems fully aware of how much depends on the personalities[18] involved when he speaks of the charm and powers of persuasion of Montagu Norman:

A man who can successively induce Mr Winston Churchill, Mr Philip Snowden, and Mr Neville Chamberlain to feed out of his hand, unfortified by success, preaching unpopular and austere courses, would be important under any form of government. With the personalities the same and knowledge no greater, it might not have made much difference if the machinery which the Labour Party desires had been in operation during the last ten years.

(Keynes 1932e, JKM 21: 132–3)

When these essentials for an efficient and democratic structure of monetary policy were written down, their author could not be sure yet that the monetary affairs of the future would be strongly influenced, at least for a while, by another man of charm and exceptional powers of persuasion, Keynes himself. For in 1931–2, when the managed sterling currency became a matter of fact, the stage was (almost) set for the Keynesian revolution in economic theory and policy.

6.4 The "Keynesian revolution" and the role of monetary policy

In fact, the above "essentials" of a sound structure of monetary policy were composed at a critical stage of the evolution of Keynes' monetary thought, namely only shortly before the time of Keynes' discovery of the "principle of effective demand," which was going to revolutionize monetary theory.[19] We know that important changes occurred between the *Treatise* and *The General Theory* at the level of theory (Bibow 2000). And we also know that Keynes' views on the appropriate role and conduct of monetary policy changed accordingly (Moggridge and Howson 1974). For aiming at stability of general prices may not be enough to counter business cycles and secure full employment, as in the *Treatise*, when the system was generally capable of getting stuck in an "unemployment equilibrium" at stable prices (or, stable inflation), as shown in *The General Theory*. In a situation of nonstructural unemployment, monetary policy might be able to permanently raise the level of activity towards its full employment potential and perhaps even without any significant price increases. Moreover, the level of structural unemployment is unlikely to be neutral with regard to monetary factors.

But these are all issues concerning the conduct of policy, the proper goals of policy in particular. And there seems to me no logical reason why these insights should have necessarily affected Keynes' views on the sound structure of monetary policy as well, in one way or another. Yet, given that Keynes' fame and influence in both theory and practical affairs is nowadays almost exclusively seen in the context of *The General Theory* and what arose out of that work, one would all the more like to be able to confirm the proposition that the Keynesian revolution left his views on the structure of policy unchanged. Unfortunately, I have not been able to unearth any evidence in this regard, in either way. Of course, *The General Theory* highlights, in a way, the technical difficulties of monetary control. For the analysis displays the key importance of guiding financial market expectations in the conduct of monetary policy, with the possibility of communication failures rendering policy ineffective (so-called liquidity traps; see Chapter 5 above). It is thus of interest that Keynes (1936a, JMK 7: 203) stressed the role of confidence in this very context:

> Thus a monetary policy which strikes public opinion as being experimental in character or easily liable to change may fail in its objective of greatly reducing the long-term rate of interest, because M_2 [liquidity held (primarily) to satisfy the speculative motive] may tend to increase almost without limit in response to a reduction of r [the long-term rate of interest] below a certain figure. The same policy, on the other hand, may prove easily successful if it appeals to public opinion as reasonable and practicable and in the public interest, rooted in strong conviction, and promoted by an authority unlikely to be superseded.

Furthermore, the analysis in *The General Theory* clearly implies that economic policies must avoid becoming a source of instability and must be closely coordinated and directed at a common goal. But Keynes' magnum opus remains generally quiet on issues of economic policy and, in particular, on the structure of monetary policy.

As the final episode of our narrative we thus briefly turn to the Bank of England's nationalization in March 1946 (see Fforde 1992; Howson 1993). For Keynes was a director of the Bank of England from October 1941 until his death on 21 April 1946 (having just been reappointed under the bank's new constitution from 1 March 1946 for a three-year period). In addition, Keynes held a highly influential, although unofficial, position at the Treasury during World War II.

In these final years of his life Keynes gained the peak of his influence, both in academia and in shaping public policy in Britain and the world (see also his role in shaping the post-war international monetary order discussed in the next chapter).

It may thus seem paradoxical that apparently Keynes was little involved in the process of the bank's nationalization, beginning in late July 1945 when the new Labour government took office. But the fact that he was abroad at the time and preoccupied with the American Loan negotiations when the Bill was prepared under Hugh Dalton in almost no time and then rushed through legislation probably explains this paradox.[20] Nevertheless, there is evidence that Keynes discussed the bank's nationalization with Graham Towers, governor of the Bank of Canada, in Ottawa in early September 1945. At Keynes' suggestion, Towers wrote a memorandum on the relationship between the Canadian government and the central bank; Towers sent the memo to Keynes in Washington, who then passed it on to Hugh Dalton at the Treasury, but not without sending a private copy to Lord Catto too (Governor of the Bank of England from 1944).

According to Towers, informally the Canadian structure of monetary policy featured a joint responsibility of the government and the central bank, with the latter being also, in a way, directly responsible to the general public. The covering letter to Catto is written in a very neutral tone, with Keynes taking no position on the issue. Towers' hand-written note attached to his memo says that its author had urged the use of the Canadian model, but thought to have failed (Bank of Canada Archives; Fforde 1992: 14–15). It is easy to see that Towers' views were in conflict with Keynes' 1932 proposal (Keynes 1932e).[21] And it is equally easy to see that the Bank of England's role as a mere instrument of the Treasury clashed with Keynes' position too.

We have already noted that Keynes was preoccupied at the time with other, more urgent matters. Perhaps Keynes thought that the course of time was such as to bring forth a structure of monetary policy which suited (old) Labour's ideas of public control anyway.[22] Maybe he thought that, being both influential at the Treasury as well as a director of the Bank of England, he would be well positioned to shape the conduct of policy under any regime.[23] But that is pure speculation. The fact is that within weeks of the enactment of the bank's new constitution Keynes was dead.

6.5 Conclusion

Keynes' pre-World War I contributions to Indian currency and financial affairs show that he attributed great importance to the existence of central banking institutions both as underwriting the stability of the financial system and as instruments of monetary policy, a given in all his later monetary works. Clearly, Keynes neither subscribed to the view that a civilized country might be better off without such an institution nor did he see any wisdom in rigid statutory rules that would unduly constrain the central bank's operational discretion and weaken its position and powers in relation to the financial system, as he thought was the case due to certain (currency school-inspired) regulations of the Bank of England.

Rather, Keynes viewed central banks as a crucial central control for the deliberate "management" of the currency and credit.[24]

On the issue of ownership of the central bank, Keynes started out in 1913 in favor of private shareholders playing a constructive part in central banking business, even when ultimate control and responsibility for the currency rested with the state. In the second half of the 1920s he more and more emphasized the importance of the central bank being seen as a national institution, acting purely with the national interest in view, and in his evidence to the Macmillan Committee in 1930 he argued that private shareholdings may therefore weaken the Bank of England. By 1932, Keynes seems to have come round to the view that this aim was probably best achieved by excluding any remaining private interests in the Bank of England's profits, endorsing Labour's position to nationalize the Bank of England. On this issue, then, there is neither any evidence nor reason to suspect that Keynes might have opposed the actualization in 1945–6 of Labour's earlier plans.

On the intricate issue of public control, Keynes from 1913 onwards disliked the idea of direct democratic control by subjecting the central bank to the general direction of a cabinet minister in turn responsible to Parliament. For one thing, he favored institutions of decentralization in controlling the economy. Moreover, in his view, democratic control over monetary policy should better be indirect, and the operations of the central bank, seen as essentially technocratic, be securely under expert control. If anything, Keynes' concern about firmly placing the central bank in a hegemonic position over the financial system, equipped with powers for effective guidance and leadership, grew stronger over time, together with his awareness of the intricacies involved and importance attached to this factor in view of his evolving monetary thought.

As to the specific arrangements for achieving a proper division of responsibilities in public control over monetary policy, Keynes was fully aware that a difficult balancing act was involved. On the one hand, he saw important merit in the decentralization in the handling of expert controls and in 1924 and 1926 rejected the idea of subordinating the central bank to the Treasury (or *vice versa*!). On the other hand, he stressed the need for close cooperation between the central bank and the Treasury, always pursuing the same policy as decided by the government. And on this last and most crucial issue, the Keynes plan of 1932 makes it clear that the independent central bank Keynes envisaged had no business in deciding the "main lines of policy."

In the managed-currency world long desired by Keynes and by then achieved, the government would have to choose from a wider array of objectives for monetary policy to meet, and its selection of policy goals (and its actual performance) would be the proper subject of parliamentary criticism. The central bank, in turn, would be held to account on its performance by the government. Interestingly, Keynes' verdict of 1932 on the poor conduct of monetary policy over recent years did not put the ultimate blame at the Bank of England's door, but at the door of the higher authorities in the state. The state might wish to delegate some aspects of responsibility in the conduct of monetary policy to an independent central bank.

But it cannot deny responsibility in the event that it (1) chooses either inappropriate goals for policy or selects incompetent technicians for pursuing them; or (2) fails to lay down clearly what the technicians' discretion should be aiming at in the first place.

I see no logical reason why Keynes should have changed his views on a sound structure of monetary policy after 1932 in light of his *General Theory*; but I was unable to uncover any conclusive evidence to either confirm or reject this proposition. No doubt though *The General Theory* significantly changed Keynes' opinions about the appropriate goals of monetary policy and the real effects of money. Given my remark at the beginning that Keynes' 1932 outline for a sound structure of monetary policy may bear some resemblance to the *structure* of monetary policy as established in the United Kingdom in 1997–8, I must therefore stress that this should not be understood as a suggested approval by Keynes of any aspect of the *conduct* of monetary policy as currently practiced in the United Kingdom. Nor is this to put forward any claim to the effect that Keynes should be seen as the godfather of the United Kingdom's new monetary arrangements.

Rather, it appears to me that both the new arrangements as well as Keynes' proposal of 1932 may simply reflect the peculiar values and traditions of a very old democracy, genuinely shared by Keynes. Other countries, then, would seem to favor different *forms and degrees* of central bank independence, including some varieties that completely de-couple monetary policy from any democratic control and accountability, and even without clearly prescribing the independent policymaker's objective function. Keynes' 1932 contribution may be seen in highlighting that a sound *structure* of monetary policy should be aiming at both efficiency in the conduct of policy as well as democratic accountability; with *no* real trade-off being involved here.

7 The international monetary order and global finance

Keynes' ideas and global vision[1]

7.1 Introduction

The analysis up to this point has followed the "closed economy" approach of *The General Theory* and largely abstracted from international considerations. In this chapter we will extend the analysis to the global context, focusing on Keynes' ideas and global vision as laid down in his plan of the early 1940s for an "International Clearing Union." This extension will not only illustrate the application of liquidity preference theory when international interdependencies are taken into account, but also the ways in which Keynes thought his ideas could be best mastered for policy purposes through design of adequate international institutions. We will then discuss the evolution of the international monetary order as actually set up at Bretton Woods and the emergence of "global imbalances" in the light of Keynes' monetary thought and Clearing Union proposals in Chapter 8.

This chapter begins with some observations on Keynes' lack of love for the gold standard, followed in Section 7.3 by a review of the evolution of his views on the international monetary order, his various reform proposals in this area, and how they relate to his advances in monetary theory. Section 7.4 then focuses more specifically on Keynes' Clearing Union plan, while Section 7.5 further discusses the notion of hoarding and the role of capital controls in the Keynes plan. Section 7.6 concludes.

7.2 The end of British supremacy and the Englishman who dethroned gold

Keynes grew up during the heydays of the gold standard, when Great Britain was the supreme global economic and financial power, the City of London at the center of global finance, and the Bank of England in the position of "conductor of the international orchestra" providing guidance for global financial conditions within the limits set by "the rules of the game."[2] Despite taking the gold standard for granted in his monetary writings until the *Treatise of Money*, the regime never struck Keynes as representing much economic wisdom. From the beginning he thought that a smarter monetary order could be devised. It is fair to say that Keynes remained a monetary reformer throughout his life, with his monetary reform proposals evolving along with his advances in monetary theory.

For instance, in his first major monetary work *Indian Currency and Finance* of 1913, Keynes judged that establishing a gold currency would have been wholly unsuitable for India, since her existing "gold-exchange standard [was putting India] in the forefront of monetary progress" (Keynes 1913a, JMK 1: 182). As to policy closer to home Keynes held out the hope that the time may not be far off when Europe "will find it possible to regulate her standard of value on a more rational and stable basis" (Keynes 1913a, JMK 1: 71). When World War I then brought the ancien régime to an abrupt end Keynes, in a commentary on wartime financial events, saw the possibility that a "new chapter of history" might open up "if it proves one of the after effects of the present struggle, that gold is at last deposed from its despotic control over us and reduced to the position of a constitutional monarch" (Keynes 1914, JMK 11: 320).

These early hopes were frustrated for sure. World War I and the Peace Treaty of Versailles left Europe in a state of economic, financial and political disarray – as acutely diagnosed and brutally criticized in *The Economic Consequences of the Peace* (Keynes 1919), a work that emphasized international economic interdependencies. While the 1920s saw vain attempts at monetary restoration that meant deflation and mass unemployment in Britain's case, the 1930s brought on even deeper and more global harm as the Great Depression hit, with soaring unemployment and protectionism nourishing the climate that would see the world end up in yet another catastrophic world war.

So it was only towards the end of his life, in the early 1940s, that Keynes finally got his chance at contributing toward putting the global economy on a "more rational" international monetary foundation. And in the script for his envisioned new and better post-war order we are thus not surprised to read that Keynes thought he had "completely dethroned gold in polite language" and effectively "substituted bank money for gold" (Keynes 1942b, JMK 25: 140). Presumably as a tribute to both his fundamental breakthroughs in monetary theory and powers of persuasion, Harrod (1951: 340) observed that "Keynes, almost single-handedly, killed that most ancient and venerable institution."

The next section reviews the evolution of Keynes' monetary thought in relation to his progressing ideas about international monetary arrangements, culminating in his proposals of the early 1940s for the post-war world – to be discussed in more detail in Sections 7.4 and 7.5.

7.3 International monetary order, national policy space and monetary theory

The immediate aftermath of World War I was characterized by economic instability of a degree unknown to the pre-war era, the stability of which was widely attributed to the gold standard order. The Zeitgeist of the early 1920s was such that political establishments felt generally disinclined toward monetary experiments, but inclined to supporting restoration of the old order. The international Brussels Conference Declaration of 1920 favored the creation of independent central banks (Kisch and Elkin [1928] 1930). The rationale was to thereby deny the state access to the printing press.[3] Another international conference followed two years later at Genoa, shortly before which Keynes had published "the first of many 'Keynes Plans' for the international monetary system" (Moggridge 1992: 377). It is noteworthy that in "The stabilization of the European exchanges: a plan for Genoa" (Keynes 1922b) Keynes still advocated a gold bullion standard as the only *practicable* solution available at the time. His key concern was to stabilize exchange rates at prevailing market rates rather than return to pre-war parities while adding flexibility to the system through wider gold points.

Britain's ambition to return to gold at sterling's pre-war parity provided Keynes' main battlefield in the years to come. One key issue was the deflation this imposed on Britain under given circumstances. Another, more general and fundamental, issue was the subordination of domestic stability to some external commitment, categorically rejected by Keynes in *A Tract on Monetary Reform*.

In the *Tract* Keynes argued strongly that monetary policy should primarily aim at domestic stability – stability of prices, credit, and employment – rather than exchange rate stability. This prescription followed from a detailed analysis of the real consequences of price level instability, both inflations and deflations. Maintaining price level stability was seen as an integral part of smoothing the business ("credit") cycle. Keynes' call for a policy focus on domestic stability did not imply a plea for flexible exchange rates though. While primarily focusing on domestic stability central banks should also anchor exchange rates and avoid purely temporary exchange rate fluctuations through foreign exchange market interventions. Gold was to be largely demonetized and only meant to serve as ultimate safeguard and reserve in the international sphere.

The advice Keynes offered in his *Tract* (dedicated to the Governors and the Court of the Bank of England) was primarily targeting the British authorities. Even as a notional war victor Britain had lost its former hegemonic position in global monetary and financial affairs to the rising power the United States of America. Internationally, the Bank of England was no longer the "conductor of the orchestra." This made a reorientation in currency management all the more urgent. Keynes (1923, JMK 4: 138) famously declared that "in truth, the gold standard is already a barbarous relic." And the following observations underline his assessment of a fundamentally changed situation: "Gold itself has become a 'managed' currency" (Keynes 1923, JMK 4: 134), changed circumstances were leaving "no escape from a 'managed' currency" (Keynes 1923, JMK 4: 136), while the "reinstatement of the gold standard means, inevitably, that we surrender the regulation of our price level and the handling of the credit cycle to the Federal Reserve Board" (Keynes 1923, JMK 4: 139). That prospect, and the upfront deflation it would entail on Britain's part, Keynes found worth warning of; but to no effect. When the dreaded monetary surrender became a reality in April 1925, Keynes launched a devastating critique at the Chancellor of the Exchequer in charge at the time.

The key innovation (and crucial breakaway from traditional quantity-theoretic reasoning) offered in "The economic consequences of Mr. Churchill" (Keynes 1925) is the emphasis on differences in speed of adjustment across different markets. In particular, Keynes argued that money wages tend to adjust much more slowly than most other prices; a fact that inspired his later emphasis in *The General Theory* on the "wage unit" and on money wages as the anchor of the whole structure of prices. Keynes deplored the idea of using tight money to deflate prices since "Deflation does not reduce wages 'automatically.' It reduces them by causing unemployment" (Keynes 1925, JMK 9: 220).

Keynes spent the next five years working on his two-volume *A Treatise on Money*. In parallel, persistently high unemployment in the depressed British economy offered him many an opportunity to address policy matters in Britain and the world.

The *Treatise* is hampered by the fact that Keynes had not fully let go of the idea of a unique natural rate of interest somehow anchored by real forces, but this deficiency does not diminish the relevance of his analysis of the case of a country that has the rate of interest fixed for it by external circumstances, and which may therefore find reaching investment equilibrium at home impracticable. The following observation nicely captures the essence of the crucial dilemma that presented the focus of Keynes' attention:

> There are, moreover, all sorts of other reasons why the day-to-day preservation of local investment equilibrium may require some departure of the local rate of interest from the international rate. This, then, is the *dilemma* of an international monetary system – to preserve the advantages of the stability of the local currencies of the various members of the system in terms of the international standard, and to preserve at the same time an adequate local autonomy for each member over its domestic rate of interest and its volume of foreign lending.
>
> (Keynes 1930b, JMK 6: 271–2)

In search of a solution for the diagnosed dilemma Keynes considered both designing instruments that could increase "local autonomy" (or, policy space) within the context of existing conditions as well as under conditions of an "ideal arrangement" that would include setting up "a supernational bank to which the central banks of the world would stand in much the same relation as their own member banks stand to them" (Keynes 1930b, JMK 6: 358). Along former lines Keynes discussed financial regulation of capital markets and institutions, discriminatory taxation, wider gold points and the operation of central banks in forward exchange markets as (complementary) ways to influence capital flows. He saw a particularly "severe technical problem" with regard to the control of international banking since "credit is like water – whilst it may be used for a multiplicity of purposes, it is in itself undifferentiated, can drip through crannies, and will remorselessly seek its own level over the whole field unless the parts of the field are rendered uncompromisingly watertight, which in the case of credit is scarcely possible" (Keynes 1930b, JMK 6: 285). In this context a widening of gold points was supposed to create scope for exchange rate uncertainty as "one of the most effective means of keeping short-term foreign lending insensitive is to allow an element of *doubt* as to the future terms of exchange between currencies" (Keynes 1930b, JMK 6: 286).

As elsewhere in the *Treatise*, Keynes was still taking the gold standard for granted in his elaborations on "ideal arrangements" including a "supernational bank" at the center of a "satisfactory system of supernational management of the value of gold" (Keynes 1930b, JMK 6: 358), though hoping that "reserve money must gradually become representative during the twentieth [century]" (Keynes 1930b, JMK 6: 355). The supernational bank would act as the central bank of central banks: "It should do no business except with central banks. Its assets should consist of gold, securities and advances to central banks, and its liabilities of deposits by central banks, such deposits we will call supernational bank money (or S.B.M. for short). (3) S.B.M. should be purchasable for gold and encashable for gold at fixed prices differing from one another by 2 per cent" (Keynes 1930b, JMK 6: 358).

These ideas may be seen as the embryo of Keynes' Clearing Union plan for the post-war international monetary order developed in the early 1940s. In the *Treatise* Keynes observed that

> it is evident that the main effect of an international gold standard (or any other international standard) is to secure *uniformity* of movement in different countries – everyone must conform to the average behavior of everyone else. The advantage of this is that it prevents individual follies and eccentricities. The disadvantage is that it hampers each central bank in tackling its own national problems, interferes with pioneer improvements of policy the wisdom of which is ahead of average wisdom, and does nothing to secure either the short-period or the long-period optimum if the average behavior is governed by blind forces such as the total quantity of gold, or is haphazard and without any concerted or deliberate policy behind it on the part of the central banks as a body.
>
> (Keynes 1930b, JMK 6: 255–6)

His emerging vision for a *managed* international standard aimed at striking a sound balance between maintaining international uniformity and sufficient national policy space. In guiding "average behavior" towards optimum outcomes both in the short and the long period, deliberate policy rather than blind forces should be trusted.

A key requirement in regime design was to secure symmetry in adjustment pressures facing both creditor and debtor countries. He was keenly aware that "the problem [of lack of policy space] presents itself in different forms to debtor and creditor nations respectively. It is likely to prove more severe and intractable in the case of a debtor nation than in the case of a creditor nation, because it is easier to lend less in an emergency than to borrow more" (Keynes 1930b, JMK 6: 276–7). He diagnosed that this very asymmetry could create a deflationary bias for the system as a whole when key creditors refused to either expand or lend sufficiently. For instance, "Great Britain in the 1890s deflated every other country in the world by refusing to lend abroad on the scale to which international economic relations had become adjusted" (Keynes 1930a, JMK 5: 305, n. 1).

A new chapter opened up as Britain went off gold for good on 21 September 1931.[4] The following years proved very fruitful to Keynes' theoretical endeavors, culminating in *The General Theory* in 1936. Keynes' immediate response to the sterling crisis was expressed in his "Notes on the currency question," in which he sought a "working compromise between the ideals of exchange stability and of price stability" (1931f, JMK 21: 21). Keynes' proposal was opportunistic, relying on the fact that other countries had not yet abandoned gold and could thus indirectly serve as external anchors as Britain was exploring its new-found monetary freedoms. Keynes recommended that Britain should stabilize sterling in terms of some commodity price standard, which itself was to be tied by some wider margin to the commodity value of gold (as supposedly stabilized by remaining gold standard members). The experiences of the early 1930s in domestic monetary management were to have a profound impact on Keynes' thinking, especially the successful reduction in long-term interest rates (see Chapter 4). It turned out that Britain avoided the worst of the Great Depression.

Keynes never lost sight of the global economic situation though. His "Means to prosperity" of March 1933 included "A proposal for the world economic conference" that reflects Keynes' theoretical breakthrough from the "banana plantation parable" of the *Treatise* to the income multiplier of *The General Theory*. Seeing little practical scope for traditional policy relief working through direct foreign loans "from the strong financial countries, which have a favorable foreign balance or excessive reserves of gold, to the weaker, debtor countries" (Keynes 1933a, JMK 9: 355), Keynes put great emphasis on loan expenditures. More precisely, he emphasized the needed "*simultaneity*" of the movement towards increased expenditure. For the pressure on its foreign balance, which each country fears as the result of increasing its own loan-expenditure, will cancel out if other countries are pursuing the same policy at the same time. Isolated action may be imprudent. General action has no dangers whatever" (Keynes 1933a, JMK 9: 356).

Additional measures included the issuance of "gold-notes" by an international authority against national government bonds at proportionate quotas for each country. The aim of this measure was to augment international reserves. Yet since the participants would accept these notes as equivalent to gold, they implied certain parities for national currencies in terms of gold and, in Britain's case, a qualified return to the gold standard, an oddity for which Keynes offered the following excuse:

> It may seem odd that I, who have lately described gold as "a barbarous relic," should be discovered as an advocate of such a policy, at a time when the orthodox authorities of this country are laying down conditions for our return to gold which they must know to be impossible of fulfillment. It may be that, never having loved gold, I am not so subject to disillusion. But, mainly, it is because I believe that gold has received such a grueling that conditions might

now be laid down for its future management, which would not have been acceptable otherwise.

(Keynes 1933a, JMK 9: 362)

In particular, Keynes favored parity adjustments "from time to time if circumstances were to require, just like bank rate – though by small degrees one would hope" and wider gold points: "The margin of 5 per cent between the gold points would be essential, in the light of recent experience, as a deterrent and a protection against the wild movements of liquid funds from one international centre to another, and to allow a reasonable independence of bank rate and credit policy to suit differing national circumstances" (Keynes 1933a, JMK 9: 362–3).

The issue of preserving sufficient policy space was further explored in an interesting lecture titled "National self-sufficiency" delivered in July 1933 (see also Crotty 1983; Dimand 2006). Keynes started his lecture explaining that he

was brought up, like most Englishmen, to respect free trade not only as an economic doctrine which a rational and instructed person could not doubt but almost as a part of the moral law. I regarded departures from it as being at the same time an imbecility and an outrage. I thought England's unshakable free-trade convictions, maintained for nearly a hundred years, to be both the explanation before man and the justification before heaven of her economic supremacy. As lately as 1923 I was writing that free trade was based on fundamental truths "which, stated with their due qualifications, no one can dispute who is capable of understanding the meaning of the words." Looking again today at the statements of these fundamental truths which I then gave, I do not find myself disputing them. Yet the orientation of my mind has changed: and I share this change of mind with many others.

(Keynes 1933c, JMK 21: 233–4)

The essence of his message is well summed up in a statement that pleads for a slow and cautious reorientation rather than abrupt break with traditions. Note that he advises finance, "above all," to be primarily national:

I sympathize, therefore, with those who would minimize, rather than with those who would maximize, economic entanglement between nations. Ideas, knowledge, art, hospitality, travel – these are the things which should of their nature be international. But let goods be homespun whenever it is reasonably and conveniently possible; *and, above all, let finance be primarily national.* Yet, at the same time, those who seek to disembarrass a country of its entanglements should be very slow and wary. It should not be a matter of tearing up roots but of slowly training a plant to grow in a different direction.[5]

(Keynes 1933c, JMK 21: 236; my emphasis)

It appears to me that the change in the orientation of Keynes' mind was both the product of a changing global political environment featuring a general movement away from the principles of *laissez-faire* capitalism as well as a reflection of his evolving monetary thought, especially as relating to the old key issue of enabling the national rate of interest to diverge from what is the case internationally. The following long quotation refers to both aspects:

> We wish – for the time at least and so long as the present transitional experimental phase endures – to be our own masters, and to be as free as we can make ourselves from the interferences of the outside world. Thus, regarded from this point of view, the policy of an increased national self-sufficiency is to be considered not as an ideal in itself but as directed to the creation of an environment in which other ideals can be safely and conveniently pursued. Let me give as dry an illustration of this as I can devise, chosen because it is connected with ideas with which recently my own mind has been largely preoccupied. In matters of economic detail, as distinct from the central controls, I am in favor of retaining as much private judgment and initiative and enterprise as possible. But I have become convinced that the retention of the structure of private enterprise is incompatible with that degree of material well-being to which our technical advancement entitles us, unless the rate of interest falls to a much lower figure than is likely to come about by natural forces operating on the old lines. Indeed the transformation of society, which I preferably envisage, may require a reduction in the rate of interest towards vanishing point within the next thirty years. *But under a system by which the rate of interest finds, under operation of normal financial forces, a uniform level throughout the world, after allowing for risk and the like, this is most unlikely to occur.* Thus for a complexity of reasons, which I cannot elaborate in this place, economic internationalism embracing the free movement of capital and of loanable funds as well as of traded goods may condemn this country for a generation to come to a much lower degree of material prosperity than could be attained under a different system.
>
> (Keynes 1933c, JMK 21: 240; my emphasis)

The reference to those "central controls" to be directed at creating a benevolent national macroeconomic environment reflects that Keynes was by this time well on track developing the key ideas and concepts of *The General Theory*. In fact, in a series of public broadcasts in 1934 entitled "Poverty in plenty: is the economic system self-adjusting?" Keynes explained that he found himself in the camp of heretics who reject the idea of automatic self-adjustment, justifying the need for deliberate use of the central controls. In view of the central theme of this book it is especially revealing that he there points his finger squarely at the theory of interest as the key flaw in *laissez-faire* orthodoxy:

> There is, I am convinced, a fatal flaw in that part of the orthodox reasoning which deals with the theory of what determines the level of effective demand and the volume of aggregate employment; the flaw being largely due to the failure of the classical doctrine to develop a satisfactory theory of the rate

of interest. … Now the school which believes in self-adjustment is, in fact, assuming that the rate of interest adjusts itself more or less automatically, so as to encourage just the right amount of production of capital goods to keep our incomes at the maximum level which our energies and our organization and our knowledge of how to produce efficiently are capable of providing. This is, however, pure assumption. There is no theoretical reason for believing it to be true.

(Keynes 1934a, JMK 13: 489)

For the diagnosed "fatal flaw" in the classical doctrine defined the very role to be played by his alternative liquidity preference theory of interest of *The General Theory*, as well summarized in a letter to Hubert Henderson of 28 May 1936:

The rate of interest is, on my theory, essentially an uncertainty phenomenon. … According to my theory, interest rates are determined by the demand and supply for money, not by the demand and supply for durable goods. During a boom the demand for money rises, and during a slump it falls off. This may be either aggravated or mitigated by changes in liquidity preference. … If the supply of money is suitably adjusted, then there is no necessary reason why interest rates need rise during a boom or fall during a depression.

(Keynes 1936e, JMK 29: 221–2)

Clearly, in Keynes' view, faith in automatic self-adjustment through interest rates as driven by natural forces in a supposedly equilibrating fashion was a lost cause. Instead, deliberate management of the central controls was needed to align interest rates with the requirements of full employment equilibrium. Unless national requirements were fully aligned with the global situation at all times, this also implies a need for sufficient policy space in this area. How could this be best achieved?

The General Theory is generally interpreted as, and often criticized for, presenting a model of a closed economy.[6] This criticism is missing the point. For it seems a very sensible starting point for an analysis of the forces that determine the level of employment in an economy at any time, to abstract from the possibility that an open economy may rely on the rest of the world to determine the level of employment for itself. Had not the 1930s provided sufficient evidence that "beggar-thy-neighbor" policies were unhelpful, to say the least, to sustain full employment, both nationally and internationally? After all, the global economy *is* a closed economy. Keynes considers diverging money wage trends (much like exchange rate changes) as affecting trade and *national* employment in Chapter 19 of *The General Theory*; just as he had already emphasized the need for *simultaneous* expansion of nations to foster global recovery from the Great Depression without trade imbalances in the years before.

In addition, *The General Theory* also sheds some important light on mercantilism as a *national* employment strategy – a crucial aspect to be kept in mind when assessing Keynes' Clearing Union plan in the next section. In laying down a vision for a new post-war order that complied with the idea of free multilateral trade, Keynes emphasized that actually reaping the full benefits of microeconomic efficiency was also conditional on the macroeconomic environment. The point is that orthodox proponents of free trade, then and now, generally fail to acknowledge that countries' options to secure macroeconomic stability, apart from allocation efficiency supposedly helped by free trade, are in important ways conditioned by the international monetary order. In Chapter 23 titled "Notes on Mercantilism" Keynes observed that

> [a]t a time when the authorities had no direct control over the domestic rate of interest or the other inducements to home investment, measures to increase the favorable balance of trade were the only *direct* means at their disposal for increasing foreign investment; and, at the same time, the effect of a favorable balance of trade on the influx of the precious metals was their only *indirect* means of reducing the domestic rate of interest and so increasing the inducement to home investment.
>
> (Keynes 1936a, JMK 7: 336)

In other words, operating under the conditions of the gold standard and free capital mobility countries had an incentive to aim at a favorable trade balance for lack of policy space that would allow them to secure domestic stability through non-mercantilistic policies. What appears to be in stark conflict with the national best interest from a Ricardian comparative-advantage perspective can make perfect macroeconomic sense.

The problem is of course that a mercantilistic strategy cannot work for the – closed! – world economy as a whole. Countries with an unfavorable trade balance would tend to face deflationary pressures. And their response could well impart an overall contractionary and deflationary bias into the system. What makes sense individually can lead to collective disaster. The new international monetary order Keynes envisioned in the light of his theoretical breakthroughs was designed to overcome this problem.

7.4 An international monetary order based on "supernational" bank money

Inspired by the insights that his *General Theory* had brought to light, Keynes was optimistic that the post-war era could be an era of wealth creation and rising incomes, provided that obstacles to free trade, constraining countries' export markets, were relieved and an expansionist bias to global demand implanted into the global monetary order, providing both the environment and the stimulus for the sought-after *simultaneous* expansion of trade and incomes.[7] He set out to establish an international monetary order that would provide both stability and symmetry in international monetary relations as well as sufficient national policy space. In essence, Keynes aimed at disabling countries to pursue mercantilist strategies while enabling them to systematically attain domestic demand-led growth through deliberate management of their economies instead.

Keynes noted that the inter-war period had provided all the unfortunate experiments of collective failure that could result when countries, desperately lacking better alternatives, judged that mercantilism was in their best national interest, featuring competitive deflation and competitive exchange depreciations, and collapse of international trade and finance. And he feared that global current account imbalances and the corresponding concentration of gold holdings in the US built up during the war could impart a contractionist bias on deficit countries and the system as a whole, risking a repeat of previous disasters featuring protectionism and beggar-thy-neighbor policies.

Arguably, Keynes' early Clearing Union (or "bancor") drafts most truly reflect his own vision for the post-war economic order.[8] As regards the new international monetary order to be established, he proposed: to create a new *international* monetary standard and system liquidity that was largely detached from gold, to implant a chiefly rule-based adjustment mechanism towards balance of payments equilibrium into the new global order featuring *symmetric* pressures for adjustment on both current account surplus and deficit countries, and to create sufficient national policy space that would enable countries to achieve domestic stability whilst abiding by the new international rules of the game at the same time, abstention from beggar-thy-neighbor strategies in particular.

At the core of Keynes' envisioned "International Clearing Union" was the international "bancor" unit of account and international liquidity in the form of (overdraft) bank money. Bancor was to be defined in terms of, but – importantly – not convertible into, gold. In contrast to the random growth in the world's gold stock, bancor supply was ultimately elastic and under deliberate international control.[9] By way of design in line with national banking principles, a credit mechanism was to overcome the "hoarding" problem afflicting the gold standard: one key matter to be discussed below.

National currencies were to have fixed parities in terms of bancor and member countries have quotas for bancor overdraft loans. Symmetry in adjustment pressures was secured as both surplus and deficit countries were to pay interest on their credit or debit balances,[10] respectively, and face quasi-automatic exchange rate realignments if their bancor clearing balances exceeded certain thresholds in terms of their defined quotas. National policy space was to be created through capital controls looking after the "hot money" problem whilst allowing countries to set interest rates in line with their respective domestic requirements: another key matter to be further discussed below.

Temporary international payments imbalances were thus to be smoothed by official and "supranational" bancor overdraft liquidity access to which would be unconditional within certain limits. Bancor liquidity would grow endogenously with trade and temporary payments imbalances, and without facing competition from either national reserve currencies or private short-term lending. Exchange rates were to be pegged but adjustable according to rules that forbid beggar-thy-neighbor style destabilization and prescribed quasi-automatic parity changes designed to keep trade balanced.[11] In essence, Keynes' bancor scheme was designed to rob countries of any mercantilist option, but grant them policy space to pursue deliberate national policy management targeting domestic stability instead; and within a symmetric and cooperative international order.

Note an important difference to today's situation here. Today, a country that allows domestic demand to stagnate typically faces currency depreciation, adding force to its improving external position. By contrast, under the bancor plan such freeloading on external growth presents no escape route as countries with a current account surplus face currency appreciation as a penalty for their failure at the home front. Similarly in the case of a country that allows its domestic demand to grow in excess of incomes and sees its external position deteriorating, exchange depreciation would give rise to or augment any inflationary pressures. In short, countries are under *extra* pressure to maintain internal balance and not become a burden on their neighbors or source of global inflation. All this runs opposite to today's arrangements. The point is that today countries at best receive *stabilizing* external support only when they are out of sync, which is not the supposed norm. The idea under Keynes' scheme is that with each country being granted the policy space that enables it to keep its own house in order, countries as a whole should tend to be in sync, yielding that *simultaneous* expansion in the world economy that was Keynes' aim.[12] In *The General Theory* Keynes observes:

> It is the policy of an autonomous rate of interest, unimpeded by international preoccupations, and of a national investment programme directed to an optimum level of domestic employment which is twice blessed in the sense that it helps ourselves and our neighbors at the same time. And it is the simultaneous pursuit of these policies by all countries together which is capable of restoring economic health and strength internationally, whether we measure it by the level of domestic employment or by the volume of international trade.
>
> (Keynes 1936a, JMK 7: 349)

In addition, Keynes envisioned complementary international institutions designed to secure a tendency towards international balance through stabilization of the international investment and credit cycle, commodity price stabilization, and supplemental international support for reconstruction and development. In fact, in the absence of a lead country playing the "*n*th country role" for the global economy (see discussion in Chapter 8), such complementary international institutions and policies would seem necessary to secure the "short-period and long-period optimum in the average behavior on the part of the central banks as a body" (each pursuing deliberate national policies) that Keynes referred to in the *Treatise* (read "central controls" in the light of *The General Theory*). Apart from exerting symmetric adjustment pressures on both deficit and surplus countries designed to hold the parts together, the international bancor system should also be "capable of deliberate expansion and contraction to offset deflationary and inflationary tendencies in effective world demand" (Keynes 1942g, JMK 25: 169).[13]

7.5 Some observations on hoarding and capital controls

After outlining the broad principles of Keynes' vision, two issues deserve further elaboration: hoarding and capital controls. In view of his liquidity preference theory of interest Keynes' observations on "hoarding" in the international context are of great interest. For instance, in his immediate response to the early US Treasury (White) Plan Keynes observes: "Since the proposed Stabilization Fund is to perform clearing functions for its members, it might seem, at first sight, to have a closer resemblance to the Clearing Union than is the case. In fact the principles underlying it are fundamentally different. For it makes no attempt to use the banking principle and one-way gold convertibility and is in fact not much more than a version of the gold standard, which simply aims at multiplying the effective volume of the gold base" (Keynes 1942f, JMK 25: 160). By contrast, a key advantage of his bancor plan was that: "The substitution of a credit mechanism in place of hoarding would have repeated in the international field the same miracle already performed in the domestic field of turning a stone into bread" (Keynes 1942b, JMK 25: 114).

Recall here Keynes' critique of the concept of hoarding as an "incomplete idea" in *The General Theory*. Distinguishing "hoarding" from the "propensity to hoard" (which he uses as a synonym for liquidity preference), Keynes emphasized that it is "impossible for the actual amount of hoarding to change as a result of decisions on the part of the public … For the amount of hoarding must be equal to the quantity of money … and the quantity of money is not determined by the public. All that the propensity of the public towards hoarding can achieve is to determine the rate of interest at which the aggregate desire to hoard becomes equal to the available cash" (Keynes 1936a, JMK 7: 174). Importantly, the term "cash," describing the object of hoarding at the national level, refers primarily to bank deposits (but may also include Treasury bills and the like). In the first instance liquidity preference theory applies to "the public's" (including non-bank financial market players) demand for bank money, in particular. And it also refers to the banks' own liquidity preference as it affects their willingness to provide liquidity to the public. But it does not refer to anything that hoarding (in some older sense) could make disappear from circulation, such as gold.[14]

At the national (or closed-economy) level and given a certain amount of liquidity as provided by the banking system, an increase in the public's propensity to hoard raises the rate of interest and depresses asset prices (and *vice versa*). In principle, the price effects can be offset if the banking system adjusts the pool of liquidity accordingly, either by taking assets off the market or by providing finance to those who are willing to do so. It may require appropriate policy reactions to induce the banks to do what seems desirable from a national macroeconomic viewpoint.[15] These are the themes of the *Treatise* and *The General Theory*.

Translated at the international level and under gold standard conditions, an increased propensity towards hoarding international liquidity, i.e. gold, requires either a current account surplus and/or a surplus on capital account (exclusive of official reserves). For an individual country the way to achieve a balance of payments surplus and gold inflow is by tightening monetary conditions (or fiscal stance). This has two effects: attracting capital flows and depressing effective demand at home. Alas, deficit countries experiencing a tendency for gold to flow out face pressures to follow suit. Following suit may cancel out any impact on the direction of capital flows, but spreads the depressing effects on effective demand throughout the system. With gold being highly inelastic in supply (in the short run), an increase in the propensity to hoard thereby creates deflationary pressures in the system as a whole (while actual hoarding remains unchanged).[16]

Note that current account imbalances do not create any such problems as long as surplus countries *automatically* lend to deficit countries, as according to Keynes was the case in "the Victorian age [when] the peculiar organization in London and to a lesser extent in Paris, the two main creditor centers, by which a flow of gold immediately translated itself, not in the first instance into a change in prices and wages, but into a change in the volume of foreign investment by the creditors, [which] caused the burden to be carried by the stronger shoulders" (Keynes 1941a, JMK 25: 30). In particular, a trade surplus triggered monetary easing from the Bank of England, thereby boosting effective demand at the center of the system; while private capital flows supposedly played a stabilizing role.

As to the envisioned post-war world, Keynes' solution to the international hoarding problem was to replace inelastic gold by elastic international liquidity in the form of bank money. In his view, not actual precautionary bank money holdings but assured access to sufficiently large overdraft loans would be key to preventing any heightened propensity to hoard from having its negative systemic effects. As Keynes explained in his maiden speech before the House of Lords on 18 May 1943:

> The margin of resources provided by the Clearing Union must be substantial, not so much for actual use as to relieve anxiety and the deflationary pressure which results from anxiety. This margin, though substantial, must be regarded solely as a reserve with which to meet temporary emergencies and to allow a breathing space. But the world's trading difficulties in the past have not always been due to the improvidence of debtor countries. They may be caused in a most acute form if a creditor country is constantly withdrawing international money from circulation and hoarding it, instead of putting it back again into circulation, thus refusing to spend its income from abroad either on goods for home consumption or on investment overseas. We have lately come to understand more clearly than before how employment and the creation of incomes out of new production can only be maintained through the expenditure on goods and services of the income previously earned. This is equally true of home trade and of foreign trade. A foreign country equally can be the ultimate cause of unemployment by hoarding beyond the

reasonable requirements of precaution. ... The present proposals avoid this by profiting from the experience of domestic banking. If an individual hoards his income, not in the shape of gold coins in his pockets or in his safe, but by keeping a bank deposit, this bank deposit is not withdrawn from circulation but provides his banker with the means of making loans to those who need them. Thus every act of hoarding, if it takes this form, itself provides the offsetting facilities for some other party, so that production and trade can continue.[17]

(Keynes 1943d, JMK 25: 272–3)

Note that the institutionalized elasticity of the object of hoarding not only prevents changes in the propensity to hoard and actual hoarding from having the price effects this would otherwise cause, but is primarily intended to discourage hoarding in the first place. On the other hand, while the international liquidity provided by the Clearing Union had to be substantial to achieve this outcome, there had to be limits to the potential temporary financing of imbalances automatically obtainable in this way: "Measures would be necessary to prevent the piling up of credit and debit balances without limit, and the system would have failed in the long run if it did not possess sufficient capacity for self-equilibrium to prevent this" (Keynes 1941c, JMK 25: 72). The point was to put *symmetric* pressures for adjustment on both surplus and deficit countries. *One-sided discipline is at risk of causing a deflationary bias.*

How do private capital flows fit into Keynes' vision? One possible reference point as international equilibrium is to require current accounts to be balanced in the medium and long term, with short-term imbalances temporarily financed by bancor overdrafts cancelling out over time. This would exclude private capital flows altogether. Yet, while Keynes emphasized capital controls as an essential ingredient of his scheme, he did see room for *long-term* private investment flows; complementing official development aid. The main objective of his scheme was to make sure that private capital flows would be stabilizing, and de-stabilizing flows be ruled out.

So one key issue was to counter "hot money," in Keynes' view posing a constant risk to economic stability since: "The whereabouts of 'the better 'ole' will shift with the speed of the magic carpet. Loose funds may sweep round the world disorganizing all steady business. Nothing is more certain than that the movement of capital funds must be regulated" (Keynes 1941a, JMK 25: 31). In fact, he thought that "central control of capital movements, both inward and outward, should be a permanent feature of the post-war system" (Keynes 1941b, JMK 25: 52).

As has become clear from his writings since the *Treatise*, the other key issue was that of retaining sufficient policy space, as Keynes once again emphasized in a letter to Harrod of 19 April 1942: "In my view the whole management of the domestic economy depends upon being free to have the appropriate rate of interest without reference to the rates prevailing elsewhere in the world. Capital control is a corollary to this" (Keynes 1942e, JMK 25: 149).[18]

While control of capital flows in general was thus deemed necessary, Keynes did not deny a positive role for genuine new investment for developing the worlds' resources. In other words, he would expect long-term private capital to flow from developed towards developing countries, as was the case in the nineteenth century, featuring "transactions between old-established and newly-developing countries where the loans were self-liquidating because they themselves created new sources of payment" (Keynes 1941a, JMK 25: 22). In any case, control over aggregate private capital outflows would be required in developed countries so as to not undermine their national policy space.[19] Furthermore, his scheme allowed for bilateral official loans between surplus and deficit countries that would help to maintain equilibrium in the Clearing Union, while permitting the two countries involved avoiding the interest charges otherwise payable to the reserve fund.

How was control to be achieved then? As foreign exchange markets are the lynchpin of the whole matter, purely private enterprise dealings in foreign exchange were not to be allowed. Instead, as Keynes explained to a meeting of European Allies in February 1943: "We contemplate the central bank or similar institutions monopolizing dealings in foreign exchange for its own nationals and an internal clearing with separate banks. Then it is left with a final balance for or against and that final balance would then be cleared with this international clearing union. That would get rid of the whole element of exchange speculation which has caused so much trouble after the last war" (Keynes 1943a, JMK 25: 212). However, it would be left to each individual country to shape its own regime of control over investment flows. Owing to the large overseas liquid funds in London Keynes thought that certainly in Britain's case "some system for the control of capital movements is absolutely indispensable the moment the war is over" (Keynes 1942e, JMK 25: 148). What he seems to have had in mind is the use of depository receipts that make investments transferable among foreign investors (and hence liquid for the individual foreign investor) but without exposing the recipient country to risks of maturity mismatches between any fixed domestic investments undertaken and the foreign financing provided for them.[20]

7.6   Conclusion: national policy space and symmetric adjustment pressures emanating within a managed international credit currency regime

Keynes' Clearing Union plan of the early 1940s marks the culmination of his monetary thought as applied to institutional and policy design in the international sphere. Based on his reading of monetary history and drawing on insights developed in *The General Theory* regarding the rationale behind, and global consequences of, national mercantilistic policies, Keynes aimed at establishing an international monetary order that would disable countries from pursuing mercantilist strategies while enabling them to systematically attain domestic demand-led growth through deliberate management of their economies instead. Apart from exerting symmetric adjustment pressures on both deficit and surplus countries designed to hold the parts together, deliberate management of the international bancor system would aim at stable global expansion and development, with additional support coming from envisioned complementary international institutions.

The discussions surrounding the establishment of a new international monetary order also shed some interesting light on hoarding and capital controls. The notion of hoarding featured prominently in Keynes' critique of the classical theory of interest and the controversies related to it. At the international level, gold or some alternative international reserve asset or currency represents "liquidity *par excellence*," the most liquid asset or object of hoarding that best satisfies liquidity preference. Keynes' aim was to discourage hoarding and forestall any price (i.e. in the first instance, exchange rate) effects of changes in the propensity to hoard by making international liquidity super-elastic. In addition, and apart from preventing *de-stabilizing* private capital flows, capital controls were also key to creating sufficient national policy space within the envisioned international monetary order that was to ban beggar-thy-neighbor policies. Each individual country could then deal with national liquidity preference along the lines discussed in *The General Theory*. As bancor was to be under international management, there was no "nth country role" to be played by any particular country on behalf of the global economy.

8 On what became of Keynes' vision at Bretton Woods and some recent issues in global finance[1]

8.1 Introduction

Following up on the previous chapter, this chapter discusses the evolution of the international monetary order as actually set up at Bretton Woods in the light of Keynes' monetary thought and Clearing Union proposal. Section 8.2 reviews the US's nth country role as key currency issuer, underwriting the international dollar standard. Section 8.3 discusses the emergence of global imbalances and paradoxical capital flows, while Section 8.4 critically investigates the Bretton Woods II hypothesis and the ongoing US financial crisis – as the culmination of global imbalances. Section 8.5 then critiques Bernanke's "saving glut hypothesis" and Greenspan's "bond market conundrum" in the light of liquidity preference theory. Section 8.6 outlines required government action to counter the credit meltdown. Section 8.7 concludes.

8.2 Bretton Woods, US dollar standard and the nth country role

Key to Keynes' vision for a sound international monetary order was the idea of symmetric pressures for adjustment facing both deficit and surplus countries alike. Balanced current account positions may be considered as an equilibrium norm in this scheme. For any particular country capital flows can play a role in the short and medium run, but not in the long run. In the short run, they can help to finance temporary current account imbalances as they regularly arise in the normal course of events, with capital flowing from current account surplus to deficit countries. Within his Clearing Union scheme this part was left to official international bancor liquidity. Reliance on private liquidity would circumscribe policy space and risk destabilizing flows. As to the medium run, Keynes saw scope for capital flowing towards "newly-developing countries where the loans were self-liquidating because they themselves created new sources of payment" (Keynes 1941a, JMK 25: 22). As to the long run, the point is that no country could really be in a *permanent* deficit or surplus position. Regarding a widely feared chronic dollar scarcity after the war, Keynes therefore observed that: "It is obvious that no country can go on for ever covering by new lending a chronic surplus on current account without eventually forcing a default from the other parties" (Keynes 1946, JMK 11: 184).

In his posthumously published article on "The balance of payments of the United States" of 1946, Keynes challenged the predominant view of a chronic dollar scarcity beyond the immediate post-war situation:

> In the long run more fundamental forces may be at work, if all goes well, tending towards equilibrium, the significance of which may ultimately transcend ephemeral statistics. I find myself moved, not for the first time, to remind contemporary economists that the classical teaching embodied some permanent truths of great significance, which we are liable to-day to overlook because we associate them with other doctrines which we cannot now accept without much qualification. There are in these matters deep undercurrents at work, natural forces, one can call them, or even the invisible hand, which are operating towards equilibrium. If this were not so, we could not have got on even so well as we have for many decades past. The United States is becoming a high-living, high-cost country beyond any previous experience. Unless their internal, as well as their external, economic life is to become paralyzed by the Midas touch, they will discover ways of life which, compared with the ways of the less fortunate regions of the world, must tend towards, and not away from, external equilibrium.
>
> (Keynes 1946, JMK 11: 185)

In retrospect, it seems fair to say that the economic life in that high-living, high-cost country the United States has indeed not become "paralyzed by the Midas touch," but has proved rather flexible and creative in preserving the system's tendency towards equilibrium most of the time.[2] By equilibrium I mean simultaneous income expansion and price stability in the global economy, whether or not external positions of individual countries, the United States in particular, are in balance or not. To understand the meaning of this notion of global equilibrium we first need to acknowledge that the regime established at Bretton Woods did *not* follow Keynes' script but differed from his vision in important ways.[3]

And Keynes himself had no trouble identifying some of the key deficiencies in the alternative American plan for the post-war order early on: excessive rigidity of exchange rates, asymmetric disciplining of debtors only[4] and the failure to create a proper international bancor standard, but grant special status to the issuer of the key currency instead.[5] Furthermore, as to global finance, the progressive easing of capital controls over time has unleashed a re-emerging international financial system, largely detached from proper international regulation and oversight.[6]

Reflecting the completion in the shift in global economic and financial power that had started with World War I, the design of the Bretton Woods order established at the end of World War II has effectively placed the United States in the position of the nth country in the international monetary order and world economy. Bretton Woods did not establish an international bancor standard, but a US dollar standard. In any pegged exchange-rate regime of n currencies there are only $n-1$ exchange rates to peg, leaving one degree of freedom concerning the regime's overall monetary stance. To the extent that the $n-1$ members' demand for international liquidity is not provided for through some common institution or mechanism that either pools and clears member currencies and/or creates liquidity on its own, a role assigned to the International Monetary Fund in the Bretton Woods regime, their demand can ultimately only be met by the nth country itself, through running a balance of payments deficit. Through its national control over the issuance of the system's key reserve currency the nth country is thereby acting both as currency anchor as well as engine (of last resort) of economic expansion. The key currency issuer's policy is thus vital for the global economy (see Terzi 2006).

I remarked above that the US has proven itself sufficiently flexible and creative in making US dollar reserves available to the rest of the world throughout the post-war period. Figure 8.1 shows the evolution of the US current account balance, (net) FDI and (net) portfolio equity flows, US private capital outflows (other than FDI and portfolio equity), and official inflows since 1960 (or later depending on data availability; all expressed as percentage of US GDP). Ignoring US official outflows, balance of payments accounting implies that deficits on current account and private capital outflows require corresponding foreign (private and/or official) flows into US assets.

Until 1970 the US actually ran a current account surplus position. In the early post-war years generous ("Marshall plan") official aid provided foreign countries with the US dollars needed for reconstruction. Then, during the 1950s and 1960s, in addition to official aid, US foreign direct investment provided the key source of US dollar reserves. While the US provided overall restraint, rapid catching-up growth in Japan and Western Europe was made possible in a low inflation, low interest rate environment. For two reasons this global constellation came under increasing stress over the course of the 1960s. First, progressive easing of capital controls and the emergence and growth of Eurocurrency markets in London allowed a rising role for private short-term funds attracted by interest rate differentials (which were adverse to the US). Second, the Vietnam War pushed the US's resource needs beyond the country's own means, so that the current account deteriorated and turned into deficit by 1971.

In the end, the Bretton Woods regime of pegged exchange rates failed for reasons of dollar abundance rather than scarcity. As Europe's refusal to either accept currency revaluation or accumulate more dollars put mounting pressure on the dollar's supposed gold backing, US President Nixon responded on 15 August 1971 by cutting the US dollar officially free from gold. The era of floating exchange rates among industrialized trading partners began. The economic and financial instabilities of the 1970s contrasted with earlier decades of brisk growth and stability.

At first, economic and political vulnerability seemed to undermine US leadership and dollar hegemony. The deutschmark and the yen emerged as competing reserve currencies. There were even initiatives for international policy coordination featuring Europe as a new global "locomotive" for recovery from the oil price shock. Lured by increased bank lending featuring in the first wave of financial globalization, Latin American and other developing countries too

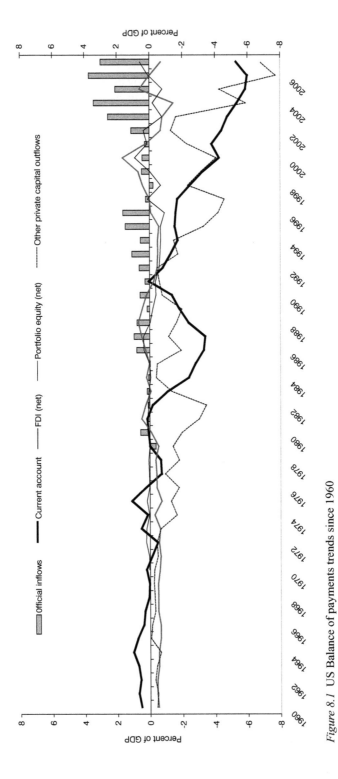

Figure 8.1 US Balance of payments trends since 1960

Sources: Bureau of Economic Analysis, International Monetary Fund, US Department of the Treasury

were welcomed to support global growth. However, in Germany, the perceived failure of the agreed macro stimulus program of the late 1970s inspired a lasting "supply-side-only" paradigm shift in economic policymaking in 1982 that is shaping European policies until this day. The impact on the developing world was profound too: the so-called "petrodollar re-cycling" set the stage for the developing country debt crises of the 1980s, triggered by short-term US interest rates reaching exorbitant levels earlier on in the decade.

While the "Volcker shock" gave rise to a global recession, miraculously, the US emerged with its global leadership role reestablished. The dollar surged on the exchanges despite the US's "twin deficits" (on both its current account and government budget). As private (non-FDI, non-equity) capital outflows from the US slowed sharply in 1982 and the US started to attract net FDI inflows throughout the 1980s, a swelling US current account deficit became the key source of foreign acquisitions of US assets.

In fact, since the early 1980s, global leadership included acting as lead driver of global demand growth for most of the time, with the US running (almost) continuous current account deficits ever since. While the US attracted large private capital inflows in the late 1990s (including net FDI and net equity inflows), since 2002 foreign official inflows have come to play a prominent role, exceeding previous episodes of dollar weakness in the late 1980s and mid 1990s. This last feature inspired the "Bretton Woods II hypothesis" (BWII) of Dooley *et al.* (2003) on global imbalances and it also relates to the "global capital flows paradox," Bernanke's "saving glut hypothesis" and Greenspan's "bond market conundrum," issues and ideas to be discussed in due course.

8.3 Global imbalances and paradoxical capital flows

Before, decomposing the US current account deficit into its key sources or counterparts, Figure 8.2 reveals that the US current account deficit of the first half of the 1980s mainly mirrored the lagging of Japan and Europe behind the US locomotive (propelled by fiscal expansion under the Reagan administration). The situation changed in the second half of the 1980s. Following the Plaza Accord the US dollar depreciated, while the oil price slumped and both Japan and Europe experienced a belated economic boom, lasting until 1990 in Japan's case and 1991 in Germany's.[7] Accordingly, the US current account deficit shrank after 1986 and even briefly disappeared by 1991. This owed to both the US experiencing a mild recession in that year and to foreign transfer payments in recognition of US military action in Iraq.

This proved a brief reversal of roles though. Since 1992 the bilateral positions with Japan and Europe have steadily deteriorated once again as both Japan and Germany got stuck in protracted domestic demand stagnation and German ("supply-side-only") policy "wisdom" was exported to Europe via the Maastricht Treaty of 1991. Apart from thus representing a *recurrent* element in the US current account imbalance, stagnation in Europe and Japan may actually be singled out as the dominant factor for the 1990s.[8] In recent years, at least the imbalance with

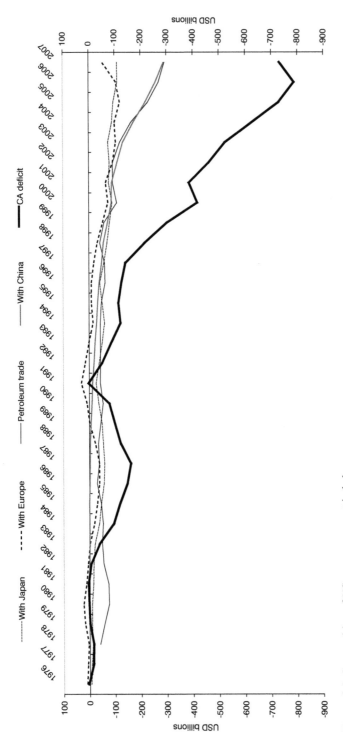

Figure 8.2 Composition of US current account imbalance

Source: Bureau of Economic Analysis

Europe has declined markedly from its peak in 2005, which owed to both a belated pickup in European growth in 2006 as well as the euro's appreciation against the dollar since 2002. By contrast, the bilateral imbalance with China, which has been the primary focus of debate in the US in recent years, has grown significantly since 2002 (although to some extent replacing deficits with other East Asian countries). And if fast industrialization and catchup in China is accepted as a key driving force behind the oil price (and more general commodity price) boom of recent years, the "China factor" would also relate to the rise in the US's petroleum trade deficit, reaching some $300bn in 2007. The composition of the US current account imbalance thus reveals that the build-up of the US's external deficit since 1991 owed to a whole variety of factors, including: protracted domestic demand stagnation in some key industrialized countries, China's emergence on the global scene and the oil price.

Figure 8.3 focuses on the other side of "global imbalances:" today's largest current account surplus countries (or groups of countries). Germany and Japan saw current account improvements of around $285bn and $90bn since 2000, respectively. Note that China only emerged as a globally significant factor as recently as 2003, with an improvement of some $350bn since that year. Saudi Arabia's sharply improved current account position (by some $80bn since 2000) is representative for oil exporters at large.

In addition, Figure 8.3 also reveals that since the late 1990s the aggregate current account position of "emerging and developing countries" as a whole has turned from deficit into surplus. In the aftermath of the Asian crises, capital flows changed direction, ever since flowing from poor to rich countries, primarily the United States. Apparently triggered by the Asian crises a conspicuous course change in behavior has turned the developing world as a whole into a net capital exporter and hoarder of surging reserve holdings in the form of US Treasury securities – a phenomenon that was dubbed the "global capital flows paradox" by former US Treasury Secretary Larry Summers (2006). This provides another contributing factor to the build-up of global imbalances.[9]

Figure 8.4 not only highlights the conspicuous turning point in the aggregate current account balance of the developing world in 1998–9, but also reveals that surging reserve accumulations in the developing world have actually been sourced from both current account surpluses as well as net *private* capital inflows. In other words, while official flows are headed north on a grand scale, net *private* capital flows *have* gone the opposite way since the early 1990s. More precisely, private flows have reached the developing world in two strong waves since capital account liberalization spread in the late 1980s and early 1990s. The first wave started in the late 1980s and abruptly ended in 1998. The second wave took off in earnest in 2002. A common element is that both waves arose in an environment of low interest rate policies by the US Federal Reserve in reaction to cyclical weakness in the US economy. The developing world's response to the two waves provided an important difference – in line with the shift in their aggregate current account position.

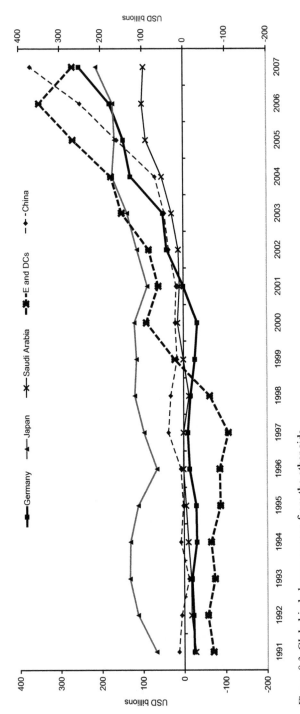

Figure 8.3 Global imbalances as seen from the other side

Source: IMF

Note: IMF classification of emerging and developing countries plus NICs but excluding China and Saudi Arabia

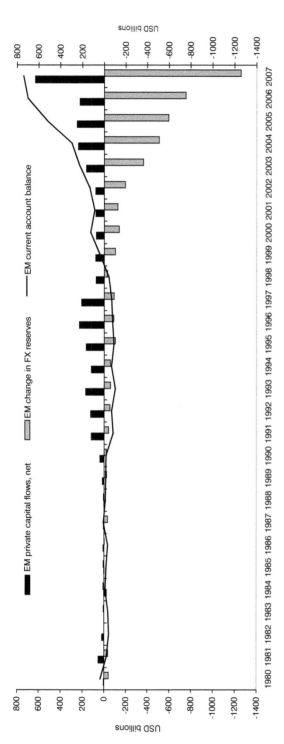

Figure 8.4 Paradoxical global capital flows from poor to rich

Source: IMF World Economic Outlook database

Notes: EM series include the WEO groups "Other emerging market and developing countries" and "Newly industrialized Asian economies"
For the "change in FX reserves" series a minus sign indicates an increase

Generally speaking, the developing world responded to the first wave in the early 1990s countries by allowing their currencies to appreciate in real terms while tolerating the emergence of rising current account deficits. Presumably this behavior followed the promise that complementing domestic saving by foreign saving would spur economic growth and development. GDP growth may have accelerated as capital inflows gave rise to asset price bubbles and consumption booms. But these gains typically proved short-lived. Financial crises occurred when private capital flows dried up or reversed, causing severe economic disruptions. Currency depreciation imposed by market forces then turned current account positions around; out of pure necessity at the start, this marked a general return to export-led growth. Ever since, countries have proved determined to *maintain* competitive exchange rates and prevent reoccurrence of external vulnerability.

So when the Federal Reserve's monetary easing in 2001 kicked off another wave of private capital flows headed towards emerging markets, countries generally resisted currency appreciation, by easing monetary policy in line with the Fed and by intervening in foreign exchange markets in support of the dollar. Maintaining competitive exchange rates became the cornerstone of their export-led development strategies, while running current account surpluses also allowed them to refill and greatly enlarge depleted foreign reserves. Apparently, experiences with financial instability and crises have taught the developing world the lesson that a competitive exchange rate may be key to *sustainable* growth under the existing US dollar standard. Seen in this light, hoarding of US dollar reserves may be interpreted as policy space insurance. Taking out insurance in this form has been on the rise since the spreading of capital account convertibility in the 1990s. Given the perception in crisis countries of insufficient multi-lateral insurance through the IMF a "self-insurance boom" followed the Asian crises.

In summary, the emergence of the US current account deficit may be interpreted as a reflection and byproduct of the US's flexible response to deficient demand elsewhere in the world economy. Essentially, in freely playing its *n*th country role, the world's key currency issuer stimulated domestic demand growth whenever deflationary pressures arrived at its shores. Such deflationary pressures can derive from two main sources: first, foreign countries' urge to export to the US at competitive prices and, second, foreign countries' urge to hoard US dollar reserves; where the former urge may also serve the latter purpose. In particular, any aggregate increase in the propensity to hoard the reserve currency (or, rise in international liquidity preference) will put upward pressure on its exchange rate and create deflationary pressures in the key country itself and potentially in the system as a whole too. To counter this threat the *n*th country has to expand domestic demand, supplying international liquidity in the process.

Maintaining internal balance in the *n*th country itself then involves spending in excess of income and tolerating the external drag and dollar liquidity outflows that such "spender and borrower of last resort" activity come along with. Since the 1990s mercantilist motives have been alive and kicking in both industrialized countries (Japan and Germany) and developing countries alike, with the hoarding motive magnifying the latter's pursuit since the Asian crises. Owing to the fact that this global arrangement worked rather well, at least until recently, an oil price boom further magnified the US current account deficit. The next section takes a closer look at the influential proposition that "global imbalances" may be sustainable since they indicate a long-lasting symbiosis of interests, also known as the BWII hypothesis.

8.4 Bretton Woods II hypothesis and the ongoing global financial crisis

Dooley *et al.* (2003) depict today's "global imbalances" as a reflection of a "revived Bretton Woods system." On their interpretation, while the US again acts as the center of global arrangements, a new periphery of Asian emerging markets has replaced the meanwhile matured former periphery of Western Europe and Japan. The periphery's primary interest is to sell its products into the large US market as a way of stimulating employment and development. Given the legendary flexibility of its markets and comparative advantage in creating *safe* financial assets, the US is in a position to tolerate the resulting quasi-permanent drag on US income growth and export of safe US dollar assets.[10]

Let us take a closer look then at those safe financial assets and how and why they are supposed to end up in foreign portfolios *in equilibrium*. Recall here a thought experiment due to Milton Friedman, which may help to illustrate the conditions under which the world's ongoing "imbalances" could indeed be sustainable. Imagine that the US Federal Reserve sent out its helicopters for cash rainfalls upon US consumers. It is easy to picture that US consumers showed no reluctance at picking up the cash notes and spending them, and to an important extent on imported goods too. The Fed's helicopter drops thus became loaded into otherwise half-empty containers returning to Asia, where they finally ended up as official reserves in the coffers of Asian central banks, forever content with holding barren pieces of paper in exchange for the products their nations shipped to the US.

For the sake of simplicity abstract from global finance and assume that the excess of US imports over exports happens to be 6 percent of GDP year after year, with US nominal GDP itself growing at a steady annual rate of 6 percent too (as roughly was the case in 2006). In steady state US external debt as a ratio of GDP would stabilize at 100 percent. The notion "external debt" suggests that the US owes to the rest of the world. But as banknotes pay no interest and are not redeemable into anything else, this looks like a bargain for the issuer of the key currency, especially if the deal continues until perpetuity. In actual fact, while more than half of US dollar banknotes do circulate outside the US, annual "shipments" of banknotes have fallen well short of the ballooning US trade deficit. So imagine instead that those helicopter banknote drops were largely converted into electronic entries of US Treasury securities. In 2003, when Treasury securities yielded 1 to 3 percent, reserves held in the form of Treasuries rather than banknotes implied only a minor qualification to our parable. For external debt to remain stable at 100 percent of GDP in steady state the US trade deficit would need to shrink somewhat to make room for the emerging negative balance on investment income account.[11]

I noted that greenbacks are not redeemable into anything else. Also, they (rather, US (net) IOUs in general) can only be "retired" from global markets and disappear from foreign portfolios if the US were to run current account surpluses in the future (in "repayment" of the goods received earlier). Just as an increase in the propensity to hoard dollars on the part of foreign investors[12] can in the first instance only impact on price, and only by driving up the dollar exchange rate (and any US policy and US bank reactions this might trigger) indirectly increase the quantity of dollars available for global hoarding, a widespread disinclination among foreign portfolio holders to hold dollars can in the first instance only depreciate the dollar, but not directly reduce hoarding of dollar reserves.[13] The latter can only occur if US banks dissolve or deleverage their international positions or, over time, if the dollar's external value gets sufficiently depressed to reverse current account positions. Apart from exchange rate effects, portfolio shifts undertaken by foreign investors between asset classes, say out of Treasuries and into US equities and properties, will affect *relative* asset prices and yield spreads if foreign holdings represent a significant factor in large US financial markets.

Now it is true that in recent years foreign investors were the dominant buyers of newly issued US Treasury (and Agency) securities. And with foreign investors buying up much of the new issuances of recent years, their shares of the total outstanding stock of US Treasury (and agency) securities has certainly gone up accordingly. But this fact as such neither confirms the supposed sustainability of imbalances as posited by Dooley *et al.* (2003) nor does it validate the above helicopter parable as a description of actual developments. For our parable suggests that US consumers were sponsored by *public* money as the driving force behind their robust spending during the period when global imbalances emerged. While expansionary fiscal policies played an important role in the recovery from the recessions in the early 1990s and 2001, it is noteworthy that the US public debt ratio has been stable or on a mild decline since the early 1990s. The true driver of US domestic demand in excess of GDP growth was not public money, but *private debts*, especially consumer debts – with mortgage debt markets as the culprit of the whole matter.

The fact that the long US expansion was essentially a consumer boom may be seen in Figure 8.5 in the fall in the personal saving rate from 7 percent of disposable income in the early 1990s to near zero by 2006 and sharp rise in the household sector mortgage debt ratio since the late 1990s.[14] To repeat, the US boom was *not* primarily financed by public money, as in the helicopter parable above, but by private debts. Whether foreign official authorities have ended up holding safe Treasuries or higher yielding assets merely affects the US's external financing cost. The key point is that the internal match to the US's external imbalance resides not with the public sector, but primarily with the US household sector. In fact, Figure 8.6 reveals a remarkably high positive correlation between the personal saving rate and the US current account balance.

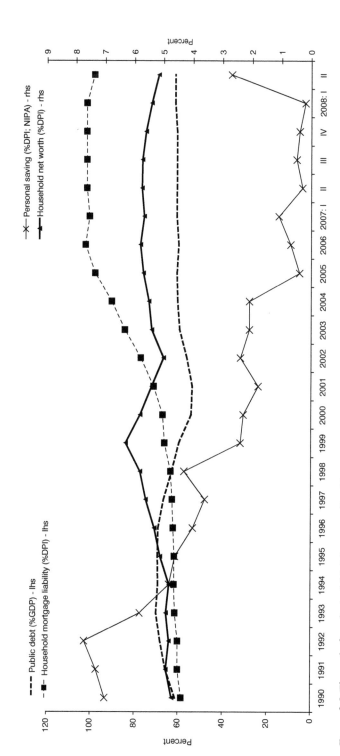

Figure 8.5 The end of a private-debt-driven spending binge

Sources: Bureau of Economic Analysis, Federal Reserve, IMF

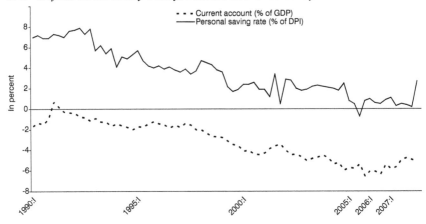

Figure 8.6 Imbalances: US household spending and external counterpart

Source: Bureau of Economic Analysis

If developments in US mortgage and property markets were key to US domestic demand and global GDP growth, as well as to the emergence of global and US imbalances, it may be less of a surprise that the crisis that hit the international financial system in the summer of 2007 originated precisely in these markets, with the US subprime mortgage sector as the epicenter of eruptions. In important ways developments followed the script of a Minskyan boom–bust cycle (see Wray 2007). After recovering from the 1990–1 recession, US property markets stabilized and the long consumer boom got off the ground, featuring a self-validating process of rising credit availability, rising asset prices and rising spending (in excess of income growth).[15] The process reflected the compound impact of: monetary policy, financial innovation, regulation and competition in the financial services industry. Both innovative processes and products played a role as banking business turned more and more into "originate to distribute," structured finance principles of "slicing and dicing" allowed the re-repackaging of large mortgage pools into collateralized debt obligations (sold on to institutional investors including unregulated hedge funds or held off bank balance sheet through "conduits" or "Special Investment Vehicles" as a kind of "shadow banking system"), while the development of credit derivatives like credit default swaps enabled an ever less transparent, but allegedly ever more efficient allocation of credit risk in the financial system.

In the process, mortgage origination moved increasingly outside the realm of regulation and mortgage credit risks apparently migrated off bank balance sheets (in avoidance of bank capital charges). Consumers – also those with "subprime" credit ratings – enjoyed easy access to mortgage finance and home equity loans, while banks and rating agencies enjoyed high fee incomes on off-balance sheet business and model-based credit risk assessments of ever-more sophisticated financial instruments, respectively. All went well as long as property prices kept on rising, validating the low risk of mortgage debt and relaxation of lending standards that was the basis for ever easier access to mortgage credit in the first place. Alas, in 2006, the property price boom that had fueled the virtuous cumulative process finally stalled, and by 2007 property prices were falling nationwide, with distress first emerging from the weakest link in the chain, subprime mortgages.

As is characteristic for the Minskyan boom phase, even borrowers who were unable to service their mortgages out of current income could finance properties, namely by taking out no-interest mortgages and relying on later refinancing at higher property values. As soon as property price rises fail to materialize such mortgages become delinquent, a clear case of "Ponzi finance" turning sour. Accordingly, the credit risk of securities backed by mortgage collateral (in whatever sophisticated ways, sliced and diced, and re-repackaged, etc.) get reassessed. When it turned out that rating agencies calibrated their models on the basis of historical data showing a marked upward trend and excluding the possibility of nationwide falling property prices, the prospect of widespread bankruptcies suddenly loomed large, both among mortgage borrowers and their lenders. As investors realized that it is not even clear on whose books risks might materialize in the end, securities prices plunged across the board (in so far as there are any prices as markets seize up in such events) and systemic risks surged – calling in the lenders of last resort as well as the "deep (Treasury) pockets" behind them.

In 2008, the US found itself in recession and the US financial system in de-leveraging mode. The BWII hypothesis correctly highlights the special status of the US dollar, suggesting continuity in this regard or at least revival since the demise of the original Bretton Woods regime of pegged exchange rates. In this respect, our analysis of the *n*th country role of the key currency issuer is in agreement with the BWII hypothesis. If anything we would go further in stressing the continuity of the international US dollar standard, with the key currency issuer's hegemonic position being further enhanced by financial globalization. But a crucial oversight afflicts BWII: while the US may well have a comparative advantage in producing safe financial assets, the very assets that were actually the culprit of the US spending growth turned out to be rather *unsafe*. And also reflecting the fact that gross financial flows and cross-border asset holdings are much larger than the net flows on which the above analysis focused, those unsafe financial assets turned out to be distributed beyond US borders nevertheless. We therefore disagree with Dooley *et al.* (2008) that the engine will be quickly fixed and BWII continue as before. Much more than a quick fix is involved, and the nature of the regime would be changing quite fundamentally too. Here we merely highlight that at least a temporary shift in global roles has occurred since 2006. Figure 8.7 shows a conspicuous reversal in the contributions of net exports to US GDP growth. With the ending of the property price boom, the US has turned from global growth engine into caboose.

Global growth held up reasonably well during the early stage of the US slowdown. But for a true "decoupling" – and sustainment of global growth – to

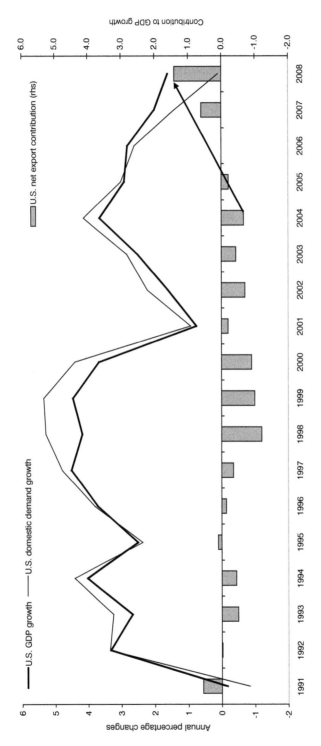

Figure 8.7 As the *n*th country ran out of steam

Source: IMF World Economic Outlook (Oct 2008)

occur while the US is in recession, adequate stimulation of domestic demand growth outside of the US would be required. Such a decoupling would also involve a reversal in global current account trends seen since the Asian crises, implying a slowdown in reserve accumulation from the current account source and unwinding of global imbalances too. This, in turn, would imply the disappearance of an alleged "global saving glut" – which is the subject of the next section.

8.5 Bernanke's "saving glut hypothesis" and Greenspan's "bond market conundrum" as seen from a liquidity preference theoretical perspective

Ben Bernanke first proposed his "saving glut hypothesis" in March 2005. And I find no fault in his starting point that "a satisfying explanation of the recent upward climb of the U.S. current account deficit requires a global perspective that more fully takes into account events outside the United States" (Bernanke 2005). But I do take issue with Bernanke's hypothesis that "over the past decade a combination of diverse forces has created a significant increase in the global supply of saving – a global saving glut – which helps to explain both the increase in the U.S. current account deficit and the relatively low level of real long-term interest rates in the world today" (Bernanke 2005). In this regard, Bernanke singles out "the recent metamorphosis of the developing world from a net user to a net supplier of funds to international capital markets" as an important source behind the rise in the global supply of saving, referring to the "series of financial crises those countries experienced" as a "key reason" for this remarkable change. Bernanke then goes seriously astray when he asserts that "in practice, these countries increased reserves through the expedient of issuing debt to their citizens, thereby mobilizing domestic saving, and then using the proceeds to buy U.S. Treasury securities and other assets. Effectively, governments have acted as financial intermediaries, channeling domestic saving away from local uses and into international capital markets" (Bernanke 2005).[16]

This last statement reveals that underlying the saving glut hypothesis is the loanable funds theory of interest – that notorious neoclassical variation on the classical theme that saving finances investment, and that a rise in thrift directly depresses interest rates, which is supposed to stimulate more investment. And I may quickly add here that the interest rate theory underlying Bernanke's saving glut hypothesis is also favored by Alan Greenspan (2007) who famously referred to a "bond market conundrum" when bond yields even *fell* in response to Fed tightening starting in June 2004.[17]

On this view, a rise in saving in much of the developing world flooded the global capital market, and the resulting excess of saving over investment in "the capital market" depressed interest rates. Developing countries' governments acted as intermediaries in the channeling of (domestic) saving into (foreign) investment, as Bernanke explains in the quotation above, by first collecting the excess saving through domestic debt issuance and then using the proceeds to buy US dollar debts. Foreign savers and their governments thereby depressed US interest rates, giving rise to increased housing investment (and consumption expenditures) by US households. In this way the "excess saving" in Asia *financed* the US boom, it seems. And as Bernanke appears to suggest, foreigners even dominated US policies since bond yields fell despite Fed tightening in 2004 – Greenspan's "bond market conundrum."

It is time to recall here Keynes' fundamental critique of classical and loanable funds theories of interest and apply his critique in the international context.[18] In the *Treatise* (and the subsequent "buckets-in-the-well" controversy) Keynes argued that an *unanticipated* rise in thrift on the part of one group of agents implies "losses" and an equivalent cash-flow shortfall on the part of another group of agents. In the national context the groups involved may be domestic consumers and producers, the unanticipated drop in spending of the former (and rise in liquidity) leaving the latter short of planned sales revenues (and liquidity) in the first instance. Saving does not lead to any new wealth creation, but a mere redistribution of existing wealth. Keynes shows that portfolio adjustments and market dealings involved in this redistribution may well affect interest rates and asset prices, but *only indirectly and in either way* depending on differences in portfolio and liquidity preferences of the two groups. There is no "excess saving" out there in some "capital market" that could *directly* depress interest rates though.

In the international context an additional level of complexity enters the analysis if different currencies are involved, featuring the exchange rate and changes in the distribution and/or the amount of international liquidity. Assume the country the nationals of which save more and spend less on imports now runs a trade surplus as a result. This implies that additional foreign exchange (international liquidity) must be held in some form by some private or official unit(s). At the same time the other country is facing an unanticipated shortfall in export earnings. Its exporters are short of planned sales revenues (and liquidity), private and/or official units of the country are losing international liquidity (or "reserves"). A common presumption would be that the country running a trade deficit and losing international liquidity would see pressures for depreciation of its (real) exchange rate emerging. At least this would seem to be the case if international liquidity consisted of gold, with the supposed adjustment pressures arising along the lines of Hume's specie-flow-price mechanism, perhaps alleviated in the short term by stabilizing capital flows (or aggravated by destabilizing ones).

Assume instead that international liquidity consists of US dollars, that international trade is transacted in terms of US dollars and that the deficit country in our example here happens to be the key currency issuer itself.[19] In this case, the amount of US dollars available in global markets would actually increase accordingly. There are two crucial issues here.

First, the dollar liquidity reaching US trade partners due to the US trade deficit is in the first instance a loss of a part of the pool of liquidity that allowed producers in the US to initiate production at a level which then turned out to be "excessive" in view of the *unanticipated* foreign rise in thrift (and disappointed sales revenues). Foreigners' income expectations and saving plans are realized, and their dollar holdings increase accordingly. If the official sector of the surplus country issues debts to its nationals, this is not as an expedient to collect any "excess saving" and then invest the saving in increased international reserves that finance increased spending in the US, as Bernanke suggests, but to "mop up" (or sterilize) domestic liquidity that arises as the foreign banking system buys dollars from exporters in excess of the dollars it sells to importers at a certain exchange rate. *Ex post* balance of payments accounting may suggest that excess saving in the surplus country "financed" excess US spending and the US trade deficit. But as Keynes' *finance motive* analysis highlighted, capitalist production requires money to go ahead when initiated. This case features US producers drawing on the pool of dollar liquidity provided by the US banking system, part of which then ends up in foreign hands. The respective banking systems in the US and abroad financed a certain level of activity resulting in incomes and saving, but US producers' income expectations got disappointed owing to a rise in thrift abroad. Importantly, and similar to the closed economy case, the (unanticipated) rise in foreign saving leads to a redistribution rather than any new creation in wealth. For US producers and the US as a whole experience a worsening in their net worth and loss in dollar liquidity corresponding to the rise in saving abroad. As in the national context, interest rates and asset prices may be affected *indirectly and in either direction*, but there is no "excess saving" to exert any *direct* downward pressure on interest rates in "the capital market."

And this leads me on to the second crucial issue. Although losing international liquidity, in a sense, the US is unlikely to experience *upward* pressures on interest rates as a result either, contrasting with gold standard conditions. For "losses in international liquidity" have a peculiar meaning for the key currency issuer, enjoying the special status that its national liquidity is also international liquidity. Even if the dollars flowing out through the current account deficit do not return as capital inflows into US securities but are held as reserves in the form of bank deposits, the liquidity "lost" in this way (i.e. bank deposits moving from domestic into foreign hands) can be easily replaced by new dollar liquidity. In contrast to countries that need to commit the "original sin" of borrowing in a foreign currency to pay for spending in excess of income, the key currency issuer enjoys the "original virtue" of paying and owing only in terms of its own currency (itself not redeemable into anything else).

It is critical to appreciate here – again – the likely response by the US Federal Reserve, which we already highlighted above in Section 8.3 when we described the role of the US as global growth engine in the emergence of global imbalances. For in following its mandate of maintaining internal balance, the Federal Reserve's policy stance will likely be eased in reaction to the fact of US producers facing a drop in sales. Easing policy is the Fed's natural response to a drop in exports that heralds weakness in US product and labor markets. And in doing so, the Fed will pay little attention to the dollar's external value. The notion of "benign neglect" has a somewhat derogatory ring to it. However, in acting as "spender of last resort" the key currency issuer is countering the deflationary effects that would otherwise arise. In particular, deflationary pressures would automatically arise under gold standard conditions whenever nations succumbed to mercantilistic motives or harbored increased desires of hoarding reserves.

This vital role of the key currency issuer's policy reaction becomes even clearer when conducting the above thought experiment of an international rise in thrift (and corresponding drop in US exports) in terms of *The General Theory* (i.e. under the assumption of correct short-term expectations). If US producers *correctly anticipate* the incipient drop in export sales and curtail production accordingly, US incomes and spending on imports would be correspondingly lower. And so would foreign incomes, with planned foreign saving turning out to be disappointed plans, a mere mirage. At lower incomes the excess saving which is supposed to depress interest rates according to the saving glut hypothesis would not arise in the first place. In fact, foreign incomes and any "excess saving" would only arise *if* US incomes and imports were somehow stimulated to offset the, in this case, anticipated drop in US exports. The flawed "loanable funds mechanism" cannot possibly bring any such relief. Instead, deliberate policy by the *n*th country is required, while the "Keynes effect" may help too.

In the closed-economy context the Keynes effect was seen in operation when the level of activity changes relative to the pool of liquidity provided by the banking system (see Chapter 5). In practice, a decline in aggregate demand depressing activity and loan demand might well induce banks to expand their business in other directions. Banks would merely be following their profit motive. And this time round their corporate borrowers are not pressured to roll-over loans to finance unplanned inventories, for instance. By taking more bonds and assets off the market bank behavior is driving up their price while the pool of liquidity rises. At the same time the monetary authorities may well react to weakness in the economy by easing monetary policy (and the banks' behavior may be inspired by the anticipation of policy easing). In the international economy context the behavior of the key currency issuer's banking system as guided by the deliberate policy of the *n*th country's authorities is key to the working of the "Keynes mechanism" (rather than effect) and provision of dollar liquidity, which is also serving as international liquidity.

In summary, I applaud Bernanke's call for a global perspective and his hints that other countries' policies may have played a part in triggering US policy reactions. But I have to reject the "saving glut hypothesis" – since it is based on a flawed interest rate theory. The alternative liquidity preference theoretical analysis elaborated above starts from the observation that expansion in the US was made possible in the first place by *dollar liquidity*. Dollar liquidity then spilled over to much of the rest of the world through the channels referred to above in Section 8.3 in a process featuring US spending growth in excess of US income growth and soaring global imbalances. From a liquidity preference theoretical perspective this was made possible to go ahead at low interest rates since both key ingredients were in place, first, low policy rates and, second, benign interest rate expectations held by financial market players. Both policy rates and interest rate expectations remained low despite rapid demand growth because of vast new global supply-side opportunities and generally weak pressures in labor markets.

Accordingly, a liquidity preference theoretical explanation for Greenspan's "bond market conundrum" attributes the very phenomenon to a *global dollar glut* arising in an environment of deficient demand in product markets. Developments in product and labor markets triggered the policy and market responses that delivered low interest rates ruling in financial markets; and whatever may be the case in the *imaginary* classical "capital market" allegedly balancing saving and investment.

And we may add here that even as inflationary pressures finally showed up in headline inflation measures in 2007, reflecting global commodity resource constraints and commodity market speculation, bond yields stayed low as markets apparently judged that the global boom and the monetary policy tightening cycle were already at or past their peak, so that inflationary pressures would soon abate again. This implied judgment became a very reasonable one especially when in August 2007 a global financial crisis shook the world economy from its Goldilocks dreams of a never-ending "Great Moderation" that for long seemed to justify relaxed risk taking in the face of extended leveraging and wildly compressed risk premiums.

As the crisis evolved, featuring spectacular failures among Wall Street investment banks, developed country government bonds once again became investors' safe havens, and risk premiums on corporate bonds and emerging market bonds soared. At first the US dollar continued to weaken further, against the euro in particular, but in the fall of 2008 the dollar's trend decline reversed. In the context of sharply rising risk aversion, triggering an equity market crash and plunging commodity prices, carry trade unwinding favored the Japanese yen and the US dollar in particular. Emerging market currencies came under pressure, reversing their appreciating trend that had been in place since 2002.

Recent exchange rate trends thus run counter to a further unwinding of global imbalances. Instead, they highlight afresh the key role of the US dollar in global finance. Apparently, emerging markets are once again experiencing pressures arising from reversals in global capital flows including a roll-back of engagement by Western banks. After years of exploding international reserve holdings, an increasing number of emerging market governments were seen intervening in foreign exchange markets in support of their currencies. Self-insurance may seem like a fine idea from the perspective of the individual developing country. It may prove less effective in a systemic global crisis. The ultimate outcome of a synchronous drawing on self-insurance plans through reserve hoarding will depend on whether emerging markets can maintain momentum in domestic demand growth and whether developed countries at the core of the global financial system succeed in stemming the ongoing "credit meltdown" that is behind the de-leveraging and repatriation of foreign financial engagements.

8.6 How to counter the "credit meltdown"

In Section 8.3 above I referred to a Minskyan boom–bust cycle as a description of developments in US property and financial markets. The Fed's "easy money" policy after 2001 surely played a role in all this, for instance through raising the attractiveness of adjustable rate mortgages and "teaser rate" features in a low interest rate environment. Yet, the above analysis emphasized that the Fed was following its mandate of fostering maximum employment and price stability when it eased policy aggressively in reaction to pronounced labor market weakness and deflation threats in 2001–3. With fiscal policy frowned upon for ideological reasons since the 1990s, the task of maintaining internal balance was primarily left to monetary policy. Attaining US internal balance required interest rates that were low enough, and asset prices that were high enough, to bring forth the private spending sufficient to also enable the US economy to play its *n*th country role. As the rest of the world over time became overly reliant on the US growth engine, the Federal Reserve had to kick the accelerator especially hard in the aftermath of the dot.com bubble burst.

Essentially, with the corporate sector in balance-sheet-repair mode, US consumers alone had to be sufficiently enticed to do the excess spending required to get the global economy back on track. The largest impact on the US economy itself came through the housing sector, the one large domestic sector in which offshoring is not an issue (while immigrant labor surely is). And in a process featuring a dynamic triangle of regulation, competition and innovation, the financial risks of mortgage financing became both ever more highly leveraged as well as widely distributed among the constituent parts of a largely unregulated shadow banking system, including its global linkages.

It is rather instructive to consider here the extent to which finance and seigniorage extraction have come full circle today. In a most rudimentary stage of development government currency note issuance provides the sole source of finance and all seigniorage goes to the state. The attraction of private banking lies in capturing the seigniorage pie, with a whole structure of finance built on top of it. In an advanced stage of banking development private credit creation becomes the primary source of liquidity, while the lender of last resort is left with merely some residual of the money business and seigniorage revenue. Meanwhile, competition between banks and markets determines to what extent seigniorage gets passed on to rentiers in line with the short-term rate of interest as set by the monetary authorities. Given the government's role in safeguarding financial stability as a prerequisite for economic stability and development, the banking system needs to be regulated to counter the inherent tendency of banking to strive on (or protect itself against) the self-fulfilling-prophecy element of credit creation (destruction) as long as the banks expand (or contract) in synchronicity; with the synchronous movement being normally assured by monetary policy. In an ideological climate that has favored deregulation by the state and "self-regulation" by the private actors concerned, competition and innovation may well have been fostered. But competition and innovation taking place largely outside the purview of regulators meant leveraging up systemic risks. Apparent microeconomic efficiency was increasingly undermining macroeconomic solidity.

As the property market bust triggered the implosion of the shadow banking system, apparent off-balance-sheet risks migrated back onto the regular (i.e.

regulated) banking systems' balance sheet. This added further pressure on bank capital, under pressure due to write-downs on whatever risks had stayed on their books anyway. Bank failures and a general breakdown in trust among banks and hence interbank lending, in turn, then saw wholesale money business increasingly moving back onto the central bank's own balance sheet; while retail money business had to be encouraged to stay with banks and money market funds by means of extended government guarantees of their safety. Yet, while finance is thus, in a sense, coming full circle, the government is not profiting from regaining market share in the money business, certainly not in the short run. Quite the opposite. For the game is one of socializing the losses after privatizing the profits. Unfortunately, socializing losses is the only game in town the government can really afford to play in the current situation. *Ex ante* sound regulation and supervision could have prevented or at least limited today's damages. *Ex post* anything but bold and aggressive action to counter the plight will turn out to be even more costly in the end.

The "crisis of confidence" analysis of Chapter 4 comes in handy here. Either because of fear and/or because of being cut off from finance, consumers, producers and entrepreneurial investors alike increasingly exercise their default option of "not spending/producing," which has direct income effects, spreading throughout the economy. At the same time portfolio investors (including nonbank financial intermediaries) become more risk averse and try to become more liquid. A rush into bank deposits and T-bills produces a surge in risk spreads and plunge in asset prices, a process feeding on itself as "forced selling" sets in. Banks can stop the downward spiral by buying or financing more risky assets, thereby providing more liquidity that can soothe other more anxious souls. Real trouble hits when the banks themselves not only fail to provide such market support line, but actually add to the liquidation of risky assets and try to become more liquid when everyone else tries to do so too. To prevent a credit crunch from turning into a full-blown debt deflation the central bank, as lender of last resort, has to substitute in for banks in providing finance to nonbanks while supplying emergency liquidity to banks. In the context of the ongoing crisis the Federal Reserve is seen as acting both as national as well as international lender of last resort, reflecting the dollars reserve currency status and the fact that distressed US assets also found their way into foreign portfolios. Not only has a good part of the US money market moved onto the Federal Reserve's balance sheet with the freezing up of domestic interbank markets as well as problems in commercial paper markets. In addition, the freezing up of the global interbank network saw the Federal Reserve enter into swap arrangements with international central banks through which dollars are made available to money markets of global systemic importance.

The evolution of the Federal Reserve System's balance sheet (though lacking full transparency in certain positions) since the start of the crisis in 2007 is a reflection of these developments. Two phases may be distinguished. In the first – pre-Lehman – phase the composition of the Federal Reserves' assets changed in favor of untypically risky assets at the expense of Treasury securities. In the second – post-Lehman – phase the size of its balance sheet has also more than doubled. The issuance of special ("Supplementary Financing Program") Treasury bills (since September 2008) and payment of interest on bank reserves (since October 2008) were added to the Fed's liability management tool arsenal as the Federal Reserve added huge amounts of risky assets to its portfolio.

We may recall here that Keynes not only fully endorsed the "Bagehot principle" of acting as lender of last resort when a liquidity squeeze was the issue, but also argued that the central bank may have to aggressively expand its own balance sheet in times when the banks refuse or are unable to expand theirs – for fear of expected losses or impaired capital owing to past losses (i.e. when solvency is the issue). In practice, liquidity and solvency problems are intimately related in systemic crises anyway. With the Fed funds rate (and interest rate paid on bank reserves) approaching zero, quantitative management methods can only increase in prominence.

The Federal Reserve can and should continue expanding its balance sheet by buying or financing whatever assets, thereby taking distressed assets off the market and storing them where "marking to market" is not a short-term threat (paired with whatever hopes for recovery of unrealized losses in the longer term). But even courageous monetary action alone is unlikely to rescue the situation and prevent a deep recession and further deterioration in the financial system. For the situation is one that also calls for bold fiscal action since both the US banking system and US consumers require large-scale balance sheet repair (Bibow 2008a).

The key challenges presented by the underlying property market bust are the following. First, as long as property prices continue to sag private households are suffering declining net worth (magnified by falling equities), with rising cases of "negative equity." This means that the for-long-reliable (credit-driven) spending engine no. 1, US consumers, has not only stalled, but is now facing a cash-flow squeeze and pressures to repay debts. Second, the more desperate the situation of household gets, the greater the deflationary pressures in property markets (through foreclosures) and product markets in general; in turn, weakening the labor market, which is thereby providing another negative feedback loop. Third, the greater the troubles of household debtors (and the related troubles spreading throughout the economy through falling household spending), the greater the troubles of their lenders (and related troubles spreading throughout the financial system through failures of lending institutions) are bound to get. Finally, the more the economy deteriorates, the greater pressures for lunatic government action (such as attempts to balance the budget) might get as the government budget and balance sheet naturally and inevitably deteriorate in a purely passive manner.

Rather than watching the public budget deteriorate in a passive manner, bold and immediate fiscal action is by far preferable. Fiscal action should partly take the form of balance sheet repair, applied to stocks of under-water units (or those at risk of becoming so). And it should partly take the form of both supporting as well as supplementing private spending by increased government spending and tax cuts. As to the latter channel, I see a strong case, for reasons of fairness, in favor of raising types of government spending with general benefits to society at large and tax cuts giving relief to taxpayers in general rather than specific measures targeting under-water households. The aim is to support spending and help the economy recover, benefiting everyone, rather than arrange redistribution towards households that ended up with excessive debts, while having the bill footed by those that did not.[20] As regards the former channel, fiscal action for balance sheet repair, measures targeting household debtors may do more to stop property market pressures arising from foreclosures, while measures targeting lenders may do more to the availability of new lending. Both types of measures are needed to stabilize property markets and the economy, and in each case the government should make sure to secure a fair share of the upside for taxpayers rather than those being bailed out.

Deciding the general nature of required fiscal action is one thing, determining the needed scale of action another. My advice is not to delay bold action. At the current juncture, risks arising from erring on the expansionary side seem low. The government budget deficit is likely to by far exceed the recent record peak of just below 6 percent of GDP in 1992 in any case. The overall national loss from economic distress will be the greater the more the situation is allowed to deteriorate when too timid action is taken.

It is instructive to briefly recall here the above helicopter parable. Essentially, fiscal action for balance sheet repair (stocks) means turning private debts into public debts *ex post*. Similarly, fiscal action in support of flows essentially means replacing private-debt-driven spending by public-debt-driven spending as key engine for recovery and future expansion. And with the short-term rate of interest approaching zero, i.e. equalling the yield on banknotes, this would make our parable become just about true. I argued above that this would also establish an important condition for a sustainable international regime à la "Bretton Woods II." A sustainable arrangement along these lines is at least conceivable as long as foreigners are willing to hold *low-yielding* US assets forever. The key currency issuer could then enjoy international seigniorage gains forever as well (although Wall Street would no longer enjoy the kind of returns that came along with financing the private spending boom; before the boom turned bust I mean). Note here that in this case the safe assets ending up in foreign portfolios are also the very debts that are actually driving the spending growth in excess of income growth of the key currency issuer acting as engine of global growth. Perhaps we might call this conceivable global arrangement "Bretton Woods III"; or at least acknowledge that what Dooley *et al.* (2003) popularized as BWII featured an important oversight that is at the heart of the ongoing global financial crisis. Alternative arrangements are surely conceivable too.

8.7 Some concluding observations

The international monetary order established at Bretton Woods did not follow Keynes' script. The world economy has operated on a US dollar standard ever since. At first this happened in the context of pegged (and all too rigid) exchange rates and including some apparent check on the key currency issuer provided by gold convertibility. Since the early 1970s the international dollar standard has featured greater degrees of exchange rate flexibility vis-à-vis the dollar. Dollar supremacy was further enhanced through the liberalization of financial markets and international capital flows. This chapter has highlighted the dual role of the key currency issuer, the nth country in the system, to act both as global currency anchor as well as global growth engine of last resort. It is noteworthy that two leading industrialized countries that pursued export-led growth strategies under conditions of "Bretton Woods I" have failed to ever grow up and let go of that strategy, but remained stuck in domestic demand stagnation since the early 1990s instead. I am of course referring to Germany and Japan. Since 1994 China essentially copied their development strategy by pegging to the dollar at a competitive exchange rate while relying on capital controls to secure national policy space. Finally, in the aftermath of the Asian crises of the late 1990s, other emerging market economies, which in contrast to China had fully embraced capital account liberalization, have (re-)embraced export-led growth strategies cum self-insurance through reserve hoarding – a lesson learned from repeated contagious crises affecting their asset class.

With much of the rest of the world becoming overly reliant on the key currency issuer as global growth engine, the latter increased its own risk exposure correspondingly, with fragile private-debt-based financing structures starting to collapse in the summer of 2007 – heralding a "Minsky moment" of truth. I diagnosed an important oversight afflicting the BWII hypothesis with its sole focus on safe financial assets produced by the US in exchange for running persistent current account deficits. US spending growth in excess of income growth proved unsustainable since it was based on ever more fragile private debt structures that were to implode as soon as the property boom stalled; the mechanism that had validated Ponzi finance as long as it lasted.

It is thus correct that "events outside the US" too played their part in the emergence of global imbalances and today's global financial crisis, but the idea of global saving glut in the capital market is not a sound one. I have rejected Bernanke's saving glut hypothesis and Greenspan's related bond market conundrum for their reliance on *flawed* loanable funds theory. My alternative "global dollar glut" hypothesis is based on Keynes' liquidity preference theory as applied at the global level and in the context of an international dollar standard. The global dollar glut hypothesis starts from the observation that expansion in the US was made possible in the first place by *dollar liquidity*. Dollar liquidity then spilled over to much of the rest of the world in a process featuring US spending growth in excess of US income growth and soaring global imbalances. All this occurred in an environment of vast new global supply-side opportunities and generally weak pressures in labor markets. Developments in product and labor markets thus triggered the policy and market responses that delivered low interest rates ruling in financial markets; and whatever may be the case in the *imaginary* classical "capital market" allegedly balancing saving and investment.

As to the global financial crisis that started in 2007 and de-railed what had been hailed as a sustainable symbiosis of interests of the US and its foreign creditors by proponents of BWII, the analysis highlighted that the private-debt-based spending engine is broke and unlikely to be restarted anytime soon. It will take bold government action to counter the credit meltdown (or debt deflation). And the Federal Reserve's balance sheet will have to continue to expand strongly as the short-term rate of interest approaches zero.

It is possible that bold US fiscal action to repair private balance sheets and bolster spending might herald a new global arrangement in which the safe assets ending up in foreign portfolios are also the actual drivers behind the spending growth in excess of income growth of the key currency issuer acting as engine of global growth. Such a "Bretton Woods III" arrangement is certainly one possible outcome, which highlights the important oversight in BWII that is at the heart of the ongoing global financial crisis: the issue of seemingly safe private debts, seemingly safe as long as the triple A convention held. However, other global arrangements are surely conceivable too, including more collaborative and symmetric ones along the lines of Keynes' original vision for a Bretton Woods order of international monetary and financial affairs.

9 Taking liquidity preference theory seriously[1]

This book set out to make the case that a proper understanding of Keynes' contribution to monetary theory requires a complete exposition and full appreciation of the essential role of liquidity preference theory in his heretical attack on the quantity theory of money. Clarifying the importance of Keynes' liquidity preference theory as the basis for understanding the role of money in a general theoretical framework of a monetary production economy is especially salient in light of the continued hegemony of the money neutrality postulate in both monetary models and the conduct of monetary policy.

While I argued there that it should not take a global financial crisis to remind us of the continued relevance of Keynes' superior contribution, I may nevertheless use some occurrences in that crisis to highlight the superiority of Keynes' analytical framework, including liquidity preference theory, over its competitors. Recall my critique of the Post Keynesian endogenous money approach as depicting banks as purely passive providers of credit to corporations through pre-arranged credit lines while drawing at its own reserves-overdraft at the central bank, albeit at the rate of interest as set by the monetary authorities.

No doubt bank overdraft facilities and pre-arranged credit lines of all sorts matter to the smooth functioning of economies. They might at first even seem to rule out the possibility of a credit crunch. And the fact that in the fall of 2008 monetary aggregates still show vivid growth (albeit much more slowly than base money) might seem to deny fears of a credit crunch. I doubt very much, though, that banks had ever anticipated such a widespread actual drawing on pre-arranged credit lines. In other words, their balance sheets are growing quite involuntarily as markets are frozen and normal channels to securitize clogged up while borrowers may even be tempted to draw on their credit lines and park the proceeds in Treasury bills for fear that credit lines might be cut back. The correspondingly emergent pressure on banks to protect the steadily depreciating value of their capital base is one of many reasons that might explain the unlikelihood of their extending *new* credit proper (including newly pre-arranged credit lines), despite their ready access to reserves. Moreover, as frozen money markets make it especially risky for any one bank to step out of line with the rest, the authorities will have to work on making a critical mass of the system more sanguine towards simultaneously increasing the rate at which they expand credit.

What all this underlines is that there is nothing passive or automatic in bank behavior at all – the Post Keynesian endogenous money view of banks as passive conduits of credit quite similarly in that respect to the traditional monetarist view of banks as passive multipliers of reserves in the transmission mechanism of monetary policy both reduce to fictions that deviate profoundly from the behaviors of banks that are currently being exhibited. Banks' assessments of credit risks vary with the state of the economy and their own liquidity preference, tempered partly by their assessment of their immediate market as well as their assessment of the state of liquidity preference for the financial system as a whole, all within the context of the necessity of their maintaining the viability of their own capital requirement. Considering these decisions in a general framework, such as the one provided by Keynes, implies that banks' and other financial intermediaries' portfolio decisions in light of their estimation of economic events significantly influence the direction of those very economic events. Furthermore, as the current crisis shows all too clearly, banks are actively engaged in financial markets and exposed to asset prices more generally, either directly or through their financing of other units, nonfinancial and financial (including hedge funds and other unregulated players, etc.). Arguably, it is impossible to make sense of the role of banks in today's crisis when viewing them as passive rather than active players; an argument that also applies to the Minskian boom phase that preceded the current bust. Keynes' liquidity preference theory and Minsky's contributions provide a suitable conceptual framework for analyzing the working of the financial system and the behavior of banks. Post Keynesian endogenous money proponents should take liquidity preference theory seriously.

My urge to take liquidity preference theory seriously of course holds for mainstream New Keynesian monetary policy modeling exercises as well. In fact, there are no banks or any financial system present in the typical mainstream modeling world in the first place: monetary policy is transmitted directly from the short-term rate of interest to the economy, with no slippage possible in between. The microeconomic foundations underlying this modeling world cannot make sense of either money or banks since Keynesian uncertainty and time are elegantly "abstracted from" (even when the terms "stochastic" and "dynamic" would perhaps suggest otherwise to the person who does not understand the critical theoretical and policy implications of the difference between the terms "risk" and "uncertainty"). The assumed characteristics of such mainstream modeling world bear little resemblance to the "economic society in which we actually live, with the result that its teaching is misleading and disastrous if we attempt to apply it to the facts of experience" (Keynes 1936a, JMK 7: 3). Admittedly, the credit rationing approach (see Stiglitz and Greenwald 2003) fares better on this count and offers valuable insights into banking and credit, but, like the mainstream in general, remains attached to the loanable funds theory of interest.

Chapter 8 has shown that continued adherence to the loanable funds theory of interest is the underlying reason for many half-baked and flawed ideas prominently featuring in today's policy debates. As Keynes pointed out, though apparently to no avail, the "saving first" view yields flawed diagnoses when applied to monetary production economies. Saving cannot be a source of finance of investment in that environment, the kind of environment we actually live in. The loanable funds theory totally misconstrues the role of the financial system, the role of liquidity provided by the banking system, in particular, in allowing capitalist production and accumulation to go ahead. In this regard, Chapter 8 highlighted the paramount role of the Federal Reserve and US banking system in today's global monetary order. Overlooking this key factor is bound to lead to poor advice on how to overcome today's global financial crisis.

In particular, proposals to apply monetary policy to pre-emptively pop perceived asset price bubbles can only overburden monetary policy even further. The issue should be taken care of by regulatory means rather than monetary policy, best as part of a more general overhaul of banking regulation that should feature built-in countercyclical (rather than procyclical) capital adequacy rules. Today's exclusively micro-focused approach of supervisors on individual institutions needs to be supplemented by a macro-prudential approach designed to detect the emergence of imbalances and build-up of systemic risk (as the aggregate outcome of individual institutions' risktaking behaviors). For the great irony of banking is that everyone may appear safe for too long despite rises in their *effective* risk exposure precisely because and as long as players are generally moving in tandem.[2] But the task of monitoring and containing excessive risktaking, and especially from a systemic perspective, is one of regulation and supervision, not of monetary policy. And I hasten to add here that while appropriate overhauls in regulation and supervision are highly desirable regarding future crisis prevention, policies to reduce leverage and strictly enforce capital requirements today would surely be counterproductive in overcoming the ongoing crisis.

Note however that constraining banks' active behavior might also dampen their responsiveness to monetary policy. I argued in Chapter 8 that the Federal Reserve was following its mandate in applying aggressively expansionary monetary policy in 2002 in response to slack in domestic labor markets that was in good part due to external reliance on the US as global growth engine; effectively on the US consumer as borrower and spender of last resort. The Federal Reserve's role of yesterday in firing the global growth engine is closely related to its role today in acting as global lender of last resort. In my view this shows that the key currency issuer's central bank has become greatly overburdened in the process.

A reassessment of the role of fiscal policy was brought upon us by the sheer scale of the emergency at hand. Note the irony that zealous attempts to minimize government intervention can end up leading to more rather than less government intervention, as governments end up owning banking systems that they withdrew from regulating because of ill-founded faith in the unguided invisible hand. Surely the usefulness of fiscal policy in stabilizing the economy needs to be reappraised beyond the resolution of the ongoing crisis as well.

Finally, in my view a reassessment of the global monetary and financial order should also be the order of the day. It is peculiar that some industrialized countries get away with notoriously freeloading on external growth to compensate their failures at home. I am referring to Germany and Japan here. And it was diagnosed as paradoxical that developing countries at large should export capital and build up immense "self-insurance" shields as protection against the hazards of global finance, contradicting promises of the blissful benefits that unregulated global finance would deliver to them (see Bibow 2009a). Apart from offering us liquidity preference theory as a suitable theoretical framework for analyzing the working of the financial system, Keynes also offered us ideas for the institutional design of an alternative global monetary and financial order that would prevent these suboptimal national policies, ideas that remain relevant today as well.

Notes

1 The triumph of Keynesianism?

1 I gratefully acknowledge comments on an earlier draft by Roy Rotheim.
2 Similarly, the *Financial Times* reports that while the International Monetary Fund assesses today's situation as the greatest shock since the 1930s, the "IMF chief economist's optimism that the world would avoid a repeat of the Great Depression of the 1930s was based on an expectation that governments would follow the right policies" (*Financial Times*, 8 Oct. 2008).
3 While few policymakers may feel inclined today to mention Keynes as their inspiration, it is noteworthy that even some conservative media commentators like Samuel Brittan came forth with calls like "Keynes, thou shouldst be living ..." (*Financial Times*, 9 Oct. 2008). Among financial market players and commentators Hyman Minsky has enjoyed a remarkable comeback; with frequent references to a "Minsky moment" appearing in the media since the beginning of the crisis (as recorded by the annual Minsky conferences organized by the Levy Economics Institute of Bard College). Minsky (1975) understood his "financial instability hypothesis" largely as an interpretation of Keynes' monetary thought.
4 In *The General Theory* he states that "it is often convenient in practice to include in *money* time-deposits with banks and, occasionally, even such instruments as (e.g.) treasury bills. As a rule, I shall, as in my *Treatise on Money*, assume that money is co-extensive with bank deposits" (Keynes 1936a, JMK 7: 167, fn. 1). Throughout this book references to *The Collected Writings of John Maynard Keynes* will be abbreviated to JMK. For purposes of chronological guidance both the year of first publication and the corresponding JMK volume and page reference will be given.
5 Keynes expressed this point perhaps most beautifully in the *Treatise*: "It is enterprise which builds and improves the world's possessions. ... If enterprise is afoot, wealth accumulates whatever may be happening to thrift; and if enterprise is asleep, wealth decays whatever thrift may be doing. Thus, thrift may be the handmaid and nurse of enterprise. But equally she may not. And, perhaps, even usually she is not. For enterprise is connected with thrift not directly but at one remove; and the link which should join them is frequently missing. For the engine which drives enterprise is not thrift, but profit. Now, for enterprise to be active, two conditions must be fulfilled. There must be an expectation of profit; and it must be possible for enterprisers to obtain command of sufficient resources to put their projects into execution. ... their power to put their projects into execution on terms which they deem attractive, almost entirely depends on the behavior of the banking and monetary system" (Keynes 1930b, JMK 6: 132–3).
6 Cf. also Clower 1967; Arrow and Hahn 1971; Hellwig 1993.
7 Pasinetti's (2007) insightful discussion of Keynes' "unaccomplished revolution" contrasts production and exchange paradigms.

8 See Bibow 2002a for a detailed discussion of the evolution of Friedman's views on monetary policy and his theoretical roots in Keynes' monetary theory.

9 Keynes made this point in more formal terms in a short note written in response to Hayek's advocacy of a commodity reserve currency as the right method to control the quantity of money and thereby preserve international price stability along quantity-theoretic lines: "On another view, however, each national price level is primarily determined by the relation of the national wage level to the national efficiency; or, more generally, by the relation of money costs to efficiency in terms of the national unit of currency. And if price levels are determined by money costs, it follows that whilst an 'appropriate' quantity of money is a *necessary* condition of stability prices, it is not a *sufficient* condition. For prices can only be stabilized by first stabilizing the relation of money wages (and other costs) to efficiency" (Keynes 1943e, JMK 26: 31).

10 In 1944 Keynes commented on the supposed "effect" as "really too fantastic for words and scarcely worth discussing" (quoted in Patinkin 1982).

11 On credit rationing see also Blinder 1987; Rotheim 2006.

12 See Tily 2006, 2007, on debt management and liquidity preference theory.

13 Paul Krugman (2008), another prominent New Keynesian and the latest winner of the "Sveriges Riksbank Prize in Economic Sciences in Memory of Alfred Nobel," puts it with his usual eloquence: "When depression economics prevails, the usual rules of economic policy no longer apply: virtue becomes vice, caution is risky and prudence is folly." While I fully agree with the thrust of his policy advice for immediate action, it may also be worth reconsidering those "usual rules of economic policy" that got us where we are.

14 See Keynes' (1936a, JMK 7: 81–5) discussion of the reconciliation of the saving–investment *identity* with "free will" in relation to the role of banks. This makes it clear both that the finance motive is implicitly taken into account in *The General Theory* and that Keynes' whole argument is based on the two-sidedness of economic transactions while having nothing to do with the supposed *ex post* nature of the saving–investment identity which his critics attributed to his argument.

2 Some reflections on Keynes' "finance motive" for the demand for money

1 This chapter appeared in the *Cambridge Journal of Economics*. Republished by permission. I have made some slight amendments. I am grateful to Wynne Godley, Michael Kuczynski, James Trevithick, and two anonymous referees for helpful comments. Special thanks are due to my research supervisor Jochen Runde. I also gratefully acknowledge ESRC Research Studentship No. R00429324032 and a Research Scholarship from Girton College, Cambridge. The paper was the joint winner of the 1993 Stevenson Prize of the University of Cambridge.

2 "There is, I think, a concealed difference of opinion, which is of very great importance, between myself and a group of economists who express themselves as agreeing with me in abandoning the theory that the rate of interest is (in Professor Ohlin's words) 'determined by the condition that it equalises the supply of and the demand for saving, or, in other words, equalizes saving and investment'. ... Nevertheless the theories are, I believe, radically opposed to one another" (Keynes 1937e, JMK 14: 201–2).

3 "The theory of the interest rate mechanism is the center of the confusion in modern macroeconomics. Not all issues in contention originate here. But the *inconclusive* quarrels – the ill-focused, frustrating ones that drag on because the contending parties cannot agree what the issue is – largely do stem from this source" (Leijonhufvud 1981: 131).

4   Cf. Runde (1994) and Ch. 4 below on the connection between Keynesian uncertainty and liquidity preference.

5   When he clarifies the connection between the two schemes of classification he uses in *The General Theory* and the *Treatise on Money* respectively he also mentions that: "I need not repeat here the analysis which I gave in Chapter 3 of that book" (Keynes 1936a, JMK 7: 195). Chapter 3 of the *Treatise* has the title "The analysis of bank money." See Shackle (1967) and Amadeo (1989) on the connection between the two books from a methodological point of view.

6   The Marshallian *k* appears in the Cambridge Cash Balance version of the equation of exchange: $M = kPY$. Cf. Bordo (1987).

7   Keynes divides money, i.e. bank deposits, into "savings deposits" and "cash deposits." The latter are held for the purpose of making payments. They are further sub-divided into "income deposits" and "business deposits A and B" (Keynes 1930a, JMK 5: 38–43).

8   This is an example of the "Index Number problem," pervasive in any aggregate variable but still generally ignored nowadays, which was probably first brought to our attention by Keynes in an undergraduate paper that won him the "Adam Smith Prize," and later on in book II of the *Treatise on Money*.

9   "For 'finance' is essentially a revolving fund. It employs no savings. It is, for the community as a whole, only a book-keeping transaction" (Keynes 1937f, JMK 14: 219).

10 See also his following remark: "The additional factor, previously overlooked, to which Professor Ohlin's emphasis on the *ex ante* character of investment decisions has directed attention, is the following. During the interregnum – and during that period only – between the date when the entrepreneur arranges his finance and the date when he actually makes his investment, there is an additional demand for liquidity without, as yet, any additional supply of it necessarily arising. In order that the entrepreneur may feel himself sufficiently liquid to be able to embark on the transaction, someone else has to agree to become, for the time being at least, more unliquid than before" (Keynes 1937f, JMK 14: 218).

11 Cf. Robertson (1940: 12–13). Keynes, by contrast, concludes: "But this only serves to buttress the liquidity theory of interest against the savings theory of interest" (Keynes 1937f, JMK 14: 221).

12 L_t^* is Davidson's modified demand for money function.

13 Tsiang (1980: 470–1) remarks in a footnote that he considers Davidson's interpretation as logically inconsistent, without however pursuing the issue any further. Nevertheless Davidson's model generally produces simultaneous shifts in both curves.

14 His discussion of the finance motive in the context of the "Keynesian cross diagram" (à la Samuelson-Hansen) is equally flawed. I shall here concentrate on the "more general" Hicksian IS/LM framework.

15 When Davidson comments on the mathematical proof of his analysis he actually says just this: it "shows that if, and only if $\alpha = \beta = k$, then the equilibrium level of output in both the traditional and finance motive systems will be identical" (Davidson 1965: 64). Apparently Davidson does not realize that there might just as well occur a simultaneous *downward* shift of the LM curve, namely in the case of a relative increase in that component of total expenditure which has the smaller Marshallian *k*. It is actually difficult to draw a singular LM curve at all, since the requirements of the active circulation *at each level of output* are now contingent upon its particular composition – we have to envisage a whole surface plane of LM curves. Furthermore, the autonomous component in Davidson's consumption function causes more trouble.

16 Shackle (1967: 138) regards Davidson's elaboration as unnecessary. Chick (1983: 200) puts it well when she says: "Transactions balances are held in anticipation of payments, and so are related to planned expenditure, every bit as much as 'finance' balances are. The difference is that no special effort is taken to acquire them: they

arise out of income or from sales." We may add that financial transactions (stock exchange turnover, roll-overs of bank loans, etc.) *at that level of actual activity* are also part of this "self-financing" continuous circular flow, or "revolving fund." See below.

17 The transient nature of the finance motive is emphasized by James Trevithick (1994) who also suggested that I illustrate my argument graphically. Fig. 2.1 illustrates an imaginary transient disequilibrium in an equilibrium model.

18 In his response to Horwich's (1966) obscure loanable funds arguments Davidson's (1967) intuitions often point in the right direction.

19 Asimakopulos 1983: 227. Cf. Keynes 1936a, JMK 7: 122–4 and Hicks 1974: ch. 1.

20 The disputants include: Asimakopulos 1983, 1985, 1986a, b, c; Davidson 1986; Graziani 1984; Kregel 1986; Snippe 1985, 1986; Terzi 1986a, b; Richardson 1986.

21 Cf. Asimakopulos 1983: 228; Richardson 1986: 191, n. 1. Keynes realized (and regretted) too late the consequences of his illustration of the finance motive as an *addendum* to the transactions motive while suppressing the discussion of the latter. Apparently he was assuming that his critics had grasped the former motive and therefore would easily understand their relation to each other. "But I did not mean to ignore the second time lag in circulation, which I had sufficiently emphasised on previous occasions" (Keynes 1938, JMK 14: 230).

22 By whom this windfall has to be borne depends on the particular institutional arrangement. The twofold process can probably still conveniently be regarded as the characteristic standard in Britain. Alternatively, the one-off provision of long-term loans by the "universal banks," i.e. a "one-stage process," may be conveniently regarded as the characteristic German standard. We may also contemplate the case where no (non-marketable) loans are provided at all but financial intermediaries invest in (marketable) securities only. As a variant hereof, to replicate the twofold process, there may be two classes of intermediaries specializing in short-term and long-term securities respectively. Also the investor may simply short hedge his open position of long-term funding in the futures market, or roll-over short-term loans in the first place. Different institutional arrangements and practices of risk sharing may well have important "real" effects but nevertheless do not affect the substance of the finance motive as a theoretical concept. Asimakopulos repeatedly conflates the two.

23 Asimakopulos (1983: 228) takes "finance" to mean (additional) bank loans. His quotation from Robertson shows that the latter made the same mistake and that Keynes was at pains to point this out (cf. for instance Keynes 1938b, JMK 29: 171). In this case Keynes *is* partly responsible for the confusion because at first he sometimes uses the word "credit" in a close context of "finance," namely when he discusses Ohlin's "credit" theory of the rate of interest. Nonetheless, Keynes made it clear right from the start that he was "concerned with changes in the *demand for money*; and those who desire to hold money only overlap partially and temporarily with those who desire to be in debt to the banks" (Keynes 1937e, JMK 14: 207). Snippe (1985: 264) is clear on this point. Furthermore, some writers (e.g. Chick 1983: 240; Richardson 1986: 192) get confused by Keynes' usage of the term "cash." Keynes states in *The General Theory*: "As a rule, I shall, as in my *Treatise on Money*, assume that money is co-extensive with bank deposits" (Keynes 1936a, JMK 7: 167n). He adhered to this convention later on too. The possibility that "cash" (money) may actually be withdrawn from the banking system and later on "returns" to it is not relevant to the issue. Indeed, the finance motive can be most easily understood in terms of a pure-chequing economy with equal (fractional) reserve requirements on active and inactive balances. As Snippe (1985: 267) points out, if they are not equal, then shifts between the two categories may affect the bank's capacity to lend. The provision of additional loans presupposes that the banking system is not fully loaned-up, i.e. that free reserves exist, or some kind of overdraft on the bank/central bank level. There is a related

issue here about the endogeneity or exogeneity of the money supply, featuring the "horizontalists versus verticalists" debate, (see Ch.. 5 below).

24 Cf. Keynes 1937f, JMK 14: 223. Again this institutional characteristic does not affect the theoretical concept of the finance motive as such. The fact that Keynes often regarded it as convenient to apply his theoretical concepts to the particular institutional setting in Great Britain, and also considering how much attention he paid to "unused overdraft facilities" in the *Treatise* (cf. Keynes 1930a, JMK 5: 36–8), might however explain why he failed to introduce explicitly in *The General Theory* what was to become the finance motive *addendum* afterwards.

25 "It may be regarded as lying half-way, so to speak, between the active and the inactive balance" (Keynes 1937e, JMK 14: 208–9).

26 There are some nods in this direction by Richardson (1986: 194), Terzi (1986: 78), and even Asimakopulos (1983: 229), but the disputants do not realize that it is pointless to discuss the finance motive on the basis of such abstractions in the first place. It is not necessary to consider here again the change-in-composition case à la Davidson (see sect. 4).

27 Cf. Tobin (1980, ch. 4) who extends the static IS/LM framework by drafting a flow-of-funds matrix, meant to represent behavioral equations, upon it. He proposes this as a framework for macroeconomic models of asset accumulation. It is often suggested that Keynes too in *The General Theory* ignores changes in wealth. Indeed, and rightly so, this is the case when he employs his principle of effective demand towards determining the level of employment at any one time. Nevertheless, changes in wealth are considered throughout the text, in particular in chs 16 and 17. For research on this kind of change-in-composition effect see Mankiw and Summers 1986, for instance.

28 For several reasons. First, Keynes' critics are preconcerned with this type of expenditure in its relation to saving. Second, Keynes thought that the revolving fund of investment finance "is subject to special fluctuations of its own" (Keynes 1937e, JMK 14: 208) which is of course apposite, given the role of investment expenditure as the *causa causans* for changes in economic activity in Keynes' scheme. Keynes did not consider consumer credit as important, which was certainly true at his time (but may no longer be true today, as the analysis in Ch. 8 highlights). In his scheme only investment expenditure is typically debt-financed spending.

29 The precautionary motive to "provide for contingencies requiring sudden expenditure and for unforeseen opportunities of advantageous purchases, and also to hold an asset of which the value is fixed in terms of money to meet a subsequent liability fixed in terms of money" (Keynes 1936a, JMK 7: 196) is on some occasions (in particular ch. 15) closely linked to the transaction motive, as the former is *partly* a result of imperfect flexibility provided by the financial system to satisfy the latter. In other contexts, namely when uncertainty comes in, the precautionary motive is grouped together with the speculative motive, as in ch. 13 of *The General Theory* and in Keynes' (1937c) *QJE* article (cf. Runde, 1994). What is more important here, however, is that the precautionary motive is also partly a function of wealth (cf. Keynes 1936a, JMK 7: 170; 1937e, JMK 14: 222; 1938a, JMK 14: 233).

30 Keynes 1930b, JMK 6: 191. Keynes remarks that: "This duality of function is the clue to many difficulties in the modern theory of money and credit and the source of some serious confusions of thought."

31 Cf. Tobin (1987). Gurley and Shaw (1960: 94) define: "Financial intermediaries are interposed between ultimate borrowers and lenders to acquire the primary securities of the borrowers and provide other securities for the portfolios of the lenders. Their revenues accrue mainly from interest on primary securities, and their costs are predominantly interest on indirect securities and expenses of administering securities."

32 "I cannot see that any revolving fund is released, any willingness to undergo illiquidity set free for further employment, by the act of the borrowing entrepreneur in spending his loan. The bank has become a debtor to other entrepreneurs, workpeople

etc. instead of to the borrowing entrepreneur, that is all. The borrowing entrepreneur remains a debtor to the bank: and the bank's assets have not been altered either in amount or in liquidity" (D.H. Robertson, Letter to Keynes from 31 Dec 1937, repr. in JMK 14: 228–9. Quoted by Asimakopulos 1983: 228; 1985: 407). See also Robertson 1938: 315.

33 Cf. e.g. Thornton and Stone (1992: 95) on the changes in sources of funds raised in debt markets by U.S. non-financial corporations.

34 Yet, to think of this revolving fund as a separate compartment of the pool of liquidity would probably not meet with Keynes' approval. For just as at the micro level, where he preferred to regard the individual's money holdings as forming "a single pool" and the "individual's aggregate demand for money in given circumstances as a single decision, though the composite result of a number of motives" (Keynes 1936a, JMK 7: 195; cf. Kahn, 1954), he sees the money stock as a single pool of liquidity at the macro level as well. Pressures on this given pool of liquidity arise owing to various motives for the demand for money discussed at the micro level, among them the finance motive (Keynes 1939b, JMK 14: 283–4). Moreover, in the case of investment finance too, the money does not disappear after being expended but flows back into the pool of liquidity, or rather remains in it in the first place though the additional temporary finance pressure disappears, and becomes available again to facilitate subsequent transactions.

35 Even though, according to our interpretation, the revolving fund of finance does *not* involve the repayment of the loan, such a case may easily be constructed where even this requirement of the Robertsonian revolving fund notion is fulfilled. Indeed, Richardson (1986: 192–4) almost does so or at least mentions it as a possibility when he says that the additional revenues arising from the expenditure of the additional loans could be used to pay back part of the outstanding loans. Unfortunately in his balance sheet examples he conflates the "dual functions of bankers" and thereby leads Asimakopulos (1986c: 199) astray once again. The constant money stock case in the IS/LM model assumes the banking system's liquidity position remains unchanged all along.

36 In the *Treatise* Keynes states that *savings deposits* may also be held as a "convenient way of holding small increments of savings with the intention of transforming them into a specific investment when they have accumulated to a sufficient sum" (Keynes 1930a, JMK 5: 32).

37 Keynes' discussion of this issue in *The General Theory* (cf. Keynes 1936a, JMK 7: 81–5) shows that the (additional) finance motive for the demand for money, although explicitly introduced only in 1937, is not at all absent from Keynes' way of thinking about this issue. Of course, the notorious ch. 17 is of crucial importance here as well.

38 It makes a big difference to investors whether they finance the investment project by a short-term bank loan or a securities issue the duration of which is more in line with the duration of the investment project undertaken. However, given the important characteristic of modern economies that tangible wealth is largely held in the form of financial assets, the whole point of this arrangement is that marketable financial assets and bank liabilities are *not* "permanent" from the point of view of the holder. But even from the point of view of the issuers of these financial assets nothing is permanent since they always have the option of changing the financial structure of the firm, and even in the case of equities, given the possibilities of equity buybacks or going private, for instance, it is difficult to make sense of what "permanent" means in this context. (Cf. Friedman 1991.)

39 Keynes (1937f, JMK 14: 222) concludes that "in general, the banks hold the key position in the transition from a lower to a higher level of activity."

40 Keynes repeatedly though unsuccessfully pointed out to his critics where their confusion stems from. His following remarks speak volumes: "It is Mr Robertson's incorrigible confusion between the revolving fund of money in circulation and the

flow of new saving which causes all his difficulties" (Keynes 1938a, JMK 14: 232–3); "We have been all of us brought up ... in deep confusion of mind between the demand and supply of money and the demand and supply of savings; and until we rid ourselves of it, we cannot think correctly" (Keynes 1939b, JMK 14: 285); "Increased investment will always be accompanied by increased saving, but it can never be preceded by it. Dishoarding and credit expansion provides not an *alternative* to increased saving, but a necessary preparation for it. It is the parent, not the twin, of increased saving" (Keynes 1939b, JMK 14: 281).

41 The late John Hicks (1974) expressed his dissatisfaction with the treatment of liquidity and investment in his IS/LM model.

3 The loanable funds fallacy

1 The chapter first appeared in *The Cambridge Journal of Economics*. Reprinted by permission. I have made some minor amendments in the text and added an appendix. I gratefully acknowledge ESRC Research Studentship No. R00429324032 and a Research Scholarship from Girton College, Cambridge. The author is grateful to Ingo Barens, Willem Buiter, Sheila Dow, Wynne Godley, Geoff Harcourt, Michael Kuczynski, Axel Leijonhufvud, Norman Miller, Tom Rymes, Jochen Runde, Harald Scherf, James Trevithick, the anonymous referees, and the participants of the 29th annual conference of the Money, Macro and Finance Research Group (Durham, 10–12 Sept. 1997) for helpful comments and discussions.

2 Keynes scholars will recognize that the framework for *disequilibrium analysis* developed in section 2 resembles the conceptual apparatus of the *Treatise on Money* and, furthermore, will not fail to notice that my application of this analytical framework to the analysis of market signals in subsequent sections traces, in effect, what I believe to be some key insights in the evolution of Keynes' monetary thought from the *Treatise* to *The General Theory* and his later "finance motive" *addendum* (subject of Ch. 2). References to Keynes' monetary thought and various contributions to the notorious LP–LF debate are largely restricted to footnotes though, as this chapter concentrates on the purely analytical aspects. The appendix to this chapter shows that Keynes' analysis in the *Treatise on Money* already establishes the logical inconsistency of what went on to become loanable funds theory; a position more fully developed in a sister paper to this chapter that appeared in *History of Political Economy* (Bibow 2000).

3 Robertson (1931, 1933, 1934, 1936, 1937, 1938a, b, 1940) and Bertil Ohlin (1937a, b) were the most prominent early proponents of loanable funds theory. Their particularly staunch followers include Tsiang 1956, 1966, 1980, 1987, 1988; Kohn 1981, 1986; Leijonhufvud 1968, 1973, 1981, 1994, 1998.

4 I shall not address the term-structure issue, and also ignore here that some (short-term) rates of interest may be policy controlled. At issue is the question whether or not *changes* in certain fundamentals *move* interest rates in any particular direction. For that purpose, we may simply start from any given level and structure of interest rates. I briefly address the separate issue of the determination of the level of interest rates in the final section. Suffice it to mention here that interest rate changes due to policy actions hardly qualify as an automatic market mechanism.

5 Internationally, there exists considerable diversity in corporate financial structures, including liquidity provisions. See Deutsche Bundesbank (1999), for instance.

6 For instance, the money buffer-stock approach seems to provide the theoretical basis for some of the applied work of the Bank of England. Interestingly, as the Bank's sectorally disaggregated analyses of "M4" and (its credit counterpart) "M4 lending" show, Private Non-Financial Corporations' (PNFCs) holdings of M4 and their (M4) borrowing from banks are particularly volatile (*Inflation Report*). Cf. also Dale and Haldane 1993, 1995; Thomas 1996.

7 Any suggestion that Tsiang's and Kohn's loanable funds models must *implicitly* assume that money holdings act as a buffer is far too generous. (Cf. Ackley 1957; Edwards 1966: 57, n. 8; Bain and McGregor 1985: 390, n. 10.) Kohn (1981: 866) almost stumbles over the fatal flaw in his preferred theory when he states that: "Current wages will be paid out of sales receipts expected to accrue by the end of the period, while last period's wages have already been paid. [*Footnote*: It is assumed in the following that firms are always able to meet their payrolls. In the deflationary situations we will consider, with shrinking dollar payrolls, that is not an unreasonable assumption. There could, in principle, be difficulties, forcing firms to borrow to meet their payrolls.]" Nowhere does Kohn or any other loanable funds theorist tell us how current wages will be paid when expected sales revenues do *not* accrue, the counterpart to the "planned saving" is simply overlooked. (See also Tsiang 1980: 477n. and Messori 1997.) By contrast, Terzi's (1986b) "flow-of-funds" demonstration of the independence of finance from saving correctly captures the flow aspects of the period 2 disequilibrium adjustments discussed in this section. While the financial buffers approach, if correctly interpreted, is adequate to illustrate the loanable funds fallacy, it shares the common limitation of modern buffer-stock approaches more generally of concentrating solely on uncertainty about net cash flows to the exclusion of uncertainty about future interest rates (in particular, Größl and Stahlecker 1997). In Ch. 4 we analyze the uncertainty aspects central to liquidity preference theory – but largely ignored by loanable funds theory. In addition, Bain and McGregor's (1985) distinction between bills and bonds confuses the loanable funds issue with the issue of the term-structure of interest rates. Of course, interest payments on deposits do not represent any problem for liquidity preference theory (cf. Keynes 1930a, JMK 5: 128n.; 1936a, JMK 7: 196, and Ch. 4 below).

8 The early Leijonhufvud (1968: 65, n. 13) mentions what he refers to as a "short run" issue: "the short run being defined as the length of lag before producers or distributors adjust their cash outflow to the new situation." In his "Wicksell connection" he expresses his firm loanable funds belief in a sweeping remark on "Robertson [being] consistently right on every aspect of the interest rate controversy" (Leijonhufvud 1981: 171, n. 58). Unfortunately, he fails to make clear there *how* the loanable funds mechanism is supposed to do the trick, at least as long as the cumulative process discussed in this section is still under way, involving, in Leijonhufvud's language, an "excess of *ex ante* saving over *ex ante* investment." (In typical loanable funds fashion, much depends on whether or not "speculators" interfere.) His argument overlooks the fact that microeconomic decisions must always be reconciled in the aggregate *in some way*, and flows always match *somehow*, in equilibrium as in any saving-*not*-equals-investment disequilibrium as well. I must stress that this has got nothing to do with the *ex post* saving–investment "identity," the villain in Leijonhufvud's (1981) story about Keynes' (1936a) straying from the Wicksellian track; but it does follow straight from the economic logic that there are always two sides to any economic transaction. Interestingly, in Leijonhufvud's view, the Keynesian problem is that there is no guarantee that the process comes to an end, and the LF mechanism thus stops working, exactly at the full employment level of activity even with flexible money wages. By contrast, his loanable funds companion Kohn (1981) claims that with flexible money wages the loanable funds mechanism would always do the trick. For a critique of Leijonhufvud (1981) see Cottrell and Lawlor (1991) and Spahn (1993). Leijonhufvud's (1998) later change in terminology, moreover, replacing "speculators" by "some sectors of the economy" which build up or restore "liquidity positions," does not change the substance of his flawed argument.

9 Both the disequilibrium case of sect. 3 and the cumulative process discussed here concentrate on the *fact* that production decisions largely involve *unconditional* commitments to payouts of sums of money (wages in particular). In addition, our

analysis implicitly *assumes* "dividend-smoothing." If, instead, firms adjust these conventionally agreed-upon payouts, (residual income earning) households' income expectations may be disappointed more immediately instead. The possibility of immediate adjustment of money payouts which are *not* contractually fixed, just like failures to meet contractually fixed payouts, does not affect the argument, representing a mixture of the disequilibrium case and equilibrium case to which we now turn – cf. Keynes' (1930a, JMK 5: 125) "widow's cruse of profits."

10 The "fundamental psychological law" (cf. Keynes 1936a, JMK 7: 96; 1936c, JMK 14: 85) provided the key insight for moving from the *Treatise*, with only one stable equilibrium and the possibility of a complete collapse in output (cf. the "banana plantation parable;" Keynes 1930a, JMK 5: 158–60), to the principle of effective demand of *The General Theory*. As a result, the rate of interest was left "in the air" (Keynes 1937e, JMK 14: 212).

11 Given his Marshallian background, of course, Keynes did not deny that producers would, in practice, have to continually adapt their short-term expectations in response to changes in demand. On the one hand, the analytical short-cut is in a way diametrically opposed not only to the *Treatise* type of disequilibrium analysis, but also to what Keynes saw as Hawtrey's preoccupation with the "higgling of the market" (cf. Keynes 1936a, JMK 7: 75). On the other hand, Keynes is at pains to emphasize the crucial role of "effective demand" as opposed to "income," a "distinction, so vital for causal analysis," in his view (1936a, JMK 7: 78; cf. also his (1937f) lecture notes on "Ex post and ex ante"). Pasinetti (1997a) offers an ingenious account of the principle of effective demand, while Hoover (1997) illuminates the issue of correct short-term expectations. Clower's (1965) dual decision hypothesis approaches effective demand from a neo-Walrasian perspective (cf. Chick 1992).

12 For instance, Tsiang (1980: 469) remarks: "But how could savings yet to materialize at some future date provide the ready finance currently needed by the investors? Keynes was certainly right in saying that the supply of finance must come out of existing cash balances or banks' credit creation."

13 In his response to Ohlin's (1937) "ex ante theory of the rate of interest," Keynes (1937f, JMK 14: 219) puts it succinctly: "The *ex ante* saver has no cash, but it is cash which the *ex ante* investor requires." Of course, Keynes has no difficulty to "readily admit that the intention to save may sometimes affect the willingness to become illiquid meanwhile" (Keynes 1937f, JMK 14: 218). Cf. McGregor (1988) on "*ex ante* saving." Within the neo-Walrasian genre, Hahn (1955) provides an "early" more thoughtful analysis of the LP–LF issue, while Ono (1994: 158) is of particular interest. See also Hellwig 1993; Hicks 1989. Interestingly, the loanable funds proponent Tsiang (1966) is rather outspoken about what he perceives as severe limitations of the neo-Walrasian paradigm.

14 As pointed out by Keynes (1938a, JMK 14: 232–3): "It is Mr Robertson's incorrigible confusion between the revolving fund of money in circulation and the flow of new saving which causes all his difficulties."

15 Lavoie (1997) reminds us, however, that there is also a modern variety of ("overdraft") endogenous money proponents who believe in the (older Wicksell-Hayek) "natural rate of interest" theme.

16 Some endogenous money proponents (such as Kaldor 1939; Moore 1988, 1991) thus fall back on the expectations theory of the term-structure (Hicks 1939) as the basis of, what amounts to, a central bank theory of interest. Unfortunately, as Keynes knew all too well, things are not that simple. Cf. Robinson 1952; Kahn 1954.

17 This argument is further developed in Bibow (1995) and Ch. 4 below. Moore (1988) completely misunderstood both Keynes' analysis of bank rate policy in the *Treatise* as well as the role of bank behavior in the theory of liquidity preference more generally. Dymski (1988), Goodhart (1989), and Arestis and Howells (1996) provide valuable criticisms of "horizontalism," while Dow (1996, 1997) offers a particularly thoughtful

criticism of, and constructive approach to, "endogenous" money. See also Tobin's (1963) classic.

18 The Keynes mechanism is *implicitly* assumed to arise whenever the analysis is carried out on the assumption that the stock of money remains constant while the level of activity and/or prices is changing. This assumption features both in discrete-time models of loanable funds theory as well as continuous-time versions (cf. Miller 1992, 1995, for instance). Interest rate changes are erroneously attributed to the non-existent loanable funds mechanism. Another popular, but empirically irrelevant, "effect" is usually called to the rescue of stability of equilibrium, the real balance effect (cf. Greenwald and Stiglitz 1993: 36).

19 New Keynesian theories of price setting behavior (cf. Romer 1993, for instance) provide explanations for observed nominal price rigidities as outcomes of optimizing behavior of producers when "menu costs" or "product reputation," for instance, are important. Interestingly, the financial counterpart of the issue is not problematized at all. Of course, the *size* of the cash-flow shortfall may be different, if goods prices are adjusted downward, depending on the price elasticity of demand, but the shortfall will not disappear altogether. The risk-aversion variety of New Keynesianism (cf. Greenwald and Stiglitz 1993, for instance) shows that financial structures may be of *real* relevance when uncertainty in the form of asymmetric information comes into play.

20 Unless we *assume* that the sought-after market signal arises *somehow* to bring forth the corresponding investment. Again, Pasinetti hits the nail on its head (and into the loanable funds coffin!): "saving decisions are simply frustrated, as long as they differ from the predetermined amount of investment" (1974: 53); and "Saving will not even materialize; it will simply be frustrated if, quite independently, a corresponding demand to invest is not being exerted" (1997b: 202).

21 In particular, we did not discuss interest rate adjustments *engineered* by the monetary authorities and their complex influences on non-policy-controlled rates (cf. Ch. 4 and Ciocca and Nardozzi 1996). Keynes' (1936a) interest rate *conventions* may even include a "loanable funds sunspot."

22 The determination of the (market) rate of interest follows these lines in the *Treatise*, and Keynes explains to Harrod in a letter of 30 Aug. 1936 (Keynes 1936c, JMK 14: 85): "the notion of interest as being the measure of liquidity preference, ... became quite clear in my mind the moment I thought of it." Cf. also Panico 1992.

23 "To speak of the 'liquidity-preference theory' of the rate of interest is, indeed to dignify it too much. ... I am simply stating what it is, the significant theories on the subject being subsequent. And in stating what it is, I follow the books on arithmetic and accept the accuracy of what is taught in preparatory schools" (Keynes 1937e, JMK 14: 215).

24 Among Keynesian reconcilers, Davidson (1965: 60; 1978) truly stands out in asserting that the LP–LF debate is merely a "semantic confusion."

25 Quite easily the prize winner in this whole muddled debate, Ahiakpor argues that Keynes misinterpreted the classics and because the classics got it right Keynes must be wrong, blissfully proclaiming (2003: 95): "The classical theory of interest makes very good sense, correctly interpreted. It is rather Keynes' money (cash) supply and demand theory of interest that is misleading and might very well be discarded from modern macroeconomics to assist better monetary policy formulations." Perhaps there is still some hope that not every 21st-century contemporary finds the fiction of living in a corn economy all that appealing, the key issue on which Ahikpor (2003: 183) expresses his strong conviction concerning a needed "recognition of classical arguments that savings are logically prior to investment spending."

4 On Keynesian theories of liquidity preference

1 I am grateful to Geoff Harcourt, Michael Kuczynski, Joseph Labia, Jochen Runde, James Trevithick, and an anonymous referee for helpful comments on an earlier version. I also gratefully acknowledge ESRC Research Studentship No. R00429324032 and a Research Scholarship from Girton College, Cambridge. This chapter appeared in *The Manchester School*, 66(2): 238–73. Reprinted by permission. I have made some slight amendments.

2 M is the stock of money while M_1 is that part of it which satisfies the requirements of the transactions (and precautionary) motives for the demand for money (the author).

3 This section concentrates on chs 13 and 15 of *The General Theory*, while the next section concentrates on chs 12 and 17. Kahn's (1954) essay "Some notes on liquidity preference" offers an outstanding account of liquidity preference, and remains a rich source of inspiration.

4 In the next section we shall highlight the feature of money as being "*par excellence* liquid*,*" where "liquidity" as a characteristic of an asset refers to that asset having a certain or predictable market value. As Keynes (1930b, JMK 6: 59) puts it, a more liquid asset, compared to a less liquid one, is "more certainly realisable at short notice without loss." If we look for a monetary aggregate as an empirical proxy for Keynes' theoretical notion of liquidity, it will have to be a broad aggregate: "It is often convenient in practice to include in *money* time-deposits with banks and, occasionally, even such instruments as (e.g.) treasury bills. As a rule, I shall, as in my *Treatise on Money*, assume that money is co-extensive with bank deposits" (Keynes 1936a, JMK 7: 167, n. 1).

5 Obviously, the question whether the monetary authority controls either the amount or the price of reserves is highly controversial. Cf. Goodhart (1994) on this issue. Schnadt (1994) offers an interesting analysis of country-specific arrangements. In practice, setting the price of reserves includes the possibility that the monetary authority "responds to market pressures." Cf. Jaenicke and Jakobs (1994) and Jaenicke (1995), for instance.

6 This is not meant as a practical rule for monetary policy in general. At the particular time Keynes was writing there was hardly any scope to loosen further the "stance of monetary policy" as defined above. Keynes' analysis in ch. 15 considers possible ways of bringing down the – conventionally determined – long rate. He stresses that institutions and practices are crucial.

7 Extreme cases such as a hyper-inflation leading to a currency crisis or a debt deflation leading to a financial crisis will not be considered here. Such episodes involve major disturbances in the "liquidity premium" (see below) on money (and money debts) while, in particular in the latter case, monetary instruments may assume unusual default risks as well.

8 I should perhaps stress that neither here nor in the previous section do we attempt to expound a theory of the term-structure. The general portfolio allocation approach may accommodate any shape of the term-structure. There may be *diversity of opinion* about the correct value of any of the elements of the "own rates" equation, just as there may be differences in attitudes towards risk (cf. Runde and Bibow 1996). A few comments may be in order here on how Keynes' "own-rates analysis" relates to the capital asset pricing model (CAPM) of the finance literature. First, (net) *yields* are default-risk adjusted. He clearly sees that what he calls "entrepreneur's or borrower's risk" (he identifies an additional "lender's risk" which is related to moral hazard) is "susceptible to diminution by averaging" (Keynes 1936a, JMK 7: 144). Second, Keynes' a terms will be zero due to the CAPM assumption of homogeneous beliefs. Third, the liquidity premium may bear some correspondence to the notion of "systematic risk" (see below). Finally, the "riskless *short-term* rate" of this partial equilibrium model is presumably set by the monetary authorities.

9 I have already mentioned that the monetary authorities may sometimes or always set this "datum" in response to what the markets expect a *credible* stance of monetary policy to be, so that, in this sense, the datum would be "market-determined." Different forms of "money," time deposits and money market mutual fund deposits, for instance, may offer different combinations of (near) money market yield and explicit charges, but their net yield will be closely related to this datum. Keynes (1936a, JMK 7: 226) is taking advantage of the particular historical circumstance when he argues that "it is characteristic of ... money ... that its yield is *nil*, and its carrying cost negligible, but its liquidity-premium substantial."

10 On our reading the underlying idea of the liquidity premium is that assets will have an "illiquidity discount" relative to money if their future price is less predictable than that of money. The point, however, is that the price may go *either way* – one simply does not know. The notion of "liquidity" (or "thickness") is also often used to describe the quality of a market in respect of the readiness it provides to take and dissolve positions and it is thereby related to cost of transactions and the "marketability" of an asset. Hahn (1990) offers an alternative explanation of a liquidity premium on money along these latter lines. If selling an asset other than money for money involves *transactions costs* (the bid-ask spread of a middleman, for instance), and if in period 1 the investor foresees that he may probably want to sell that asset in period 2, then, Hahn finds, money *may* command a "liquidity premium," provided that the transactions costs entering into this intertemporal optimization problem are large enough. Transactions costs à la Hahn lead to an "illiquidity discount" of another sort, even when their size and actual occurrence are *uncertain*. They make arbitrage and portfolio reshuffling more costly. In my view transactions costs of this type come under Keynes' "carrying cost" element, a clear-cut *one-way* guess. Both Kahn (1954) and Tobin (1958) regard transactions costs as affecting the length of the planned investment horizon, i.e. at what interval it is worthwhile to consider reshuffling a portfolio. In the case of institutional investors the costs of trading financial instruments are negligible, while the fixed costs of sustaining the financial superstructure (which has to remunerate itself somehow) are immense. These two concepts of liquidity premia may be related nevertheless, as Keynes (1936a, JMK 7: 159–60, 170) identifies a "dilemma" in the organization of securities markets. On the one hand liquid markets tend to encourage the willingness of investors to part with money (due to the precautionary motive), while on the other hand liquid markets invite, in modern terms, excess volatility, bubbles and over-shooting (due to the speculative motive). For a discussion of this dilemma in the context of foreign exchange markets see e.g. Eichengreen *et al.* 1995; Garber and Taylor 1995; Kenen 1995.

11 Equities are not normally repaid and hence do not have to be rolled-over, while in some countries firms may buy back their equities, thereby adjusting their gearing ratio. In terms of the general constraint faced by the management as described above, debt and equity instruments are very similar and the widely observed "dividend smoothing" is important here. Although raising finance for new start-ups involves special informational problems, the "view of continuance" remains important as well. It is always possible to deliberately issue a bad debt *once*, or to sign a cheque that will bounce *once*. We are not concerned here with fraud. Cf. Kahn (1971).

12 When Keynes (1936a, JMK 7: 228) translates his "own-rates analysis," yielding a structure of asset demand prices, into a proper perspective of how actual decisions influence economic activity, he puts it in this way: "[T]hose assets of which the normal supply-price is less than the demand-price will be newly produced; and these will be those assets of which the marginal efficiency would be greater (on the basis of their normal supply-price) than the rate of interest (both being measured in the same standard of value whatever it is)." Apart from the effects of the general level of interest rates on overall economic activity, special opportunities for take-overs may arise in the occasion of depressed securities prices. In the opposite case high valuations may

encourage a management to embark on business expansions, as is reflected in Keynes' (1936a, JMK 7: 151) remark which inspired Tobin's (1969, 1978) q-theory: "For there is no sense in building up a new enterprise at a cost greater than that at which a similar existing enterprise can be purchased whilst there is an inducement to spend on a new project what may seem an extravagant sum, if it can be floated off on the Stock Exchange at an immediate profit."

13   Clearly views may diverge in either direction, i.e. the markets may get the general level of interest rates "wrong" in either direction, deflationary or inflationary. Keynes' account (ch. 12 of *The General Theory*) of the working of financial markets in this respect is unsurpassed. See also Wojnilower (1980) and Soros (1987). We ignore here the possible role of "wealth effects" in the context of consumption spending (cf. Keynes 1936a, JMK 7: 92–4, 319).

14   Those who argue that supply prices would also fall and re-establish equilibrium would commit a fallacy of composition, not to mention the potentially disastrous effects of a "debt deflation" on the financial superstructure.

15   We thus obtain another perspective (see sect. 4.2 above) on the part played by the banking system, the specialist provider of financial instruments which are *par excellence* liquid. The banking system issues its liabilities by buying assets. It may do so, as in our example above, by taking (additional) securities off the market. Alternatively, the banking system may indirectly finance this process by providing additional credit to other (specialist) institutions or wealth holders. The banking system may also enlarge the pool of liquidity by making additional bank advances to business borrowers, for instance, thereby reducing the extent to which these borrowers need to have recourse to securities issues. Of course, not all firms have a choice between bank credit and securities markets. In addition, the allocation of bank credit will typically involve a process of credit rationing, and there will normally be what Keynes (1930b, JMK 6: 326–9) calls a "fringe of unsatisfied borrowers."

16   Notice that in the case of fixed income securities, for instance, market prices and relative net yields may change although the individual investor's expectations about the relative net yields on different forms of wealth $(q_i - c_i)$ as well as the a_i terms were unchanged initially. Furthermore, while we defined a crisis in confidence as not involving any definite view on the a_i terms (*expected* relative price changes), *actual* changes in market prices may lead to definite views on subsequent price changes. The increase in yield differentials necessary to establish a new equilibrium of own rates would be reduced if the own rates calculus of some investors (within the public and/or the banking system) includes rising positive a_i terms. Notwithstanding the fact that the loss in confidence must be widespread to affect market prices, once market prices are affected such "news" may be interpreted differently by investors. Furthermore, even if the banking system did meet the rise in liquidity preference, the latter may continue to change.

17   Earlier on we concentrated on the way in which the banking system affects the general level of interest rates. We now added an aspect which refers primarily to the risk structure of interest rates and involves credit rationing of a sort that may also have strong allocative effects. The New Keynesians concentrate on this latter aspect, but ignore that the former is required as well (Stiglitz and Weiss 1981). Recall that we are only looking at the onset of a disequilibrium where bankers' confidence may represent the sole trigger which initiates the trouble. In other words, a pre-emptive rise in bankers' liquidity preference may give rise to a "credit crunch" (cf. Wojnilower 1980). Once a disequilibrium is initiated the (perhaps forced) opt-out effects in the sphere of spending and production will impinge on the bank's loan portfolio performance and the increased desire to "stay liquid" in the sphere of the portfolio decision may further damage the value of collateral of these loans. A Fisher-like (1933) debt deflation would represent an extreme outcome, requiring special preconditions, of our more general crisis in confidence. Minsky (1975, 1982), starting from Keynes' distinction between

"borrower's risk" and "lender's risk," attaches an important role to the banking system in explaining the (inherent) instability of investment spending. According to his "financial instability hypothesis," moreover, the special preconditions for a financial crisis arise endogenously. Cf. also Fazzari and Papadimitriou (1992).

18 Both assets are free of default risk, but "cash" (i.e. bank deposits) is also "riskless" in the sense that its nominal market value does not fluctuate. Tobin (1958: 67) makes the simplifying assumption that cash pays no interest, but stresses that "it is the current and expected differentials of consols over cash that matter." Liquidity preference theory must therefore be "regarded as an explanation of the existence and level not of the interest rate but of the differential between the yield on money and the yields on other assets" (Tobin 1958: 65). "Consols" are "risky" in the sense that their market value fluctuates inversely with their current yield. Tobin derives a "separation theorem" and shows that his consols may well be understood as a portfolio of securities, a portfolio with some undiversifiable market risk. The "investment balances" are assumed to be available over the investment period with certainty.

19 It is not only that some investors must be sufficiently bullish about securities for an inverse term-structure to come about in the first place. Once it has come about, and at any point in time as long as the term-structure remains inverse, it will still be required for some investors to be sufficiently bullish.

20 Other authors have rejected Tobin's approach on the ground that it fails to give a proper account of Keynes' speculative motive. For instance, Gilbert (1982: 158), Chick (1983: 213) who argues that the portfolio-theoretic approach should be treated as complementary to Keynes' speculative motive, and Runde (1994) who relates Tobin's analysis to the "precautionary motive."

21 B.M. Friedman (1985) and Woodford (1990) echo these results. This interpretation lends support to Tobin's view that, if nothing else, his risk aversion theory widens the applicability of comparative statics to the macroeconomic analysis of stationary equilibrium states. Although we reject Tobin's risk aversion theory as an elaboration on Keynes' speculative motive and as an explanation of the latter's aggregate liquidity preference schedule, this is by no means supposed to demean the importance of Tobin's contribution in its own right. Indeed Tobin is quite modest in the claims he makes about his theory of risk aversion. One must bear in mind that his approach is partly a response to that notorious criticism leveled against the (im)plausibility of Keynes' speculative motive, in particular, by Leontief (1947) who contends that investors learn from experience and, hence, in equilibrium, in a stationary state, liquidity preference would not exist. In Tobin's (1958: 85) view "so stationary a state is of very little interest." The aggregation of Tobin's *essentially microeconomic* analysis in the form of the CAPM has difficulties in handling heterogeneous beliefs, but we offered a possible alternative macroeconomic interpretation above.

22 Hicks distinguishes between, what he calls a "pure auto-economy," in which firms show financial (reserve) assets on their balance sheets, on the one end of the possible spectrum of arrangements, and a "pure overdraft economy" in which firms' "liquid positions" solely consist of prearranged automatic access to overdraft credit provided by the banking system, as the other extreme. As long as the provision and use of overdraft facilities were purely (credit) demand driven, liquidity could not possibly pose a constraint on the firm's *expansion* of its business (cf. pp. 83–84 above).

23 I argued further above (see n. 10) that this type of liquidity premium relates to Keynes' "carrying-costs" element. Jones and Ostroy's analysis of the effects of changes in the variability of beliefs on asset demands, for instance, refers to a given level of switching cost while risk aversion is altogether excluded (linear utility function). Interestingly, Hicks (1989: 142) – in what is probably his final published sentence – maintains that "[r]isk-aversion is a consequence of rational behavior." Hahn (1990), a proponent of the "transactions-costs liquidity premium," criticizes Jones and Ostroy not only for ignoring risk aversion but also for their neglect of the "saving decision." The reader

may have noticed that a saving decision does not feature among the types of decisions discussed here. *Motives* to save affect the propensity to consume (spending decision), and agents may even solve their lifetime consumption pattern by having a dynamic programming scheme in the back of their mind. But a saving *decision* is not actually made by anyone except by infinitely lived representative agents "living" in continuous market-clearing equilibrium. More generally, saving is a mere residual (cf. Keynes 1936a, JMK 7: 84–5; Bibow 1995). While we concentrate on investment spending here, the argument applies to consumption spending on durable goods as well. The precautionary saving *motive* (Deaton 1992) is important here, which is often linked to the idea that more precautionary saving *somehow* leads to more investment.

24 The orthodox SEU approach to uncertainty distinguishes between "terminal moves" and "informational moves," the former referring to situations in which the decision maker must make an immediate bet, the latter to situations where the decision maker may opt for obtaining additional information first. Only in the realm of situations where informational moves are available is the decision maker's "confidence in his beliefs," measured by the tightness of the (prior) subjective probability distribution, believed to make any "action-relevant difference" (cf. Hirshleifer and Riley 1992: 11).

25 This is not to suggest that Hicks (1974) is wrong in arguing that in Keynes' theory the marginal efficiency of capital and the theory of money "belong together." He expresses his dissatisfaction, in this respect, about his own older interpretation, i.e. the *IS/LM* model. Hicks proposes to develop a "theory of liquidity" as a link between the marginal efficiency of capital and the theory of money. But we need to get the *time* element right, otherwise "liquidity slips through" (again?).

26 Hirshleifer and Riley (1992: 170) not only fail to distinguish between different types of decisions but, moreover, present "(1) taking immediate terminal action, versus (2) acquiring better information first" as simple alternatives; where information may, first, be newly generated by an informational action or, second, be acquired via a transaction from some expert provider or, third, emerge autonomously simply with the passage of time, like tomorrow's weather (cf. ibid., p. 204). Their last example illustrates, for one thing, that no (income-generating) informational actions may occur either. But their weather example is also suggestive in another way. For it appears that we need only wait to see what tomorrow is like, as if there is one particular predetermined world out there. In capitalistic economies, however, it is largely entrepreneurial investors who determine – in the form of today's investment spending decisions – what shape the future (capital stock) will take. Indeed, this is the whole point: the interdependence between investors' behavior and the shape of the evolution of the economy. In the process of shaping our future material world, they also determine today's level of economic activity. Keynes (1937c, JMK 14: 113–14; my emphasis) explains that: "By 'uncertain knowledge' ... I do not mean merely to distinguish what is known for certain from what is only probable. The game of roulette is not subject, in this sense, to uncertainty ... the expectation of life is only slightly uncertain. *Even the weather is only moderately uncertain.* The sense in which I am using the term is that in which the prospect of a European war is uncertain, ... or the obsolescence of a new invention, or the position of private wealth owners in the social system in 1970. About these matters there is no scientific basis on which to form any calculable probability whatever. We simply do not know."

27 Makowski (1990) seems to be aware of some of these problems. Starting from the Hicksian idea of waiting, he defines uncertainty as "risk plus the possibility of learning," and describes the impact of an increase in uncertainty on investors as follows: "*when uncertainty is high, then the desire for investment is temporarily low*" (p. 472). The impact of uncertainty on savers' liquidity preference, in his account, is however somewhat curious. Savers just happen to *know* when investors are struck by uncertainty, and they *know* also that *uncertain* situations, as opposed to risky situations, have "built-in dynamics;" uncertainty is expected to be resolved in the future (a one-

way bet). Effectively Makowski's built-in dynamics of uncertain situations yield a rationale for a loanable funds version of the "liquidity trap" à la Hicks (1937) in which uncertainty does not play any part at all.
28 Clearly, this does *not* imply that the financial system and monetary policy would not matter. Throughout this chapter I have treated the role of the *behavior* of financial intermediaries much along the lines of Keynes' (1936a) simplifying assumption of a constant stock of money, amended by the "finance motive" (Keynes 1937e). In the "finance motive debate" Keynes stresses the pivotal role of the banking system (cf. Chs 2 and 5). Cf. Moore (1988) on the alternative "endogenous money" view.

5 On exogenous money and bank behavior

1 The author is grateful for comments from Andrew Bain, Sheila Dow, Geoff Harcourt, Jochen Runde, Tom Rymes, Olaf Schlotmann, the participants (particularly Meyer Burstein) of the History of Economics Society Conference 1997 held at the College of Charleston, SC, USA, the participants (particularly Cristina Marcuzzo and Harald Hagemann) of the European Society for the History of Economic Thought Conference 1998 held at the University of Bologna, Italy, the participants of the Money, Macro and Finance Conference 1998 held at Imperial College, London, UK, and two anonymous referees. I also benefited from correspondence on the issue of money endogeneity with James Tobin. This paper appeared in 2000 in the *European Journal of the History of Economic Thought*. Republished by permission. I have made some minor amendments and added a postscript.
2 Keynes (1923, JMK 4: 134) observes that: "Gold itself has become a 'managed' currency." A return to gold was unacceptable to him at any parity, since "[w]ith the existing distribution of the world's gold, the reinstatement of the gold standard means, inevitably, that we surrender the regulation of our price level and the handling of the credit cycle to the Federal Reserve Board of the United States" (ibid., p. 139).
3 This view probably only became part of monetary orthodoxy after the Radcliffe Report (Kahn 1958) but monetary practice followed this line earlier; for long hindered by limitations on the fiduciary issue. Cf. Feavearyear 1963: 400–2.
4 Keynes (1936a, JMK 7: 195) explains the relationship between the two books in this regard, stressing that: "Money held for each of the three purposes forms, nevertheless, a single pool."
5 Notice that this leaves the possibility of what Keynes calls "income inflation," the analysis of which he considers to be outside the scope of monetary theory (Keynes 1930a, JMK 5: 140, 150–1).
6 As the public's use of cash is of no relevance in Keynes' monetary theory (Keynes 1930a, JMK 5: 27), the note issue is not an essential function of what Keynes calls here a central bank either. Recall that already in his *Tract* he suggested that "cash, in the form of … currency notes [be] supplied *ad libitum*." His *Treatise* analysis assumes that the central bank is also the note-issuing authority or, alternatively, that, for purposes of exposition, "the balance sheets of the central bank and of the note-issuing authority are amalgamated" (Keynes 1930b, JMK 6: 201). With the Currency and Bank Notes Act of 1928 the two issues were amalgamated and the Currency Note Issue transferred to the Bank of England. Formerly the Currency Note Account was under the auspices of the Treasury (cf. Feavearyear 1963: 359).
7 The important point is that banks pay attention to their "liquid resources" (whatever may serve as banks' "reserves") *relative* to their overall balance sheet (cf. Keynes 1930a, JMK 5: 24). Keynes is certainly aware of the variety of alternative institutional arrangements between the central bank and the member banks, and the role of clearing and money market arrangements in this context. Banks' conventional ratios at the time exceeded these requirements, in his view (Keynes 1930b, JMK 6: 48, 62), and they

were also excessive with regard to prudential considerations. For he thought that a serious run on the British banking system had become "improbable" (Keynes 1930b, JMK 6: 48).

8   Keynes refers to "the normal level of bankers' deposits, required to make the Bank of England strong beyond a doubt and able in all circumstances to impose its will on the market without straining its own earning capacity unduly" (Keynes 1930b, JMK 6: 64). The exceptional circumstances he has in mind describe a case where a "lack of ammunition" would otherwise hinder her in carrying out open-market operations *à outrance*.

9   This is correctly interpreted by Hicks (1989) who, however, failed to see how this relates to the "liquidity theory of interest" of *The General Theory*.

10 Keynes distinguishes a third category of assets "which the central bank cannot create itself, but from or (and) into which it is bound by law to convert its legal-tender money." This is of direct relevance in a commodity money system, but complications arising from international monetary arrangements may be subsumed under this heading too. Keynes favored capital controls in order to maximize the room for maneuver of monetary policies aimed at domestic objectives, but thought that "the only adequate remedy could be found in a system of supernational management" (Keynes 1930b, JMK 6: 336). The international dimension of monetary policy is taken up again in Ch. 7.

11 Active use of bank rate began in 1838 (Homer and Sylla 1996). Short bills were only exempted from the usury laws in 1833, and between 1714, when the usury limit was reduced to 5%, and the late 1830s, bank rate was pegged at 5% for most of the time. Feavearyear (1931: 281–8) argues that an important change in management occurred in 1878 when "the Bank took a definite step to change its position in the money market," namely to largely withdraw from the discount business by publishing a discount rate that exceeded the market rate (cf. Hawtrey 1962). Rymes (1998) has an interesting argument here concerning the size of the base in Keynes' argument about making bank rate "effective." Moore (1988) completely misses the point about making bank rate effective in Keynes' analysis.

12 Keynes criticizes Hawtrey's "monetary theory of the credit cycle" for solely focusing on the impact of short-term interest rates on dealers' "liquid capital," whilst neglecting the role of longer term rates and "fixed investment."

13 In the *Treatise* Keynes still took the neoclassical view that flexible money wages would do the trick, mainly through improving net exports and supported by monetary factors (much along the lines of the "Keynes mechanism;" see below). Thus, an unemployment equilibrium was only possible due to rigid money wages. In this case, but only as a last resort, he recommended public works. In *The General Theory* flexible money wages may not only *not* do the trick, but may actually make things worse. And the potentially beneficial effects of increasing the money stock in terms of wage units may be more easily obtained by pursuing appropriate monetary policies in the first place.

14 The verdict is that CMSA was a tactical mistake. Cf. Harcourt 1987; Kaldor 1983; Thirlwall 1983; Tobin 1983.

15 In what appears to be a fragment from his 1932 lecture notes Keynes speaks of a "large class of possible monetary policies – indeed all or most of those in which the total supply of money is not perversely correlated with the demand for money in the active circulation, a perverse correlation in this case being a tendency for the former to change in the same direction as the latter and perhaps at a faster rate" (Keynes 1932a, JMK 29: 55–6). The CMSA stands for any *particular* banking policy in which "the total supply of money is not perversely correlated." Cf. also Rymes 1989: 63–77.

16 This bank-driven interest rate channel is not to be confused with the "loanable funds mechanism" (Leijonhufvud 1981) which loanable funds theorists believe to move interest rates in the right direction when changes in the real forces of productivity

and thrift occur (cf. Kahn 1954; Pasinetti 1974; Panico 1992; Bibow 2000, and Ch. 3 above). Nor is it to be confused with the "real balance effect" popularized by Patinkin (1958) and believed by some to have proved Keynes theoretically wrong (Friedman 1968, 1971). As regards the latter "effect," Greenwald and Stiglitz (1993: 36) put it mildly when they remark: "The enormous attention the real balance effect has received over the years hardly speaks well for the profession" (cf. Tobin 1980). In contrast to textbook presentations of real balance and Keynes effects, featuring general money wage and price deflations, the suggested analytical generality of the Keynes mechanism precludes major price deflations, as these would easily ruin the banking system (cf. Keynes 1931a, JMK 9).

17 I am grateful to an anonymous referee for bringing the statistics in Nevin and Davis 1970 to my attention. Some key features of the period of Keynes' monetary trilogy are summarized in Table 5.1 (see appendix), showing both the rise in the banks' securities portfolios of the 1930s (in line with his *General Theory*) as well as significant variations in the banks' asset composition (as already observed in the *Tract* and *Treatise*). Cf. also Nevin 1955; Feavearyear 1963.

18 Leijonhufvud (1981) may have been misled by widespread US bank failures. But UK developments were different: money supply fell continuously during the deflationary period of 1920 to 1925, and then grew slowly until 1930. After a *minor* decline in 1931, money grew *faster* for the rest of the 1930s (cf. Howson 1975; Friedman and Schwartz 1982). In 1931 Keynes observed: "Fortunately our own domestic British Banks are probably at present – for various reasons – among the strongest. But there is a degree of Deflation which no bank can stand" (Keynes 1931a, JMK 9: 157). The US experience may have been a very important inspiration behind Friedman's monetarism though.

19 Bank rate was pegged to 2% for 18 years from 1932 onwards, except for a brief episode in 1939 (Homer and Sylla 1996: table 61). Homer and Sylla (1996: 455) report that short-term market rates were even below 1% from 1932 onwards. According to Feavearyear (1963: 373–6) Treasury bills sometimes yielded as little as 3/16%. Keynes certainly takes advantage of the historical incidence of very low short-term rates, in particular in his polemical attacks on the "classics:" "who outside a lunatic asylum would hold barren money?" (Keynes 1937c, JMK 14: 115). Yet, interest payments on money do not represent any problem for liquidity preference theory (cf. Kahn 1954 and Ch. 4 above).

20 Cf. Feavearyear 1963; Howson 1975, 1988; Moggridge 1997; Moggridge and Howson 1974; Nevin 1955. Keynes' views on the future of the rate of interest over the period from sterling's departure from gold and the War Loan conversion until 1936 are reflected in Keynes 1932b, 1932d, 1934b, 1935, 1936f; all in JMK 21.

21 It must be stressed that Keynes' analysis in ch. 15 of *The General Theory* is carried out mainly in the form of *thought experiments* which take the yield on liquidity as *given* (rather than *nil*; see n. 18). In practice, banks may not actually depart from their normal reserve ratio, and pile up "cash;" much depends on institutional arrangements and practices. Past (rather than expected) losses provide another reason why banks might fail to follow suit. The discussion refers to the general case of a largely intact banking system. Even in the special case of greatly impaired bank capital the monetary authorities might still succeed in reducing the risk-free rate of interest on government debts (and through both the liquidity and expectational channels), while banks may however refuse to extend new credit and take risky loans and assets onto their balance sheets. Accounting and regulatory rules are highly relevant here too.

22 The view of banks as presiding over a balance sheet which they regard as being in overall "equilibrium," in some sense, includes the possibility of their regret about some illiquid or "frozen" business they have locked-in on their books. Past mistakes are reflected in today's balance sheets and may well pose important constraints on business, but nevertheless one may presume that banks try their best in the light of

whatever damage past mistakes have left on their books. Wojnilower (1980) offers a most interesting account of "credit crunches." See also Wolfson (1996).

23 Contrary to the widely held view that Keynes "sanctioned" Hicks' (1937) *IS/LM* interpretation, the correspondence between the two men between Aug. 1936, starting right after Hicks' (1936) first, less well-known review of *The General Theory*, and April 1937 clearly shows their disagreement on the interest rate issue (cf. Keynes 1936b, 1937a; Kregel 1988). In my view, their disagreement – which remained unresolved – features *two* distinct, albeit related aspects of the interest rate issue. One, subject of this chapter, concerns the "elasticity" of money supply and the "Keynes mechanism," the other the loanable funds debate. In a way, the finance motive (cf. Ch. 2) illustrates both of these aspects and their relationship.

24 Keynes (1936a, JMK 7: 174) states succinctly: "the quantity of money is not determined by the public." And: "no amount of anxiety by the public to increase their hoards can affect the amount of hoarding, which depends on the willingness of the banks to acquire (or dispose of) additional assets beyond what is required to offset changes in the active balances" (Keynes 1937e, JMK 14: 213). Cottrell (1994: 599) points out correctly the implausibility of the idea of changes in the liquidity preferences of the general public being accommodated via overdrafts.

25 Tobin (1991) criticized Kaldor for his attack on *The General Theory*. Tobin (1963, 1982) illuminates important aspects of bank behavior.

26 By contrast, the modeling approach to bank behavior chosen in sect. 10.7.5 of Godley and Lavoie (2007) seems unappealing to me. A rise in banks' liquidity preference is shown there to induce a higher ratio of liquid assets (bills) to deposits (or total liabilities), with the size of the banks' balance sheet *growing* at the same time. To begin with, the focus on liquid assets seems somewhat odd in view of the emphasis on liability management in the endogenous money approach (although asset management has made a great comeback in the context of the credit crisis and breakdown of trust between banks and hence seizing up of money markets). More important, I would associate an increased liquidity preference of banks primarily with a reduced urge to expand risky business by extending credit (either new or roll-overs) or taking securities off the market and onto the balance sheet (or shoveling them into off-balance-sheet vehicles or conduits that involve explicit or implicit liquidity support). In principle, then, this would make for a *reduced* growth (or even decline) in bank balance sheets; and whatever may happen to some directly measurable liquidity ratios. However, an expansion of bank balance sheets may still result, if banks anticipate easier monetary policy and rising government bonds, with other (non-bank) units becoming keener to hold liquidity in the face of a slowing economy and falling bond yields. Recall that the Keynes mechanism only requires liquidity to grow *relative* to incomes. In Godley and Lavoie (2007) bank portfolios are limited to loans and bills. Following the same stock-flow consistent macroeconomic modeling methodology, Le Heron and Muoakil (2008) use a richer set of bank assets to illuminate bank behavior.

27 "Other things equal, a larger quantity of money means lower interest rates, because it means that the banking system is taking a larger quantity of securities off the market, is assisting in greater measure in financing the holding of securities, and is reducing the extent to which securities have to be issued on the market in order to secure finance. … If the quantity of money is increased, this means that the banks have increased their assets, and in doing so they will have bid up the prices of securities, i.e. lowered rates of interest" (Kahn 1958: 146–7).

6 Keynes on central banking and the structure of monetary policy

1 The author gratefully acknowledges helpful comments from Sheila Dow, Charles Goodhart, Geoff Harcourt, Don Moggridge, Jochen Runde, T. K. Rymes, the

participants (particularly Hansjörg Klausinger) of the ESHET Conference 2000 held at the University of Graz, the participants of a workshop held at the University of Toronto on 24 Nov. 2000, and two anonymous referees. Furthermore, I am grateful to John Fforde and Corinna Balfour for kindly providing me with information relating to the Keynes–Towers discussion in 1945, and to Jacky Cox and Rosalind Moad (Modern Archives, King's College), Sarah Millard (Bank of England Archives), and Corrinne Miller (Bank of Canada Archives) for their kind support in tracing the relevant archive sources. Last, but not least, the author is grateful for the hospitality and financial support provided by the Levy Economics Institute during the final stages of his work on this chapter. This chapter appeared in the *History of Political Economy*. Republished by permission. I have made some minor amendments.

2 Bibow (1999), Blinder (1998), Forder (1998) and Goodhart (1994) critically discuss this literature. Matters of structure and conduct of monetary policy are not generally treated as distinct issues in the literature.

3 Keynes (1913a, JMK 1: 115) would "emphatically apply to India the well-known doctrine which the powerful advocacy of Mr Bagehot raised in England many years ago to an impregnable position in the unwritten constitution of this country – the doctrine, namely, that in a time of panic the reserves of the Bank of England must, at a suitably high rate, be placed at the disposal of the public without stint and without delay." See Bagehot (1873) and, on the "victory of the Bagehot principle," Fetter (1965); see also Vicarelli 1988 and Chandavarkar 1985.

4 In a private letter dated 12 Aug. 1913, Austen Chamberlain, the commission's chairperson, tells Keynes that he had deliberately put the latter's *Indian Currency and Finance* aside when it appeared in June in order to form some opinions of his own. Having read the book from cover to cover only after the commission adjourned, Chamberlain ([1913] 1971: 99–100) comments: "You will certainly be considered the author of the Commission's report whenever that document sees the light. I am amazed to see how largely the views of the Commission as disclosed by our informal discussions are a mere repetition of the arguments and conclusions to which your study had previously led you."

5 The memorandum arose in consultation with Sir Ernest Cable, was finished by Keynes on 6 Oct. 1913, and appeared with the report on 2 March 1914.

6 The three presidency banks of Bengal, Bombay and Madras were established in the first half of the 19th century, having a semiofficial character under control of the East India Company. They became purely privately owned under imperial reign and lost any official character they might have had, together with the right of note issue in 1876, but their position and role remained a piece of machinery peculiar to India and its colonial political arrangements. The presidency banks were both the largest commercial banks of Royal India and fulfilled, at least to some extent, certain central banking functions as bankers' bank and government's banker (see Keynes 1913a; Chandavarkar 1983).

7 The secretary of state (for India) was a minister of the British cabinet in London who, in subordination to the cabinet, represented the fount of authority as well as the director of policy in India. The secretary of state exercised his authority via the governor-general (and "viceroy"), the personal representative of the crown in India and head of the government of India (i.e. the viceroy's council).

8 Keynes' careful elaboration on this argument may have been partly motivated by a perceived diplomatic need to appease the government of India's opposition to the central bank plan. Applying the argument to bank rate policy, Keynes (1913b, JMK 15: 196) argues that "whenever the bank rate was high, there would be a clamour that the Government were not lending all they might." Keynes also tries to allay the banks' fears of a new competitor, stressing that there was no need for the central bank to enter into normal banking business at any scale. Instead the central bank should aim at rediscount business as its channel of accommodation. This would have the additional

advantage that admitting a bank to the rediscount list would go hand in hand with a supervisory role and thus deter unsound banking practices.

9   Kisch and Elkin ([1928] 1930: 17) report a marked change in attitude towards the government–central bank relationship following the inflationary aftermath of World War I: "The pre-war tendency, particularly as regards actual statutory provisions, was somewhat to stress the control of the State over the Central Bank. ... The war exhibited in extreme terms the danger of this system. Since the war the tide has set strongly against granting the State power to interfere with the functioning of a Central Bank. The Brussels Conference Resolution of 1920 in favor of the creation of independent Central Banks crystallized the general feeling" (see also Sayers 1938: ch. 4). It is thus noteworthy that already in the *Tract* Keynes (1923, JMK 4: 154) regarded the note issue as a purely passive agent in the scheme, "supplied *ad libitum*" either by the Treasury or the central bank. His following dismissive report from the Genoa conference of 1922 (*Manchester Guardian,* 15 April 1922) also well reflects both his frustration about the participants' failure to agree on any particular common policy as well as his attitude towards certain timeworn ideas in currency (some of which still enjoy much popularity today, being typically expressed in the same general terms): "Nothing is being considered at present but a series of pious declarations of general principles. Many of these are old and stale. It does not help much to repeat in general terms that currencies should be stable, that budgets should balance, and that banks of issue should be free from political pressure. ... In short some day, somehow, at some parity we must have gold again. But when, how, or at what parity Genoa shrinks from declaring" (Keynes 1922a, JMK 17: 382–3). Shortly before the Genoa conference Keynes had published (*Manchester Guardian,* 6 April 1922) "the first of many 'Keynes Plans' for the international monetary system" (Moggridge 1992: 377; see Keynes 1922b, JMK 17: 355–69) in which he still advocated a gold bullion standard as the only practicable solution, aiming at exchange stabilization at prevailing market rates though (rather than at pre-war parities). See Moggridge 1986 and Ch. 7 below on Keynes' evolving views on the international monetary system.

10 Similarly, when summoned to give evidence to the Committee on the Currency and Bank of England Note Issues, in July 1924, Keynes denied the Treasury power to veto the Bank of England's interest rate policies. The clear distinction between, in modern language, goal and instrument independence that characterizes his proposal of 1932 is evident in his thinking on the matter from early on: "I think that the function of the Government and of the Treasury is to determine the policy, whether it is to be a gold standard or whatever it is to be, but the technical means of achieving that ought to be left to a body in the position of the Bank of England" (Keynes 1924, JMK 19: 255).

11 Defined as "bodies whose criterion of action within their own field is solely the public good as they understand it, and from whose deliberations motives of private advantage are excluded, ... – bodies which in the ordinary course of affairs are mainly autonomous within their prescribed limitations, but are subject in the last resort to the sovereignty of the democracy expressed through Parliament" (Keynes 1926a, JMK 9: 288). Keynes (ibid., p. 290) also refers to "big undertakings" which would still need to be socialized, arguing that "we must probably prefer semi-autonomous corporations to organs of the central government for which ministers of State are directly responsible."

12 In his appreciation of *Lombard Street*, on the occasion of the centenary of Bagehot's birth, Keynes attributes to Bagehot the proposition that, by force of circumstance, the Bank of England had become a national institution with national responsibilities: "Bagehot's view has long prevailed, but even now we sometimes speak in the old way. Labour politicians demand the nationalization of the Bank of England; Dr Leaf predicts that appalling disasters would ensue from such an act. They both waste their words. Bagehot nationalized the Bank of England fifty years ago. We may differ about what our monetary policy ought to be, but whatever it is, the Bank of England stands

as an instrument of incomparable power to carry it out" (Keynes 1926b, JMK 19: 468).

13 In a letter to Winston Churchill (Chancellor of the Exchequer) of 13 May 1928, Keynes (1928b, JMK 19: 749–50) argues that the Bank of England's position might be strengthened in the short run due to the tendency of rising unemployment to reduce the circulation and hence to enlarge the bank's reserves, but stresses that "you cannot rely on this as a permanency. It is NOT TRUE in the long run that the maximum of imbecility is wisdom."

14 Thirty years later Milton Friedman (1960) devised an "auto-pilot" scheme whereby the central bank's discretion at the operational level would be reduced to zero by legislating a fixed rate of growth for the monetary base.

15 More precisely, by preventing saving–investment disequilibria (in *Treatise* terms), or deviations of the market rate of interest from the natural rate, monetary policy would avoid "profit inflations/deflations," seen as the driving force behind the credit cycle. By contrast, "income inflation" (essentially rising efficiency wages and unit labor costs) cannot be controlled by monetary means – other than by deliberately causing unemployment. Given the difficulties of forcing down money wages, Keynes thought that some degree of income inflation should be allowed to assist the redistribution of productive resources between different uses (see Keynes 1930a).

16 In his evidence to the Macmillan Committee, Keynes deliberately kept the general question of sufficiency of the Bank of England's total resources and earning power separate from the more specific issue of her resources for meeting any external drain, as the issue of hidden capital reserves was more intimately related to the ownership question and the central bank's powers in relation to the markets in conducting domestic monetary policy. The commissioners' speculations about these issues (and Keynes' general concern about the lack of statistics and secrecy in central banking) were not at all academic as, in actual fact, the Bank of England managed to keep substantial *hidden* foreign exchange reserves between 1925 and 1931, using them to increase her room for discretion in relation to the Treasury (cf. Moggridge 1972: 160–1, 176–85).

17 The Macmillan Report (Committee on Finance and Industry 1931) made no specific proposals for changing the existing structure of monetary policy and for bringing the Bank of England under public ownership and control (cf. Moggridge 1972: 159; Sayers 1976: 362; Cairncross 1988; Dodwell 1934). It must also be borne in mind that the *Treatise* and the Macmillan Report took sterling's link to gold as a datum.

18 This is noteworthy for the fact that Milton Friedman's main economic objection to central bank independence is that monetary policy would thereby be made highly dependent on personalities, thus risking "accidents of personality" (Friedman [1962] 1969). Friedman later altered his views about the importance of personalities in light of subsequent US experience (see Friedman 1984), but he certainly stuck to his central proposition that "money is much too serious a matter to be left to the central bankers" (Friedman 1992: 261).

19 The exact dating of Keynes' discovery of the principle of effective demand is controversial. (For a discussion, see Moggridge 1992: ch. 21.) And a related controversy concerns possible anticipations of the principle of effective demand and *The General Theory* (see, for instance, Patinkin 1982 and Laidler 1999, the latter reserving a special role for Ralph Hawtrey). Of course, there is also considerable controversy about what the principle of effective demand and the essence of the Keynesian revolution were all about (see the thoughtful account by Pasinetti 1997a).

20 The new Parliament was opened on 15 Aug. and the king's speech included the measure of bringing the Bank of England under public control, which came as no surprise, as the Labour Party had campaigned to do exactly that (Fforde 1992). On 16 Aug. 1945 was the final court meeting at which Keynes was present, and according to the minutes the issue was not being discussed. The minutes (and additional records)

indicate that the issue was first discussed at the court of 23 Aug., with discussions continuing until Nov. Keynes' final meeting with Prime Minister Clement Attlee and Hugh Dalton before leaving for the negotiations took place in the evening of 23 Aug. 1945 (Moggridge 1992). Keynes left London on the morning of 27 Aug. He stayed in Ottawa between 2 and 4 Sept., before traveling on to Washington for the loan negotiations. Keynes departed from New York on 11 Dec., returning home on 17 Dec. On 20 Dec. 1945, the day of the third reading of the bill in the House of Commons and the first court at which Keynes was present again, the bank's new constitution was no longer an issue at the court's meeting (Bank of England Archives). Keynes' files at King's College contain copies of the Bank of England bill as brought from the Commons on 20 Dec. 1945 and the parliamentary debates in the House of Lords on 22 Jan. 1946 (Keynes Papers, King's College). There are no markings in the text of these documents. However, Susan Howson (1993: 116) reports a note "literally on the back of an envelope" as indicating that Keynes gave "some support" to Lord Piercy's interpretation of clause 4(3) of the Bank of England bill as aired in the House of Lords on 22 Jan. 1946. Piercy argued that clause 4(3) foresaw that the right of initiative for making recommendations or issuing directions to any banker was left to the bank (rather than the Treasury).

21 At least this is my clear impression, being wholly based though on the earlier evidence discussed in this chapter. Towers' note may not make it clear whether its author thought to have failed to convince Keynes in particular. By contrast, there is indisputable evidence that Towers' views were not greeted with any sympathy at the Bank of England (see Bank of England Archives, G1/261). We may note here that in 1943 Graham Towers, apparently on the advice of Keynes, was discussed and "sounded out" as a possible candidate for replacing Montagu Norman. Apparently the fact that Towers was the governor of a government-owned central bank partly explained the hostility against him prevalent at the Bank of England, where he was also seen as being "too Keynesian" (see Fullerton 1986: 190–5, kindly brought to my attention by Robert Dimand). Furthermore, it is also noteworthy that the "Canadian model" faced a severe crisis under the governorship of Towers' successor, James Coyne. On the one hand, the so-called Coyne affair featured a government that seemed keen to deny its responsibility for monetary policy (passing the buck to the Bank of Canada for carrying out unpopular policies). On the other hand, the affair involved a central bank governor apparently not indisposed to imposing his personal views on general economic policies upon Canada rather than sticking to his monetary policy mandate (which was not particularly clearly laid down for him in the first place). A situation then arises in which the central bank both lacks any clear democratic legitimacy for what it is doing, but cannot be held to account for whatever it may decide to do either – given that responsibility for monetary policy was positioned in some kind of democratic vacuum. It seems to me that Keynes' monetary structure was designed exactly to prevent a situation from arising in which it was not clear at all times that the government was in fact in charge of economic and monetary policies. On the Coyne affair, see Gordon 1961; Howitt 1993; Royal Commission on Banking and Finance 1964; Rymes 1994.

22 Since the establishment of the Exchange Equalization Account in 1932 (see Keynes 1932e) and the War Loan Conversion Scheme of that year (see Keynes 1932b), the cooperation between the Treasury and the bank seems to have been very close, with debt management issues being the dominant factor in "cheap money" both during the recessionary 1930s as well as the "3% war" (see Howson 1975, 1988). The situation was such that Montagu Norman described himself as "an instrument of the Treasury," and during the debates on the bank's nationalization in 1945–6 many saw the measure as merely bringing the *de jure* situation back in line with what had *de facto* emerged already. It is noteworthy that the alleged "bankers' ramp of 1931," related to Labour's fall from government in that year, still featured in the parliamentary debates of the

Bank of England bill in 1945–6. In Fforde's (1992) history of the "nationalization of Norman's Bank," the Bank of England appears to have been anything but eager at the time to be given stated objectives and to bear responsibility in relation to the Treasury.

23 It was probably clear that debt management concerns would dominate policy for quite some time; Keynes participated in debt management talks at the Treasury until shortly before his death (Moggridge 1992; Howson 1993). See also Tilly (2006, 2007).

24 At least on one occasion, though, the case of North Russia of 1918, Keynes recommended (and devised a scheme for) the setting up of a currency board. See Spring Rice 1919; Schuler 1992; Walters and Hanke 1992; Ponsot 2002.

7 The international monetary order and global finance

1 I gratefully acknowledge comments on an earlier draft by Jürgen Krompardt and Andrea Terzi.

2 "During the latter half of the nineteenth century the influence of London on credit conditions throughout the world was so predominant that the Bank of England could almost have claimed to be the conductor of the international orchestra. By modifying the terms on which she was prepared to lend, aided by her own readiness to vary the volume of her gold reserves and the unreadiness of other central banks to vary the volume of theirs, she could to a large extent determine the credit conditions prevailing elsewhere. ... But today, unfortunately, the position is considerably changed" (Keynes 1930b, JMK 6: 274–5). And more succinctly, also concerning the crucial change in circumstances: "Before the war Great Britain and since the war the United Sates have had a considerable power of influencing the international situation to suit themselves" (Keynes 1930a, JMK 5: 148).

3 Keynes analyzed the printing press link between fiscal and monetary policies in ch. 2 of his *Tract on Monetary Reform* titled "Public finance and changes in the value of money." He had little sympathy for governments' use of the "inflationary tax" in paying their ways. But he also took despair at the burden of the debt inherited from a war financed at high interest rates, as was the case for Britain, observing that: "The powers of uninterrupted usury are too great. If the accretions of vested interest were to grow without mitigation for many generations, half the population would be no better than slaves to the other half. Nor can the fact that in time of war it is easier for the State to borrow than to tax, be allowed permanently to enslave the taxpayer to the bond-holder" (Keynes 1923, JMK 4: 56). Later, in "How to pay for the war?," Keynes (1939a) was going to advise that Great Britain should fight World War II while maintaining low interest rates and using taxation as the key expenditure-changing instrument for keeping inflation in check without rewarding rentiers at taxpayers' expense. His plan was only followed to some small degree (Skidelsky 2000).

4 While Keynes as a member of the Macmillan Committee still supported the official gold standard policy he was not surprised by Britain's exit, as expressed in a letter to Richard Kahn of 13 Aug. 1931: "We should be off [gold] ... within a month unless heroic measures are taken" (Keynes 1931e, JMK 20: 594–5).

5 I highlight here the issue of financial organization as this matter is at the heart of Keynes' vision for the post-war world as discussed below. Preceding the above statement Keynes offered a judgment that is pertinent to international portfolio investment, singling out the "remoteness between ownership and operation [as] an evil in the relations between men," a principle that, when applied internationally, would "in times of stress [be] intolerable – I am irresponsible towards what I own and those who operate what I own are irresponsible towards me" (Keynes 1933c, JMK 21: 236).

6 For instance, Meltzer (1988: 311) comments "Keynes's neglect of the open-economy aspects of the policies recommended in the *General Theory* is inexplicable."

7   "The plan aims at the substitution of an expansionist, in place of a contractionist, pressure on world trade, especially in the first years" (Keynes 1941b, JMK 25: 46). Keynes was not denying that "the risk of inflationary conditions in the immediate post-war period is a real one" (Keynes 1942a, JMK 25: 104). He also observed that "there is no countervailing objection [to a supernational bank money] except that which applies equally to the technique of domestic banking, namely that it is capable of the abuse of creating excessive purchasing power and hence an inflation of prices. In our efforts to avoid the opposite evil, we must not lose sight of this risk" (Keynes 1942g, JMK 25: 192). Meltzer (1989) appears to imply that Keynes pushed expansionism for tactical reasons, fearing that the Americans would be too timid.

8   See JMK 25: ch. 1. In particular, these are the first draft titled "Post-war currency policy" of 8 Sept. 1941 (Keynes 1941a), the second ("grammor") draft titled "Proposals for an international currency union" of 18 Nov. 1941 (Keynes 1941b), the third ("bancor") draft titled "Proposals for an international currency union" of 15 Dec. 1941 (Keynes 1941c), and its redrafted version (or fourth draft) of Jan. 1942 that formed part of a memorandum by the Treasury on External Monetary and Economic Problems (Keynes 1942b). As Keynes wrote in a letter to R. F. Kahn of 11 May 1942, "my currency schemes, which you saw in an early version, have gone through a vast number of drafts without, in truth, substantial change" (Keynes 1942d, JMK 25: 143). The later drafts are certainly of great interest too, especially since in them Keynes clarified a number of institutional aspects and how they related to his monetary thought and, moreover, often highlighted the differences between his own ("Currency Union") and American ("Stabilization Fund") ideas and plans, the latter becoming known to him at first unofficially in July 1942 (Horsefield 1969a: 16). But the later drafts, starting with the August 1942 one sent to Harry Dexter White and including the British Treasury's White Paper of April 1943 bearing Keynes' name, are also increasingly influenced by strategic considerations in the discussions with the Americans and ultimately the need to find a common line. Take for instance his admission in a speech given on 26 Feb. 1943 that "We have been very gentle towards the creditors because we are a little scared of them" (Keynes 1943a, JMK 25: 211). In a letter of 27 April 1943 to Roy Harrod Keynes wrote "I fully expect that we shall do well to compromise with the American scheme and very likely accept their dress in the long run. But I am sure that it would be premature to do so at present. For one thing, their plan is very far from being a firm offer. The real risk, I always have thought, is that they will run away from their own plan, let alone ours" (Keynes 1943c, JMK 25: 268).

9   The preface to Keynes' memo of Aug. 1942 comparing the British and American proposals reads: "We need a quantum of international currency, which is neither determined in an unpredictable and irrelevant manner as, for example, by the technical progress of the gold industry, nor subject to large variations depending on the gold reserve policies of individual countries; but is governed by the actual currency requirements of world commerce, and is also capable of deliberate expansion and contraction to offset deflationary and inflationary tendencies in effective world demand (Keynes 1942g, JMK 25: 168–9).

10 The first and second drafts even foresaw that in cases where any credit balance at yearend exceeded the full amount of a country's index quota "the excess shall be transferred to the Reserve Fund of the Clearing Bank" (Keynes 1941a, JMK 25: 36; 1941b, JMK 25: 64). In the "bancor plan" this penalty for surplus countries turned into an interest charge (Keynes 1941c, JMK 25: 79). As Keynes explained the point was to put "at least as much pressure of adjustment on the creditor country, as on the debtor" and that "the creditor should not be allowed to remain passive. For if he is, an impossible task is laid on the debtor country, which is for that very reason in the weaker position, so that the evils with which we are familiar are very likely to ensue" (Keynes 1941b, JMK 25: 48–9).

11 On this matter, the third draft, which in contrast to the second draft was leaning towards discretion rather than rules and general principles, states that: (6) "A member state may not depreciate the rate of exchange of its local currency in terms of bancor, unless it is a Deficiency Country; and the amount of the depreciation within a year shall not exceed 5 per cent without the permission of the Governing Board. The Governing Board may require a stated measure of depreciation as a condition of allowing an overdraft in excess of half of a member's quota, if it deems that to be the suitable remedy. By making possible rules as to when changes in the rates of exchange of a national currency are allowed or prescribed, it much increases the efficiency of small changes such as 5 or 10 per cent; and it protects any permitted change from being neutralized by an unjustified competitive depreciation elsewhere. (7) A Surplus Country shall discuss with the Governing Board (but shall retain the ultimate decision in its own hands) what measures would be appropriate to restore the equilibrium of its international balances, including (a) measures for the expansion of domestic credit and domestic demand; (b) the appreciation of its local currency in terms of bancor, or, if preferred, an increase in money-wages; (c) the reduction of excessive tariffs and other discouragements against imports; (d) international loans for the development of backward countries" (Keynes 1941c, JMK 25: 79–80).

12 Note that even if countries were cyclically in step, their "efficiency wage rates" (or, unit labor cost trends) could still be out of step (reflecting diverging "income inflation" and/or productivity trends). Keynes (1943e, JMK 26: 33) was optimistic that "if the initial exchange rates are fixed correctly, this is likely to be the only important disequilibrium for which a change in exchange rates is the appropriate remedy" – a statement that assumes successful domestic demand management.

13 Vines (2003: F350) has an interesting discussion on the apparently missing "control mechanism" or discipline in Keynes' scheme. In Vines' interpretation national fiscal policies were supposed to ensure both national full employment as well as – in the aggregate – the right level of global aggregate demand. While I agree that Keynes in *The General Theory* and after put more emphasis on the role of fiscal policy Vines pays too little attention to both national monetary policies (and the related role of capital controls) as well as the element of international monetary policy that Keynes envisioned. Meltzer (1989: 133) is quiet on this point but observes that "the limitation on [bancor] supply came from the rules setting a country's maximum indebtedness in relation to its quota."

14 Cf. Keynes (1930a, JMK 5: 27) on bank money. Except for retail bank runs it is convenient to completely ignore bank notes, which are endogenously provided anyway (cf. Keynes 1923, JMK 4: 145).

15 And one may usefully distinguish here "business as usual" policy conduct and exceptional crisis situations involving the central bank as "lender of last resort," extending additional liquidity in the form of bank notes (retail bank run) or central bank deposits (wholesale bank run), or even the deep pockets of the Treasury in cases of insolvency. In the case of wholesale bank runs the "credit mechanism" may break down and money markets freeze, with an increased propensity to hoard liquidity that can only be met by the monetary authorities.

16 In the longer run deflation may encourage the production of gold, stimulating employment. Some economists would also mention the real balance effect here, assuming there is no banking system to be destroyed.

17 Similarly, in a note in reaction to an article by Hayek in the *Economic Journal*, Keynes observed: "The peculiar merit of the Clearing Union as a means of remedying a chronic shortage of international money is that it operates through the velocity, rather than through the volume, of circulation. A *volume* of money is only required to satisfy hoarding, to provide reserves against contingencies, and to cover inevitable time lags between buying and spending. If hoarding is discouraged and if reserves against contingencies are provided by facultative overdrafts, a very small amount of

actually outstanding credit might be sufficient for clearing between well-organized central banks. The C.U., if it were fully successful, would deal with the quantity of international money by making any significant quantity unnecessary. The system might be improved, of course, by further increasing the discouragement to hoarding" (Keynes 1943e, JMK 26: 31).

18 Both key issues feature most clearly in Keynes' observation that control of capital movements "is not merely a question of curbing exchange speculations and movements of hot money, or even of avoiding flights of capital due to political motives, though all these it is necessary to control. The need, in my judgment, is more fundamental. Unless the aggregate of the new investments which individuals are free to make overseas is kept within the amount which our favorable trade balance is capable of looking after, we lose control over the domestic rate of interest. ... But we cannot hope to control rates of interest at home if movements of capital moneys out of the country are unrestricted" (Keynes 1943d, JMK 25: 275–6; cf. Moggridge 1986).

19 Bibow 2009a argues that developing countries (as host countries of foreign investment) should follow comprehensive management of their capital account to protect their policy space.

20 Keynes suggested applying this approach to both existing stocks as well as any new flows. For instance: "Foreign-owned balances and investments held within the jurisdiction of a central bank at the date of the establishment of the International Clearing Bank shall be frozen in the sense that they shall not be withdrawn thereafter except by permission of the central bank concerned or under the general license [that a Surplus Bank shall grant for the withdrawal of foreign-owned balances and investments within its jurisdiction]. The same shall apply to subsequent remittances on capital account but the title to such balances and investments may be freely transferred as between foreign nationals" (Keynes 1941a, JMK 25: 37–8). He thought that even unilateral control could be made effective as long as a record were kept of inward capital movements and made available to the country from which the capital was flowing, the government of which had to have at its disposal the powers of confiscation (see Keynes 1942f, JMK 25: 165). See also n. 5 on portfolio investment.

8   On what became of Keynes' vision

1 I gratefully acknowledge comments on an earlier draft by Jürgen Krompardt and Andrea Terzi. Bibow 2009a investigates the global monetary and financial order more specifically from the perspective of developing countries.

2 Much has been made of Keynes' final words including that reference to "the invisible hand." Cesarano (2003: 509) expresses surprise that Keynes "revindicates some fundamental hypotheses of the classical theory, which he mostly helped to explode." *The General Theory* clearly distinguished between the workings of the invisible hand at the microeconomic level and the "central controls" that were needed at the macroeconomic level to assure overall efficiency (i.e. including avoidance of waste of resources through idleness). At the international level too he hoped that favorable global aggregate demand conditions would yield simultaneous expansion and render microeconomic interferences (trade restrictions) superfluous. I disagree with Cesarano's (2003: 511) Keynes interpretation that the solution of the dollar shortage was supposed to be "given by the classical adjustment mechanism operating through a change in the price level." Keynes' reference to the "Midas touch" refers to spending, be it home spending on imports into the "high-living" country, official aid to poorer countries or foreign investments made by a "high-cost" country in lower cost locations. Keynes had no desire to see the US price level driven up along classical lines.

3 See Cesarano 2006; Isard 2005.

4 See his "comparative analysis" of the two plans of Feb. 1943, for instance. "The means of disciplining a creditor country is sadly lacking under [the White Plan]" (Keynes 1943b, JMK 25: 220).

5 Gold was only incompletely dethroned under Bretton Woods as long as gold convertibility of the US dollar remained officially in place, which led to the interpretation of the system as a "gold exchange standard" rather than a dollar standard (see e.g. Triffin 1960; Williamson 1983). While this was supposedly meant as a check on the international monetary powers of the key currency issuer, I have my doubts that in actual fact it ever had much of that kind of effect. After all, the apparent check was relieved step by step and finally gotten rid off altogether as it became increasingly inconvenient. It is true though that the increased precariousness in the global economic environment due to market liberalization, flexible exchange rates and especially capital account convertibility have further magnified the powers of the lead country under the international US dollar standard.

6 See Blecker (1999) and Eatwell and Taylor (2000) for a regime critique following the occurrences of the emerging market crises of the 1990s.

7 On Japan's experience see Werner 2003. Germany's export-driven recovery occurred in the context of the "hardening" of the European Monetary System in the late 1980s. A clash between the (always-too-eager-to-tighten) Bundesbank and (more balanced) US authorities preceded the stock market crash of October 1987, which gave way to more cautious tightening, allowing stronger growth even before unification. Applying careless monetary overkill, the Bundesbank then pushed Germany into protracted domestic demand stagnation in the aftermath of the historical unification challenge in the early 1990s (see Bibow 2003).

8 Referring to the period between 1995 and 2000, the IMF observed in its May 2001 World Economic Outlook that "rapid U.S. GDP growth and relatively weaker growth in other parts of the world, notably Europe and Japan, as well as a sharp increase in the real foreign exchange value of the dollar driven in large part by capital inflows, contributed to the rise in the deficit" (IMF 2001: 14). And in Sept. 2002 the Fund observed that "external imbalances across the main industrial country regions widened steadily during the 1990s [with these imbalances being] dominated by the euro area and Japan, respectively" (IMF 2002: 65–7).

9 Emerging and developing countries include "newly industrialized Asian countries" but exclude China and Saudi Arabia (shown separately). Henning (2000) estimates that almost $100bn of the rise in the US current account deficit in the aftermath of the Asian crises was a consequence of allowing Asian and other crisis economies to see their current account positions turn into surplus.

10 Kregel 2007 makes the case that BWII may be closer to Keynes' Clearing Union plan than the actual original regime set up at Bretton Woods, highlighting the automatic credit extension from current account surplus to deficit countries under BWII.

11 As Sovereign Wealth Funds (SWFs) increasingly take over the job of investing reserves for higher yields this factor is becoming more of a qualification and, accordingly, arrangements less of a bargain to the key currency issuer in terms of debt service costs.

12 The focus here is on foreign investors while of course US investors' portfolio choices regarding currencies and different types of financial instruments and assets in general have the same kinds of effects too. Considering short sales and derivative markets would add another layer of complexity.

13 This illustrates the international equivalent to Keynes' "constant money stock assumption" in *The General Theory*. In this case it is the US Federal Reserve and US banking system that can through their response change the "pool of (international) liquidity" available, apart from longer term current account trends.

14 Note also that as the household sector leveraged up net worth continued to grow until 2007, when this trend started to reverse as well.

15 In the 1990s the US also experienced an investment boom, which ended with the dot. com bust in 2001.
16 Bernanke (2007) gives an update of developments.
17 Among many other mainstream economists, I suppose, the authors of BWII too subscribe to loanable funds theory. Dooley *et al*. (2008: n. 3) assert that "the advent of the [BWII] system persistently lowered the long term rate of interest at every stage of the business cycle because of the large scale supply of net savings that emerging market countries were pushing into the industrial countries," developments which they attribute to the "historically unusual decision of many EM governments to place a substantial share of national savings in international financial assets."
18 See Ch. 3 above for a full step-by-step analysis of the closed economy case.
19 For external imbalances among all other countries adjustments would still essentially run along the above gold standard lines except for regional arrangements featuring reserve pooling and liquidity creation.
20 Put differently, as regards property markets and the pressing need to avoid overshooting of property prices, the choice is to either address the excess supply problem by reducing supply (through helping homeowners as potential sellers) or by boosting demand (through helping potential buyers).

9   Taking liquidity preference theory seriously

1 I am grateful for comments on an earlier draft by Roy Rotheim.
2 I am reminded here of Keynes' (1931a, JMK 9: 156) observation that "a 'sound' banker, alas! is not one who foresees danger and avoids it, but one who, when he is ruined, is ruined in a conventional and orthodox way along with his fellows, so that no one can really blame him." And I may add that Keynes' (1936a, JMK 7: 156) suggestion of the game of Musical Chairs as describing the behavior of professional financial market players found an interesting echo just before the outbreak of the ongoing financial crisis in the words of Citigroup's former Chief Executive Officer Charles O. Prince III: "When the music stops, in terms of liquidity, things will be complicated. But as long as the music is playing, you've got to get up and dance. We're still dancing."

Bibliography

Ackley, G. (1957) 'Liquidity preference and loanable funds theories of interest: a comment', *American Economic Review*, 47: 662–73.

Ahearne, A. *et al.* (2002) 'Preventing deflation: lessons from Japan's experience in the 1990s', *Board of Governors of the Federal Reserve System, International Finance Discussion Paper*, 729 (June).

Ahiakpor, J.C.W. (2003) *Classical Macroeconomics: Some Modern Variations and Distortions*, London: Routledge.

Allsopp, C. and Vines, D. (2000) 'The assessment: macroeconomic policy', *Oxford Review of Economic Policy*, 16(4): 1–32.

Amadeo, E.J. (1989) *Keynes's Principle of Effective Demand*, Aldershot: Edward Elgar.

Arestis, P. (1988) 'Post Keynesian theory of money, credit and finance', in P. Arestis (ed.), *Post-Keynesian Monetary Economics: New Approaches to Financial Modeling*, Aldershot: Edward Elgar, pp. 41–71.

Arestis, P. and Howells, P. (1996) 'Theoretical reflections on endogenous money: the problem with "convenience lending"', *Cambridge Journal of Economics*, 20: 539–51.

Arestis, P. and Sawyer, M. (2005) 'New consensus monetary policy: an appraisal', in P. Arestis, M. Baddeley and J. McCombie (eds), *The New Monetary Policy*, Cheltenham: Edward Elgar.

Arrow, K. J. and Hahn , F. A. (1971). *General Competitive Analysis*, Amsterdam: North-Holland.

Asimakopulos, A. (1983) 'Kalecki and Keynes on finance, investment and saving', *Cambridge Journal of Economics*, 7(3/4): 221–33.

Asimakopulos, A. (1985) 'Finance, saving and investment in Keynes's economics: a comment', *Cambridge Journal of Economics*, 9(4): 405–7.

Asimakopulos, A. (1986a) 'Finance, investment and saving: a reply to Terzi', *Cambridge Journal of Economics*, 10(1): 81–2.

Asimakopulos, A. (1986b) 'Richardson on Asimakopulos on finance: a reply', *Cambridge Journal of Economics*, 10(2): 199–201.

Asimakopulos, A. (1986c) 'Finance, liquidity, saving, and investment', *Journal of Post Keynesian Economics*, 9(1): 79–90.

Bain, A.D. and McGregor, P.G. (1985) 'Buffer-stock monetarism and the theory of financial buffers', *Manchester School*, 53: 385–403.

Bagehot, W. (1874) *Lombard Street: A Description of the Money Market*, London: Kegan, Paul & Co.

Ball, L. (1997) 'Disinflation and the NAIRU', in C.D. Romer and D.H. Romer (eds), *Reducing Inflation*, Chicago: University of Chicago Press, pp. 167–85.

Bank of Canada Archives, Towers Papers, Memo dated 5 Sept. 1945.

Bank of England Archives, Files G1/261; G18/1; G1/15; G1/16; ADM11/1; ADM11/2; ADM11/3; ADM11/4; G4/168; G4/169; G2/33; G19.

Bernanke, B.S. (2002) 'Asset-price "bubbles" and monetary policy', Remarks made before the New York Chapter of the National Association for Business Economics, New York, October 15, The Federal Reserve Board, http://www.federalreserve.gov/BoardDocs/ Speeches/2002/20021015/default.htm

Bernanke, B.S. (2005) 'The global saving glut and the U.S. current account deficit', Federal Reserve Board, Remarks, 10 March.

Bernanke, B.S. (2007) 'Global imbalances: recent developments and prospects', Federal Reserve Board, Remarks, 11 Sept.

Bernanke, B.S. and Blinder, A.S. (1988) 'Credit, money and aggregate demand', *American Economic Association Papers and Proceedings*, 78: 435–9.

Bernanke, B.S. and Blinder, A.S. (1992) 'The Federal Funds Rate and the channels of monetary transmission', *American Economic Review*, 82: 901–22.

Bernanke, B.S. and Gertler, M. (1995) 'Inside the black box: the credit channel of monetary policy transmission', *Journal of Economic Perspectives*, 9(4): 27–48.

Bibow, J. (1995) 'On Keynesian Theories of Liquidity Preference', unpublished Ph.D. thesis, University of Cambridge.

Bibow, J. (2000) 'The loanable funds fallacy in retrospect', *History of Political Economy* 32(4): 789–831.

Bibow, J. (2002a) *What has Happened to Monetarism? An Investigation into the Keynesian Roots of Milton Friedman's Monetary Thought and its Apparent Monetarist Legacies*, Annandale-on-Hudson, N.Y: Levy Economics Institute, Working Paper, 347.

Bibow, J. (2002b) 'The markets versus the ECB, and the euro's plunge', *Eastern Economic Journal,* 28(1): 45–57.

Bibow, J. (2003) 'On the "burden" of German unification', *Banca Nazionale del Lavoro Quarterly Review*, 61(225): 137–69.

Bibow, J. (2004a) 'Reflections on the current fashion for central bank independence', *Cambridge Journal of Economics*, 28(4): 549–76.

Bibow, J. (2004b) *Assessing the ECB's Performance since the Global Slowdown: A Structural Policy Bias Coming Home to Roost?*, Annandale-on-Hudson: Levy Economics Institute, Working Paper, 409 (July).

Bibow, J. (2006a) 'Inflation persistence and tax-push inflation in Germany and the euro area: a symptom of macroeconomic mismanagement?', Institute für Makroökonomie und Konjunkturforschung, *IMK Studies*, 1/2006.

Bibow, J. (2006b) 'Liquidity preference theory', in P. Arestis and M. Sawyer (eds), *Handbook of Alternative Monetary Economics*, Cheltenham: Edward Elgar, pp. 328–45.

Bibow, J. (2007) 'Global imbalances, Bretton Woods II, and Euroland's role in all this', in J. Bibow and A. Terzi (eds), *Euroland and the World Economy: Global Player or Global Drag?* Basingstoke: Palgrave (Levy Economics Institute, Working Paper, 486), pp. 15–42.

Bibow, J. (2008a) 'The international monetary (non-)order and the "global capital flows paradox"', in E. Hein, T. Niechoj, P. Spahn and A. Truger (eds), *Finance-led Capitalism?*, Marburg: Metropolis (Levy Working Paper, 531), pp. 219–48.

Bibow, J. (2008b) 'Zur (Re-) Etablierung zentralbankpolitischer Institutionen und Traditionen in Westdeutschland: Theoretische Grundlagen und politisches Kalkül (1946–67)', forthcoming in C. Scheer (ed.), *Studien zur Entwicklung der Ökonomischen*

Theorie XXII: Die deutschsprachige Wirtschaftswissenschaft nach 1945, Schriften des Vereins für Socialpolitik, Berlin: Duncker & Humblot.

Bibow, J. (2009a) 'Insuring against private capital flows: is it worth the premium? What are the alternatives?', *International Journal of Political Economy*, 37(4): 5–30.

Bibow, J. (2009b) 'On the origin and rise of central bank independence in West Germany', *European Journal of the History of Economic Thought*, 16(1): 155–190.

Bindseil, U. (2004) *Monetary Policy Implementation: Theory, Past and Present*, Oxford: Oxford University Press.

Black, F. (1987) *Business Cycles and Equilibrium*, Oxford: Basil Blackwell.

Black, F. (1995) 'Interest rates as options', *Journal of Finance*, 50(7): 1371–6.

Blanchard, O.J. and Fischer, S. (1989) *Lectures on Macroeconomics*, Cambridge, MA: MIT Press.

Blecker, R.A. (1999) *Taming Global Finance: A Better Architecture for Growth and Equity*, Washington DC: Economic Policy Institute.

Blinder, A.S. (1987) 'Credit rationing and effective supply failures', *Economic Journal,* 97(June): 327–52.

Blinder, A.S. (1997) 'What central bankers can learn from academics – and *vice versa*', *Journal of Economic Perspectives*, 11(2): 3–19.

Blinder, A.S. (1998) *Central Banking in Theory and Practice*, Cambridge, MA: MIT Press.

Blinder, A.S. and Maccini, L.J. (1991) 'Taking stock: a critical assessment of recent research on inventories', *Journal of Economic Perspectives*, 5: 73–96.

Bloomfield, A.I. (1959) *Monetary Policy under the International Gold Standard: 1880–1914*, New York: Federal Reserve Bank of New York.

Bordo, M.D. (1987) 'Equation of exchange', in J. Eatwell, M. Milgate and P. Newman (eds), *The New Palgrave: Money*, London: Macmillan.

Borio, C.E.V. (1997) 'The implementation of monetary policy in industrial countries: a survey', *BIS Economic Papers*, 47 (July).

Bridel, P. (1987) *Cambridge Monetary Thought: The Development of Saving-Investment Analysis from Marshall to Keynes*, London: Macmillan.

Buiter, W.H. (1980) 'Walras' law and all that: budget constraints and balance sheet constraints in period models and continuous time models', *International Economic Review*, 21: 1–16.

Cairncross, A. (1988) 'The Bank of England: relationships with the Government, the Civil Service, and Parliament, in G. Toniolo (ed.), *Central Banks' Independence in Historical Perspective*, Berlin: WDG.

Carabelli, A. (1988) *On Keynes's Method,* London: Macmillan.

Cesarano, F. (2003) 'Keynes's revindication of classical monetary theory', *History of Political Economy,* 35(3): 491–519.

Cesarano, F. (2006) *Monetary Theory and Bretton Woods: The Construction of an International Monetary Order*, Cambridge: Cambridge University Press.

Chamberlain, A. ([1913] 1971) Letter to John Maynard Keynes, 12 Aug., in *The Collected Writings of John Maynard Keynes*, ed. Elizabeth Johnson, London: Macmillan, vol. 15, pp. 99–100.

Chandavarkar, A.G. (1983) 'Money and credit (1858–1947)', in Dharma Kumar (ed.), *The Cambridge Economic History of India*, Cambridge and New York: Cambridge University Press, vol. 2.

Chandavarkar, A.G. (1985) 'Keynes and central banking', *Indian Economic Review,* 20(2): 283–97.

Chick, V. (1983) *Macroeconomics after Keynes*, Cambridge, MA: MIT Press.

228   *Bibliography*

Chick, V. (1992) *On Money, Method and Keynes*, London: Macmillan.

Chick, V. (1993) 'The evolution of the banking system and the theory of monetary policy', in S.F. Frowen (ed.), *Monetary Theory and Policy: New Tracks for the 1990s*, London: Macmillan.

Chick, V. and Dow, S.C. (2002) 'Monetary policy with endogenous money and liquidity preference: a nondualistic treatment', *Journal of Post Keynesian Economics*, 24(4): 587–607.

Ciocca, P. and Nardozzi, G. (1996) *The High Price of Money: An Interpretation of World Interest Rates*, Oxford: Clarendon Press.

Clarida, R., Gali, J. and Gertler, M. (1999) 'The science of monetary policy: a new Keynesian perspective', *Journal of Economic Literature*, 37: 1661–1707.

Clarke, P. (1988) *The Keynesian Revolution in the Making*, Oxford: Clarendon Press.

Clower, R. (1965) 'The Keynesian counter-revolution', in F.H. Hahn and F.P.R. Brechling (eds), *The Theory of Interest Rates*, London: Macmillan.

Clower, R. (1967) 'A reconsideration of the microfoundations of monetary theory', *Western Economic Journal*, 6: 1–9.

Committee on Finance and Industry [Macmillan Committee] (1931) *Report*, Cmd. 3897. London, HMSO.

Cottrell, A. (1993) 'Keynes's theory of probability and its relevance to his economics', *Economics and Philosophy*, 9(1): 25–51.

Cottrell, A. (1994) 'Post-Keynesian monetary economics', *Cambridge Journal of Economics*, 18: 587–605.

Cottrell, A. and Lawlor, M.S. (1991) 'Natural rate mutations: Keynes, Leijonhufvud and the Wicksell connection', *History of Political Economy*, 23: 625–43.

Crotty, J.R. (1983) 'On Keynes and capital flight', *Journal of Economic Literature* 21(1): 59–65.

Dale, S. and Haldane, A.G. (1993) 'Bank behaviour and the monetary transmission mechanism', *Bank of England Quarterly Bulletin*, 73: 478–91.

Dale, S. and Haldane, A.G. (1995) 'Interest rates and the channels of monetary transmission: some sectoral estimates', *European Economic Review*, 39: 1611–26.

Dalziel, P. (2002) 'The triumph of Keynes: what now for monetary policy research', *Journal of Post Keynesian Economics*, 24(4): 511–27.

Davidson, P. (1965) 'Keynes' finance motive', *Oxford Economic Papers*, 17(1): 47–65.

Davidson, P. (1967) 'The importance of the demand for finance', *Oxford Economic Papers*, 19(2): 245–53.

Davidson, P. (1978) *Money and the Real World*, 2nd edn, London: Macmillan.

Davidson, P. (1986) 'Finance, funding, saving, and investment', *Journal of Post Keynesian Economics*, 9(1): 101–10.

Davidson, P. (1988) 'A technical definition of uncertainty and the long-run non-neutrality of money', *Cambridge Journal of Economics*, 12(3): 329–37.

Davidson, P. (1991) 'Is probability theory relevant for uncertainty? A post Keynesian perspective', *Journal of Economic Perspectives*, 5(1): 129–43.

Davidson, P. (1994) *Post Keynesian Macroeconomic Theory*, Aldershot: Edward Elgar.

Davis, E.G. (1980) 'The Correspondence between R. G. Hawtrey and J. M. Keynes on the *Treatise*: The Genesis of Output Adjustment Models', *Canadian Journal of Economics*, 13(4): 716–24.

Deaton, A. (1992) *Understanding Consumption*, Oxford: Clarendon Press.

De Cecco, M. (1974) *Money and Empire: The International Gold Standard, 1890–1914*, Oxford: Basil Blackwell.

Deleplace, G. and Nell, E.J. (eds) (1996) *Money in Motion: The Post Keynesian and Circulationist Approaches*, London: Macmillan.

De Long, B. (2000) 'The triumph of monetarism?', *Journal of Economic Perspectives*, 14(1): 83–94.

Desai, M. (1989) 'Endogenous and exogenous money', in J. Eatwell *et al.* (eds) *The New Palgrave: Money*, London: Macmillan.

Deutsche Bundesbank (1999) 'Zur Unternehmensfinanzierung in Deutschland und Frankreich: eine vergleichende Analyse', *Monatsbericht* (Oct.).

Deutscher, P. (1990) *R.G. Hawtrey and the Development of Macroeconomics*, London: Macmillan.

Dimand, R.W. (1988) *The Origins of the Keynesian Revolution*, Aldershot: Edward Elgar.

Dimand, R.W. (2006) 'Keynes on global economic integration', *Atlantic Economic Journal*, 34: 175–82.

Dixit, A.K. and Pindyck, R.S. (1992) *Investment under Uncertainty*, Princeton, NJ: Princeton University Press.

Dodwell, D.W. (1934) *Treasuries and Central Banks*, London: P.S. King & Son.

Dooley, M.P., Folkerts-Landau, D. and Garber, P. (2003) *An Essay on the Revived Bretton Woods System*, NBER Working Paper, 9971.

Dooley, M.P., Folkerts-Landau, D. and Garber, P.M. (2008) *Will Subprime be a Twin Crisis for the United States?*, NBER Working Paper, 13978.

Dow, S.C. (1996) 'Horizontalism: a critique', *Cambridge Journal of Economics*, 20: 497–508.

Dow, S.C. (1997) 'Endogenous money', in G. C. Harcourt and P. Riach (eds), *A 'Second Edition' of The General Theory*, London: Routledge, pp. 61–78.

Dow, S.C. (2006) 'Endogenous money: structuralist', in P. Arestis and M. Sawyer (eds), *Handbook of Alternative Monetary Economics*, Cheltenham: Edward Elgar.

Dymski, G. (1988) 'A Keynesian theory of bank behavior', *Journal of Post Keynesian Economics*, 10: 499–526.

Eatwell, J. and Taylor, L. (2000) *Global Finance at Risk: The Case for International Regulation*, Oxford: Polity Press.

Edwards, E.O. (1966) 'The interest rate in disequilibrium', *Southern Economic Journal*, 23: 49–57.

Eichengreen, B., Tobin, J. and Wyplosz, C. (1995) 'Two cases for sand in the wheels of international finance', *Economic Journal*, 105(428): 162–72.

Eucken, W. (1952) *Grundsätze der Wirtschaftspolitik*, Tübingen and Zürich: Mohr Siebeck.

Fazzari, S. and Papadimitriou, D.B. (1992) *Financial Conditions and Macroeconomic Performance: Essays in Honor of Hyman P. Minsky*, London: M.E. Sharpe.

Feavearyear, A.E. ([1931] 1963) *The Pound Sterling*, Oxford: Oxford University Press, 2nd edn.

Fetter, F.W. (1965) *Development of British Monetary Orthodoxy: 1797–1875*, Cambridge, MA: Harvard University Press.

Fforde, J. (1992) *The Bank of England and Public Policy: 1941–1958*, Cambridge: Cambridge University Press.

Fisher, I. (1933) 'The debt-deflation theory of great depressions', *Econometrica*, 1: 337–57.

Foley, D.K. (1975) 'On two specifications of asset equilibrium in macroeconomic models', *Journal of Political Economy*, 83: 303–24.

Fontana, G. (2003) 'Post Keynesian approaches to endogenous money: a time framework explanation', *Review of Political Economy*, 15(3): 291–314.

Fontana, G. and Palacio-Vera, A. (2007) 'Are long-run price stability and short-run output stabilization all that monetary policy can aim for?', *Metroeconomica*, 57(2): 269–78.

Forder, J. (1998) 'Central bank independence: conceptual clarifications and interim assessment', *Oxford Economic Papers*, 50(3): 307–34.

Friedman, B.M. (1985) 'Effects of large budget deficits', *Oxford Review of Economic Policy*, 1(1): 58–71.

Friedman, B.M. (1991) 'The risks of financial crisis', in M. Feldstein (ed.), *The Risk of Economic Crisis*, Chicago, IL: University of Chicago Press.

Friedman, M. (1960) *A Program for Monetary Stability*, New York: Fordham University Press.

Friedman, M. (1968) 'The Role of Monetary Policy', *American Economic Review*, 58(1): 1–17.

Friedman, M. ([1962] 1969) 'Should there be an independent monetary authority?', repr. in *Dollars and Deficits*, Chicago, IL: Aldine.

Friedman, M. (1970) 'A theoretical framework for monetary analysis', *Journal of Political Economy*, 78(2): 193–238.

Friedman, M. (1971) *A Theoretical Framework for Monetary Analysis*, NBER Occasional Paper, New York, 112.

Friedman, M. (1975) 'How to hit the money target', *Newsweek* (8 Dec.).

Friedman, M. (1984) 'Monetary policy for the 1980s', in J.H. Moore (ed.), *To Promote Prosperity: U.S. Domestic Policy in the Mid–1980s*, Stanford, CA: Hoover Institution Press.

Friedman, M. (1992) *Money Mischief: Episodes in Monetary History*, San Diego, CA: Harvest Brace & Co.

Friedman, M. (2002) 'Comment on Gaspar and Issing', *Australian Economic Papers*, 41(4): 366–8.

Friedman, M. and Schwartz, A.J. (1982) *Monetary Trends in the United States and the United Kingdom*, Chicago, IL: University of Chicago Press.

Fullerton, D.H. (1986) *Graham Towers and his Times: A Biography*, Toronto: McClelland & Stewart.

Garber, P. and Taylor, M.P. (1995) 'Sand in the wheels of foreign exchange markets: a sceptical note', *Economic Journal*, 105(428): 173–80.

Gertler, M. and Gilchrist, S. (1994) 'Monetary policy, business cycles, and the behavior of small manufacturing firms', *Quarterly Journal of Economics*, 109: 309–40.

Ghosh, A. and Phillips, S. (1998) 'Warning: inflation may be harmful to your growth', International Monetary Fund, *IMF Staff Papers*, 45(4): 672–710.

Gilbert, J.C. (1982) *Keynes' Impact on Monetary Economics*, London: Butterworth Scientific.

Godley, W. and Lavoie, M. (2007) *Monetary Economics: An Integrated Approach to Credit, Money, Income, Production and Wealth*, London: Palgrave Macmillan.

Godley, W., Papadimitriou, D.B., Hannsgen, G. and Zezza, G. (2007) *The U.S. Economy: Is there a Way Out of the Woods?*, Annandale-on-Hudson: Levy Economics Institute, Strategic Analysis, Nov.

Goodhart, C.A.E. (1989) 'Has Moore become too horizontal?', *Journal of Post Keynesian Economics*, 12: 29–34.

Goodhart, C.A.E. (1994a) 'Game theory for central bankers: a report to the governor of the Bank of England', *Journal of Economic Literature*, 32(1): 101–14.

Goodhart, C.A.E. (1994b) 'What should central banks do? What should be their macroeconomic objectives and operations?', *Economic Journal*, 104(6): 1424–36.

Gordon, H.S. (1961) *The Economists versus the Bank of Canada*, Toronto: Ryerson Press.

Graziani, A. (1984) 'The debate on Keynes' finance motive', *Economic Notes*, 1: 5–33.

Graziani, A. (1989) 'The theory of the monetary circuit', *Thames Papers in Political Economy* (Spring): 1–26.

Greenspan, A. (1998) 'Problems of price measurement', Chairman's remarks on deflation at the AEA annual meeting (Chicago), http://www.bog.frb.fed.us/boarddocs/speeches/19989193.htm

Greenspan, A. (2007) *The Age of Financial Turbulence: Adventures in a New World*, London: Penguin.

Greenwald, B.G. and Stiglitz, J.E. (1993) 'New and Old Keynesians', *Journal of Economic Perspectives*, 7: 23–44.

Größl, I. and Stahlecker, P. (1997) *A Simultaneous Treatment of the Liquidity and Portfolio Motive with Implications for Monetary Demand*, Discussion paper, 18, University of Hamburg, ISTÖ.

Gurley, J.G. and Shaw, E.S. (1960) *Money in a Theory of Finance*, Washington, DC: Brookings Institution.

Hahn, F.H. (1955) 'The rate of interest and general equilibrium analysis', *Economic Journal*, 65(1): 52–66.

Hahn, F.H. (1982) *Money and Inflation*, Oxford: Blackwell.

Hahn, F.H. (1990) 'Liquidity', in F.H. Hahn and B.M. Friedman (eds), *Handbook of Monetary Theory*, Amsterdam: Elsevier Science Publisher BV, pp. 63–80.

Harcourt, G.C. (1987, 1992) 'The legacy of Keynes: theoretical methods and unfinished business', repr. in C. Sardoni (ed.), *On Political Economists and Modern Political Economy*, London: Routledge.

Harcourt, G.C. (1994) 'Kahn and Keynes and the making of *The General Theory*', *Cambridge Journal of Economics*, 18(1): 11–24.

Harrod, R.F. (1951) *The Life of John Maynard Keynes*, New York and London: W. W. Norton & Co.

Hawtrey, R. (1962) *A Century of Bank Rate*, 2nd edn, London: Frank Cass & Co.

Hayek, F.A. von (1931) 'Reflections on the pure theory of money of Mr. J.M. Keynes', *Economica*, 11 (Aug.): 270–95.

Hayek, F.A. von ([1976] 1990) *Denationalization of Money: The Argument Refined*, 3rd edn, Hobart Special Paper, 70, London: Institute of Economic Affairs.

Hayes, M.G. (2006) *The Economics of Keynes: A New Guide to The General Theory*, Cheltenham: Edward Elgar.

Hellwig, M.F. (1993) 'The challenge of monetary theory', *European Economic Review*, 37: 215–42.

Henning, C.R. (2000) 'External relations of the euro area', in R. Mundell and A. Clesse (eds), *The Euro as a Stabilizer in the International Economic System*, Boston, MA, and London: Kluwer Academic.

Hewitson, G. (1995) 'Post-Keynesian monetary theory: some issues', *Journal of Economic Surveys*, 9: 285–310.

Hicks, J.R. (1936) 'Mr. Keynes' theory of employment', *Economic Journal*, 46: 238–53.

Hicks, J. (1937) 'Mr. Keynes and the "Classics": a suggested interpretation', *Econometrica*, 5(2): 147–59.

Hicks, J.R. (1939) *Value and Capital*, Oxford: Clarendon Press.

Hicks, J. (1974) *The Crisis in Keynesian Economics*, Yrjö Jahnsson Lectures, Oxford: Basil Blackwell.

Hicks, J.R. (1989) *A Market Theory of Money*, Oxford: Clarendon Press.

Hirshleifer, J. and Riley, J.G. (1992) *The Analytics of Uncertainty and Information*, Cambridge: Cambridge University Press.

Homer, S. and Sylla, R. (1996) *A History of Interest Rates*, 3rd edn, New Brunswick, NJ: Rutgers University Press.

Hoover, K.D. (1997) 'Is there a place for rational expectations in Keynes's *General Theory?*', in G.C. Harcourt and P. Riach (eds), *A 'Second Edition' of The General Theory*, London: Routledge, pp. 219–37.

Horsefield, K.J. (1969a) *The International Monetary Fund 1945–1965: Twenty Years of International Monetary Cooperation*, vol. 1. Washington, DC: IMF.

Horsefield, K.J. (1969b) *The International Monetary Fund 1945–1965: Twenty Years of International Monetary Cooperation*, vol. 3, *Documents*, Washington, DC: IMF.

Horwich, G. (1966) 'Keynes's finance motive: comment', *Oxford Economic Papers*, 18(2): 242–51.

Howells, P.G.A. (1995) 'Endogenous money', *International Papers in Political Economy*, 2(2): 1–41.

Howitt, P.W. (1993) 'Canada'. in Fratianni and Salvatore (eds) *Monetary Policy in Developed Countries: Handbook of Comparative Economic Policies,* Vol. 3: 459–508, Westport, CT: Greenwood Press.

Howson, S. (1975) *Domestic Monetary Management in Britain 1919–38*, Cambridge: Cambridge University Press.

Howson, S. (1988) 'Cheap money and debt management in Britain 1932–1951', in P.L. Cottrell and D.E. Moggridge (eds), *Money and Power: Essays in Honor of L.S. Pressnell*, London, Macmillan, pp. 227–289.

Howson, S. (1993) *British Monetary Policy: 1945–51*, Oxford: Oxford University Press.

Hubbard, R.G. (1994) 'Investment under uncertainty: keeping one's options open', *Journal of Economic Literature*, 32(4): 1816–31.

Huizinga, J. (1993) 'Inflation uncertainty, relative price uncertainty, and investment in U.S. manufacturing', *Journal of Money, Credit and Banking*, 25(3): 521–49.

IMF (2001) *World Economic Outlook*, Washington, DC: IMF.

IMF (2002) *World Economic Outlook*, Washington, DC: IMF.

Isard, P. (2005) *Globalization and the International Financial System: What's Wrong and What Can be Done*, Cambridge: Cambridge University Press.

Issing, O. (2000) 'Walter Eucken: Vom Primat der Währungspolitik', speech, Walter-Eucken-Institute, Freiburg, 17 March.

Issing, O. (2001) 'Why price stability?', in Alicia Garcia Herrero, Vítor Gaspar, Lex Hoogduin, Julian Morgan and Bernhard Winkler (eds.), *Why Price Stability?* First ECB Central Banking Conference, Frankfurt am Main: European Central Bank..

Jaenicke, J. (1995) 'Wertpapierpensionsgeschäfte', *Jahrbücher für Nationalökonomie und Statistik*, 214: 209–25.

Jaenicke, J. and Jakobs, H.T. (1994) 'Das Zinstenderverfahren: Institutionelle Gestaltung und Einfluß auf die Geldmarktzinsen', *Zeitschrift für das gesamte Kreditwesen*, 634–41.

Johnson, H.G. (1951–2) 'Some Cambridge controversies', *Review of Economic Studies*, 19: 93–104.

Johnson, H.G. (1962) 'Monetary theory and policy', *American Economic Review*, 52: 335–84.

Jones, R.A. and Ostroy, J.M. (1984) 'Flexibility and uncertainty', *Review of Economic Studies*, 51: 13–32.

Kahn, R.F. ([1929] 1989) *The Economics of the Short Period*, Basingstoke: Macmillan.

Kahn, R.F. (1954) 'Some notes on liquidity preference', *Manchester School*, 22(3): 229–57; repr. in Kahn, *Selected Essays on Employment and Growth*, Cambridge: Cambridge University Press, 1972.

Kahn, R.F. ([1958] 1972) Memorandum of evidence submitted to the Radcliffe Committee, reprinted in *Selected Essays on Employment and Growth*, pp. 124–152, Cambridge: Cambridge University Press, 1972.

Kahn, R.F. ([1971] 1972) 'Notes on the rate of interest and the growth of firms', repr. in *Selected Essays on Employment and Growth*, Cambridge: Cambridge University Press, 1972.

Kahn, R. F. (1976) 'Historical origins of the International Monetary Fund', in A. P. Thirlwall (ed.), *Keynes and International Monetary Relations*, London, Macmillan, pp. 3–35.

Kahn, R.F. (1978) 'Some aspects on the development of Keynes's thought', *Journal of Economic Literature*, 16(3): 545–59.

Kahn, R.F. (1984) *The Making of Keynes's General Theory: Raffaele Mattioli Lectures*, Cambridge: Cambridge University Press.

Kahn, R.F. (1985) 'The Cambridge Circus (1)', in G.C. Harcourt (ed.), *Keynes and his Contemporaries*, Basingstoke: Macmillan.

Kaldor, N. (1939) 'Speculation and economic stability', *Review of Economic Studies*, 7(1): 1–27.

Kaldor, N. (1970) 'The new monetarism', *Lloyds Bank Review* (July), pp. 1–18.

Kaldor, N. (1982) *The Scourge of Monetarism*, Oxford: Oxford University Press.

Kaldor, N. (1983) 'Keynesian economics after fifty years', in G.D.N. Worswick and J.A. Trevithick (eds), *Keynes and the Modern World*, Cambridge: Cambridge University Press.

Kashyap, A.K., Lamont, O.A. and Stein, J.C. (1994) 'Credit conditions and the cyclical behavior of inventories', *Quarterly Journal of Economics*, 109: 565–92.

Kenen, P.B. (1995) 'Capital controls, the EMS and EMU', *Economic Journal*, 105(428): 181–92.

Keynes, J.M. ([1913a] 1971) *Indian Currency and Finance*, repr. in *The Collected Writings of John Maynard Keynes*, London: Macmillan, vol. 1.

Keynes, J.M. ([1913b] 1971) 'Memorandum on proposals for the establishment of a state bank in India', repr. in E. Johnson (ed.), *The Collected Writings of John Maynard Keynes*, London: Macmillan, vol. 15, pp. 151–211.

Keynes, J.M. ([1914] 1983) 'The prospects of money', repr. in D. Moggridge (ed.), *The Collected Writings of John Maynard Keynes*, London: Macmillan, vol. 11, pp. 299–328.

Keynes, J.M. ([1919] 1971) 'The economic consequences of the peace', repr. in *The Collected Writings of John Maynard Keynes*, London: Macmillan, vol. 2.

Keynes, J.M. ([1921] 1973) *A Treatise on Probability*, repr. in *The Collected Writings of John Maynard Keynes*, London: Macmillan, vol. 8.

Keynes, J.M. ([1922a] 1977) 'The finance experts at Genoa', repr. in E. Johnson (ed.), *The Collected Writings of John Maynard Keynes*, London: Macmillan, vol. 17, pp. 380–3.

Keynes, J.M. ([1922b] 1977) 'The stabilization of the European exchanges: a plan for Genoa', repr. in E. Johnson (ed.), *The Collected Writings of John Maynard Keynes*, London: Macmillan, vol. 17, pp. 355–69.

Keynes, J.M. ([1923] 1971) *A Tract on Monetary Reform*, repr. in *The Collected Writings of John Maynard Keynes*, London: Macmillan, vol. 4.

Keynes, J.M. ([1924] 1981) 'Minutes of evidence: Committee on the Currency and Bank of England Note Issues', repr. in D. Moggridge (ed.), *The Collected Writings of John Maynard Keynes*, London: Macmillan, vol. 19(1), pp. 239–61.

Keynes, J.M. ([1925] 1972) 'The economic consequences of Mr Churchill', repr. in *The Collected Writings of John Maynard Keynes*, London: Macmillan, vol. 9.

Keynes, J.M. ([1926a] 1972) 'The end of laissez-faire', repr. in *The Collected Writings of John Maynard Keynes*, London: Macmillan, vol. 9, pp. 272–94.

Keynes, J.M. ([1926b] 1981) 'Bagehot's *Lombard Street*', repr. in D. Moggridge (ed.), *The Collected Writings of John Maynard Keynes*, London: Macmillan, vol. 19(2), pp. 465–72.

Keynes, J.M. ([1926c] 1981) 'Minutes of evidence: Royal Commission on Indian Currency and Finance', repr. in D. Moggridge (ed.), *The Collected Writings of John Maynard Keynes*, London: Macmillan, vol. 19(2), pp. 477–524.

Keynes, John M. ([1928a] 1981) Letter to *The Times* (18 May), repr. in D. Moggridge (ed.), *The Collected Writings of John Maynard Keynes*, London: Macmillan, vol. 19(2), pp. 750–2.

Keynes, J.M. ([1928b] 1981) Letter to Winston Churchill, repr. in D. Moggridge (ed.), *The Collected Writings of John Maynard Keynes*, London: Macmillan, vol. 19(2), pp. 749–50.

Keynes, J.M. ([1930a] 1971) *A Treatise on Money: The Pure Theory of Money*, repr. in *The Collected Writings of John Maynard Keynes*, London: Macmillan, vol. 5.

Keynes, J.M. ([1930b] 1971) *A Treatise on Money: The Applied Theory of Money*, reprinted in *The Collected Writings of John Maynard Keynes*, London: Macmillan, vol. 6.

Keynes, J.M. ([1930c] 1981) 'Minutes of evidence: Committee on Finance and Industry', repr. in D. Moggridge (ed.), *The Collected Writings of John Maynard Keynes*, London: Macmillan, vol. 20, pp. 38–311.

Keynes, J. M. ([1931a] 1972) 'The consequences to the banks of the collapse of money values', repr. in *The Collected Writings of John Maynard Keynes*, London: Macmillan, vol. 9, pp. 150–8.

Keynes, J. M. ([1931b] 1973) 'The pure theory of money: a reply to Hayek', *Economica* (Nov.), repr. in *The Collected Writings of John Maynard Keynes*, London: Macmillan, vol. 13, pp. 243–56.

Keynes, J.M. ([1931c] 1973) Letter to D. H. Robertson, 6 Oct., repr. in D. Moggridge (ed.), *The Collected Writings of John Maynard Keynes*, London: Macmillan, vol. 13, pp. 272–4.

Keynes, J.M. ([1931d] 1973) 'A rejoinder', in D. Moggridge (ed.), *The Collected Writings of John Maynard Keynes*, London: Macmillan, vol. 13, pp. 219–36.

Keynes, J.M. ([1931e] 1981) Letter to R. F. Kahn, 13 Aug., repr. in D. Moggridge (ed.), *The Collected Writings of John Maynard Keynes*, London: Macmillan, vol. 20, pp. 594–5.

Keynes, J.M. ([1931f] 1982) 'Notes on the currency question', 16 November, repr. in D. Moggridge (ed.), *The Collected Writings of John Maynard Keynes*, London: Macmillan, vol. 21, pp. 16–28.

Keynes, J.M. ([1932a] 1979) 'Fragment', repr. in D. Moggridge (ed.), *The Collected Writings of John Maynard Keynes*, London: Macmillan, vol. 29, pp. 54–7.

Keynes, J.M. ([1932b] 1982) 'Reflections on the sterling exchange', *Lloyds Bank Review* (April), repr. in *The Collected Writings of John Maynard Keynes*, London: Macmillan, vol. 21, pp. 63–82.

Keynes, J.M. ([1932c] 1982) 'This is a budget of excessive prudence', repr. in D. Moggridge (ed.), *The Collected Writings of John Maynard Keynes*, London: Macmillan, vol. 21, pp. 102–7.

Keynes, J.M. ([1932d] 1982) 'A note on the long-term rate of interest in relation to the conversion scheme', *Economic Journal* (Sept.), repr. in D. Moggridge (ed.), *The Collected Writings of John Maynard Keynes*, London: Macmillan, vol. 21, pp. 114–25.

Keynes, J.M. ([1932e] 1982) 'The monetary policy of the Labour Party', repr. in D. Moggridge (ed.), *The Collected Writings of John Maynard Keynes*, London: Macmillan, vol. 21, pp. 128–45.

Keynes, J.M. ([1933a] 1972) 'The means to prosperity', *The Times*, repr. in *The Collected Writings of John Maynard Keynes*, London: Macmillan, vol. 9, pp. 335–66.

Keynes, J.M. ([1933b] 1973) 'A monetary theory of production', repr. in D. Moggridge (ed.), *The Collected Writings of John Maynard Keynes*, London: Macmillan, vol. 13, pp. 408–11.

Keynes, J.M. ([1933c] 1982) 'National self-sufficiency', *The New Statesman and Nation* (8 and 15 July), repr. in D. Moggridge (ed.), *The Collected Writings of John Maynard Keynes*, London: Macmillan, vol. 21, pp. 233–46.

Keynes, J.M. ([1934a] 1973) 'Poverty in plenty: is the economic system self-adjusting?', *The Listener* (21 Nov.), repr. in D. Moggridge (ed.), *The Collected Writings of John Maynard Keynes*, London: Macmillan, vol. 13, pp. 485–92.

Keynes, J. M. ([1934b] 1982) *Excerpts from Speech*, National Mutual Annual Meeting, repr. in *The Collected Writings of John Maynard Keynes*, London: Macmillan, vol. 21, pp. 312–17.

Keynes, J. M. ([1935] 1982) *Excerpts from Speech*, National Mutual Annual Meeting, repr. in *The Collected Writings of John Maynard Keynes*, London: Macmillan, vol. 21, pp. 349–52.

Keynes, J.M. ([1936a] 1973) *The General Theory of Employment, Interest and Money*, repr. in *The Collected Writings of John Maynard Keynes*, London: Macmillan, vol. 7.

Keynes, J.M. ([1936b] 1973) Letter to J.R. Hicks, 31 Aug., in D. Moggridge (ed.), *The Collected Writings of John Maynard Keynes*, London: Macmillan, vol. 14, pp. 71–2.

Keynes, J.M. ([1936c] 1973) Letter to R.F. Hawtrey, 30 Aug., in D. Moggridge (ed.), *The Collected Writings of John Maynard Keynes*, London: Macmillan, vol. 14, pp. 84–6.

Keynes, J.M. ([1936d] 1973) Letter to D.H. Robertson, 31 Dec., in D. Moggridge (ed.), *The Collected Writings of John Maynard Keynes*, London: Macmillan, vol. 14, pp. 89–95.

Keynes, J.M. ([1936e] 1979) Letter to Hubert Henderson, 28 May, repr. in D. Moggridge (ed.), *The Collected Writings of John Maynard Keynes*, London: Macmillan, vol. 29, pp. 221–4.

Keynes, J. M. ([1936f] 1982) *Excerpts from Speech*, National Mutual Annual Meeting, repr. in *The Collected Writings of John Maynard Keynes*, London: Macmillan, vol. 21, pp. 374–9.

Keynes, J.M. ([1937a] 1973) Letter to J.R. Hicks, 31 March, in D. Moggridge (ed.), *The Collected Writings of John Maynard Keynes*, London: Macmillan, vol. 14, pp. 79–81.

Keynes, J.M. ([1937b] 1973) 'The theory of the rate of interest', repr. in D. Moggridge (ed.), *The Collected Writings of John Maynard Keynes*, London: Macmillan, vol. 14, pp. 101–8.

Keynes, J.M. ([1937c] 1973) 'The General Theory of employment', *Quarterly Journal of Economics*, 51(2), repr. in *The Collected Writings of John Maynard Keynes*, London: Macmillan, vol. 14, pp. 109–23.

Keynes, J.M. ([1937d] 1973) 'Ex post and ex ante', lecture notes, in *The Collected Writings of John Maynard Keynes*, London: Macmillan, vol. 14, pp. 179–83.

Keynes, J.M. ([1937e] 1973) 'Alternative theories of the rate of interest', *Economic Journal*, 47(2), repr. in *The Collected Writings of John Maynard Keynes*, London: Macmillan, vol. 14, pp. 201–15.

Keynes, J.M. ([1937f] 1973) 'The "ex ante" theory of the rate of interest', *Economic Journal*, 47(4), repr. in *The Collected Writings of John Maynard Keynes*, London: Macmillan, vol. 14, pp. 215–23.

Keynes, J.M. ([1938a] 1973) 'Mr. Keynes and "finance"', *Economic Journal*, 48(2), repr. in D. Moggridge (ed.), *The Collected Writings of John Maynard Keynes*, London: Macmillan, vol. 14, pp. 229–33.

Keynes, J.M. ([1938b] 1973) Letter to R.F. Harrod of 4 July, repr. in D. Moggridge (ed.), *The Collected Writings of John Maynard Keynes*, London: Macmillan, vol. 14, pp. 295–7.

Keynes, J.M. ([1938c] 1979) 'Finance', Letter to D.H. Robertson of 22 May, repr. in D. Moggridge (ed.), *The Collected Writings of John Maynard Keynes*, London: Macmillan, vol. 29, p. 171.

Keynes, J.M. ([1939a] 1972) 'How to pay for the war', *The Times* (14 and 15 Nov.), repr. in *The Collected Writings of John Maynard Keynes*, London: Macmillan, vol. 9, pp. 367–439.

Keynes, J.M. ([1939b] 1973) 'The process of capital formation', *Economic Journal*, repr. in D. Moggridge (ed.), *The Collected Writings of John Maynard Keynes*, London: Macmillan, vol. 14, pp. 278–85.

Keynes, J.M. ([1941a] 1980) 'Post-war currency policy', 8 Sept., repr. in D. Moggridge (ed.), *The Collected Writings of John Maynard Keynes*, London: Macmillan, vol. 25, pp. 21–40.

Keynes, J.M. ([1941b] 1980) 'Proposals for an international currency union', 18 Nov., repr. in D. Moggridge (ed.), *The Collected Writings of John Maynard Keynes*, London: Macmillan, vol. 25, pp. 42–66.

Keynes, J.M. ([1941c] 1980) 'Proposals for an international currency union', 15 Dec., repr. in D. Moggridge (ed.), *The Collected Writings of John Maynard Keynes*, London: Macmillan, vol. 25, pp. 68–94.

Keynes, J.M. ([1942a 1980) 'Notes on "Critical Observations on the Clearing Bank Plan"', 22 Jan., in D. Moggridge (ed.), *The Collected Writings of John Maynard Keynes*, London: Macmillan, vol. 25, pp. 103–8.

Keynes, J.M. ([1942b] 1980) 'Plan for an international currency (or clearing) union', 25 Jan., repr. in D. Moggridge (ed.), *The Collected Writings of John Maynard Keynes*, London: Macmillan, vol. 25, pp. 108–39.

Keynes, J.M. ([1942c] 1980) 'Minutes of a meeting of the War Cabinet Committee on reconstruction problems', 31 March, repr. in D. Moggridge (ed.), *The Collected Writings of John Maynard Keynes*, London: Macmillan, vol. 25, pp. 139–42.

Keynes, J.M. ([1942d] 1980) Letter to R.F. Kahn, 11 May, repr. in D. Moggridge (ed.), *The Collected Writings of John Maynard Keynes*, London: Macmillan, vol. 25, pp. 143–4.

Keynes, J.M. ([1942e] 1980) Letter to Roy Harrod, 19 April, repr. in D. Moggridge (ed.), *The Collected Writings of John Maynard Keynes*, London: Macmillan, vol. 25, pp. 146–51.

Keynes, J.M. ([1942f] 1980) 'Notes on the memorandum for post-war currency arrangements transmitted by Sir F. Phillips', 3 Aug., repr. in D. Moggridge (ed.), *The Collected Writings of John Maynard Keynes*, London: Macmillan, vol. 25, pp. 160–7.

Keynes, J.M. ([1942g] 1980) 'Proposals for an international clearing union', 28 Aug., repr. in D. Moggridge (ed.), *The Collected Writings of John Maynard Keynes*, London: Macmillan, vol. 25, pp. 168–95.

Keynes, J.M. ([1943a] 1980) 'Speech to a meeting of the European Allies', 26 Feb., repr. in D. Moggridge (ed.), *The Collected Writings of John Maynard Keynes*, London: Macmillan, vol. 25, pp. 206–15.

Keynes, J.M. ([1943b] 1980) 'A comparative analysis of the British project for a clearing union (C.U.) and the American project for a stabilization fund (S.F.)', 1 March, repr. in D. Moggridge (ed.), *The Collected Writings of John Maynard Keynes*, London: Macmillan, vol. 25, pp. 215–26.

Keynes, J.M. ([1943c] 1980) Letter to Roy Harrod, 27 April, repr. in D. Moggridge (ed.), *The Collected Writings of John Maynard Keynes*, London: Macmillan, vol. 25, p. 268.

Keynes, J.M. ([1943d] 1980) Speech before the House of Lords, 18 May, repr. in D. Moggridge (ed.), *The Collected Writings of John Maynard Keynes*, London: Macmillan, vol. 25, pp. 269–80.

Keynes, J.M. ([1943e] 1980) 'The objective of international price stability', *Economic Journal*, repr. in D. Moggridge (ed.), *The Collected Writings of John Maynard Keynes*, London: Macmillan, vol. 26, pp. 30–3.

Keynes, J.M. ([1943f] 1980) Letter to Benjamin Graham, 31 Dec., repr. in D. Moggridge (ed.), *The Collected Writings of John Maynard Keynes*, London: Macmillan, vol. 26, pp. 36–8.

Keynes, J.M. ([1944] 1980) 'Note by Lord Keynes [on "Keynes vs. Hayek on a commodity reserve currency"]', *Economic Journal,* 54 (Dec.), repr. in D. Moggridge (ed.), *The Collected Writings of John Maynard Keynes*, London: Macmillan, vol. 26, pp. 39–40.

Keynes, J.M. ([1946] 1983). 'The balance of payments of the United States', *Economic Journal,* 56(222): 172–87, repr. in *The Collected Writings of John Maynard Keynes*, London: Macmillan, vol. 11.

Keynes Papers, Modern Archives, King's College, Cambridge, files: BE/1.

Kisch, C.H. and Elkin, W.A. ([1928] 1930) *Central Banks: A Study of the Constitutions of Banks of Issue, with an Analysis of Representative Charters*, 3rd edn, London: Macmillan.

Kohn, M. (1981) 'A loanable funds theory of unemployment and monetary disequilibrium', *American Economic Review*, 71: 859–79.

Kohn, M. (1986) 'Monetary analysis, the equilibrium method, and Keynes's "General Theory"', *Journal of Political Economy*, 94(6):1191–1224.

Kohn, D.L. (2008) 'Monetary policy and asset prices revisited', Speech delivered at the Cato Institute's 26th Annual Monetary Policy Conference, Washington DC, November 19, Federal Reserve Board, http://www.federalreserve.gov/newsevents/speech/kohn20081119a.htm *BIS Review,* 144.

Kregel, J.A. (1984–5) 'Constraints on the expansion of output and employment: real or monetary?', *Journal of Post Keynesian Economics*, 12(2): 139–52.

Kregel, J.A. (1986) 'A note on finance, liquidity, saving, and investment', *Journal of Post Keynesian Economics*, 9(1): 91–100.

Kregel, J. (1988) 'The multiplier and liquidity preference: two sides of the theory of effective demand', in A. Barriere (ed.), *The Foundations of Keynesian Analysis*, London: Macmillan.

Kregel, J. (1998) 'Aspects of a post Keynesian theory of finance', *Journal of Post Keynesian Economics*, 21(1): 111–33.

Kregel, J. (2007) 'Financial flows and international imbalances: the role of catching up by late industrializing developing countries', in E. Hein, T. Niechoj, P. Spahn and A. Truger (eds), *Finance-led Capitalism?*, Marburg: Metropolis.

Krugman, P. (2008) 'Depression economics returns', *The New York Times* (14 Nov.).

Labour Party (1932) *Currency, Banking and Finance,* London: Labour Party (3 July).

Laidler, D. (1984) 'The "buffer stock" notion in monetary economics', *Economic Journal Conferences Papers*, 94: 17–34.

Laidler, D.E.W. (1999) *Fabricating the Keynesian Revolution*, Cambridge: Cambridge University Press.

Lavoie, M. (1992) *Foundations of Post-Keynesian Economics*, Aldershot: Edward Elgar.

Lavoie, M. (1996) 'Horizontalism, structuralism, liquidity preference and the principle of increasing risk', *Scottish Journal of Political Economy*, 43(Aug.): 275–300.

Lavoie, M. (1997) 'Loanable funds, endogenous money and Minsky's financial fragility hypothesis', in A.J. Cohen, H. Hagemann and J. Smithin (eds), *Money, Financial Institutions and Macroeconomics*, Amsterdam: Kluwer Nijhoff Boston, pp. 67–82.

Lavoie, M. (2004) 'The new consensus on monetary policy seen from a post-Keynesian perspective', in M. Lavoie and M. Seccareccia (eds), *Central Banking in the Modern World*, Cheltenham: Edward Elgar, pp. 15–33.

Lavoie, M. (2006a) 'A post-Keynesian amendment to the new consensus on monetary policy', *Metroeconomica*, 57(2): 165–92.

Lavoie, M. (2006b) 'Endogenous money: accommodationist', in P. Arestis and M. Sawyer (eds), *Handbook of Alternative Monetary Economics*, Cheltenham: Edward Elgar.

Lavoie, M. (2008) *Taming the New Consensus: Hysteresis and Some Other Post-Keynesian Amendments*, University of Ottawa, mimeo.

Lawson, T. (1985) 'Uncertainty and economic analysis', *Economic Journal*, 95(4): 909–27.

Le Heron, E. and Mouakil, T. (2008) 'A post-Keynesian stock-flow consistent model for dynamic analysis of monetary policy shock on banking behavior', *Metroeconomica*, 59(3): 405–40.

Leijonhufvud, A. (1968) *On Keynesian Economics and the Economics of Keynes*, New York: Oxford University Press.

Leijonhufvud, A. (1973) 'Effective demand failures', *Swedish Journal of Economics*, 75(3): 27–28.

Leijonhufvud, A. (1981) *Information and Coordination*, New York: Oxford University Press.

Leijonhufvud, A. (1994) 'Hicks, Keynes and Marshall', in H. Hagemann and O. F. Hamouda (eds), *The Legacy of Hicks*, London: Routledge.

Leijonhufvud, A. (1998) 'Mr. Keynes and the moderns', *European Journal of Economic History*, 5: 169–88.

Leontief, W. (1947) 'Postulates: Keynes' General Theory and the classicists', in S. Harris (ed.), *The New Economics*, New York: Knopf, pp. 232–42.

Liberal Industrial Inquiry (1928) *Britain's Industrial Future*, London: Ernest Benn Ltd.

McGregor, P.G. (1988a) 'The demand for money in a period analysis context, the irrelevance of the "choice of market," and the loanable funds–liquidity preference debate', *Australian Economic Papers,* 27(2): 136–41.

McGregor, P.G. (1988b) 'Keynes on ex-ante saving and the rate of interest', *History of Political Economy*, 20(1): 107–18.

Maclachlan, F.C. (1993) *Keynes's General Theory of Interest: A Reconsideration*, London: Routledge.

Makowski, L. (1990) 'Keynes's liquidity preference theory; a suggested reinterpretation', in F.H. Hahn (ed.), *The Economics of Missing Markets, Information, and Games*, Oxford: Clarendon Press, pp. 468–75.

Mankiw, N.G. (2009) *Principles of Economics*, 5th edn, Mason, OH: South-Western Cengage Learning.

Mankiw, N.G. and Summers, L.H. (1986) 'Money demand and the effects of fiscal policies', *Journal of Money, Credit, and Banking*, 18(4): 415–29.

Meade, J. (1975) 'The Keynesian revolution', in M. Keynes (ed.), *Essays on John Maynard Keynes*, Cambridge: Cambridge University Press, pp. 82–8.

Meltzer, A.H. (1988) *Keynes's Monetary Theory: A Different Interpretation*, Cambridge: Cambridge University Press.

Meltzer, A.H. (1989) 'Keynes on monetary reform and international economic order', in F. Capie and G. E. Wood (eds), *Monetary Economics in the 1980s*, London: Macmillan.

Messori, M. (1991) 'Keynes' *General Theory* and the endogenous money supply', *Economie Appliquee* (Jan.).

Messori, M. (1995) 'Own rate of own interest and the liquidity preference', *Economic Notes*, 24(2): 375–404.

Messori, M. (1997) 'Keynesians, New Keynesians and the loanable funds theory', in A.J. Cohen, H. Hagemann and J. Smithin (eds), *Money, Financial Institutions and Macroeconomics*, Boston: Kluwer Nijhoff, pp. 33–54.

Miller, N.C. (1992) 'Cash-in advance, buffer-stock monetarism, and the loanable funds–liquidity preference debate in an open economy', *Journal of Macroeconomics*, 14: 487–507.

Miller, N.C. (1995) 'Towards a loanable funds/amended-liquidity preference theory of the exchange rate and interest rate', *Journal of International Money and Finance*, 14: 225–45.

Minsky, H.P. ([1975] 2008) *John Maynard Keynes*, New York: McGraw-Hill.

Minsky, H.P. (1982) *Can 'IT' Happen Again? Essays on Instability and Finance*, Armonk, NY: M.E. Sharpe.

Minsky, H.P. ([1986] 2008) *Stabilizing an Unstable Economy*, New York: McGraw-Hill.

Moggridge, D.E. (1972) *British Monetary Policy 1924–1931: The Norman Conquest of $4.86*, Cambridge: Cambridge University Press.

Moggridge, D.E. (1986) 'Keynes and the international monetary system 1909–46', in J. Cohen and G. Harcourt (eds), *International Monetary Problems and Supply-Side Economics: Essays in Honor of Lorie Tarshis*, New York: St Martin's Press.

Moggridge, D.E. (1992) *Maynard Keynes: An Economist's Biography*, London: Routledge.

Moggridge, D.E. (1997) 'Keynes and the post-war world', paper presented at the 1997 HES conference.

Moggridge, D.E. (2001) '"Maynard would not have wished"?: second-guessing the author of "The balance of payments of the United States"', *History of Political Economy* 33(4): 815–24.

Moggridge, D.E. and Howson, S. (1974) 'Keynes on monetary policy, 1910–1946', *Oxford Economic Papers*, 26(2): 226–47.

Moore, B.J. (1988) *Horizontalists and Verticalists: The Macroeconomics of Credit Money*, Cambridge: Cambridge University Press.

Moore, B.J. (1991) 'Money supply endogeneity: "reserve price setting" or "reserve quantity setting"?', *Journal of Post Keynesian Economics*, 13(3): 404–13.

Nevin, E.T. (1955) *The Mechanism of Cheap Money*, Cardiff: University of Wales Press.

Nevin, E.T. and Davis, E.W. (1970) *The London Clearing Banks*, London: Elek.

O'Donnell, R.M. (1989) *Keynes: Philosophy, Economics and Politics*, Basingstoke: Macmillan.

O'Donnell, R. M. (1991). 'Keynes on probability, expectations and uncertainty', in R. M. O'Donnell (ed.) *Keynes as Philosopher-Economist*, London: Macmillan.

Ohlin, B. (1937a) 'Some notes on the Stockholm theory of savings and investments II', *Economic Journal*, 47(2): 221–40.

Ohlin, B. (1937b) 'Alternative theories of the rate of interest: rejoinder', *Economic Journal*, 47(3): 423–7.

Ono, Y. (1994) *Money, Interest, and Stagnation: Dynamic Theory and Keynes's Economics*, Oxford: Clarendon Press.

Orphanides, A. and Wilcox, D.W. (2002) 'The opportunistic approach to disinflation', *International Finance*, 5(1): 47–71.

Palley, T.I. (1991) 'The endogenous money supply: consensus and disagreement', *Journal of Post Keynesian Economics*, 13: 397–403.

Palley, T.I. (2007) 'Macroeconomics and monetary policy: competing theoretical frameworks', *Journal of Post Keynesian Economics*, 30(1): 61–78.

Panico, C. (1992) 'Liquidity preference', in P. Newman, Murray Milgate and John Eatwell (eds), *The New Palgrave: A Dictionary of Money and Finance*, London: Macmillan.

Pasinetti, L.L. (1974) *Growth and Income Distribution*, Cambridge: Cambridge University Press.

Pasinetti, L.L. (1997a) 'The principle of effective demand', in G.C. Harcourt and P. Riach (eds), *A Second Edition of The General Theory*, London: Routledge, pp. 93–104.

Pasinetti, L.L. (1997b) 'The marginal efficiency of investment', in G.C. Harcourt and P. Riach (eds), *A 'Second Edition' of The General Theory*, London: Routledge, pp. 198–218.

Pasinetti, L.L. (2007) *Keynes and the Cambridge Keynesians: A Revolution in Economics to be Accomplished*, Cambridge: Cambridge University Press.

Patinkin, D. ([1956] 1965) *Money, Interest and Prices*, 2nd edn, New York: Harper & Row.

Patinkin, D. (1958) 'Liquidity preference and loanable funds: stock and flow analysis', *Economica*, 38(4): 300–318.

Patinkin, D. (1976) *Keynes' Monetary Thought*, Durham, NC: Duke University Press.

Patinkin, D. (1982) *Anticipations of the General Theory*, Chicago, IL: University of Chicago Press.

Pindyck, R.S. (1991) 'Irreversibility, uncertainty, and investment', *Journal of Economic Literature*, 29(3): 1110–48.

Pollin, R. and Zhu, A. (2006) 'Inflation and economic growth: a cross-country nonlinear analysis', *Journal of Post Keynesian Economics*, 28(4): 593–614.

Ponsot, J.-F. (2002) 'Keynes and the "National Emission Caisse" of North Russia: 1918–1920', *History of Political Economy*, 34(1): 177–206.

Presley, J.R. (1979) *Robertsonian Economics: An Examination of the Work of Sir D.H. Robertson on Industrial Fluctuation*, London: Macmillan.

Presley, J.R. (1992) 'Robertson and Keynes: three phases of collaboration', in *Essays on Robertsonian Economics*, London: Macmillan.

Ramsey, F.P. (1926) 'Truth and probability', in D.H. Mellor (ed.), *Foundations: Essays in Philosophy, Logic, Mathematics and Economics*, London: Routledge & Kegan Paul, pp. 58–100.

Reuters (2008) 'ECB's Trichet holds the line on rates, inflation', 24 Jan.

Richardson, D.R. (1986) 'Asimakopulos on Kalecki and Keynes on finance, saving and investment', *Cambridge Journal of Economics*, 10(2): 191–8.

Robertson, D.H. (1926) *Banking Policy and the Price Level*, London: P. S. King & Son.

Robertson, D.H. (1931) 'Mr. Keynes' theory of money', *Economic Journal*, 41: 395–411.

Robertson, D.H. (1933) 'Saving and hoarding', *Economic Journal*, 43(Sept.): 399–413.

Robertson, D.H. (1934) 'Industrial fluctuation and the natural rate of interest', *Economic Journal*, 44(Dec.): 650–6.

Robertson, D.H. (1936) 'Some notes on Mr Keynes' General Theory of Employment', *Quarterly Journal of Economics*, 51(1): 168–91.

Robertson, D.H. (1937) 'Alternative theories of the rate of interest: rejoinder', *Economic Journal*, 47(3): 428–36.

Robertson, D.H. (1938) 'Mr. Keynes and "finance"', *Economic Journal*, 48(2): 314–18.

Robertson, D.H. (1940) 'Mr. Keynes and the rate of interest', in *Essays in Monetary Theory*, London: Staples Press, pp. 1–39.

Robinson, J. (1952) *The Rate of Interest and Other Essays*, London: Macmillan.

Robinson, J. (1970) *Economic Heresies*, London: Macmillan.

Rochon, L.P. (1999) *Credit, Money and Production: An Alternative Post-Keynesian Approach*, Cheltenham: Edward Elgar.

Rochon, L.P. and Rossi, S. (eds) (2003) *Modern Theories of Money: The Nature and Role of Money in Capitalist Economies*, Cheltenham: Edward Elgar.

Romer, D. (1993) 'The New Keynesian synthesis', *Journal of Economic Perspectives*, 7: 5–22.

Romer, D. (2000) 'Keynesian macroeconomics without the LM curve', *Journal of Economic Perspectives*, 14(2): 149–69.

Rotheim, R. (2006) 'Credit rationing', in P. Arestis and M. Sawyer (eds), *Handbook of Alternative Monetary Economics*, Cheltenham: Edward Elgar, pp. 307–27.

Royal Commission on Banking and Finance [The Porter Commission] (1964) Ottawa: Queen's Printer.

Runde, J.H. (1990) 'Keynesian uncertainty and the weight of arguments', *Economics and Philosophy*, 6(3): 275–92.

Runde, J.H. (1994) 'Keynesian uncertainty and liquidity preference', *Cambridge Journal of Economics*, 18(2): 129–44.

Runde, J.H. (1996) 'Uncertainty, Keynesian/Knightian', in J. Davis, W. Hands and U. Mäki (eds), *Handbook of Economic Methodology*, Aldershot: Edward Elgar.

Runde, J.H. and Bibow, J. (1996) 'Expectations and the price of equities', in R. Koppl and G. Mongiovi (eds), *Essays in Honor of L.M. Lachmann*, London: Routledge, pp. 183–200.

Rymes, T.K. (1998) 'Keynes and anchorless banking', *Journal of the History of Economic Thought* (March) 20(1): 71–82.

Rymes, T.K. (1994) 'On the Coyne-Rasminsky Directive and responsibility for monetary policy in Canada', in P.L. Siklos (ed.), *Varieties of Monetary Reforms: Lessons and Experiences on the Road to Monetary Union*, Boston, MA: Kluwer Academic Publishers.

Sargent, T. (1987) *Dynamic Macroeconomic Theory*, Cambridge, MA: Harvard University Press.

Savage, L.J. (1954) *The Foundations of Statistics*, New York: John Wiley & Sons.

Sayers, R.S. (1938) *Modern Banking*, Oxford: Oxford University Press.

Sayers, R.S. (1957) *Central Banking after Bagehot*, Oxford: Clarendon.

Sayers, R.S. (1976) *The Bank of England: 1891–1944*, Cambridge: Cambridge University Press.

Schnadt, N. (1994) *The Domestic Money Markets of the UK, France, Germany and the US*, London: London Business School, City Research Project; Subject Report VII (Paper 1).

Schuler, K.A. (1992) 'Currency Boards', Ph.D. diss., George Mason University, Fairfax, VA.

Setterfield, M. (2002) 'Introduction: a dissenter's view of the development of growth theory and the importance of demand-led growth', in M. Setterfield (ed.), *The Economics of Demand-led Growth: Challenging the Supply-side Vision of the Long Run*, Cheltenham: Edward Elgar.

Setterfield, M. (2006) 'Is inflation targeting compatible with Post Keynesian economics?', *Journal of Post Keynesian Economics*, 28(4): 653–71.

Shackle, G.L.S. (1961) 'Recent theories concerning the nature and role of interest', *Economic Journal*, 71(2): 209–54.

Shackle, G.L.S. (1967) *The Years of High Theory*, Cambridge: Cambridge University Press.

Shackle, G.L.S. (1972) *Epistemics and Economics*, Cambridge: Cambridge University Press.

Shefrin, H. (1999) *Beyond Greed and Fear: Understanding Behavioral Finance and the Psychology of Investing*, Oxford: Oxford University Press.

Shiller, R.J. (2000) *Irrational Exuberance*, Princeton, NJ: Princeton University Press.

Shleifer, A. (2000) *Inefficient Markets: An Introduction to Behavioral Finance*, Oxford: Oxford University Press.

Skidelsky, R. (2000) *John Maynard Keynes: Fighting for Britain 1937–1946*, London: Macmillan.

Smithin, J. (1994) *Controversies in Monetary Economics: Ideas, Issues and Policy*, Aldershot: Edward Elgar.

Snippe, J. (1985) 'Finance, saving and investment in Keynes's economics', *Cambridge Journal of Economics*, 9(3): 257–69.

Snippe, J. (1986) 'Finance, saving and investment in Keynes's economics: a reply', *Cambridge Journal of Economics*, 10(4): 373–7.

Soros, G. (1987) *The Alchemy of Finance*, 2nd edn, New York: John Wiley & Sons.

Spahn, H.-P. (1993) 'Liquiditätspräferenz und Geldangebot: Schritte zu einer keynesianischen Kreditmarkttheorie des Zinses,' in H.-J. Stadermann and O. Steiger (eds), *Der Stand und die nächste Zukunft der Geldforschung*, Berlin: Duncker & Humblot.

Spahn, H.-P. (2007) 'Realzins, intertemporale Preise und makroökonomische Stabilisierung: Ein Streifzug durch die Theoriegeschichte,' *Hohenheimer Diskussionsbeiträge*, 202.

Spring Rice, D. (1919) 'The North Russian currency', *Economic Journal*, 29(115): 280–9.

Stiglitz, J.E. and Greenwald, B. (2003) *Towards a New Paradigm in Monetary Economics*, Cambridge: Cambridge University Press.

Stiglitz, J.E. and Weiss, A. (1981) 'Credit rationing in markets with imperfect information', *American Economic Review*, 71(2): 393–410.

Summers, L.H. (2006) 'Reflections on global account imbalances and emerging markets reserve accumulation', L.K. Jha Memorial Lecture, *Reserve Bank of India* (March).

Taylor, J.B. (2000) 'Teaching modern macroeconomics at the principles level', *American Economic Review*, 90(2): 90–4.

Terzi, A. (1986a) 'Finance, saving and investment: a comment on Asimakopulos', *Cambridge Journal of Economics*, 10(1): 77–80.

Terzi, A. (1986b) 'The independence of finance from saving: a flow-of-funds interpretation', *Journal of Post Keynesian Economics*, 9(2): 188–97.

Terzi, A. (2006) 'International financial instability in a world of currencies hierarchy', in L.-P. Rochon and S. Rossi (eds), *Monetary and Exchange Rate Systems: A Global View of Financial Crises*, Oxford: Edward Elgar.

Thirlwall, A. (1983) 'Comment on Kaldor', in D. Worswick and J.A. Trevithick (eds), *Keynes and the Modern World*, Cambridge: Cambridge University Press.

Thomas, R. (1996) 'Understanding broad money', *Bank of England Quarterly Bulletin* (May): 163–79.

Thornton, D.L. and Stone, C.C. (1992) 'Financial innovation: causes and consequences', in K. Down and M.K. Lewis (eds), *Current Issues in Financial and Monetary Economics*, London: Macmillan.

Tily, G. (2006) 'Keynes's theory of liquidity preference and his debt management and monetary policies', *Cambridge Journal of Economics*, 30(4): 657–70.

Tily, G. (2007) *Keynes's General Theory, the Rate of Interest and 'Keynesian' Economics: Keynes Betrayed*, London: Palgrave Macmillan.

Tobin, J. (1958) 'Liquidity preference as behavior towards risk', *Review of Economic Studies*, 25(1): 65–86.

Tobin, J. ([1963] 1965) 'Commercial banks as creators of money', repr. in W.L. Smith and R.L. Teigen (eds), *Readings in Money, National Income and Stabilization Policy*, Homewood, IL: Richard D. Irwin.

Tobin, J. (1969) 'A general equilibrium approach to monetary theory', *Journal of Money, Credit, and Banking*, 1(1): 15–29.

Tobin, J. (1978) 'Monetary policies and the economy: the transmission mechanism', *Southern Economic Journal*, 44(3): 421–31.

Tobin, J. (1980) *Asset Accumulation and Economic Activity*, Oxford: Basil Blackwell.

Tobin, J. (1982) 'The commercial banking firm', *Scandinavian Journal of Economics*, 84(4): 495–539.

Tobin, J. (1983) 'Comment on Kaldor', in G.D.N. Worswick and J.A. Trevithick (eds), *Keynes and the Modern World*, Cambridge: Cambridge University Press.

Tobin, J. (1987) 'Financial intermediaries', in J. Eatwell, M. Milgate and P. Newman (eds), *The New Palgrave: Money*, London: Macmillan.

Tobin, J. (1991) 'On the endogeneity of money supply', in E. Nell and W. Semmler (eds), *Nicholas Kaldor and Mainstream Economics*, London: Macmillan.

Townshend, H. (1937). 'Liquidity-premium and the theory of value', *Economic Journal*, 47(March): 157–69.

Trevithick, J.A. (1992) *Involuntary Unemployment: Macroeconomics from a Keynesian Perspective*, New York: Harvester Wheatsheaf.

Trevithick, J. (1994) 'The monetary prerequisites for the multiplier: an adumbration of the crowding-out hypothesis', *Cambridge Journal of Economics*, 18(1): 77–90.

Triffin, R. ([1960] 1961) *Gold and the Dollar Crisis*, New Haven, CT: Yale University Press.

Tsiang, S.-C. (1956) 'Liquidity preference and loanable funds theories, multiplier and velocity analyses: a synthesis', *American Economic Review*, 46: 539–64.

Tsiang, S.-C. (1966) 'Walras' law, Say's law and liquidity preference in general equilibrium analysis', *International Economic Review*, 7: 329–45.

Tsiang, S.-C. (1980) 'Keynes's finance demand for liquidity, Robertson's loanable funds theory, and Friedman's monetarism', *Quarterly Journal of Economics*, 94(3): 467–91.

Tsiang, S.-C. (1987) 'Liquidity', in J. Eatwell, M. Milgate and P. Newman (eds), *The New Palgrave*, London: Macmillan.

Tsiang, S.-C. (1988) 'The flow formulation of a monetary model for an open economy and the determination of the exchange rate', in M. Kohn and S.-C. Tsiang (eds), *Finance Constraints, Expectations, and Macroeconomics*, Oxford: Clarendon Press.

Vicarelli, F. (1984) *The Instability of Capitalism*, Philadelphia: University of Philadelphia Press.

Vicarelli, F. (1988) 'Central bank autonomy: a historical perspective', in G. Toniolo (ed.), *Central Banks' Independence in Historical Perspective*, Berlin: WDG.

Vines, D. (2003) 'John Maynard Keynes 1937–1946: the creation of international macroeconomics', *Economic Journal*, 113 (June): F338–F361.

Walters, A. and Hanke, S.H. (1992) 'Currency boards', in P. Newman, M. Milgate and J. Eatwell (eds), *The New Palgrave Dictionary of Money and Finance*, London: Macmillan.

Weisman, D.L. (1984) 'Tobin on Keynes: a suggested interpretation', *Journal of Post Keynesian Economics*, 6(3): 411–20.

Werner, R. (2003) *Princes of the Yen: Japan's Central Bankers and the Transformation of the Economy*, Armonk, NY: M.E Sharpe.

Williamson, H. (1983) 'Keynes and the international economic order', in D. Worswick and J. Trevithick (eds), *Keynes and the Modern World*, Cambridge: Cambridge University Press.

Wojnilower, A.M. (1980) 'The central role of credit crunches in recent financial history', *Brookings Papers on Economic Activity*, 2: 277–326.

Wolfson, M.H. (1996) 'A post Keynesian theory of credit rationing', *Journal of Post Keynesian Economics*, 18(3): 443–71.

Woodford, M. (1990) 'Public debt as private liquidity', *American Economic Review*, 80(2): 382–8.

Woodford, M. (2003) *Interest and Prices: Foundations of a Theory of Monetary Policy*, Princeton, NJ: Princeton University Press.

Wray, L.R. (1990) *Money and Credit in Capitalist Economies*, Aldershot: Edward Elgar.

Wray, L.R. (1992) 'Alternative theories of the rate of interest', *Cambridge Journal of Economics*, 16(1): 69–89.

Wray, R. (2007) *Lessons from the Subprime Meltdown*, Annandale-on-Hudson: Levy Economics Institute, Working Paper, 522.

Index

Routledge
Taylor & Francis Group

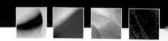

International Journal of the Economics of Business

EDITOR:
Eleanor Morgan, *University of Bath, UK*

NORTH AMERICAN EDITOR:
H.E. Frech III, *University of California, Santa Barbara, USA*

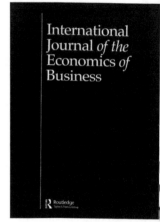

International
Journal *of the*
Economics *of*
Business

Routledge

International Journal of the Economics of Business presents
original, peer reviewed research in economics that is clearly
applicable to business or related public policy problems or issues.
The term 'business' is used in its widest sense to encompass both
public and private sector - governmental, private non-profit and
cooperative organizations, as well as profit-seeking enterprises.
Services and distribution are included along with manufacturing and
extractive industries. Coverage includes the less developed and
former Eastern Bloc countries, as well as industrialized countries.

International Journal of the Economics of Business carries papers relating to three main spheres:
The organization - to analyse and aid decision making and the internal organization of the business;
The industry - to analyse how businesses interact and evolve within and across industries; The external
environment - to show how public policy, technological developments and other outside forces affect
business behaviour.

SUBSCRIPTION RATES
Volume 15, 2008, 3 issues per year
Print ISSN 1357-1516
Online ISSN 1466-1829
Institutional rate (print and online): US$686; £426; €549
Institutional rate (online access only): US$651; £404; €521
Personal rate (print only): US$173; £107; €138

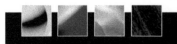

Routledge
Taylor & Francis Group

Review of Political Economy

Increase in pages for 2008

EDITORS:
Gary Mongiovi, *St John's University, USA*
Steve Pressman, *Monmouth University, USA*

The **Review of Political Economy** is a peer-reviewed journal welcoming constructive and critical contributions in all areas of political economy, including the Austrian, Behavioral Economics, Feminist Economics, Institutionalist, Marxian, Post Keynesian, and Sraffian traditions. The **Review** publishes both theoretical and empirical research, and is also open to submissions in methodology, economic history and the history of economic thought that cast light on issues of contemporary relevance in political economy. Comments on articles published in the **Review** are encouraged.

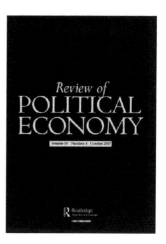

SUBSCRIPTION RATES
Volume 20, 2008, 4 issues per year
Print ISSN 0953-8259
Online ISSN 1465-3982
Institutional rate (print and online): US$836; £487; €669
Institutional rate (online access only): US$794; £462; €635
Personal rate (print only): US$194; £120; €155

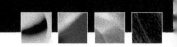

Applied Mathematical Finance

EDITORS-IN-CHIEF:
Ben Hambly, *University of Oxford, UK*
William Shaw, *King's College London, UK*

The journal encourages the confident use of applied mathematics and mathematical modelling in finance. The journal publishes papers on the following:

- modelling of financial and economic primitives (interest rates, asset prices etc);
- modelling market behaviour;
- modelling market imperfections;
- pricing of financial derivative securities;
- hedging strategies;
- numerical methods;
- financial engineering.

The journal encourages communication between finance practitioners, academics and applied mathematicians. Both theoretical and empirical research welcomed, as are papers on emerging areas of mathematical finance and interdisciplinary topics. The journal seeks papers reviewing the development of significant practical tools, algorithms and new products. The modelling or solution of problems should demonstrate the capacity for generalization. Original and substantial pieces of research resulting in open problems are welcome; this will also be a forum for the airing of new problems and new areas of activity.

SUBSCRIPTION RATES
Volume 15, 2008, 6 issues per year
Print ISSN 1350-486X
Online ISSN 1466-4313
Institutional rate (print and online): US$1623; £975; €1298
Institutional rate (online access only): US$1541; £926; €1233
Personal rate (print only): US$214; £128; €171

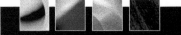

View an online sample issue at:
www.informaworld.com/AMF

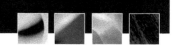

Journal of Chinese Economic and Business Studies

The international scholarly journal of the Chinese Economic Association UK (CEA-UK)

Increase in frequency for 2008

MANAGING EDITOR:

Xiaming Liu, *Birkbeck College, London, UK*

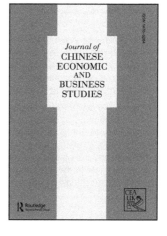

Journal of Chinese Economic and Business Studies is a peer-reviewed journal aiming to publish current and relevant findings from cutting edge research in Chinese economic, business and related issues. More specifically, it aims:

- to provide a forum for exchange of information and ideas among people in academic, business and government professions who are interested in the Chinese economy.
- to foster and enhance research activities that advance knowledge in transition economies.
- to discuss the relevance of Chinese economic and business studies to our society.

The journal specialises in both theoretical and empirical research on the Chinese economy, business and related issues including economic theories and policies for transition economies, economic reforms in the agricultural sector, state-owned enterprises, financial and fiscal systems and management styles, R&D and technology, marketing, human resources, business strategy, business culture and ethics, foreign trade and direct investment, similar issues for Hong Kong and Taiwan, and their relevance to other parts of the world.

SUBSCRIPTION RATES
Volume 6, 2008, 4 issues per year
Print ISSN 1476-5284
Online ISSN 1476-5292
Institutional rate (print and online): US$515; £311; €412
Institutional rate (online access only): US$489; £295; €391
Personal rate (print only): US$157; £95; €126

View an online sample issue at:
www.informaworld.com/jcebs

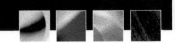

The European Journal of Finance

EDITOR:

Chris Adcock, *University of Sheffield, UK*

The European Journal of Finance publishes a full range of research into theoretical and empirical topics in finance. The emphasis is on issues that reflect European interests and concerns. The journal aims to publish work that is motivated by significant issues in the theory or practice of finance.

The journal promotes communication between finance academics and practitioners by providing a vehicle for the publication of research into European issues, stimulating research in finance within Europe, encouraging the international exchange of ideas, theories and the practical application of methodologies and playing a positive role in the development of the infrastructure for finance research, teaching and practice throughout Europe.

SUBSCRIPTION RATES
Volume 14, 2008, 8 issues per year
Print ISSN 1351-847X
Online ISSN 1466-4364
Institutional rate (print and online): US$1908; £1157; €1526
Institutional rate (online access only): US$1812; £1099; €1449
Personal rate (print only): US$204; £124; €163

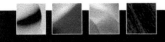

Routledge
Taylor & Francis Group

The Journal of International Trade & Economic Development

An International and Comparative Review

Now included in the Thomson ISI Social Sciences Citation Index ©

EDITORS:
Professor Pasquale M. Sgro, *Deakin Business School, Australia*
Professor Bharat R. Hazari, *City University of Hong Kong,*
Hong Kong

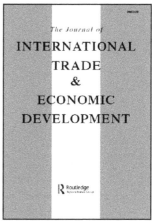

The Journal of International Trade & Economic Development, a peer-reviewed journal, focuses on international economics, economic development and, more importantly, the interface between trade and development. The links between trade and development economics are critical at a time when both fluctuating commodity prices and trade liberalisation and agreements can radically affect the economies of developing countries.

The Journal of International Trade & Economic Development is designed to meet the needs of international and development economists, economic historians, applied economists and policy makers. The international experts who make up the journal's Editorial Board encourage contributions from economists world-wide.

SUBSCRIPTION RATES
Volume 17, 2008, 4 issues per year
Print ISSN 0963-8199
Online ISSN 1469-9559
Institutional rate (print and online): US$931; £564; €745
Institutional rate (online access only): US$884; £535; €707
Personal rate (print only): US$142; £97; €114

informaworld

A world of specialist information for the academic, professional and business communities. To find out more go to: **www.informaworld.com**

updates
Taylor & Francis Group

Register your email address at **www.informaworld.com/eupdates** to receive information on books, journals and other news within your areas of interest.

For further information, please contact Customer Services at either of the following:
T&F Informa UK Ltd, Sheepen Place, Colchester, Essex, CO3 3LP, UK
Tel: +44 (0) 20 7017 5544 Fax: 44 (0) 20 7017 5198
Email: tf.enquiries@informa.com Website: www.tandf.co.uk/journals
Taylor & Francis Inc, 325 Chestnut Street, 8th Floor, Philadelphia, PA 19106, USA
Tel: +1 800 354 1420 (toll-free calls from within the US)
or +1 215 625 8900 (calls from overseas) Fax: +1 215 625 2940
Email: customerservice@taylorandfrancis.com Website: www.taylorandfrancis.com

When ordering, please quote: XJ04201A

View an online sample issue at:
www.informaworld.com/JITED

For Product Safety Concerns and Information please contact our EU
representative GPSR@taylorandfrancis.com
Taylor & Francis Verlag GmbH, Kaufingerstraße 24, 80331 München, Germany

www.ingramcontent.com/pod-product-compliance
Ingram Content Group UK Ltd.
Pitfield, Milton Keynes, MK11 3LW, UK
UKHW021617240425
457818UK00018B/613